F. D. R.

His Personal Letters

Franklin D. Roosevelt

EARLY YEARS

Foreword by

ELEANOR ROOSEVELT

Edited by

ELLIOTT ROOSEVELT

DUELL, SLOAN AND PEARCE

New York

E
807
R649

F. D. R.
His Personal Letters

EARLY YEARS

To the Memory of

SARA DELANO ROOSEVELT

ACKNOWLEDGMENT

IN THE PREPARATION of this book many persons, friends and strangers alike, gladly responded to requests for assistance. To all of them I extend my thanks. In particular the contributions of the research supplied by two members of the editorial staff of my publishers, Miss Mary C. Mahoney and Mr. Edmund W. Nash, Jr., who devoted a large portion of their time and energy to checking on various sources for verification of many of the facts. Miss Malvina Thompson, secretary to Mrs. Franklin Delano Roosevelt, also was instrumental in providing much of the important material contained herein.

I am especially grateful to Frank D. Ashburn for permission to use material from his excellent *Peabody of Groton: A Portrait;* and to Edmund P. Rogers, not only for his help in explaining details of Franklin Roosevelt's early life, but also for the use of two interesting early letters from his personal collection.

Miss Margaret Suckley of the staff of the Franklin Delano Roosevelt Memorial Library was very generous in giving her time and advice in obtaining material for checking purposes.

Many members of the family also contributed; the assistance provided by Miss Laura Delano and Miss Ellen Roosevelt was of particular value.

In addition I wish to thank Dr. C. Rankin Barnes, Dr. W. Russell Bowie, Leverett Bradley, Herbert Burgess, Guy F. Cary, W. Sheffield Cowles, John C. Dolan, Kimball C. Elkins, Helen S. Farr, Edward J. Flynn, James L. Goodwin, Alden D. Groff, Dr. Frank L. Janeway, R. Scot Leavitt, Roger William Loewi, Marian Lawrence Peabody, Mr. and Mrs. Henry H. Richards, Dr. Edwin J. van Etten, William P. Wharton, and the research staff of *The New York Times*.

—E. R.

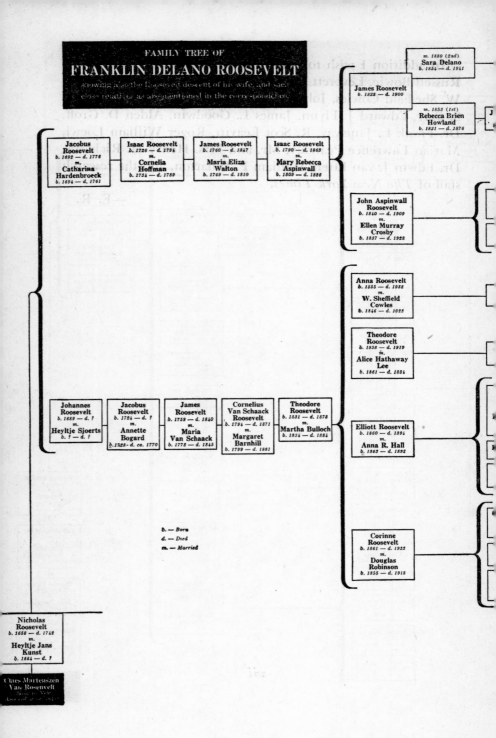

FAMILY TREE OF
FRANKLIN DELANO ROOSEVELT

showing also the Roosevelt descent of his wife, and such close relatives as are mentioned in the correspondence.

m. 1880 (2nd)
Sara Delano
b. 1854 — d. 1941

James Roosevelt
b. 1828 — d. 1900

m. 1853 (1st)
Rebecca Brien Howland
b. 1831 — d. 1876

J

Jacobus Roosevelt
b. 1692 — d. 1776
m.
Catharina Hardenbroeck
b. 1694 — d. 1761

Isaac Roosevelt
b. 1726 — d. 1794
m.
Cornelia Hoffman
b. 1734 — d. 1789

James Roosevelt
b. 1760 — d. 1847
m.
Maria Eliza Walton
b. 1769 — d. 1810

Isaac Roosevelt
b. 1790 — d. 1863
m.
Mary Rebecca Aspinwall
b. 1809 — d. 1886

John Aspinwall Roosevelt
b. 1840 — d. 1909
m.
Ellen Murray Crosby
b. 1837 — d. 1928

Anna Roosevelt
b. 1855 — d. 1932
m.
W. Sheffield Cowles
b. 1846 — d. 1923

Theodore Roosevelt
b. 1858 — d. 1919
m.
Alice Hathaway Lee
b. 1861 — d. 1884

Johannes Roosevelt
b. 1689 — d. ?
m.
Heyltje Sjoerts
b. ? — d. ?

Jacobus Roosevelt
b. 1724 — d. ?
m.
Annette Bogard
b. 1728 — d. ca. 1770

James Roosevelt
b. 1759 — d. 1840
m.
Maria Van Schaack
b. 1773 — d. 1845

Cornelius Van Schaack Roosevelt
b. 1794 — d. 1871
m.
Margaret Barnhill
b. 1799 — d. 1861

Theodore Roosevelt
b. 1831 — d. 1878
m.
Martha Bulloch
b. 1834 — d. 1884

Elliott Roosevelt
b. 1860 — d. 1894
m.
Anna R. Hall
b. 1863 — d. 1892

Corinne Roosevelt
b. 1861 — d. 1933
m.
Douglas Robinson
b. 1855 — d. 1918

b. — Born
d. — Died
m. — Married

Nicholas Roosevelt
b. 1658 — d. 1742
m.
Heyltje Jans Kunst
b. 1664 — d. ?

Claes Martenszen Van Rosenvelt

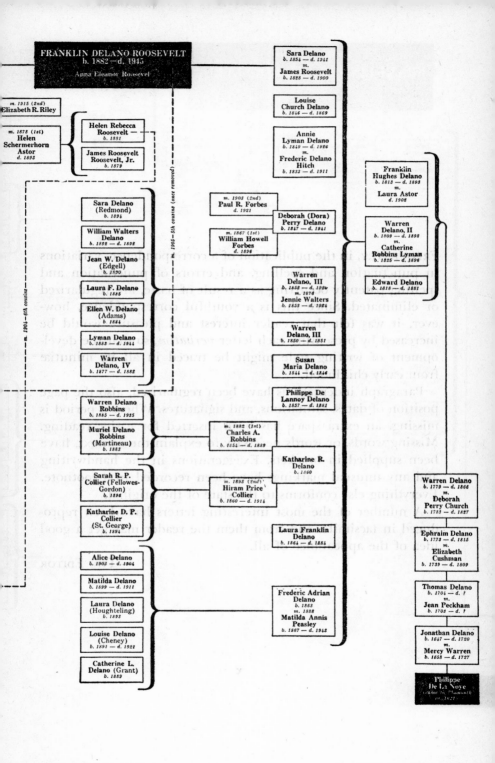

FRANKLIN DELANO ROOSEVELT
b. 1882 — d. 1945

Anna Eleanor Roosevelt

m. 1915 (2nd)
Elizabeth R. Riley

m. 1878 (1st)
Helen Schermerhorn Astor
d. 1893

Helen Rebecca Roosevelt
b. 1881

James Roosevelt Roosevelt, Jr.
b. 1879

Sara Delano (Redmond)
b. 1894

William Walters Delano
b. 1892 — d. 1892

Jean W. Delano (Edgell)
b. 1890

Laura F. Delano
b. 1885

Ellen W. Delano (Adams)
b. 1884

Lyman Delano
b. 1883 — d. 1944

Warren Delano, IV
b. 1877 — d. 1882

Warren Delano Robbins
b. 1885 — d. 1935

Muriel Delano Robbins (Martineau)
b. 1883

Sarah R. P. Collier (Fellowes-Gordon)
b. 1896

Katharine D. P. Collier (St. George)
b. 1894

Alice Delano
b. 1903 — d. 1904

Matilda Delano
b. 1899 — d. 1911

Laura Delano (Houghteling)
b. 1893

Louise Delano (Cheney)
b. 1891 — d. 1921

Catherine L. Delano (Grant)
b. 1889

Sara Delano
b. 1854 — d. 1941
m.
James Roosevelt
b. 1828 — d. 1900

Louise Church Delano
b. 1846 — d. 1869

Annie Lyman Delano
b. 1849 — d. 1926
m.
Frederic Delano Hitch
b. 1853 — d. 1911

m. 1903 (2nd)
Paul R. Forbes
d. 1921

Deborah (Dora) Perry Delano
b. 1847 — d. 1941

m. 1867 (1st)
William Howell Forbes
d. 1896

Warren Delano, III
b. 1852 — d. 1920
m. 1874
Jennie Walters
b. 1853 — d. 1924

Warren Delano, III
b. 1850 — d. 1851

Susan Maria Delano
b. 1844 — d. 1846

Philippe De Lannoy Delano
b. 1857 — d. 1881

m. 1882 (1st)
Charles A. Robbins
b. 1854 — d. 1889

Katharine R. Delano
b. 1860

m. 1893 (2nd)
Hiram Price Collier
b. 1860 — d. 1914

Laura Franklin Delano
b. 1864 — d. 1884

Frederic Adrian Delano
b. 1863
m. 1888
Matilda Annis Peasley
b. 1867 — d. 1943

Franklin Hughes Delano
b. 1813 — d. 1893
m.
Laura Astor
d. 1902

Warren Delano, II
b. 1809 — d. 1898
m.
Catherine Robbins Lyman
b. 1825 — d. 1896

Edward Delano
b. 1818 — d. 1881

Warren Delano
b. 1779 — d. 1866
m.
Deborah Perry Church
b. 1783 — d. 1827

Ephraim Delano
b. 1773 — d. 1815
m.
Elizabeth Cushman
b. 1739 — d. 1809

Thomas Delano
b. 1704 — d. ?
m.
Jean Peckham
b. 1705 — d. ?

Jonathan Delano
b. 1647 — d. 1720
m.
Mercy Warren
b. 1658 — d. 1727

Philippe De La Noye
(came to Plymouth in 1621)

m. 1905 — 5th cousins (once removed)

m. 1905 — 5th cousins

m. 1905 — 6th cousins

Frequently, in the publication of a correspondence, variations in punctuation and spelling, and errors of punctuation and spelling patently occurring as a result of haste, are regularized or eliminated. Since this is a youthful correspondence, however, it was felt that reader interest and pleasure would be increased by presenting each letter *verbatim*, so that the development of writing style might be traced in all its minutiæ from early childhood.

Paragraph indentations have been regularized, also the page position of dates, salutations, and signatures. Where a period is missing, an extra space has been inserted for easier reading. Missing words, or words necessary to explain the context, have been supplied in brackets. Exaggerations in the handwriting and any unusual markings have been recorded in a footnote. Everything else conforms to the state of the original.

A number of the most interesting letters have been reproduced in facsimile, and from them the reader may get a good idea of the appearance of all.

—The Editor

CONTENTS

Sixty-four Pages of Illustrations

AN
INTRODUCTORY
NOTE

SINCE the death of Franklin Delano Roosevelt, there has been a growing demand for details of his private life, an interest reflected in the many inquiries which have been received by members of his family. Extensive documentation while he was alive has provided rich and readily available sources for the historian of his public career; there is, on the other hand, no such mass of material at the service of those concerned with him as an individual—the biographer, the student, the general reader alike. Herein has been the impetus for *F.D.R.: His Personal Letters.*

It is contemplated that these papers will be published in three volumes: the first, containing correspondence with his family and friends from the time he wrote his first letter, at the age of five, to his graduation from Harvard in 1904; the second, correspondence from 1905 to 1928, the period bounded respectively by his marriage to Anna Eleanor Roosevelt and his election as Governor of New York State; and the third, letters and other personal material covering the Governorship and the Presidency, up to his death in 1945.

This first volume of the three, *Early Years*, exists at all because of the preoccupation which Sara Delano Roosevelt had for the future of her only child. In common with so many mothers then and now, she preserved every youthful letter and document of her son's which she could lay hands upon; in her case, the motherly conviction of destiny proved especially fortunate. Because of it, there is now available an invaluable legacy from which readers may extract the formative influences of Franklin Roosevelt's life.

The correspondence in this volume has been presented chronologically, and in three main divisions: *Boyhood, Groton,* and *Harvard.* Short commentaries before each section serve to give the reader a time-and-place background. The letters themselves have been individually annotated, with the careful assistance of members of Franklin Roosevelt's family and of boyhood friends, to explain the various references to occasions, persons, and events. Brief historical and biographical notes have also been furnished, where necessary, and to enrich the material. The effort has been to trace each one of the many allusions, yet at the same time keep the annotations short enough to satisfy clarity without gratifying pedantry.

It should be noted that while the letters preserved by Sara Delano Roosevelt represent unquestionably the great bulk of her son's youthful correspondence, certain gaps, certain unexplainable references, indicate that a small number of the letters addressed to his parents must have been lost, or were not collected at all.

Finally, it was decided that every letter available should be published. During his years at Groton, for instance, Franklin Roosevelt wrote voluminously, often several times a week, and there is repetition in this correspondence when read consecutively. Certainly, a number of his letters home throw little additional light upon the development of his character, and there was the temptation to eliminate these in the interests of readability. But since, at base, it was the purpose of this book to render a service to historians, that solution was rejected and the material set forth *in toto*. The only exceptions to this are the (indicated) deletions of certain proper names for obvious reasons.

—THE EDITOR

FOREWORD

AFTER my husband's death, when we were going through the various things in the house at Hyde Park which we were not leaving there permanently, my husband's secretary, Miss Grace Tully, told me that in the little study which he always used when he was home there were a great many red cardboard cases, on the backs of which was written: "Family Papers." He had always intended to go through them at some time, but he said that if anything happened to him, I was the one to have these particular cases.

I moved them over to the upper part of my garage near my cottage, and it was not until the spring of 1947 that I finally began to go through the cases. Then I found that I had all or nearly all of the letters which my husband had ever written to his mother, and all the letters which my own children had ever written to their grandmother, and quite a number of other items of business and of purely family interest.

As I began to read these letters, I realized that probably my husband had intended some day to go through them and put them in order as an interesting record over a fairly long span of years. Whether he intended to publish them, I do not know, but I feel sure that to many people who were fond of my hus-

xv

band in this country and abroad, a record such as these letters make will be of great interest.

My son Elliott agreed to do the editing and write the necessary explanations, consulting other members of the family, and lifelong friends of my husband, wherever he did not himself have information of the people referred to, or of the correct sequence of the letters or of the events which occurred in be tween, when the family was united and letters were not written.

From several points of view I think these letters are interesting. The chief interest of this first volume lies in the fact that it makes clear some of the training and background which went into preparing a man to meet the problems which were to face him in his public life. It is not only, of course, the education you are given, or the opportunities which you have, but it is how you profit by the education and how you grasp the opportunities which count in the ultimate use of the tools which the years of preparation have given you.

Here in these letters, I think, one can watch the growth of knowledge, the development of a personality, the training of a mind, and the influence of environment and of contacts with other people on human material.

I hope that in sharing these letters with the world we can make a contribution which will be of use to historians and educators, and which will give pleasure to many who felt Franklin D. Roosevelt was in truth their friend.

—ANNA ELEANOR ROOSEVELT

James Roosevelt and Franklin (16 months old), June 1883.

*Two studio portraits taken
in England during his first
trip abroad when F.D.R. was
three years old, June 1885.*

*The first letter Franklin ever wrote was addressed to his
mother, written in ink, and illustrated with sailboats.*

*Dear Sallie I am very sorry you
have a cold and you are in
bed I played with Mary today
for a little while I hope by tomorrow
you will be able to up I am glad
to say that my cold is letter your
loving Franklin D. Roosevelt*

1887

Sara Delano Roosevelt, called "Sallie" by friends, was
so addressed by her five-year-old son in his first letter.

One of the two ink drawings enclosed in the letter was
a detailed study of a boat under full steam and full sail.

*Written in the spring of 1888
when Hyde Park was in bloom.*

My dear Mama.
Thank you so much
for the looly soldiers.
Brother Roxy may
take a picture of our
gardans because it
takes looks so nice.
We are going to have
a big bush in our

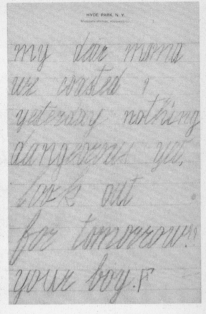

*Written on New
Year's Day, 1888.*

gardans and it nearly
two feet high. I take
my rest eory day but
I am not out much
We have battles with
the soldiers eory day.
and they are so nice.
Good bye dear Mama
Your loving little

Franklin.
P.S. Give my love
to papa and
Uncle Frank and
Aunt Laura.
Franklin
1888

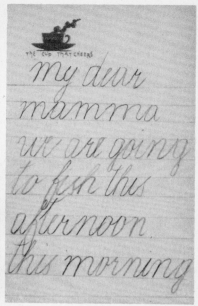

THE CUP THAT CHEERS

My dear
mamma
we are going
to fish this
afternoon.
this morning

Franklin sat for this portrait in Poughkeepsie in January 1887. The letter was written four months later.

I take the
goat-cart, to
give, mary
newbold, a
drive, we
miss you

very much.
your
affectionate
son
Franklin

may 10 1898

My dear
mamma I
went fishing
yesterday
after noon
with papa a
we caught a
dozen of
minnows
we left them
on the bank
papa told
me it would
frighten
the fish to
put them
on the hand
how is dear
grandpapa
I hope he
is better dear
mamma I
send you
a kiss your
loving son
Franklin

The first letter he ever dated in his own hand was addressed to his mother at "Algonac" where she was visiting her father.

My dear Mama.
I am in a great
hurry. I found
two birds nests
I took one egg
we are all

well. I am going
to the Millie
Rogers Party.
and to meet
Papa. Good
bye your loving
Franklin P S
love to all

To his mother, on hobby-horse paper, and to his grandfather,
Warren Delano II, between carefully pencil-ruled lines.

My dear Grandpapa
I am very glad
that you are better.
it is Beatrice Stur-
gis birthday and I
am going there to
tea I send you a

book mark which
I worked for you
with my love.
Your loving
Franklin

around August 1888

my dear mama I went to my lessons this morning. this afternoon I played with mary newbold. her mama says mary can come to morrow, but I dont know if the rodgers can come. their mama went this morning to new york I send love to mama and papa and uncle Fred adrian harticular. and his Intended western wife, I hope dear grandpapa is well and grandmama with love to you and papa. your own loving little Franklin

Franklin's early lessons were taken with the children of the neighboring Archibald Rogers family at their home.

ALDWYN TOWER.

GREAT MALVERN.

MY DEAR MAMA, WE HAVE NOT BEEN ABLE
ABLE TO GO OUT TODAY. WE HAVE BEEN PLAYING
GAMES. ONE GAME WAS STEEPLECHASE THE
OTHER WAS SOLDIERS THE OTHER DOMINOES
AND IT TOOK UP ALL THE MORNING. WE PLAYED
SOME MORE THIS AFTERNOON. WE MADE A
GREAT DISCOVERY OF A BOX OF DOMINOES
AND DRAUGHTS WITH THE RED AND WHITE
KINGS AND QUEENS JUST LIKE THAT BOOK
THROUGH THE
LOOKING GLASS
TURN OVER

WE NEARLY WENT TO THE BEACON
THIS MORNING AND WE PICKED A LOT OF
WILD FLOWERS.
YOUR LOVING FRANKLIN

From Great Malvern, Wor-
cestershire, England, where,
in the care of his governess,
Franklin was convalescing
from typhoid contracted just
before sailing from New York.

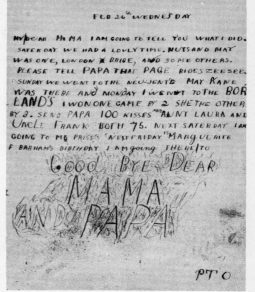

FEB 26th WEDNESDAY

MY DEAR MAMA I AM GOING TO TELL YOU WHAT I DID.
SATERDAY WE HAD A LOVLY TIME. NUTS AND MAY
WAS ONE, LONDON X BRIGE, AND SOME OTHERS.
PLEASE TELL PAPA THAT PAGE RIDES ZEE SEE.
SUNDAY WE WENT TO THE NEU-JENTS MAY KANE
WAS THERE AND MONDAY I WENT TO THE BOR
LANDS I WON ONE GAME BY 2 SHE THE OTHER
BY 3. SEND PAPA 100 KISSES AND AUNT LAURA AND
UNCLE FRANK BOTH 75. NEXT SATERDAY I AM
GOING TO MY PRISES NEXT FRIDAY IS MARGUERITE
F BARHAM'S BIRTHDAY I AM going THERE TO
GOOD BYE DEAR
MAMA
AND PAPA

PTO

urlier that year (1889), two hun-
ed fifty kisses for Papa, Aunt
aura, and Uncle Franklin H.
elano for whom he was named.

New York 4 1889

Liebe Mama!

Ich will dir sagen,
daß ich auch schon
deutsch schreiben
kann. Ich will
aber versuchen es noch
immer besser zu ler-
nen, daß du dich
nicht freuen sollst.
Nun bitte ich dich,
schreibe mir auch
einen brief, in deut-
scher Schrift und
Sprache.
Dein Dichliebender
Sohn Franklin D.R.

Pencil drawing on foolscap, a single-masted sailboat with flags.

He and his governess collaborate on a letter in German.

A card from her son on Sara D. Roosevelt's thirty-fifth birthday.

Signed drawings of a dock-
tailed horse with two-wheeled
buggy and a well-heated house
near by a blossoming tree.

One of "the beautiful Delano sisters" — Franklin's mother.

Debby, his lively dock-tailed Welsh pony, wore a curb bit.

James Roosevelt, Hudson Valley patroon, good Union Democrat, railroad and shipping magnate, was a widower with a son aged twenty-six when he married twenty-six-year-old Sara Delano.

June 7ᵗʰ 90

My dear Papa.

I hope you are well
I am at algonac
and Lyman and
Laura and Ellen
and the baby
are coming today

at twelve oclock.
Mama left this
morning and I am
going to take
my bath alone.
I have jumped
from five to
six feet today.
Good Bye your loving Frank

At "Algonac" awaiting
the arrival of the four
Delanos, his first cous-
ins and playmates.

THE HYDE PARK DAILY HERALD.
JAN. 1. 1891.
THE GRAPHIC HAS ARRIVED THIS MORNING.
IT SNOWED THIS MORNING.
THE THERMOMETER IS 14 DEGREES. PROBABLY IT WILL
FREEZE TO MORROW. GOOD COASTING AT HYDE PARK ON
THE HUDSON N. Y.   JAS. ROOSEVELT UPSET A LARGE
BOB WITH 6 LADIES AND 1 BOY. THE BOY SCRAPED HIS
LEG A LITTLE, BUT IT IS NOT A VERY BAD WOUND.
MRS JAS. ROOSEVELT AND MISS ANNA ROOSEVELT
BOTH HURT THEIR HIPS. THEY PROBABLY WILL BE WELL
IN TWO WEEKS.
MISS A. ROOSEVELT IS STAYING WITH MR. AND MRS
JAS . ROOSEVELT. MISS SANDS HAS LEFT MR. AND MRS
ROGERS. THERE WAS A COASTING PARTY AT MR ......
PLACE TODAY.
HARD RAIN TOMORROW.
MR AND MRS . J. ROOSEVELT WILL PROBABLY NOT GO
TO NEW . YORK TOMORROW.
NOT MUCH SNOW MELTED.. HARD RAIN IN NEW YORK
DAY BEFORE YESTERDAY. A BOY WAS KICKED IN THE
HEAD BY A HORSE WHILE HE WAS COASTING.

On a child's typewriter,
nine-year-old Franklin's
first journalistic effort.

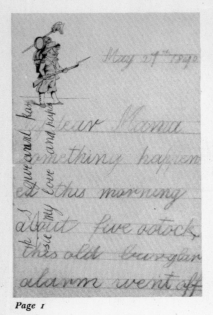

Page 1

May 2?ᵗʰ 1890

Dear Mama
something happen
ed this morning
about five oclock,
this old burglar
alarm went off

Page 3

saying he would
come with pleasure
MONDAYS REPORT
pretty good in the
morning but very
mischievous.
MONDAYS REPORT
very good in the
afternoon. Good
bey your loving
franklin

Page 2

I was hardly awake Mamie went
down stairs but she could
not turn it off and I had to go
down and turn it off. Mary
did not come over yesterday.
we played "steeple chase" and
my horse & won every race.
I just got a letter from Edmond

The first page of this letter was penciled in smooth, careful strokes. The second and third pages were written with a pen.

BOYHOOD

BOYHOOD

FRANKLIN DELANO ROOSEVELT was born on January 30, 1882, in the house then known as "Springwood" and which he himself later called "Krum Elbow," at Hyde Park in Dutchess County, New York.

The Hyde Park house is today the property of the people of the United States; in 1882, it was the typical spacious home of an affluent Hudson Valley landowner. It had been acquired by James Roosevelt in 1867 from the Josiah Wheelers, and to it he brought his second wife, Sara Delano, following their marriage in 1880. James Roosevelt was then a man of fifty-two, a widower with a grown son. His new bride was exactly half as old as he was (and exactly the same age as James Roosevelt Roosevelt, her stepson). She became the great concern of her husband's life; he largely retired from active business, though retaining his position as director of a number of companies, and settled down to the life of a country gentleman. The birth of Franklin Roosevelt provided the second interest of his later years.

The environment in which young Franklin grew up was one of comfort and security. It was the "landed gentry" tradition of the Hudson Valley aristocracy, with atmosphere and customs whose American roots were in the seventeenth century, and whose European origins traced farther back still. It was a tradition well maintained by his parents. James Roosevelt, seventh of his line in America, was a graduate of Union College and the holder of a law degree from Harvard who did not pursue that profession but entered business instead, and increased his own fortune through shrewd investments in the then-expanding iron and railroad industries. Sara Delano came from a family of merchants whose interests were scattered throughout the world, particularly in the China trade. As a natural consequence, they traveled widely; at the age of eight, Sara Delano sailed with her mother and several of her brothers and sisters on the clipper ship *Surprise* to Hong Kong, to join her father who was then repairing war-damaged fortunes in the firm of Russell and Company. Travel and the sea, history and geography became her natural interests. After her marriage, she and her husband went on frequent trips to Europe, often taking their son along; his first voyage was made at the age of three. Thus, to the atmosphere of Hyde Park was added the influence of broader horizons.

There were other parental directions. Recognizable in Franklin Roosevelt's early letters is their influence—in knowledge of nature, in love for horses and dogs, for outdoor sports, hunting, riding, sailing. James Roosevelt taught his son to recognize the various birds whose habitat was the Hudson Valley, and to make a collection of their eggs. In the hall of the Hyde Park house today there is another collection, of stuffed and mounted birds, further product of the instruction which Franklin Roosevelt received from his father. Magnificent trees adorned the Hyde Park countryside; here again, parental teaching aroused a boyish interest later to be reflected not only in tree plantations at Hyde Park, but in reforestation on a national scale. Cruises on his father's auxiliary cutter, the *Half Moon*, and sailing his own knockabout during the summer off Campobello Island on the New Brunswick coast, all provided practical experience of the sea, and an intensification of the attachment to it that was to have well-known results.

As for formal education, not until he entered Groton at the age of fourteen did Franklin Roosevelt "go to school." Prior to that time, there was a blend of teaching and upbringing not unusual in the era and the society—a French governess, a German governess, and several gentlemen tutors who prepared him for boarding school. Aside from the neighbors' children mentioned often in his early letters, therefore, this only child was less with those his own age than most young boys.

Thus, briefly, background factors. To what extent the conditions of growth shaped the tree, is largely a matter of individual interpretation. The letters speak for themselves.

*The first letter of which there is any record was written in
1887, when Franklin Roosevelt was five. It was an intra-mural
communication. His mother was ill in her room at Hyde Park,
and he wrote to her from another part of the house.*

1887

Dear Sallie

I am very sorry you have a cold and you are in bed   I
played with Mary today for a little while   I hope by tomorrow you will be able to be up   I am glad tosay that my cold
is better   your loving

FRANKLIN D. ROOSEVELT

The letter was written in ink and enclosed in an envelope
bearing the address: "Mrs. James Roosevelt / Hyde Park /
N Y" in his own handwriting. The date "1887" is in his
mother's hand, apparently added later as she began her collection. The letter also enclosed a page of his ink drawings
of sailboats. The salutation "Sallie" refers to his mother; she
was called so by father and friends, and his childhood ear
had doubtless picked this up as a form of address. The
"Mary" was Mary Newbold, daughter of a neighbor, Thomas
Newbold.

*The second known letter was
written in 1888, shortly before
his sixth birthday.*

HYDE PARK, N. Y.
TELEGRAPH STATION, POUGHKEEPSIE

my dear mama

we coasted! yesterday   nothing dangerous yet, look out for
tomorrow!!   your boy.

F

This letter was written in pencil with pencil-ruled lines for
guides. The letter heading is printed family stationery. On

the reverse of the single sheet his mother noted in ink: "Written by Franklin when 5 years and 11 months old. He knew his letters but was told how to spell the words—Jan 1st 1888."

∽∾

"We have battles with the sol-
diers evry day . . ."

My dear Mama.

Thank you so much for the lovly soldiers. Brother Rosy may take a pictuer of our gardans because it looks so nice. We are going to have a big bush in our gardans and it's nearly two feet high. I take my rest evry day but Iam not out much   We have battles with the soldiers evry day. and they are so nice. Good bye dear Mama   Your loving little

FRANKLIN

P. S. Give my love to papa and Uncle Frank and Aunt Laura.

FRANKLIN

1888

This letter was written in longhand script, in ink. The date "1888" was added in his mother's hand. "Brother Rosy" is a reference to his half-brother, James Roosevelt Roosevelt (the son of James Roosevelt and his first wife, Rebecca Howland), who was twenty-eight years older than he. "Uncle Frank and Aunt Laura" were his maternal great-uncle, Franklin Hughes Delano, after whom he was named, and the latter's wife, the former Laura Astor, a granddaughter of John Jacob Astor. The probable date of this letter was the spring of 1888.

∽∾

"I found two birds nests . . ."

My dear Mama.

I am in a great hurry. I found two birds nests   I took one egg   we are all well. I am going to the Millie Rogers Party. and to meet Papa. Good bye   your loving

FRANKLIN

P S   love to all

7

Again written in the spring of 1888. The letterhead shows a little boy with helmet and saber riding a hobby-horse, printed in gold, blue-green, gray, and flesh colors. The letter was written in ink. "Millie Rogers" was Emily Rogers, daughter of the Henry Pendleton Rogers', Hudson River neighbors.

∽

"We are going to fish this after-
noon . . ."

My dear mamma
   we are going to fish this afternoon, this morning I take the goat-cart, to give, mary newbold, a drive, we miss you very much. your affectionate son

FRANKLIN

Written in pencil. The letterhead shows a steaming cup and saucer engraved in silver, with the inscription "The Cup That Cheers." The "goat-cart" was a pony cart and not, as the description implies, one drawn by a goat. The date is again the spring of 1888.

∽

"We caught a dozen of min-
nows . . ."

MAY 18   1888

My dear mamma
   I went fishing yesterday after noon with papa   we caught a dozen of minnows   we left them on the bank   papa told me it would frighten the fish to put them in the pond   how is dear grandpapa   I hope he is better dear mamma   I send you a kiss   your loving son

FRANKLIN

Written in pencil on the same letterpaper as the preceding, with the date in his own hand. "Dear grandpapa" refers to Warren Delano II, his maternal grandfather, who in 1848 had settled at Newburgh, N. Y., south of Hyde Park and on the opposite bank of the Hudson. His mother was at this time visiting there at the Delano family home, "Algonac."

~~

"I send you a book mark . . ."

My dear Grandpapa

I am very glad that you are better. it is Beatrice Sturgis birthday and I am going there to tea. I send you a book mark which I worked for you with my love. Your loving

FRANKLIN

This penciled letter was sent to his Grandfather Delano from Campobello Island. Following the signature there is the ink notation (in another hand): "received August 1888." His parents had purchased land at Campobello in 1883, and became permanent summer residents by 1886, when their house was completed. Since members of the Sturgis family appear frequently in this correspondence, a word of explanation is appropriate at this point. The Delano-Sturgis acquaintanceship originated in the halcyon days of the China trade, and was—as might be expected—bound up with the firm of Russell and Company. Of this notable house, Mary Caroline Crawford (in her *Famous Families of Massachusetts*) said: "From first to last there were forty-eight members in the firm of Russell and Company, all of whom lived in China a portion of the time . . . no organization exerted a more powerful influence on Boston society than this wealthy and highly successful house." Nathaniel Russell Sturgis (whose first wife was a cousin of Catherine Lyman) went to China in 1833 and became a partner in the firm of Russell, Sturgis and Company of Canton, retaining his position when the latter was incorporated into Russell and Company in 1840. At this same time Warren Delano II was a young man in the Canton offices of the company, his job to check the lading bills of the wondrous clipper ships as they came to anchor off Whampoa Island, ten miles downriver. Russell Sturgis (he dropped the name Nathaniel in later life) returned to Boston, married for the

9

third time in 1846, and contemplated passing the rest of his business career in native climes. But in 1849, delayed a few days in London during a trip by the dilatoriness of a luggage expressman, he made the acquaintance of a senior member of Baring Brothers, was offered and accepted a position with that great British bank. He passed the remainder of his life in England, succeeding Thomas Baring as head of the firm in 1873, and dying in 1887 at the age of eighty-two. Two of his grandchildren, Edward and S. Warren Sturgis, were among F.D.R.'s masters at Groton; another, fifth Russell Sturgis in the line, was a near neighbor of the James Roosevelts at Campobello, and father of the Beatrice Sturgis mentioned here. It is possible to date this letter accurately from her second birthday, which fell on August 7th.

〰

". . . and his Intended western
wife . . ."

TELEGRAPH
POUGHKEEPSIE (WESTERN UNION)

POST OFFICE
HYDE PARK ON THE HUDSON, N. Y.

NOV 20 1888

my dear mama

I went to my lessons this morning. this afternoon I played with mary newbold. her mama says mary can come to morrow, but I dont know if the rodgers can come. their mama went this morning to new york   I send love to mama and papa and uncle Fred adrian particular and his Intended western wife. I hope dear grandpapa is well and grandmama   with love to you and papa. your own loving little

FRANKLIN

In pencil. The date is in his own hand; the post-office and telegraph addresses are printed on the letterhead. Near neigh-

bors were the Archibald Rogers family, which included a
number of boys and girls around his age; a sort of kinder-
garten was held at their home, which he attended. "Uncle
Fred Adrian" was his maternal uncle, Frederic Adrian Delano,
who had gone into railroading some years before with the
Chicago, Burlington & Quincy Railroad. In November of
1888 he married Matilda Annis Peasley, daughter of James
C. Peasley, vice-president of the C.B.&Q. Frederic Delano
lived for many years in Chicago, rose to become general man-
ager of the C.B.&Q., and president successively of the
Wheeling, the Wabash, and the Monon railways. During
World War I he was a vice-governor of the Federal Reserve
Board; he served for eighteen years on the National Capital
Park Commission in Washington; and, in 1934, F.D.R. ap-
pointed him chairman of the National Resources Planning
Board. The "Grandmama" of this letter was Mrs. Warren
Delano II, the former Catherine Lyman.

∽∾

*"Send Papa 100 kisses and Aunt
Laura and Uncle Frank both
75 . . ."*

FEB 26TH   WEDNESDAY

My dear Mama
    I am going to tell you what I did. Saterday we had a lovely
time. Nuts and May was one, London Brige, and some others.
Please tell Papa that Page rides ZeeZee. Sunday we went to
the Neu-jent's May Kane was there and Monday I went to
the BORLAND'S I won one game by 2 she the other by 3.
Send Papa 100 kisses and Aunt Laura and Uncle Frank both
75. Next Saterday I am going to Mr Prise's Next Friday is
Marguerite F Barham's birthday I am going there to
            GOOD BYE DEAR MAMA AND PAPA
PTO
P S Thank you for the lovly photos

In ink, with printed characters. His mother noted on the back of the sheet: "1889—Park." "Nuts and May," like "London Brige," was a children's game. "Page" was possibly a groom on the Hyde Park estate, but the reference has not been traced. "ZeeZee" was one of James Roosevelt's favorite riding horses. The "Neu-jent's" (probably "Nugents") and "Mr. Prise" remain obscure. "May Kane" was most likely Marian Sybil Kane, his own age, one of the five daughters of the Grenville Kanes of Tuxedo Park and a niece of S. Nicholson Kane (vide infra). There were two girls, Maud and Ella, in the Borland family of nearby New Hamburgh.

∽∽

"We are going to see Barnoms Circus . . ."

AND
MAR 22/89

My dear

We are going to see Barnoms Circus and it is going to march through the streets and we are going to see it. We are coming home the eleventh of April. I am very sorry you hurt your arm. I forgot to put your name in it   Send love to Edmund   good bye   your loving

FRANKLIN D. ROOSEVELT

From the collection of Edmund P. Rogers. This letter was sent from New York to Archibald Rogers, Jr., at Hyde Park. The Barnum circus paraded then, as it does today, from its railroad cars through the streets of the city to the show grounds. The childhood friendship with young Archibald Rogers ended when the latter died of diphtheria the following December. "I forgot to put your name in it" probably refers to the salutation.

∽∽

*Translation of a letter written
in German script*

NEW YORK 4/889

Dear Mama!

I will show you, that I can already write in German. But I
shall try always to improve it, so that you will be really pleased.
Now I want to ask *you* to write me a letter in German script
and language. Your loving son

FRANKLIN D. R.

The German script (see pictorial section) shows, from handwriting variations, that this letter was something of a col-
laborative effort. At this period in his life he was studying
German with his governess, Fraulein Reinhardt, and spoke it
with a certain facility. Across the face of the envelope his
mother noted: "Letter from Franklin written when he was 6
years and 10 months old"—which would place the date in
November of 1888, conflicting with the written date of April
1889.

∽

"We made a great discovery of a
box of Dominoes . . ."

1889 ALDWYNTOWER
GREAT MALVERN

My Dear Mama.

We have not been able to go out today. We have been playing games. One game was Steeplechase the other was Soldiers
the other Dominoes, and it took up all the morning. We played
some more this afternoon. We made a great discovery of a box
of Dominoes and draughts with the red and white kings and
queens just like that book THROUGH THE LOOKING-
GLASS

turn over

13

We nearly went to the beacon this morning and we picked a lot of wild flowers. Your loving

FRANKLIN

*(Across outside of letter, to show
when folded in four, he wrote:)*

FROM
FRANKLIN

In the summer of 1889 he went abroad, and the slight illness with which he boarded the boat was soon diagnosed as typhoid fever, necessitating his going to the Royal Infirmary in Liverpool immediately after landing. He convalesced under the care of his governess at Great Malvern, in Worcestershire, while his parents were away visiting various friends —hence this letter. It was printed in ink, and the date "1889" added by his mother.

∽∽

*For his mother's birthday on
September 21, 1889, he made a
birthday card, roughly square,
with red letters pasted on heavy
white paper. The front reads:*

FOR
DEAR
MAMA

The double inside spread:

A HAPPY
BIRTHDAY

And the back:

1889

∽∽

Also extant from this period in his life are three sheets of foolscap with drawings, showing:

1) **Pencil drawing of a single-masted sailboat** with flags, and, on the reverse side, a two-masted schooner with flags and lifeboats in davits.

2) **Ink drawing of house** with two smoking chimneys, porch showing two figures at table, a blossoming tree with a ladder set against the trunk and a figure climbing up. This has a decorative whorled border and is signed in the lower lefthand corner "FDR."

3) **Ink drawing of a horse and buggy** with driver in black, wearing black stovepipe hat, holding reins and whip. This has a similar decorative border and the same signature in the same place.

∽∾

"I had to go down and turn it off . . ."

MAY 27TH 1890

My dear Mama

something happened this morning about five oclock, this old burglar alarm went off   I was hardly awake   Mamie went down stairs but she could not turn it off and I had to go down and turn it off. Mary did not come over yesterday. We played "steeple chase" and my horse won every race. I just got a letter from Edmond saying he would come with pleasure.

MONDAYS REPORT. pretty good in the morning but very mischievous.

MONDAYS REPORT   very good in the afternoon.

Good bey   your loving

FRANKLIN

P S   give aunt Kassie my love and papa

The letterhead shows the colored figure of a soldier. The first page was written in pencil, the remainder in ink, in his large but very clear script. "Mamie" was the name by which he called his nurse Ellen, who came to the James Roosevelts shortly after his birth and stayed many years. "Edmond" was Edmund P. Rogers, son of Archibald Rogers. "Aunt Kassie" was his maternal aunt, Katharine Delano, whose first husband, Charles A. Robbins, had died the year before. In 1893 she married Hiram Price Collier.

〜

"I am going to take my bath alone . . ."

JUNE 7TH 1890

My dear Papa

I hope you are well. I am at algonac and Lyman and Laura and Ellen and the baby are coming today at twelve oclock. Mama left this morning and I am going to take my bath alone. I have jumped from five to six feet today   Good bye   your loving

FRANKLIN

The personal references here are to Lyman Delano (who, like his uncle Frederic Adrian Delano, became prominent in railroading, and was chairman of the board of the Atlantic Coast Line); to Miss Laura F. Delano (who, it will be recalled, was with F.D.R. at Warm Springs when he died); to Ellen W. Delano (later married to Frederick B. Adams, director of Air Reduction Corporation); and to Jean W. Delano ("the baby" —afterward the wife of the head of the Boston Museum of Fine Arts, George Harold Edgell)—all children of F.D.R.'s maternal uncle, Warren Delano III.

〜

16

The cast of features and facial expression Sara D. Roosevelt
shared with her son can readily be seen in this oil portrait.

Algonac.
Dec. 9th 1890

My dear Mom,

I arrived here safely and found all well. We went out coasting in the afternoon after having talked with grandpa.

This morning I went out coasting again and spilt Mad^elle^ twice. I fastened our sleds to a carriage and it pulled us up the hill. I cannot write more as I am going out coasting again. I hope you arrived all right in N. Y. and enjoyed the ball. Good bye. Love to papa.

Your loving

Franklin.

F.D.R. and a Campobello playmate at the
helm in a stiff Bay of Fundy breeze.

With his mother on the porch of the original
frame house on the Hyde Park estate.

April 10th 1891

My dear Aunt Doe,

We are having a very early Spring and the ride to Algonac as we did last summer. I am to have a little farm and chicken house of my own. I hope you and Uncle Will will come

Papa is going to buy a cutter that will go by naphtha and we are going to sail in it at Campobello and

To Aunt Doe and Uncle Will Forbes, abroad—" . . . any foreign stamps . . . as I have begun to make a collection."

wild flowers are beginning to come up in the woods. My pony Deb by is well and I rode 12 miles today with Papa and we are going to

home soon. Please tell Uncle Will that if he has any foreign stamps I should like to have them as I have begun to make a collection.

here. With much love and many kisses to you both.
I am your affectionate nephew
Franklin.

Gruss aus BAD NAUHEIM

To his first cousins, Muriel and Warren Delano Robbins, with a message for his Aunt Katherine Delano Robbins.

May 30th 1891

My dear Muriel and Warren. We are staying in Bad Nauheim Germany. It is lovely here and on this paper is picture of the big lake on which we row and Papa got me a great big boat and I sail it every day. I am sending you a drawing of the boat. Tell Aunt Kassie that I am drawing her a little book with skeches of Nauheim and other places where we go to. I have a splendid bow and arrow and I shoot in the park. It is raining now. I go to the public school with a lot of little mickies and we have German reading, German dictation, the history of Siegfreed, and arithmetic in which I am to 14 X 71 on paper. and I like it very much. Give my love to Grandpa and Grandma and say I wish they were here. Good bye your affectionate Franklin D. R.

P.S. Give my love to Aunt Kassie and write soon. F. D. R.

Hyde Park
Feb 27th 1892

My darling mumkin & Pak!

Good morning I hope you have used Pears soap & are flourishing now.

I am dying of school fever & you will be horrified to hear that my temperature is 150°. But really I have got a "petit rhume" only

I am in the hands of the celebrated Dr Sandoz — He came up to see me this morning & ordered 5 drops of camfer on sugar twice in the mornin; a hot toe bag, breakfast in bed & stay at home all day if not clear of the disease. I went to play with E. yester

terday & rided o=
ver there—Today
the whole army
of carpenters come
to lunch—We got
12 eggs yesterday
and there is no
clocking hen.

N'ayez au moins pas peur,
je ne laisserai pas sortir Franklin
& j'en aurai bien soin, il est gai
comme un pinson ainsi il n'est
guère malade — Il a changé
hier en rentrant & je ne vois pas
qu'il ait un rhume mais
il dit qu'il en a un — Je me
méfie un petit peu parce
que hier il m'a dit en riant
qu'il serait malade & ne
pourrait pas aller à l'église
Il fait beaucoup de vent
& assez froid
Je vous ai écrit hier, vendredi
vous envoyant la mesure
des nappes

I can't write any more, last night
So good bye. Your   High wind all night
 affectionate   FDR
Roosevelt Delano
Franklin
P.S. The thermometer
went down to 10°

A "petit rhume" treated by the celebrated Dr. Sandoz.

". . . and spilt Mad^elle twice . . ."

My dear Mom,

I arrived here safely and found all well. We went out coasting in the afternoon after having talked with grandpa. This morning I went out coasting again and spilt Mad^elle twice. I fastened our sleds to a carriage and it pulled us up the hill. I cannot write more as I am going out coasting again. I hope you arrived all right in N.Y. and enjoyed the ball. Goodbye . . Love to papa.

Your loving

FRANKLIN.

"Mad^elle" thus dumped in the snow was his Swiss governess, Mlle. Jeanne Sandoz, who later left him to take care of his Aunt Kassie's children at Tuxedo Park.

~~

"A boy was kicked in the head
by a horse . . ."

The Hyde Park Daily Herald.
Jan. 1. 1891.

The Graphic has arrived this morning.

It snowed this morning.

The thermometer is 14 degrees. Probae [probable] it will freeze to morrow. Good coasting at Hyde Park on the Hudson N.Y. Jas. Roosevelt upset a large bob with 6 ladies and 1 boy. The boy scraped his leg a little, but it is not a very bad wound. Mrs Jas. Roosevelt and Miss Anna Roosevelt both hurt their hips. They probably will be well in two weeks.

Miss A. Roosevelt is staying with Mr. and Mrs Jas. Roosevelt. Miss Sands has left Mr. and Mrs. Rogers. There was a coasting party at Mr. . . . . place today.

Hard rain tomorrow.

Mr and Mrs J. Roosevelt will probably not go to New. York tomorrow.

Not much snow melted . . Hard rain in New York day before yesterday. A boy was kicked in the head by a horse while he was coasting.

First aspirations toward a journalist's career, written on a child's typewriter. It contains the first of many references to the *Survey Graphic,* a magazine he greatly admired. Miss Anna Roosevelt was his fifth cousin, a sister of Theodore Roosevelt, and a close friend of Mr. and Mrs. James Roosevelt Roosevelt, who lived next door to F.D.R.'s parents. "Miss Sands" was Miss Louise Sands of New York, a frequent visitor at the Archibald Rogers' home. The boy kicked by a horse was F.D.R.

∞

"I have begun to make a collection . . ."

APRIL 10TH 1891

My dear Aunt Doe,

We are having a very early Spring and the wild flowers are beginning to come up in the woods. My pony Debby is well and I rode 12 miles today with Papa and we are going to ride to Algonac as we did last summer. I am to have a little farm and chicken house of my own. I hope you and Uncle Will will come home soon. Please tell Uncle Will that if he has any foreign stamps I should like to have them, as I have begun to make a collection.

Papa is going to buy a cutter that will go by naphtha and we are going to sail in it at Campobello and here. With much love and many kisses to you both.

I am your affectionate nephew   FRANKLIN.

The "Aunt Doe" to whom this letter was addressed was his maternal aunt, Deborah Perry (Dora) Delano. She married William Howell Forbes, a partner in Russell and Company, and lived for over thirty years at "Rose Hill," the Warren Delano house in Macao, across the bay from Hong Kong. After her husband's death in 1896, she married his younger brother, Paul Forbes. "Debby" was a Welsh pony, F.D.R.'s first. The "cutter that will go by naphtha" materialized into the fifty-one-foot sailing yacht *Half Moon,* launched in July of 1891.

〜〜

"I had a fight with a big boy of
eleven . . . and I beat him . . ."

My dear Edmond,   R.M.S. "TEUTONIC"
    I am writing to you on the "Teutonic." She is the largest ship I ever saw. She is 582 feet long and 56 feet broad and 39 feet depth of hold. She has almost everything on board there is a library, a barber shop, lots of baths, and lots of other things where you get quite lost. We are rolling so now I can hardly write. The waves are quite high. When one is sitting down one has to take care one does not slip off. I can not write more now. Please write soon. Good. bye I am your affec^nate
                                                FRANKLIN
P.S. I had a fight with a big boy of eleven because he cheated and I beat him.
                                                F.D.R.

   From the collection of Edmund P. Rogers, to whom it was addressed. The letter was mailed from Queenstown (Cobh), Ireland, postmarked May 13th, 1891. The "Teutonic" of the White Star Line was carrying James Roosevelt and his family to their annual cure at Bad Nauheim, in the agreeable Germany of the third year of Wilhelm II's reign.

〜〜

"I am to '14 x 71' on paper . . ."

My dear Muriel and Warren.   MAY 30TH 1891
    We are staying in Bad Nauheim Germany. It is lovely here and on this paper is a picture of the big lake on which we row and Papa got me a great big boat and I sail it every day. I am sending you a drawing of the boat. Tell Aunt Kassie that I am drawing her a little book with skeches of Nauheim and other places where we go to. I have a splendid bow and arrow

and I shoot in the park. It is raining now. I go to the public school with a lot of little mickies and we have German reading, German dictation, the history of Siegfried, and arithmetic in which I am to "14 x 71", on paper, and I like it very much. Give my love to Grandpa and Grandma and say I wish they were here. Good bye   your affectionate

FRANKLIN. D. R.

P.S. Give my love to Aunt Kassie and write soon.

F.D.R.

The letterhead bears an engraving of the lake here mentioned, with the legend *"Gruss aus Bad Nauheim."* Nauheim was a health resort about forty miles east of the Rhine, near Frankfurt, where treatment baths in carbonated water, supplemented by graded physical exercises, were given James Roosevelt, who suffered from heart disease. "Muriel and Warren," to whom the letter was addressed, were Muriel Delano Robbins and Warren Delano Robbins, Aunt Kassie's children by her first marriage. The former married Cyril Martineau and lives in London; Warren Robbins entered the diplomatic service, became chief of protocol in the State Department, and in 1933 was appointed minister to Canada by his first cousin. To improve his German, F.D.R. was on this trip placed in the Nauheim *Volksschule.*

∽

A message tossed to the waves

7 COLLEGE GREEN,
TOWYN, R.S.O.,
MEIRIONETHSHIRE

White Star Line Office,
Liverpool.

Gentlemen:
The enclosed bottle & paper was picked up on the beach at Towyn by Mr. Morris Jones, Creigfor, Dinasmawddwy. Kindly send him particular of same if there is any.

Yours truly
H. W. GRIFFITHS

(and clipped to the above letter
was the following slip of paper,
written in ink by F.D.R.):

If this is picked up please return to White Star Line Office
Liverpool   May 12 1892

                    F D ROOSEVELT, P. BABCOCK

Off Queenstown

                             per "Germanie" from
                                   New York
                                 May 4, 1892

The above material was enclosed in an envelope forwarded to
"Master Franklin Roosevelt, R.M.S. Majestic," by the White
Star Line office, and he received it on his way back from
Europe in 1892. He and his co-signatory had enclosed the
message in a bottle and tossed it overboard on their trip
across.

〜〜

"We got 12 eggs yesterday and
there is no clocking hen . . ."

                                   HYDE PARK
                           FEB. 27TH   1892

My darling mumkin and Pap!

Good morning   I hope you have used Pear's Soap & are
flourishing now. I am dying of school fever and you will be
horrified to hear that my temperature is 150°   But really I
have got a "petit rhume" only I am in the hands of the celebrated Dr. Sandoz— He came up to see me this morning &
ordered 5 drops of camfer on sugar twice in the mornin; a
hot toe bag, breakfast in bed & stay at home all day tomorrow
and today if not clear of the disease. I went to play with E.
yesterday and *rided* over there— Today the whole army of
carpenters come to lunch— We got 12 eggs yesterday and there

is no clocking hen. I can't write any more, So Good bye. Your afectionate

ROOSEVELT DELANO FRANKLIN

P.S. The thermometer went down to 10° last night   High wind all night

FDR

"The celebrated Dr. Sandoz" refers to his governess, Mlle. Sandoz. "E." was Edmund P. Rogers. The phrase "tomorrow and today" in the fifth sentence was inserted interlinear in another hand, presumably his governess', who wished his parents to be confident their son was having the best of care. Apparently she wanted to be *absolutely* sure, for she wrote on the reverse of the letter sheet, in French, the following additional message:

> *Do not concern yourselves in the least, I won't let Franklin go out and will take good care of him; he is as gay as a finch ["il est gai comme un pinson"] and actually he is hardly sick at all— He changed his clothes yesterday when he came in and I couldn't see that he had a cold but he said he had one—I was a little distrustful because yesterday he had told me laughingly that he would be ill and wouldn't be able to go to church—*
>
> *It is very windy and quite cold.—*
>
> *I wrote you yesterday, Friday, sending you the measurements of the tablecloths.*

◇◇

"How are the dead rats getting on? . . ."

Hyde Park on the Hudson, N. Y.   1893

My dear Mammy   APRIL 18TH

I hope you are much better today & that you will be able to go out today. How are the dead rats getting on? Have you all my things down? If not, just telegraph to me & I will come to help you. Have you as fine a day as we have, it is elegant up here. Yesterday I worked all the morning on joice [joists] for the Club House & in the afternoon Edmond & I put two of

22

them up. I dined and supped at Edmond's but Melle got there at 6.40 so we had not any time to play. Today Edmond is coming to lunch & we will get the other joice up.

Please thank Pippy for the nails & tell him to send in his bill very soon. On Wednesday we will begin to put the back and sides on. Melle lost her purse in N.Y. containing about $6 & two zither-rings, she is quite broken hearted. Melle has changed her mind about crinoline & wears skirts 7 yards in circumference. I am flourishing & have only fallen 3 times from the top story window.

With bales of love to everybody   Your devoted baby

NILKNARF

Of the incident of the "joice," Edmund Rogers recalls: "We built a small boat-club house and planned to dam a small field below the Roosevelt house, on which to sail and race small model yachts. We finished the Club House—all but the roof—and then had to leave." As for "Pippy" who supplied the nails for this enterprise, he remains an indistinct figure. "Nilknarf" is a further progression of the signature to the previous letter, and can be deciphered without too great difficulty.

〜〜〜

"I have brushed my teeth and said my prayers . . ."

HYDE PARK/1893

Darling Mumpy,

I am going to get up at half past six to make your Xmas present it is going to be lovely!!! Please don't forget to get the stamps for Muriel [and] Warren ready for the mail I have brushed my teeth & said my prayers, & as it is quater past eight I must stop.

Loveingly

FDR

A very rough pencil scrawl, not employing the usual ink and the ruled guide-lines. The place and date were added on the reverse of the sheet by his mother.

Translation of a letter written
in French

Dear Mumsy & Pupsy.

I hope that you are well. I know what kind of skates you should buy, ask for Peck & Snider's American Club Skates, Size N° 10. We skated yesterday but it began to rain & we came home. My soldiers and the ba-dog for Hermon came yesterday; my soldiers are magnificent, beautiful and not expensive. *If* you want to give me a Christmas present give me 2 boxes of soldiers like the ones I bought the other day; you can tell them apart from the others because they have two little cannons hitched to horses & 10 little soldiers with white trousers and blue jackets like this [at this point he drew a sketch of one of the soldiers, and below it wrote: "LIFE SIZE"]

They are the best soldiers I have ever seen. Mr. Nick (Cane) came to see us yesterday & he couldn't get in because the piazza had been varnished. I can't write any more because I have to go riding.

Your unhappy son

TLEVESOOR D. NILKNARF

"Springwood" was the old original name of the Hyde Park house; in later years F.D.R. spoke of it as "Krum Elbow," thereby encountering considerable disagreement over the historical justification for this name from neighbors, and, it may be added, from his mother. The "Hermon" referred to here was Herman Livingston Rogers, another son of Archibald Rogers (and who, it will be recalled, was in later years host to the Duke and Duchess of Windsor at his chateau in France). Herman Rogers was a godchild of Mrs. James Roosevelt; at this time he was a little over two years old. "Nick (Cane)" was Mr. S. Nicholson Kane of New York, an elderly bachelor and a great friend of the Rogers' and Roosevelts; he was for many years on the Regatta and Race Committees of the New York Yacht Club. The signature here reaches an ultimate point in the experimentation. On the reverse of the sheet of letter-paper, his governess added, in French: "This was in place of French composition. Franklin wrote it all by himself, except for 4 spelling mistakes which I corrected."

∽∽

"I have just finished a success-ful game of Flip . . ."

CHAMPLAIN TRANSPORTATION COMPANY
Lake George Steamboat Company

Jas. Roosevelt,
President.
                                    HYDE PARK, JAN. 8TH, 1895
                                    WEDNESDAY EVENING
Darling Mum,

It is 8.15, & I am just going to bed; Elsie is making my bed & I have just finished a successful came [game] of "Flip" with Mr. Dumper in which I beat 9 games out of 10. I have been in bed all day, & my cold is really better. Rosine has gone to "dine" at the Scholl's, & is coming home at 10 p.m. I hope this will reach you tomorrow

I think I will be all right tomorrow, but I shall not go out in the morning & only in the afternoon, if the weather is fine. With loads of love,
                                    F.D ROOSEVELT

The printed letterhead reveals one of the business interests which James Roosevelt retained in his later years, and those who can recall the now-ended period when paddle-wheel steamers competed for business on the Adirondack lakes may imagine that the demands upon his time were less arduous than enjoyable. The Champlain Transportation Company had been born out of competition and amalgamation, but the rail-roads were at this time already pointing out the end of its prosperity. "Elsie" was a Roosevelt housemaid and laundress who later became a sort of general factotum. This letter contains the first reference to the tutor who stayed longest with him, Mr. Arthur Dumper of Cleveland, who joined the house-hold in 1893. "Rosine" and the "Scholls" remain obscure.

25

GROTON

GROTON

In a book about private schools of America [1] published three years after Franklin Roosevelt graduated from Groton, the following passage occurs. It seems to convey aptly not only the topographical appearance of Groton School, as it was then, but also something of its atmosphere:

> To the north and west of the school the land descends in wooded slopes to the valley of the Nashua River, while far to the north are the rolling waves of the Pack Monadnock range in New Hampshire, and above and beyond them Grand Monadnock itself. But no village or city is visible in all the wide prospect, and only to the eastward is there a hint of anything but entire seclusion from the world at large, for in that quarter, two miles away, is the village of Groton, not wholly invisible, yet rather guessed at than actually seen.

It was while still a senior at Episcopal Theological School in Cambridge, Massachusetts, that Endicott Peabody began to raise the money to found a preparatory school. He himself had been educated at Cheltenham, in England, and it was the strong influence of the English public schools—most particularly, of Rugby and of Rugby's great headmaster, Thomas Arnold—that drove his ambition and molded his concept of Groton. Within a short time, that concept became a reality.

[1] *Some Famous American Schools,* by Oscar Fay Adams, Boston, 1903.

29

James and Prescott Lawrence donated approximately one hundred acres of land on Farmer's Row in the very quiet village of Groton, Massachusetts, some thirty-five miles north of Boston. Forty thousand dollars was raised. There was set up a board of trustees calculated to give confidence to prospective supporters, and to parents with sons to be appropriately educated. Its president was the noble and inspiring rector of Trinity Church in Boston, Phillips Brooks, later to become Bishop of Massachusetts. William Lawrence, then dean of Episcopal Theological School and Brooks's eventual successor as bishop, was secretary. The founder's father, Samuel Endicott Peabody, a successful businessman and former member of J. S. Morgan and Company in London, was treasurer. J. Pierpont Morgan himself graced the board. The prospectus that these trustees issued said in part:

> *Every endeavor will be made to cultivate manly, Christian character, having regard to moral and physical as well as intellectual development.*

In 1883 construction of a schoolhouse began. Tuition was set at $500 (in 1947 it was $1400); Peabody's salary as headmaster was to be $1200 and those of Reverend Sherrard Billings and William Amory Gardner, the two original masters, $800. On October 15, 1884, the school formally opened.

Other buildings were soon added: Brooks House (after Phillips Brooks) in 1884; two years later the first small gymnasium, tennis courts, and the boathouse, given by that great patron of Harvard, Augustus Hemenway; the first chapel, a gift of William Amory Gardner; in 1890 the fives courts; in 1891 Hundred House (so called because it was built to house one hundred boys.) Thus they were when Franklin Roosevelt entered Groton in 1896—characteristically ranged around a circular expanse of lawn, with Hundred House to the south, Brooks House to the north, the old schoolhouse to the west, and the gym and chapel to the east. The color scheme, with the exception of the chapel, was (and remains) red brick with white trim. "Inside," as Frank Ashburn, the noted chronicler of the school,[1] says, "the arrangement of the buildings was almost Spartan. The predominating color was a brown stain or a varnished finish which was durable but in no sense sybaritic."

The daily routine of that period consisted of breakfast at 7:30, chapel services at 8:15, classes from 8:30 to noon, two afternoon school periods of forty-five minutes each, followed by athletics. In the evening there was chapel again, after supper, then a study period in the schoolroom, following which the Rector and Mrs. Peabody shook the hands of each and every boy as they filed out to their dormitories. At night stiff white collars and evening shoes were worn; blue suits were the order on Sunday. The routine was strict, tardiness fatal. The Spartan atmosphere extended to sleeping arrangements, Ashburn notes:

> All boys, in whatever form, slept in cubicles except for the senior and at times the junior prefect. A cubicle was a narrow alcove, about six feet wide and nine or ten feet deep, opening on a broad corridor. The walls of each cubicle were about seven feet high, above which there was a vacant space to a tall ceiling. There was no door to a cubicle, but a cloth curtain. . . . In the cubicle was a bed, a bureau, a chair, and a small rug. Suits were hung on hooks on the cubicle wall.

And to washing:

> Attached to each dormitory was a lavatory, with showers (a cold one was required of every boy every morning), black soapstone sinks, and tin basins for washing.

The curriculum was in the classical vein, with Latin, Greek, English Literature and Composition, and Mathematics dominant, plus the modern languages of German and French, and with the grudging intrusion of one or two science courses. The Rector taught Sacred Studies. From him emanated the strong

---

[1] *Peabody of Groton; A Portrait,* by Frank D. Ashburn, New York, 1944.

religious atmosphere of the school, whose charter provides that none but a Protestant Episcopal clergyman may become its headmaster. Life centered around the chapel to a very considerable extent. The importance which Endicott Peabody attached to religion in the education of Groton boys was reflected in a letter he wrote to Franklin Roosevelt years later, in 1935:

> I venture to think that your going to Church means more to the people throughout the land than almost anything else that you can do. . . . To us in the School, it is a great thing to be able to point to a Groton graduate, now in the highest position in the country, believing in the Church and devoted to its interests.

A word should be said about the man whose personality was Groton's from 1884 to his retirement in 1940. The Reverend Endicott Peabody was a big, broad-shouldered man, with blond hair and blue eyes; he inspired awe by his looks as much as by his words. He was an enthusiastic sportsman, participating (as was the custom then) in the school athletics. In 1882, before the idea of Groton had been advanced and he was a student at Episcopal, he spent a year in charge of a church at Tombstone, Arizona, in order to get some practical experience for the ministry. The *Tombstone Epitaph* recorded: "Well, we've got a parson who doesn't flirt with the girls, who doesn't drink beer behind the door, and when it comes to baseball, he's a daisy."

His sternness and his adherence to certain principles of conduct were famous, and extended beyond the school limits to graduates, whom he was not loath to reprimand when divers actions of their later lives departed from what he considered proper standards. He guided his school in a very definite path. Through the years, his inflexibility brought him often into sharp conflict with both educators and parents; his decisions were not necessarily always for the best, and yielded little to modern points of view, but they were invariable. In 1941, when he was eighty-four years old, Franklin Roosevelt wrote him:

POST OFFICE
HYDE PARK
ON THE HUDSON, N.Y.

TELEGRAPH
POUGHKEEPSIE

1893.

April 18th

My dear Mammy
I hope you are
much better to
-day & that you
will be able to
go out today.
How are the dear

rats getting on?
Have you all
my things down?
If not, just tele-
-graph to me & I
will come to help
you. Have you as
fine a day as we
have, it is elegant

but Mlle got there
at 6.40 so we had
not any time to
play. Today
Edmond is com
ing to lunch
& we will get
the other joice up

up here. Yesterday
I worked all the
morning on joice
for the Club
House & in the af
-ternoon Edmond
& I put two of them
up. I dined & sup
-ped at Edmond's

Edmond Rogers and Franklin succeeded in getting the
"joice" up, and finished their clubhouse, all but the roof.

POST OFFICE
HYDE PARK
ON THE HUDSON, N.Y.

TELEGRAPH
POUGHKEEPSIE

Please thank
Peppy for the
nails & tell him
to send in his
bill very soon.
On Wednesday
we will begin

to put the back &
sides on. Mᴸˡᵉ
lost her purse in
N. Y. containing
about $6 & two
zither-rings, she
is quite broken
hearted. Mˡˡᵉ has

changed her
mind about cri-
noline & wears
skirts 7 yards
in circumference
I am flourishing
& have only fal-
len 3 times from

the top story win-
dow.
With bales of love
to everybody
Your devoted baby
Nilknarf.

"Nilknarf," another variant of the signature, can
be deciphered without a great deal of difficulty.

"I have brushed my teeth & said my prayers...."

A message tossed to the waves off Queenstown and found on the coast of Wales.

Hyde Park - 1893.
Springwood Dec. 7ᵈ

Dear Mumsy e Papsy.

J'espère que vous êtes
bien. Je sais quelle sorte
de patkins il faut acheté,
demandez pour Peck e
Snider's American Club

Skates, Size N° 10. Nous
avons patinés hier mais
il a commencé de pleu
voir e nous sommes
rentrés. Mes soldats e
le ba-chien pour Hermo,
sont venus hier; mes
soldats sont magni-

-fiques, splendides e pas
chers. Si vous voulez
me donner un cadeau
de Noël donnez moi
2 boîtes de soldats
comme j'ai acheté
l'autre jour; on peut
les distinguer des autres

parcequ'ils ont deux
petits canons attelés à
des chevaux e 10 petits
soldats avec les panta-
-lons blancs e les jaquettes
bleues comme ceci
Ce sont les meilleurs
soldats que j'ai
jamais vus. M. Nick
(Dane)

LIFE SIZE

*In place of French composition, a five-page letter from
Tlevesoor D. Nilknarf with a postscript from Mlle. Sandoz.*

nous a visités hier et il n'a pas pu entrer parce que la piazza était ... Je ne peux plus écrire, il faut que j'aille à cheval. Votre malheureux fils Flevesoor D. Nelknarf

Ceci était au lieu de composition — Franklin l'a écrit tout seul à part 4 fautes d'orthographe que j'ai corrigées

Wednesday Noon
Oct. 14th /96

Dear Papa & Mama,

I have just got your letter and I hope you will be able to come soon. I should very much like a red turtle neck sweater for skating and coasting. You can get them at any dry goods store; they are much warmer than other sweaters, on account of the double neck, they look like this

I have everything I need, but cake, candy or any delicacy would be acceptable (Taddy also agrees to this)! My finger is all right now. I had some iodine painted on it and my hand looked like a large ball for a day or two. I am afraid that this would not reach you at Hyde Park, as it does not leave here till tonight or tomorrow morning, so I am sending it to Algonac.

With much love
F. D. Roosevelt

"... cake, candy, or any delicacy would be acceptable (Taddy also agrees to this)!"

Franklin's first report

GROTON SCHOOL,

GROTON, MASS.

Report of _F. Roosevelt_ III Form

for the month ending _Oct. 7 – 1896_

Rank in Class of _19_ Boys _4_

		MONTHLY AVERAGE.	EXAMINATION MARKS.
Latin,		7.70	
	Composition,		
Greek,		6.75	
	Composition,		
Mathematics,	Trigonometry,		
	Geometry,		
	Algebra,	9.75	
	Arithmetic,		
English,	Literature,	8.50	
	Composition,	8.40	
	Grammar,		
	Reading,		
French,		8.00	
German,			
History,		7.33	
Science,		7.50	
Physics,			
Sacred Studies,		8.00	
Punctuality,		10.00	
Neatness,		9.68	
Decorum,			
AVERAGE MARK FOR THE MONTH,		7.79	
AVERAGE MARK FOR THE TERM,			

REMARKS. _Very good. He strikes me as an intelligent & faithful scholar, & a good boy._

E. Peabody.

From Groton, at the end of the first month.

En route to Groton in the fall of 1897, Franklin visited with his Grandfather Delano at Fairhaven, Massachusetts.

November 5th 1896

Hurrah, Hurrah, Hurrah

Groton

46

St Marks

O

I am hoarse, deaf, and ready to stand on my cocoanut! Our team played a wonderful game and the victory was ours after the first five minutes. St Marks seemed to be asleep during the first half & she let us get a score of 28 0 In the second half she braced up a little but did not prevent us from scoring 18 more. Our fellows played without a fault, and the inter-

-ference was especially good. "Dave" Hawkins surprised everyone with wonderful runs. He made 7 touchdowns and Auchincloss made the other one. I lunched with Mrs. Lawrence yesterday, and came to the game with them afterwards.

The pictures came from Boston today and some of them are splendid. Has the bill been sent to you? I ordered some

mounting paste & a brush with them.

It is raining here today and it is our hardest study day in the whole week as we have two periods at latin two at Greek and three at Algebra

I am going to get a boy to print some of my pictures for me so that I can send you some

With love

T D Roosevelt

In 1896 touchdowns were worth four points, field goals five, safeties two, and goals after touchdown two.

I count it among the blessings of my life that it was given to me in formative years to have the privilege of your guiding hand and the benefit of your inspiring example.

Mr. and Mrs. James Roosevelt were friends of the James Lawrences of Groton, and in 1883, before the school had yet begun to function, Franklin Roosevelt was put down on its waiting list. In accordance with what the Rector desired for his students—a full six years of Groton training in the six forms—he should have entered in 1894, but there was a strong tendency on Sara Delano Roosevelt's part to have the company of her only child for as long as possible, and his departure was put off. A classmate, James L. Goodwin, recalls:

> Franklin D. and I entered Groton School in September, 1896, in the third form. We were the only two boys to enter that form that year, and so, being new boys in a class of sixteen, became quite friendly.

Goodwin then goes on to make some revealing observations:

> When a boy goes to school or college his first months are greatly helped or hindered by the reputation of near relatives who have preceded him. When Franklin D. entered he had a nephew, James R. Roosevelt, Jr., who was in the fourth form; he was a queer sort of boy, and was much made fun of by his classmates. He was nicknamed "Rosy." Franklin D. therefore had much to contend with, following after his nephew. Furthermore, Franklin D. before he went to Groton had never been with other boys very much, had had tutors at home and besides had a father who was quite well on in years when he went to school. He therefore found it difficult at first with these handicaps to adjust himself to boarding school life.

The volume of letters F.D.R. wrote home from Groton would seem to attest to some degree of homesickness, though the subject was never mentioned. Goodwin adds:

33

As time went on and we proceeded into the fourth, fifth, and sixth forms and Franklin D. became better known by his classmates he developed an independent, cocky manner and at times became very argumentative and sarcastic. In an argument he always liked to take the side opposite to that maintained by those with whom he was talking. This irritated the other boys considerably. He was bright however and in his studies did very well and often stood near the top of his form.

During the four years at Groton, Franklin Roosevelt's health was normal, with the usual measles, scarlet fever, and other school afflictions. Despite the very considerable space given over in his letters to cavities and straightenings and changes of dentist, his teeth gave him no unusual trouble, beyond imperiling his managership of the baseball nine in his sixth-form year. He took part in all the school sports, including boxing and golf; submitted contributions to the school magazine; joined and participated in the debating groups; was usually looking forward to or back upon a vacation, but wrote when he graduated: "I feel awfully to be leaving here for good." Endicott Peabody's recollection is revealing. In a letter to another Groton graduate in 1932, the Rector said:

> There has been a good deal written about Franklin Roosevelt when he was a boy at Groton, more than I should have thought justified by the impression that he left at the school. He was a quiet, satisfactory boy of more than ordinary intelligence, taking a good position in his form but not brilliant. Athletically he was rather too slight for success. We all liked him. So far as I know that is true of the masters and boys alike.

"I am getting on finely both mentally and physically . . ."

GROTON SCHOOL
SEPT. 18, 1896,
FRIDAY.

Dear Mommerr & Popperr

I am getting on finely both mentally and physically. I sit next a boy named A. Gracie King at meals, he is from Garrisons and knows the Pells and Morgans. Do you know about him?

I am still in the 3rd A & I think I am about half way up. I am all right in Latin, Greek, Science and French; a little rusty in Algebra but not more so than the others I played football today on the 4th twenty-two (7th eleven) & tackled Taddy twice successfully. I play right halfback or fullback Saturday—

Just got your letter & also one from Mr. Dumper. He is in Mt. Vernon & well. It rained this morning, but it has stopped now

We have just had Latin and Algebra, and we study French tonight. We went to Mrs. Peabody's Parlor last night for half an hour and played games.

I got the shoes last night with the tooth-powder; the shoes are just right

We are off to dinner now so I cannot write more but I will write you Sunday.

With lots of love to Pa & yourself

F.D.R.

This is the first letter written from Groton. Archibald Gracie King of Garrison on the Hudson was in the class of 1902 at Groton but did not graduate; he was fatally burned in 1909 and died within a few days. The mention of the "Pells and Morgans" refers to the Alfred Pell family of Highland Falls, N.Y., and to the family of Gerald Morgan who was later to marry Mary Newbold, the childhood playmate mentioned in F.D.R.'s very first letter. The various Groton football teams were grouped for purposes of practice into groups of two elevens each, known as "twenty-twos." The "Taddy" whom he tackled successfully was James Roosevelt Roosevelt, Jr., his half-nephew; this was a family nickname. It will be noted hereinafter that the letters contain numerous requests for and acknowledgments of the receipt of toothpowder, toothbrushes, and articles of a similar nature. This did not betoken the non-existence of such necessities in the region; there was, however, no school store, and the walk into Groton village was (particularly in winter) something to be avoided whenever possible. Finally, a word should be said about the institution of "Mrs. Peabody's Parlor." There the Rector's wife entertained boys and visiting parents at tea, and smoothed over many an early homesickness. Fanny Peabody was her husband's first cousin, and married him in 1885, shortly after the school opened. Frank Ashburn has written of her: "It is hard for a Grotonian to imagine Groton without Mrs. Peabody. Masters and boys fell in love with her at once and have remained so ever since. Her touch was felt in all phases of school life and yet it was never obviously so in any way. That was one of the things that made it so good and sure. It was always there, one was aware of it, yet somehow took it for granted, as one takes what he loves in his own home. The early Groton generations always addressed her and spoke of her as 'The Madam.' When the children came [the Peabodys had five daughters and a son], they seemed a natural part of Groton too. It was a home, a family."

〜〜

"I have not been put in the boot-box yet . . ."

GROTON SCHOOL
SEPT. 20, 1896,
SUNDAY.

My dear Aunt Annie

I have put off writing to you until I could tell you something about the school.

The manicure case is delightful, and I am tempted to use

it all the time. Please thank Uncle Fred very much for the patent nail clippers, and tell him that I think them better than scissors.

I am getting on very well and I have not been put in the boot-box yet! I have been playing foot-ball every day, but I have escaped serious injury so far. I am in the choir, and expect to make my début in a few hours. Edmund Rogers is in the choir also, and is doing very well.

The buildings are built on three sides of a square; the new building, where we eat, sleep, and study at night, on one side, the old building, now used as the study and recitations building on the other, and the gymnasium and fives court between.

There are three football fields, one used by the first twenty-two, another by the second twenty-two and the third, a larger field than the others, is used by both the third and fourth.

I play on the fourth 22 with Edmund, and Taddy plays on the opposite team.

With a great deal of love I am your affectionate nephew

FRANKLIN D. ROOSEVELT.

"Aunt Annie," to whom this letter was addressed, was his maternal aunt, Annie Lyman Delano, a family favorite. She, like her sister Dora, married a Russell and Company associate, Frederic Delano Hitch, who was a distant cousin. She lived most of her life at Algonac, being a great benefactress of the town of Newburgh. As for the dread "boot-box," one may note that each boy had a locker in the basement of his dormitory where he was required to deposit his outdoor boots. These lockers were not very large, but sufficiently so to receive the doubled-up figure of the average "new boy" when he had been acting "fresh" and upperclassmen felt some private disciplining was indicated. To this letter, as to most of those she collected, his mother added whatever portions of the date—day, month, or year—F.D.R. had left out and which were necessary to keep a correct record. In this case it was the figures "96."

[GROTON SCHOOL]
SEPT. 21, 1896,
MONDAY.

Dear Mama—

I got your letter at noon and was very sorry to hear that Papa's cold was worse, but as I have not heard anything more, I trust he is better today. We are off to bed and I will finish tomorrow morning

Tuesday.

I am in the choir and sang Soprano twice on Sunday. The same evening I went to Mrs. Peabody's parlor where we all sang hymns

I am going Mrs. Lawrence's to-morrow afternoon.

I am getting on very well and so far I have not had any warnings, latenesses or marks. Mr. Gladwin reads to us for fiteen minutes every evening before we go to bed in a very funny book, called "The Casting Away of Mrs. Lecks and Mrs. Ailshine."

Billy Wright sits next me at table, did I know him in Washington?

Your lovely letter just received and I was much relieved to hear that papa was better. I wrote you on Saturday to Fair Haven but I suppose it got there too late

I am getting on quite well in my studies, and about half way up in my class, I think.

Please thank Papa very much for sending me the Ill. London News and the Scientific American   They are very nice.

I wrote a letter to Aunt Annie on Sunday thanking her for the manicure case, and Uncle Fred for the nippers.

I am very well, and quite warm, although I have not put on the medium flannels.

I have not needed them so far, but I will change next Sunday

With a great deal of love to Papa and yourself—

I am affectionately

FRANKLIN D ROOSEVELT

The boys call me Uncle Frank, but I would sooner be Uncle
Frank, than Nephew Rosy as they have been calling Taddy!

Mrs. James Lawrence lived near the school, and often asked
some of the boys in for tea or a meal—considering the usual
flavor of the school's board, this was an invitation to be striven
for. Irving C. Gladwin, known as "Max," was a master at
Groton from 1887 to 1926; he taught F.D.R. French. "Billy
Wright" was William M. Wright, a member of the class of
1903, who did not graduate; he came of a Long Island, not a
Washington family. F.D.R. had not been any length of time
resident in Washington since the winter of 1887, which his
family passed in a house on K Street, and during which time
occurred the fabled presentation to President Cleveland. The
reference to "Fair Haven" is important in family history. The
original Warren Delano, F.D.R.'s great-grandfather, was a New
Bedford whaling captain who, in the early years of the nine-
teenth century, built a house at Fairhaven, Mass., which came
to be known as "The Homestead." It was willed to the whole
of his family, but since none of his children other than Warren
Delano II had any offspring, it descended to the latter's family
and through the years was a favorite visiting-place of Sara
Delano Roosevelt and her brothers and sisters. It was always
open. F.D.R. spent many weekends there when he was at
Harvard. Eventually, in 1942, Frederic A. Delano, acting on
behalf of the whole family, sold the old place, and it was
demolished. The *Illustrated London News* and the *Scientific
American*, along with the previously mentioned *Survey
Graphic*, were sent F.D.R. regularly by his mother, and were
periodicals he particularly delighted in.

∽

GROTON SCHOOL
SEPT. 27, 1896,
SUNDAY.

Dear Papa and Mama

I am getting on very well so far. Thanks very much for your letters; the more the better.

I have not had any blackmarks or latenesses yet and I am much better in my studies.

I got the best mark in Algebra yesterday yesterday [*sic*] morning and the day before I got the best in English Composition. Yesterday afternoon our 1st Eleven played the Brookline High School team, a lot of toughs, and beat them quite badly, the score was 16–0 and for the first game of the season it was very good.

I cheered myself hoarse so that I was quite croaky at choir practice.

I like Greek very much, it is very easy so far, and Mr. Abbott, a young Englishman just come to the school, gives us very short lessons. I am going to try for the punctuality prize, but it will be hard work, as one lateness will spoil.

The Biddle boy is quite crazy, fresh and stupid, he has been boot-boxed once and threatened to be pumped several times. Our 4th twenty-two play four times a week, and we have had some very desperate battles. My head is a little bunged up, but otherwise I am all right. Mr. Peabody read to us in his study several evenings in the week after supper. I eat a great deal and I have gained several pounds.

I am going to Groton on Wednesday for the second time. A number of boys have fruit sent them and it is kept in the fruit closet and given out three or four times a week. Could you send me some grapes or other small fruit? It would be very nice.

With lots of love to Muriel and Warren and papa and yourself

affectionately
FRANKLIN D. ROOSEVELT

40

"Black-marks" were a famous Groton institution, and were bestowed (up to a maximum of six at a time) by masters upon the boys for any of a wide variety of breaches of discipline. They had to be "worked off" weekly, by doing copying or other tasks at the discretion of the master in charge on the day set, usually Saturday afternoon, which was a half-holiday. A too-large accumulation of black-marks resulted in an invitation "to see the Rector in his study." "Latenesses" were in a different category from the black-marks, and counted as part of the regular "Punctuality" grade on the monthly reports; too many, however, could also lead to a Peabody interview. The "Mr. Abbott" here mentioned was none other than the famous "Bott" of Lawrenceville. Mather Almon Abbott was born in Halifax, educated in England, and came to Groton as a master in 1896; in 1915 he left to enter Yale as a graduate student, where he performed the unparalleled feat of attaining a professorship in three years. In 1919 he was invited to become headmaster of Lawrenceville School in New Jersey, where he remained till his death in 1934. For a book about Abbott (*Bott: The Story of a Schoolmaster*, by William H. Husted, New York, 1936) F.D.R. was later asked to contribute a brief reminiscence, and wrote: ". . . he horrified us all the first few weeks by 'soaking' us six black marks apiece—the maximum penalty—for the most trivial offenses! He did this, of course, before he understood the system and I well remember, first, our indignation and then our admiration when he told us in class that he had made a mistake, that he now understood the system, and that he would not repeat the mistake." Mention is made of the trials of "the Biddle boy"; this was Moncure Biddle, Groton 1901, and not Francis Biddle, later Attorney General under F.D.R., who was in the class of 1905. As for "pumping," here was an even more horrendous form of disciplining than the use of the boot-box. It was administered with great formality and in absolute silence by the sixth-formers, who would enter (usually during a study period when all the lower forms were gathered together) and call out the name of some boy who had perhaps been cheating or who had merely been acting bumptious and neglecting to address his remarks to upperclassmen with the proper respect. The poor paralyzed wretch was then removed, under the terrified gaze of his fellows, to a lavatory where basinfuls of water were poured over him and down his throat, practically to the point of drowning. The practice was neither acknowledged nor prevented by the faculty. (The English school system of "fagging" was, however, definitely forbidden.)

~~~

"I am getting on very well with the fellows . . ."

GROTON
OCT. 1, 1896,
THURSDAY.

Dear Mama

Thank you very much for the grapes, they are delicious. Please do not send any more, because Mr. P. says that they make to much of a mess on the floors.

I have had the blue trousers and the umbrella marked in the sewing room. The note paper and the hymnal are very nice. I had to get a large "Church Hymnal" for singing in the choir but I use the small one for prayers. On Parlor nights Mrs Mc.Murray and Edmund play whist against the younger Rainsford boy and myself.

I am getting on very well with the fellows although I do not know them all yet.

The football teams have been made up into elevens yesterday, Edmund and Taddy play on the same team and opposite me. Poor Taddy is on the lowest team, he could be on a much higher one if he only kept his wits about him! He has been very nice to me, although I see very little of him.

I am in a great hurry so excuse scrawl

FRANKLIN D ROOSEVELT

"Mr. P." was the Rector. One of the whist partners mentioned was Mrs. McMurray; this lady was the school housekeeper and a very stiff, dignified person most positive in her likes and dislikes, in whose good graces it was well to be. "The younger Rainsford boy" was W. Kerr Rainsford, also Groton 1900, who later became head of the School of Architecture at the Carnegie Institute of Technology.

∽∽

"It was a desperate game throughout . . ."

GROTON SCHOOL
OCT. 4, 1896,
SUNDAY.

Dear Mama and Papa,

I got your letter last night and was surprised to hear that you had not got my letter of Thursday.

I take milk and crackers, every night. I asked Mr. Peabody about it and he told me to have my name put on the list.

On going to the fruit-closet last night, I found a large army of ants in my grapes, they were all rotten!

Yesterday our team played the English High School eleven, a lot of toughs again. They disputed every point of the game and made Mr. Peabody quite angry. Neither side scored and it was a desperate game throughout.

I had a very nice time at the Joy's on Wednesday Edmund, Roger Derby and Lorrie Rainsford were there. Yesterday I lunched at Mrs. Whitney's cottage with Mrs. Draper and had a very nice time.

Mrs. Lawrence was out when I called the other day but I am going again on Wednesday.

While I was watching the game yesterday, I was much surprised to see Miss. Morton drive up. I had a little talk with her, but I do not know where she is staying.

The Scientific Americans are very welcome and everybody is trying to borrow them.

I will write to Aunt Dora this afternoon and also to Muriel if I have time.

We go to Mr. Gardner's on Sunday afternoons and have cake and google. The time seems to pass very fast now but the first week seemed interminable. I have not had any black-marks yet and have been on time for everything.

We play footbal only four times a week and I am very well

Excuse scrawl

With love

F. D ROOSEVELT

My name has been mixed up with Taddy's several times, much to the amusement of the schoolroom

FD.R

Mr. and Mrs. Charles Joy were the parents of Benjamin Joy, who was in the form below F.D.R.; they lived in a large house just beyond the school. Mrs. Joy and Mrs. James Lawrence were sisters. The two other boys who visited the Joys with F.D.R. and Edmund Rogers were Roger A. Derby, Groton 1901, and (Dr.) Laurence F. Rainsford, Kerr's brother. Mrs. Whitney, wife of the carpenter who did woodworking and repair jobs for the school, ran a small inn across from Hundred House and ran it with an iron hand, turning away those she disliked no matter who they were. Whitney's was one of the two places parents stayed when they visited their sons. Later on it was enlarged and became the present-day "Parents' House." The Draper reference is to Mrs. William H. Draper, daughter of the founder of the *New York Sun*, who would then have been up visiting her son George, in the form ahead of F.D.R. As to "Miss. Morton," she was Miss Mary Morton, the daughter of Levi P. Morton, governor of New York State and vice-president of the United States from 1889-1893. The Mortons lived at Rhinebeck, on the Hudson, and were friends of the Roosevelt family. A note should be added about "Mr. Gardner" and "google," two essential and inseparable Groton institutions. William Amory Gardner, more familiarly known as "Uncle Billy Wag," was a cousin of the Rector's, and the nephew of one of the most startling of Bostonians, Isabella Stewart ("Mrs. Jack") Gardner, who brought him up. At an early age he and his two brothers were orphaned and had rather a lonely childhood in the home of their aunt and uncle. He was also a very rich young man. These two circumstances combined to make Groton a perfect object for his lifelong devotion. He was one of the "Triumvirate" of original masters, along with Peabody and Billings; he was only twenty-one when the school opened, and he died forty-six years later, in 1930, still actively a part of the school. His largess provided both the original timber-and-plaster chapel and the famous Gothic building that replaced it, and extended to other gifts. A bachelor, he built himself a capacious mansion at the school and staffed it with a corps of servants. He attached to his house a curious construction containing a stage, a swimming pool, a squash court, and a maze, which was known as the "Pleasure Dome." There boys came Sunday afternoons to be served "google," a form of sicky-sweet pink lemonade. He was the owner of the Cup Defender sailing yacht *Mayflower;* he was also a famous knitter of socks and mufflers. An exceptional Greek scholar, he held hilarious classes in that subject (to the disapproval of the Rector), and was especially skilled in the recondite art of punning in Greek.

∽

"The food tasted perfectly de-
licious after the school . . ."

[GROTON]
OCT. 11, 1896,
SUNDAY.

Dear Papa and Mama

Many thanks for your letters, I would have written before but I had nothing to write about.

Mrs. Minturn is here and I went to supper with her last evening; I could not stay long, as we had choir-practice at seven. The food tasted perfectly delicious after the school food.

We have sausages or sausage-croquettes for the last three days, but I have managed to keep perfectly well.

45

We played the weekly game with the Boston Latin School and beat them 12–0. We have not been scored against this year, although our team is the lightest that we have ever had

On Thursday afternoon the choir voted for a half holiday, we have two each term and I managed to dislocate my fourth finger in a small football game. I have not been able to play since, in consequence, but I shall begin again tomorrow.

This coming Thursday is the School's birthday and we expect to have a high old time.

I am getting on pretty well with my lessons, I am about top in Algebra and about middle in other studies

The Scientific American has not come yet, but I expect it tomorrow morning. I had a letter from Mr. Dumper yesterday, he is getting on very well. Edmund is doing quite well, I think, in everything except Latin. I am glad the Rogers have a decent tutor this time, it would not take much to improve over Mr. Bunny!

With lots of love

F.D.R.

P.S. Stamps are always acceptable

There were two Minturns, cousins, in his form: Hugh and John W. From the fact that special mention is made to his mother, it may be assumed that the "Mrs. Minturn" in this case was Mrs. John W. Minturn, the former Louisa Aspinwall and a cousin of James Roosevelt. The rewards of choir service were half-holidays and the purpose of the vote was to pick the day. The School Birthday fell on October 15, and was the occasion of considerable celebration, of which more is revealed in ensuing letters. "Mr. Bunny" was the Archibald Rogers' tutor, Leon Durand Bonnet; he later became headmaster of a school at Tuxedo Park, N.Y. Lest one be persuaded F.D.R. was avidly attending to his famous stamp collection during this period, it should be noted that the postscript refers to stamps for his letters home—a request competing in frequency with that for dental articles.

~~

"I should very much like a
red turtle *neck sweater . . ."*

Dear Papa & Mama,

I have just got your letter and I hope you will be able to
come soon. I should very much like a red *turtle* neck sweater
for skating and coasting You can get them at any dry-goods
store; they are much warmer than other sweaters, on account
of the double neck, they look like this! [followed by a drawing.]

I have everything I need, but cake, candy or any *delicacy*
would be acceptable (Taddy also agrees to this)!

My finger is all right now; I had some iodine painted on it
and my hand looked like a large ball for a day or two.

I am afraid that this would not reach you at Hyde Park,
as it does not leave here till tonight or tomorrow morning, so
I am sending it to Algonac.

With much love   F D ROOSEVELT

The signature to this letter was scribbled over, as if he were
experimenting with different handwritings.

〜〜

"Many thanks for the nose-guard . . ."

[GROTON]
OCT. 21, 1896,
WEDNESDAY.

[No salutation]

Many thanks for the nose-guard and your letter. I managed
to get a small cut on both eyelids of my left eye yesterday, I
think from a shoe-heel, but it is all right now. Don't forget my
report! I think I may get 3rd or 4th in the form

FDR.

47

This was a U.S. one-cent postal sent to his mother. Each student's average monthly mark was posted for the school to see, but the actual reports, with individual grades and comments from the Rector, were sent home; therefore, in order to know his grade in any particular subject he had to get it from his mother. This first Groton report was dated Oct. 17, 1896; F.D.R. stood fourth in a class of nineteen; his average mark was 7.79 on the 10.00 decimal basis; individual grades were: Latin, 7.70; Greek, 6.75; Mathematics (Algebra), 9.75; English Literature, 8.50; English Composition, 8.40; French, 8.00; History, 7.33; Science, 7.50; Sacred Studies, 8.00; Punctuality, 10.00; and Neatness, 9.68. The Rector always added a remark at the end of a report, usually one or at the most two succinct words. This being a first report, he expanded, and said: "Very good. He strikes me as an intelligent & faithful scholar, & a good boy."

〜〜

"Send me my watch as I need it when I go far from the buildings . . ."

GROTON
OCT. 25, 1896,
SUNDAY.

Dear Papa & Mama

I have nothing much to tell you this week. Mr and Mrs Henry Rogers are here and I lunched with them today. Poor Edmund could not be there as he had another upset.

He is in the infirmary and has a little fever. He thinks it is from a pie that we had for supper.

He slept a good deal and the nurse says that he will be better tomorrow.

Monday morning

Edmund is better today but is going to stay in the infirmary all day as he feels rather shaky still.

Mrs Wright and the younger boy are staying at Mrs. Powell's and they came to the parlor last night.

48

Don't forget my report, I think I got forth place in the form, not much but better than I expected. Please send me my watch and chain as I need it when I go far from the buildings.

The candy and prunes are delicious and I am about half way through them

With love   Excuse scrawl

F D Roosevelt

Mr. and Mrs. Henry Pendleton Rogers, first cousins of Edmund Rogers, are those referred to here; their son, Henry Pendleton Rogers, Jr., was then in the class of 1897. Mrs. Isaac Wright was the mother of William M. Wright, mentioned previously. Mrs. Powell was the wife of Mr. Gardner's coachman, and ran an inn much similar to Whitney's, just outside what is now the school gate.

"There is very little to write about in the middle of the week . . ."

[GROTON]
OCT. 29, 1896,
THURSDAY.

Dear Papa & Mama

Many thanks for your letters and the papers. There is very little to write about in the middle of the week. We played foot-ball today as usual and I found the nose-protector a great use, for my nose is still rather tender from a whack I got the other day.

You write that my algebra-mark was 9.75; if so it was about the highest in the school for last month.

The candies are delicious and I still have quite a lot left.

With lots of love

F D Roosevelt

Dear Papa and Mama

I got the bible, prayer-book and watch on Friday; thank you very much for them   The bible is very nice and the type is large enough even for a Groton dark day!

I have been singing and reading all day and I feel rather lazy and stupid, for there is not much to do. I wrote to Aunt Laura this morning and I am going to write to Aunt Doe this evening. I am going to hire a wagon with Taddy on Thanksgiving morning, with two horses and we may take two other fellows   We play St Marks next Wednesday and if we win I shall telegraph you.

We expect the game to be very close and if anything we have the better team.

Have you found a Van Daeal's French Composition, if you have please send it to me as we use it every Saturday night.

Edmund is all right now, but he has to be careful what he eats.

There is really nothing to write about now but I will tell you all about the St. Mark's game on Thursday

With loads of love

Υρανκλιν Δελανω Ρωσενελτ

(Papa can read this!)

The "French Composition" was probably *An Introduction to the French Language—Being a Practical Grammar with Exercises,* by Alphonse Naus Van Daell, published that same year by Ginn and Company. The signature in Greek is a phonetic version with some slight errors—the use of the letter "U" in the first name and the letter "D" in the second, in place of the Greek symbols for *phi* and *delta.*

"I am hoarse, deaf, and ready
to stand on my cocoanut! . . ."

[No salutation]

Hurrah,   Hurrah,   Hurrah

G   R   O   T   O   N

46

St. Marks

0

I am hoarse, deaf, and ready to stand on my cocoanut!
OUR team played a wonderful game and the victory was ours
after the first five minutes. St. Marks seemed to be asleep
during the first half and she let us get a score of 28–0 In the
second half she braced up a little but did not prevent us from
scoring 18 more.

Our fellows played without a fault, and the interferance
was especially good. "Dave" Hawkins surprised everyone with
wonderful runs. He made 7 touchdowns and Auchincloss made
the other one.

I lunched with Mrs. Lawrence yesterday, and came to the
game with them afterwards.

The pictures came from Boston today and some of them
are splendid. Has the bill been sent to you? I ordered some
mounting-paste & a brush with them.

It is raining here today and it is our hardest study day in
the whole week as we have two periods at latin, two at Greek
and three at Algebra.

I am going to get a boy to print some of my pictures for me so that I can send you some

With love

F D ROOSEVELT

To penetrate the mysteries of the football scores quoted liberally throughout these letters, it should be noted that in 1896 touchdowns were worth 4 points, goals after touchdown 2, field goals 5, and safeties 2. The two heroes mentioned were David S. Hawkins, Groton 1898, and (Dr.) Hugh Auchincloss of the class of 1897, the noted New York surgeon. The mention of getting pictures printed should be clarified. Photography was then a craze, and darkrooms were constructed in various obscure corners of the school; it is recalled by contemporaries that there was a "cabinet" used for the purpose in the basement of Hundred House at one time. There was no official school darkroom; boys chipped in to make their own. Mr. Griswold, one of the more scientifically given masters, was an enthusiastic partisan.

〜〜

"We had a grand bonfire after the game . . ."

GROTON

NOV. 8, 1896,

SUNDAY.

Dear Papa & Mama

Many thanks for the Van Daell. It came just in time for evening school.

We had a grand bonfire between the two buildings after the game on Wednesday and Mr. Gardiner [Gardner] got some firecrackers and Roman candles, and a big barrel of figbiscuits. We marched all about and shouted and sang until nine p.m.

I went to Mrs Wharton's to lunch today & had a very nice time. Edmund went too & we played games afterwards.

We will be very careful on Thanksgiving day and Edmund is going with us. I am sure that we can manage two horses.

52

It is pouring here and there is very little to do.

I have nothing to write about and as the football season is practically over we have not many games.

We expect to have skating very soon as it freezes nearly every night.

With love

F D ROOSEVELT

The personal reference here is to Mrs. William P. Wharton, of a Groton family who lived on Farmer's Row; she was the stepmother of a fourth-former, William P. Wharton, Jr.

∽

"We have several very pretty songs . . ."

[GROTON]
NOV. 12, 1896,
THURSDAY.

Dear Papa & Mama

We expect Mr and Mrs Rogers here soon and I am to lunch with them on Saturday.

I am doing very well in Algebra and I think a good deal better in Greek. The month ends on Saturday and you will get the report about a week later. I am dying to see it and I hope my mark will be better than last month. There is very little to do now, and the weather is horrid. We have sun one moment and rain the next.

We had a Glee Club practice last night and it was great fun.

We are to sing at Christmas and we have several very pretty songs

With loads of love

Φρανκλιν.

The Greek signature had by now been properly amended.

∽

"I am looking forward to your
visit with much pleasure . . ."

Dear Papa and Mama,

We had an exciting game yesterday with the Harvard Freshmen, and we beat them 14–0. Dave Hawkins got a sprained ankle after a beautiful run and touchdown, so he could not play in the second half. Guy Cary took his place and played beautifully making another touchdown. Mrs Rogers watched the game from the Powell pony-cart. Mr Rogers got quite excited over the game and he talked with Mr. G. all the time.

Rosey and I lunched with them and I went back to afternoon-tea.

I am looking forward to your visit with much pleasure and I shall come to the Lawrences about 1 o'clock. Are Edmund and Taddy to come to lunch or dinner?

Edmund cannot go with us as he is going to Boston with the Derbys but I shall get two other fellows who have nothing else to do.

The singing was much better today and Mrs Rogers liked it very much.

Be sure you send me my report. Please! as I am very anxious to hear it.

I have bought six pictures of the school for $1 from another boy, and I will show them to you on Thankgiving.

With love

FDR.

Guy Fairfax Cary was in the class of 1898. "Mr. G." was a very common nickname for Mr. Gardner. "Rosey" and "Taddy," it should be repeated, were one and the same person: his half-nephew, James Roosevelt Roosevelt, Jr. "The Derbys" were the parents of Richard, Roger, and Lloyd, all Groton contemporaries; the family lived in the Hudson Valley.

The "FDR" signature to this letter is conceived with extremely fancy flourishes. On his November 1896 report, he ranked second in a class of nineteen boys with an average of 8.33. His worst grade was a 5.66 in English Composition; his best a 9.92 in Algebra, which drew the marginal notation of "Excellent" from Mr. Peabody. All other marks except for Latin were above 8.00, with a 9.67 in Neatness and another devastating 10.00 in Punctuality. The Rectorial comment was: "Very creditable."

∽∾

*"The Roller Skates are not very
good for ice! . . ."*

[GROTON]
NOV. 19, 1896,
THURSDAY.

Dear Papa & Mama

Many thanks for the ulster but I think that I had better wear a sweater and covert-coat instead as the ulster is awfully heavy.

We are going to take a boy named Goodrich and someone else with us. There is very little to say this week except that I heard from Mr Dumper on Sunday, and he is very well.

I got 2nd place this month as you have doubtless seen from my report.

My mark 8.33 was the third highest in the lower school, only Krumbhaar and the leader of the 2nd form beating me.

What, wherefore and why in the name of all that's strange and curious!

The Roller Skates are very nice but they are not *very* good for ice! I shall keep them till you come but please bring some real ones as the skating will be here in a few weeks

The red sweater is very nice, and is just right

With love

FDR

P.S stamps are acceptable!

"A boy named Goodrich" was Caspar Goodrich of the class of 1899; heterodoxly, he later entered Annapolis. "Krumbhaar" was Edward Bell Krumbhaar, in F.D.R.'s form, today a distinguished Philadelphia doctor. The signature is a quite illegible grouping of flourishes.

∽∽

"My supply of stamps has run short . . ."

Dear Papa and Mama

I was very much pleased to get your telegram last night saying that Aunt Dora had arrived in New York. I have written her today.

Please bring me a pair of three buckle arctics and some decent skates (!!!).

I have just finished the chocalate you gave me and the prunes dissappeared about a week ago.

A Mrs. Erving Winslow read the "Merchant of Venice" to the School last Tuesday, and Taddy and one other boy were the only ones who did not grace the big hall with their presence. They thought it would be dull and thought it would be nicer to *"loaf for once"*! It will be charged for $.50 on the bill, but I hope you do not mind.

Please don't forget my marks, and my supply of stamps has run short.

We have not yet decided on a fourth boy for our drive, but we shall get one who cannot do anything else

Poor Biddle has been sent to bed for being saucy to one of the masters and is now in the infirmary. I found it necessary to chastise him yesterday, but he is just as fresh again today!

I am looking forward every moment to seeing you on Thursday.

With love

F.D.R.

Catherine Reignolds Winslow, daughter of a British army officer, came to America in 1850 at the age of fourteen and found an almost immediate success in the theatre. She was a beautiful woman, an excellent actress: for many years during the height of her career she was a member of the stock company of the Boston Art Museum. After her retirement she continued to live in Boston, occasionally giving dramatic readings in various Eastern cities, and training pupils for the stage. Through these latter she promoted Ibsen's plays, and the Norwegian dramatist once had occasion to thank her publicly for her advocacy of his work. In 1861 she married Erving Winslow, Bostonian of Bostonians and a *Mayflower* descendant, who performed even more prominently than his wife, though upon slightly different boards. He was the son of a wealthy merchant family, and took up a literary career which eventually led him to the ardent support of various causes. He promoted free trade, social service, Henry George, Americanism, and Christianity, but reached his finest flower with the formation, late in 1898, of the Boston Anti-Imperialist League, to combat empire instincts aroused by the Spanish-American War. The League shortly became national in scope; Winslow was secretary of the New England branch (whose president was Groton village's leading citizen, George Sewall Boutwell—*vide infra*), and the most active and audible of its workers. He contributed his time, money, letter-writing and speech-making abilities in support of its conviction "that any attempt to conduct an imperial or military government in alien tropical colonies would be inevitably destructive of republican government at home." His protest rose most flame-like in 1899 over the annexation of the Philippines; on November 29th of that year the *New York Tribune* (which took polite but distinct pleasure in using Winslow as a whipping boy) printed a Thanksgiving greeting which he had addressed to President McKinley: "Lovers of liberty who would rather be the hunted patriot than the blood-guilty usurper today, will nevertheless use it to pray that he who has given America her first thanksgiving of shame may be brought to repentance, and a better mind." The *Tribune* utilized this message as the *point d'appui* for an editorial two days later, entitled "Poor Erving!" and full of late-Victorian sarcasm.

∽∾

"Only one Sunday more! . . ."

[GROTON]
DEC. 6, 1896,
SUNDAY.

Dear Papa and Mama

Many thanks for your lovely letters and the Graphic. I got the receipt for my A.O.U. dues and the Check-List yesterday.

On Thursday evening a Mr Bühler gave a lecture, illustrated with stereoptican pictures, on the Battle of Gettysburg. It was perfectly splendid, and lasted for over two hours.

Taddy is in the infirmary suffering from a stomach-ache, but the nurse says his condition is not very critical (!) and that he will be well in a few ~~months~~, hours I mean.

A new kid has come from Fitchburg whose name is Crocker, and we hope he will turn out better than Biddle!

The skates have not come yet but I have used Taddy's twice. The first skating was on Wednesday but the ice got very soft yesterday, and today it is again warm.

Only one Sunday more!

Nothing to say

With love

FRANKLIN.

The "A.O.U." was the American Ornithologists Union. "Mr. Bühler" was Huber Gray Buehler (pronounced "Beeler"); he was born and spent the first twenty-eight years of his life in Gettysburg, went to Hotchkiss School in Connecticut as an English master in 1891, and from 1904 to his death in 1924 was headmaster of that school. The "new kid from Fitchburg" was Alvah Crocker, Jr., of the class of 1901. He was the eldest of three sons of the Fitchburg paper family who went to Groton; his younger brother, Reverend John Crocker, succeeded the Rector as headmaster of the school.

"Exams begin on Monday . . .
we have nine of them . . ."

Dear Papa & Mama

The lovely skates came this morning with the watch; the skates are great and have been much admired by all the boys. We have had warm weather but I hope we will be able to skate again tomorrow as it is much colder now

The Graphics were very welcome and I have a small mob round me when they come. Taddy is all right again now, but there are quite a number of other boys in the infirmary, suffering from indigestion, tonselitice, jaundice etc.!—

Exams begin on Monday and last till Friday we have nine of them and I expect to pass all right

With haste & love

FD.R.

〜〜

"The Rector's father read the
'Christmas Carrol' . . ."

[GROTON]
DEC. 13, 1896,
SUNDAY.

Dear Papa & Mama,

Less than a week and I shall be home!

I am just home from the Xmas service; it was very nice and the Chapel was decorated with greens, which the boys prepared on Thursday and Friday evenings.

The hymns went quite good & the anthem was splendid.

We begin our exams tomorrow; the Monday exam is Sacred Studies, on Tuesday we have Latin Comp.; on Wednesday, English & Science; on Thursday, Latin, Political Economy and Greek, and on Friday, Mathematics and French.

I shall finish this after Afternoon Service as it is lunch time now and we are going to feast on turkey and cranberry-sauce.

Shall I bring my ulster home? and my waterproof?

The Rector's father read the "Christmas Carrol" to the school after lunch and he is going to finish it after supper.

The singing was rather weak this afternoon as all the hymns were difficult and unfamiliar.

The new Crocker kid had 8 blackmarks & 1 lateness last week & he was pumped yesterday

With love

F.D.R.

The Rector's father, Samuel Endicott Peabody, was present at the school on most of its festive occasions; his reading of Dickens' famous tale became a Groton custom continued by his son, who would read it over a period of several evenings to the whole of the school gathered in his own home. The final report of F.D.R.'s first term was dated Dec. 15, 1896; he stood fourth in the class of nineteen with an average of 7.79. "Very good," commented the Rector. This mark included the aforementioned examinations; he got a 75 in Latin, 76 in Greek, 85 in Algebra, 80 in English Literature, 95 in French, 90 in History, 88 in Science, and 78 in Sacred Studies. The master who made out this report wrote on the reverse of it: "Do you wish your son to take dancing lessons next term? Please send for the boys 2 pairs each of thick boots for general use. We like to have the boys' boots cleaned and this can only be done when they have 2 pairs to wear alternately."

∽∽

"*. . . a McCormick boy from Chicago . . .*"

[GROTON]
JAN. 5, 1897,
TUESDAY.

Dear Papa & Mama

We arrived safely at six o'clock after a pleasant journey on.

I sat with Buell Hollister coming on and we did not have to change cars at all.

60

Two new boys have come to the School, Edwin Corning, whom you know, and a McCormick boy from Chicago.

I am going to write to Mrs. Pell tomorrow as I forgot all about it at home.

I shall try to buy a share in a dark room, and if I can, I will get you to send on the chemicals.

Our table is terribly crowded on account of the new boys and I would give anything to be moved up a table, where I really belong.

My cold is already better I think but I shall be careful until it has entirely gone. Mr. Billings was very sorry he could not stay with us in the holidays.

Please send my toboggan & snowshoes as soon as possible as we may have snow anyday.

With much love

FRANKLIN D ROOSEVELT

P.S Excuse blots, but as I have no blotting-paper out I have to use fingers

Buell Hollister was in the class of 1901, and later graduated from Yale. Together with a Harvard and a Princeton man he formed the New York securities firm of Pyne, Kendall & Hollister, in 1909. Edwin Corning, two years behind F.D.R. at Groton, came of a prominent Albany family. After college he entered a family business, the Ludlum Steel Company, one of the oldest American tool-steel manufacturers. His interests soon turned to another field, and in 1912 he went into Albany County politics. In 1926 he became chairman of the New York State Democratic Committee, and in November of that year was elected lieutenant governor on the ticket with Alfred E. Smith. This of course put him in a prominent position to receive the gubernatorial nomination in 1928, the year Smith ran for President, and one wonders if there was any conflict with the old schoolmate who eventually received that nomination. Edward J. Flynn, however, recalls that "the friendship between Franklin D. Roosevelt and Corning was more or less a social one. At no time do I think that their

political careers conflicted. I am certain that Mr. Corning
had no part in persuading President Roosevelt to run for
Governor in 1928. My recollection is that Mr. Corning decided that he was more or less through with politics, and I
am not sure whether it was his health or his personal desires
that influenced him." Edwin Corning, who died in 1934, was
the father of Mayor Erastus Corning of Albany. As for the
"McCormick boy from Chicago," this was none other than
Col. Robert R. McCormick, the owner and publisher of
the *Chicago Tribune*. While at Groton he was known
as "Rufus." His class was 1899, *ex*. There were many nick-
names for the Reverend Sherrard Billings—"Mr. B.," "Beebs,"
"the Little Man"—and all of them affectionate. His small size
was the most conspicuous thing about him, together with a
very black beard, which he retained until it began to gray,
and then reduced to a stiff little brush on his upper lip. Like
Peabody, he was a graduate of Episcopal; he was twenty-seven
when Groton opened, with one year's teaching experience
behind him, and he remained at the school until his death in
1933. He was the Rector's second-in-command, taking charge
of the school in the latter's absences. He was a fine preacher,
and had a gift for making his Latin and Greek classes both
instructive and entertaining.

∿

". . . thankful I am to get away
from the kid table . . ."

[GROTON]
JAN. 7, 1897,
THURSDAY.

Dear Papa & Mama
    Thank you so much for your letters.
    When I got into the car on Tuesday I went to the window
several times to see you, but you had disappeared entirely, and
I supposed you had left the platform.
    I think I could accept Dr. Dwights offer if he makes the

price $35. As the original is worth about $10 more than a set with two reprinted volumes and the binding would bring it up another $10.

The price last year was $30 for the original *unbound* so $35 would not be at all out of the way, for a bound set this year.——

It is a pity Aunt Nelly mistook the date of my going back, for she had a message for you in her letter. I return her letter for you to read & destroy.

I have at last been moved up a table, and thankful I am to get away from the kid table where I suffered three months.

I now sit at Mr. Gladwin's table and next to Ben Joy.

We began Geometry this morning and I think I shall like it.

Edwin Corning is rather homesick I think, when he was asked how he enjoyed the food, his eyes began to water.

With loads of love

FRANKLIN D ROOSEVELT

"Aunt Nelly" was Miss Eleanor Blodgett, perhaps his mother's closest friend. She was F.D.R.'s godmother, but no actual relation. (His godfather was Elliott Roosevelt, father of his future wife.) The interval between this letter and the one following was taken up by measles. His mother came up to Groton to be near him, and took him home to convalesce.

$\sim\!\!\sim$

"My tail is better but the hard
benches hurt it a little . . ."

GROTON SCHOOL
FEB. 18, 1897,
WEDNESDAY.

Dear P & M.

The train was on time last night and the journey was uneventful and seemed fearfully long. I am really very well and I think I shall pick up my lessons soon.

63

I arrived here just in time to hear a Mr. Zenoni a Polish or Russian Jew. and a mind reader. His performance was better than Miss Lancaster's and he was much quicker in his work.

The boys have taken up up [*sic*] skiing. Will you get the footholders on my pair repaired and send them to me?

My tail is better but the hard benches hurt it a little. I rub it with Arnica, but it is not easy.

Bad pen & with love   FDR

〰️

*"We are all looking forward
to the play . . ."*

[GROTON]
FEB. 19, 1897,
THURSDAY.

Dear Papa & Mama

Taddy is in the infirmary with an abscess in his ear; the doctor cut it yesterday and he is better today. I was not the first boy back as J. L. Goodwin got here two hours before me. He left N.Y at 9 a.m. arriving at Ayer Junction at 4 p.m. Wednesday.

The sled is perfectly lovely and I think it was very good of you to give it to me.

My tobboggan smashed the first time I used it but Whitney may be able to mend it.

Young Corning got 1st place in the second form last month but it will not be as easy for him after Wright comes back. We are all looking forward to the play on the 22nd. The stage is being put up in the gymn. and the 6th Form have been rehearsing for some time.

With loads of love   F. D ROOSEVELT

P.S. Taddy is better today but still in the infirmary. With haste—   FDR

P.P.S. Taddy may come out of the infirmary tonight.

64

James L. Goodwin has been previously mentioned as the other "new boy" who entered the third form with F.D.R. His mother was if anything even more solicitous of her son's school welfare than Mrs. James Roosevelt, and when he came down with the measles at the same time as F.D.R., he also enjoyed a convalescence at home. Ayer was the town where the Boston & Albany Railroad deposited travelers to the school; from there one completed the journey of four miles by horse carriage.

〜〜

"I have not much opportunity
for observing birds here . . ."

[GROTON]
FEB. 21, 1897,
SUNDAY.

Dear Papa and Mama,

We have had about two inches of snow here and it is quite cloudy today.

Taddy came out of the infirmary yesterday morning and is all right now.

He received your letter yesterday; and at the same time I received a letter from the Department of Agriculture asking me to fill out some enclosed papers about the birds I see every day. As I have not much opportunity for observing birds here, I shall wait until I get to Campobello.

There are loads of parents and graduates here for the 22nd, and we have three graduates in our dormitory, who sleep in cubicles vacated by sick boys.

We have had a terrible epidemic of grippe, and there are about ten boys in the infirmary now. There have been four cases of ear trouble besides Taddy's and one or two cases of jaundice.

Cryder has just come back and is looking rather thin.

. I have got my ticket for the play in the third row and next to Goodwin.

65

The play is called "False Pretentions," and Mr. Gar. is to have one of the principal parts.

Mrs. Robeson, the mother of a boy in my form, read to the School in the study last night We all enjoyed it immensly but Taddy thought it w'd be a bore so he did not go in.

With loads of love

F.D.R.

Washington's Birthday was the occasion for much school celebration; the sixth form always put on a play, at the school and later in Groton village; and parents and faithful graduates appeared, straining the capacities of Powell's and Whitney's. "Cryder" was Ogden Cryder of the class of 1902. Mrs. Robeson, the mother of Andrew Robeson, Jr., 1900, is recalled as having been a frequent visitor to the school who enjoyed reading to the boys—it was not an unusual custom for a parent to do so.

∾

*"I take my C.L.O. after break-
fast and supper . . ."*

[GROTON]
FEB. 25, 1897,
THURSDAY.

Dear Papa and Mama

The play on Monday night was a great success and a lot of people were there.

All the sixth form acted and they gave several good songs. I will show you the program and tell you all about it at Easter.

Thank you very much for your letters and the newspaper clippings they are very interesting

We are having splendid coasting and tobogganing on the crust and I have just come back from Joy's Hill. The skis came all right and I went out on them yesterday.

I was very sorry to hear about Aunt Tilly's illness but I trust she is much better now

I am glad to hear that Rubber Boots was induced to sail as I was afraid he would back out at the last moment.

I hope you will seal up my birds before the babies come to stay with you or else I should be afraid of the consequences.

I take my C.L.O. after breakfast and supper as Mrs. Wagner says it is bad to take it after a hearty meal like dinner.

I am not tutored in anything and I get on all right in everything except Geometry, in which I am rather behind hand.

With loads of love

FRANKLIN D ROOSEVELT

By now the "intended western wife" had become his Aunt Tilly. "Rubber Boots," from evidence contained in later letters, appears to have been his half-brother, James Roosevelt Roosevelt, although the point of the nickname is quite lost. The reference in the seventh paragraph is to the collection of mounted birds which can be seen in Hyde Park today; the "babies" were the two youngest daughters of Warren Delano III—Jean (mentioned earlier), and Sara, born in 1894, who later married Roland L. Redmond, president of the Metropolitan Museum of Art, and senior partner in the same New York law firm of Carter, Ledyard & Milburn where F.D.R. had his first job. "C.L.O." was the inevitable cod-liver oil; as for Mrs. Wagner, there is some dispute among Groton historians as to whether she was the regular school nurse at the time—if not the head nurse, she may have been one of the special nurses who came to help out whenever there was a good deal of sickness at the school.

〜〜

"I made a two-minute speech . . ."

[GROTON]
FEB. 28, 1897,
SUNDAY.

Dear Papa and Mama

Edmund arrived last night and is very well.

We have had splendid coasting and toboganning on the

67

crust, which is very thick and perfectly smooth. We go about a quarter of a mile perfectly straight on Joys Hill, and my toboggan got the second record yesterday.

Taddy's new Poland bob is splendid, and the fastest in the school.

My debate comes on the 22nd of March and is the last one of the season.

The debate last Thursday was on the Nicaragua Canal Bill and I made a two-minute speech; I was rather nervous at first, but I want to get accostomed to it so as to be all right for my debate.

Polly Wharton is the president of the Junior Debating Society, and is very dignified in the chair.

Only twenty-nine days more and we shall be coming home!

I have begun the big bottle of CL.O. and it is kept outside the Dispensary window to keep cool.

Rawle and Ben Joy are back, but as fast as one boy gets well another gets sick and about eight boys are still in the Infirmary

With love

F D ROOSEVELT

At Groton there were debating groups for both lower- and upper-classmen; after the formal debate and rebuttals had been concluded by the scheduled participants, the argument was thrown open to members of the audience, and it was on one of these occasions that F.D.R. made what was possibly his first political speech. A brief note on the Nicaraguan Canal issue— In 1889 the Maritime Canal Company of Nicaragua, a private enterprise, had been incorporated by Congress, and in the summer of that year work had begun on the construction of a canal across the Nicaraguan Isthmus. Operations were suspended in 1893, when a break on the New York stock market forced the company into bankruptcy. Congress, however, continued to take an interest in the project, appointing boards of engineers to report on the cost of completion in 1895, and again in 1897, at the time of this reference. By 1899 the Panama scheme superseded it. "Polly Wharton" was William Pickman Wharton, Jr., Groton 1899, the stepson of the Mrs. Wharton mentioned in an earlier letter. He was a nephew by marriage of Edith Wharton. His father had been Assistant Secretary of State under Benjamin Harrison, and he was very greatly excited about politics all through his school career—Mr. Gardner, in one of his celebrated School Birthday poems, referred to him as "young Politics Wharton," whence the lifelong nickname of "Polly." Later on in life Wharton became prominent in the same American Ornithologists Union which is mentioned in a previous letter; he took a great interest in conservation, and this brought him occasionally into contact with F.D.R. The reference in the final paragraph of the letter is to Henry R. Rawle, of the class of 1902.

∽∾

". . . whether we should increase
the size of our Navy . . ."

[GROTON]
MARCH 4, 1897,
THURSDAY.

Dear Mom,

My thank (!) for your German letter. I read it, but it is very difficult   I have not yet read Miss Kreusberg's letter, but I will try to do it tonight. [This much of the letter, including the date and salutation, were written in German script.]

Blease expoctorate me on ze dwendy ninse. [This sentence in a form of English.]

The pictures which you sent to Mr. Taddy are very pretty and [I] love them also. [Back to German.]

The subject of my debate will probably be the question of whether we shall increase the size of our Navy, but we have not decided yet. [This sentence shifts to French.]

I shall write Sunday to Toutou and Muriel, and I am very glad that Muriel and Warren are coming during my vacation.

[In German again, with the exception of the one word "vacation."]

The first Lenten Service is to be held in the Chapel this afternoon. There are to be three of them this Lent, and a clergyman will address us this time. The attendance is not compulsory, I do not expect to see my nephew there, who by the way is suffering from an acute attack of lumbago and spent last night in the infirmary.

Excuse French, German & English & a bad pen
With love [Final section of letter in English.]

F D ROOSEVELT

F.D.R. was by now scheduled as a member of a team for a regular debate; it will be recalled, in reference to the proposed subject, that at this time Theodore Roosevelt was Assistant Secretary of the Navy under McKinley, and was ardently (and disconcertingly) espousing "preparedness"—reorganization of the Navy, increased size, and so on. "Toutou" was F.D.R.'s half-niece, Helen Rebecca Roosevelt, "Taddy's" sister. She married a sixth cousin from the same side of the family as Anna Eleanor Roosevelt—Theodore Douglas Robinson, son of Theodore Roosevelt's sister Corinne.

〜〜

"Please give me permission to
go in a canoe . . ."

[GROTON]
MARCH 7, 1897,
SUNDAY.

Dear Papa and Mama

I am sending you a circular about the School Camp. Can you spare $10 annually for 3 years?

I am trying to do a Prize Puzzle with Goodwin, which came out in the St. Nicholas

It is about the Statesmen of America & we have found most of them.

We are having horrible weather here, yesterday it rained & today everything is frozen tight. The river broke up on Monday but it is still full of ice.

Please give me permission to go in a canoe as I would have to keep off the river until swimming time in June otherwise.

I have put my name down for the Winter Sports & I am going to try for the standing high, running high and standing broad jump, as well as the ten yards dash and the potato race. The Sports are to be held in a few weeks and I am going to train for them soon.

The pussywillows are coming out here and I have seen robins & songsparrows.

If you want to get any pussywillows, there are two or three very good bushes in the swamp by Brother Rosy's greenhouse, which are very easy to get at.

I have written to Muriel & shall write Toutou this afternoon.

I am delighted with the plans for the Easter vacation, only the sooner I get away from New York the better.

Last Sunday as the Chapel was so cold we had afternoon service in the Schoolroom

With love by loads

F. D. ROOSEVELT

The circular concerning the School Camp is available; it reveals admirably the feeling about social problems and charity which was characteristic of the society of the time, admixed with some typical Groton attitudes. It says in part:

"The Missionary Society of Groton School owns a small island in Lake Asquam, New Hampshire, where, for the past four years, it has maintained a summer camp for poor boys of Boston and New York. The aim of the camp has been to provide a vacation for boys who have no other opportunity to escape from the heat of the city, and lists of such boys are obtained each year from those in charge of various city missions. The boys come in squads of twenty or twenty-five, and, in most cases, spend a fortnight at the camp, where they row, swim, etc., and also do some regular work each day, such as wood cutting, road making or carpentering.

". . . The 'Faculty' as the boys call it, consists regularly of two graduates of the school, one master, and two members of the Missionary Society from the Fifth and Sixth Forms. The Faculty usually changes each fortnight, but there is in addition one who stays permanently at the camp and attends to the business management. The boys received must be at least ten and not more than fourteen years old. In case of good behavior they are invited for two successive years.

"This camp has been most successful. Many boys from wretched homes arrive with pale faces, looking worn, dirty, and old, and go back after a fortnight completely transformed in appearance, and furthermore with a new idea of the possibilities of cleanliness, decency and civilization.

"For the Faculty, too, the fortnight is not without its lessons of simplicity, patience, and, above all, fraternal feeling for those who, with all the differences of environment and education, are yet moved by the same hopes and fears and temptations as they. The ultimate equality of human beings is impressed in a way not likely to be forgotten in the years when these members of the Faculty become men in the community. . . ."

〜〜

*"I am going to write my speech
. . . then learn it by heart . . ."*

[GROTON]
MARCH 11, 1897,
THURSDAY.

Dear Papa and Mama

The Final Doubles of the Fives Tournament was played off this morning between Mr. Peabody and Devens and Geo. Clark and Birckhead, and resulted in a victory for Clark and Birckhead. The scores were 15-9 and 15-8.

I am to debate on the 22nd with Caspar Goodrich against Goodwin and Thorndyke. The question is: Resolved that the U.S. increase the navy. We are pro, or for it.

72

Please send any points that you find, no matter if they are on my side or not.

I am going to write my speech out and then learn it off by heart.

My speech is the first of the four and I think the sides are pretty even. The snow has almost gone and the chute was taken down today.

I am to be in 8 events in the games next Wednesday although I do not expect to get a single thing.

What with training, debating and studying for the exams I find my time pretty well taken up.

Many thanks for the Graphic and Scientific Americans

I have just come back from the second Lenten Service in the Chapel We had a very good Sermon, really an address, from some Mr. Thingummy I went to Groton yesterday and ate about two lbs. of vile peanut candy, had a head & belly ache in consequence but am cheerful as a cricket today.

With tons of love

FRANKLIN D. ROOSEVELT

Do you like this signature better than other?

"Fives," being typically Groton, deserves some words of explanation. It is a form of handball played at various English public schools; the construction of the court and the rules of the game vary, and the fives played at Groton follows the style at Rugby. The court is approximately twenty feet long and ten feet wide, completely enclosed on three sides by high walls, and to the rear by a low wall about four and one-half feet high. The ball can be struck against any of the four walls but must finish up against the forward wall, which is equipped with a tell-tale approximately three feet above the floor. Scoring is the same as in regular handball. The ball itself is made of twine covered with leather, and players customarily wear padded gloves for protection. The game can be played either singles or doubles, the court for the latter being wider in measurement. As has been previously noted, masters participated in the school sports, which explains the Rector's presence as a doubles partner. "Devens" was Arthur L. Devens, Jr., Groton 1898, whose son Charlie was later to have a brief but interesting career as a pitcher for the New York Yankee baseball club. The victorious pair were George C. Clark, Jr., Groton 1897, afterward of Clark, Dodge & Co., notable as the oldest New York securities firm still doing business under its original name; and Malbone H. Birckhead, Groton 1898. "Thorndyke" was John R. Thorndike, in F.D.R.'s form. The signature to this letter begins to show a close resemblance to the familiar hand of later years.

~~

"I am rather backward in Geometry . . ."

[GROTON]
MARCH 15, 1897,
MONDAY.

My Dear Papa and Mama

It snowed here yesterday and we now have about 2½ inches, just enough to spoil everything and to little for tobogganing.

My debate comes in a week and I have written a little on it already. Goodrich's father sent him some points, and we have got a good many from the library.

We do not go home til the 30th, I made a mistake in the date. I suppose we are to go with the other boys to New York.

I shall tell Mr Jefferson to send you Catalogue if he has any more left.

Do you think you could get a tailor to put a pair of extensions on my new spring & autumn suit or rather on one pair of pantys. I want one pair left as they are, so that I can change them when I wear very thin stockings

I am not being tutored in anything and although I am rather backward in Geometry, I shall study up at Easter

With great haste & love

FRANKLIN D R.

P.S Just had letter from Aunt Annie & Papa & you   Many thanks for all the valuable points and letters

Will miss mail

FDR

74

George D. Jefferson was at Groton from 1896 to 1908; he served as secretary to the Rector and was in charge of the school office. From a comparison of ink and handwriting, it can be seen that F.D.R.'s mother added the letters "ue" to the end of the word "Catalogue" in the fourth paragraph. Similar improvements or corrections on her part "for the record" can be noted in later letters.

〜〜

"The 1st heat of the potatoe race was run today . . ."

[GROTON]
MARCH 18, 1897,
THURSDAY.

Dear P. & M.

Yesterday afternoon the Bishop of Mass came up and several boys were confirmed. The choir took part in the service, which was very pretty.

We had our half holiday today instead of yesterday. The 1st heat of the potatoe race was run today and as there were over 70 entries Edmund and I lost; indeed there were only about 10 Winners, who are to run for the Championship on Saturday. The dining table a[t] which the winner eats receives a turkey as a prize. Ben Joy is in the finals and we are hoping that the turkey will come to our table.

The Fives Tournament Singles Finals was played off this afternoon between Devens and Birckhead which Devens won easily. The Ten yards dash is to come off tomorrow and the other sports are arranged for Saturday and next Wednesday.

I have nearly finished my debate and I find your points very valuable.

I do not expect to pass all my exams which begin next Thursday, but I shall cram as much as possible after my debate

I have very little spare time now

With love

FRANKLIN D ROOSEVELT

"The Bishop of Mass," William Lawrence, was a close friend of the Rector's for sixty years, having been dean of Episcopal Theological School when Peabody was there, and being one of Groton's original trustees. He held the Massachusetts episcopate from 1893 to 1927, succeeding Phillips Brooks and being in turn succeeded by his own son-in-law, Bishop Charles L. Slattery. Another of his children (he had eight in all), William Appleton Lawrence, became Bishop of Western Massachusetts in 1936. Lawrence was always actively interested in school affairs, and retired from his position as a trustee only after Peabody resigned, in 1940 at the sprightly age of ninety. His book, *Memories of a Happy Life* (Boston, 1926), conveys much of the flavor of educational, religious, and social life in Boston during the period when F.D.R. was at Groton and Harvard.

～～

"Tomorrow evening will find
me on the floor . . ."

[GROTON]
MARCH 21, 1897,
SUNDAY.

Dear Mama and Papa

I have finished my debate and tomorrow evening will find me on the floor. I do not expect to be very nervous as I have made several two minute speeches already.

We have the III Class Broad Jump on Friday & also the ten yard dash which was won by Dave Hawkins our star football player. I got 4th or 5th (!) place in the Standing Broad Jump and we have not had any other III Class events yet but they are to come off next Wednesday   Yesterday we had the different boxing matches.

In the Heavy-weight Class we had three fine rounds between Geo. Clarke and Joe Swan which was won by the former.

In a Featherweight round between Thorndyke and Lathrop Brown, Brown slipped and fell on the floor of the Gym. putting his knee out of joint. He is better today and may be able to walk about tomorrow. Owing to some mistake, all the boxing came off yesterday so we did not have any III Class events.

I expect to fail on at least three of my exams and I shall have to study at Easter. If my debate had come earlier I would have been able to study hard for the exams, but the debate and the Sports take up all my spare time.

I have been given 2 black-marks since I came back, both from Mr. Abbott but as they were given for no fair reason he took them both off! I have not had any latenesses, so I stand a pretty good show for getting a prize.

We are to have the last Lenten Service next Friday when Mr. Thayer is going to address us.

Has my necktie come from Brooks Bros? If so, please bring it to N.Y. so that I can wear it when there. Can't you arrange to go to Hyde Park before Saturday? The less I have of N.Y. the better.

With loads of love & looking forward to seeing you in a little over a week

FRANKLIN D. ROOSEVELT

Among those participating in the boxing matches were Joseph R. Swan, Jr., senior prefect of the class of 1898, and Lathrop Brown, Groton 1900, who became one of F.D.R.'s most intimate friends and roomed with him all four years at Harvard. Mr. Abbott's early errors in the giving of black-marks have been noted; concerning latenesses, Bishop Lawrence recalled an incident which well illustrates the importance with which the Rector regarded punctuality. He and Theodore Roosevelt were staying at the school in June of 1900. Early one morning, T.R. burst into his room half dressed, and before Lawrence was fully awake, shouted: "Bishop, can you tell a bewildered Governor what time it is? My watch has stopped, and if I am late to breakfast in this school, I may be disciplined." The Reverend William Greenough Thayer had been a master at Groton from 1886 to 1894; at the time of this reference, he had completed the first two years of his notable headmastership of St. Mark's School, Groton's great rival at Southboro, Mass.

77

[GROTON]
MARCH 24, 1897,
WEDNESDAY.

Dear Papa and Mama

Last Monday was a red letter day for me; in the morning after school we had the III Class High Kick. There were about 15 Entries, Edmund among others. A tin pan was suspended from the ceiling of the Gym, about 3½ feet from the floor at first. As it rose the contestants dropped out one by one until I found myself one of the only three left, the other two being A. Crocker and Robeson. At the next rise in the pan Crocker dropped out and at the next rise Robeson missed the kick 3 time and I twice. As we were only allowed 3 tries, Robeson was out of it and at my 3rd kick I just touched the pan which secured 1st prize to me. My kick was 7 feet 3½ inches from the floor & Robeson's was 7 ft. 2⅜ inches   I kicked just 2 feet over my head.

At every kick I landed on my *neck* on the left side so the result is that the whole left side of my body is sore and my left arm is a little swollen!

In the evening after school Goodrich and I read over our debates to ourselves. I was not at all nervous in the chair as Goodrich and Goodwin debated first. Their debates were very good, only Goodwin did not speak his very well. My debate came next and lasted about 6 minutes and came out without a hitch. Thorndike the next debater was cut short in his speech by Polly Wharton the president, and requested not to read his speech. He got very confused and tried to speak from notes, but the result was a failure and "he quit." Several two minute speeches were made afterwards but as the meeting grew very uproarious it was adjourned.

Over 30 votes were cast out of which our opponents received three! I think it is about the biggest beating that has been given this year. I expected that we would win, but I did not think we would get as many votes as we did.

Mr. Gladwin has bought an Aeolian Grand. It is the rage of the school & our dormitory is always crowded with boys who want to hear it. Mr Gladwin has "Die Walküre" & "Siegfried" for it and although they do not sound very well on the Aeolian, they seem quite familiar to me.

I will be able to pass my exams as long as they cover work done since I came back, but I shall probably fail on at least three as I have not been able to make up the six-week's work which I lost.

I hope Warren will be all right in time to come to H.P.

I have had two letters from Aunt Annie but I am so awfully busy that I am afraid I shall not have time to answer.

I shall write you to the Rennaissance on Saturday which you may get before you see me.

With loads of love

F.D.R.

The James Roosevelts and many other Hudson Valley people habitually stayed at the Hotel Renaissance when they came to New York. F.D.R.'s parents kept an apartment in the hotel, which was located at 2-10 West 43rd Street, on the corner of Fifth Avenue. Following this letter came the Easter vacation. His winter term report, dated March 30, placed him fifth in a class of seventeen with an average mark of 7.74, despite some rather distressing examination marks which included a 45 in Algebra and a 48 in History. The overall Peabody comment: "This is very creditable."

〜〜

"I do not intend to overwork myself . . ."

[GROTON]
APRIL 13, 1897,
TUESDAY.

Dear Papa and Mama

We arrived here safely after a comfortable journey on. The sandwiches were delicious, and the ginger-snaps did not last

79

more than ten minutes. We did not wait more than ten minutes at Worcester as the train was a little late. My trunk came all right, and I shall unpack tomorrow morning.

Will you write to Mr. Peabody to give me permission to go on the river as it will be better coming straight from you.

Please leave an order in the Post Office to send anything that comes for me including *any newspapers or advertisements,* while you are away, and I think it would be better to send word to the Scientific American to change my address as it will be quicker and surer than coming via Hyde Park.

Nat Emmons and Postlethswaite are back but several others are not coming for some weeks on account of teeth.

I studied a good deal on the train & I think I shall be able to pass my Latin.

I do not intend to overwork myself, as I did last term, but I shall do my best to keep well up in my form and keep free from latenesses.

I shall feel fearfully lonely when you are abroad but I shall expect to hear from you at least twice a week and I shall write you on Sundays and Thursdays as usual. Please don't forget to send me some one cent stamps, and I should like to have a few fives in case of need.

With tons of love and thousands of kisses   affectionately

FRANKLIN D ROOSEVELT

P.S. I still smell the oleo-margerine on my hair.

"Nat Emmons and Postlethswaite" were Nathaniel F. Emmons, Groton 1903, who courted and married a local maiden, Elizabeth Prescott Lawrence, daughter of the James Lawrences; and J. Ellis Postlethwaite, Groton 1897. The previous term's examination mark in Latin had been a failing 50, hence the necessity for taking it again. As for the oleomargarine, that had been an attempt to control his hair which was then somewhat unruly.

Thursday
March 11ᵗʰ

Dear Papa and Mama

The Final Doubles of the Fives Tournament was played off this morning between Mr Peabody and Devens and Geo Clark and Birckhead, and resulted in a victory for Clark and Birckhead. The scores were 15-4 and 15-8.

I am to debate on the 22ⁿᵈ with Caspar Goodrich against Goodwin and Shorndyke. The question is: Resolved that the U.S. increase the navy. We are pro, or for it

Please send any points that you find, no matter if they are on my side or not

I am going to write my speech out and then learn it off by heart.

My speech is the first of the four and I think the sides are pretty even. The snow has almost gone and the chute was taken down today.

I am to be in 2 events in the games next Wednesday although I do not expect to get a single thing.

What with training, debating and studying for the exams I find my time pretty well taken up.

Many thanks for the Graphic and Scientific Americans

I have just come back from the second Lenten service in the Chapel where We had a very good Sermon, really an address, from some Mr Thingummy

I went to Groton yesterday and ate about two lbs of vile peanut candy, had a head + belly ache in consequence but am cheerful as a cricket today

With tons of love
Franklin D. Roosevelt

Do you like this signature better than others?

The signature to this letter begins to resemble the familiar hand of later years.

→ Franklin D Roosevelt

November 1ˢᵗ Sunday
/96

Dear Papa and Mama
    I got the bible,
prayer-book and watch
on Friday, thank you
very much for them
The bible is very nice
and the type is large
enough even for a
Groton dark day!
I have been singing
and reading all day
and I feel rather
lazy and stupid, for

there is not much to
do. I wrote to Aunt
Laura this morning
and I am going to
write to Aunt Doe
this evening.
I am going to hire
a wagon with Taddy
on Thanksgiving
morning, with two
horses and we may
take two other fellows
We play St Marks
next Wednesday and
if we win I shall

telegraph you.
We expect the game
to be very close and
if anything we have
the better team.
Have you found a
Van Daeal's French
Composition, if you
have please send it
to me as we use
it every Saturday
night.
Edmund is all right
now, but he has
to be careful what

he eats.
There is really nothing
to write about now
but I will tell you
all about the St.
Marks game on
Thursday
        With loads of
        love
Υραυκλιν Δελανω
    Ρωοεϝελτ
(Papa can read this!)

Further experimentation with his signature, a phonetic version in Greek.

This family portrait taken during F.D.R.'s final year at Groton was the last to be made before the death of James Roosevelt in December 1900.

Messrs. Barbour, Ir. and the mid-nineG. 1890 baseball team.

At Campobello, the schooner Half-Moon *at her mooring.*

At Hyde Park for Christmas, a free ride for F.D.R.'s dog.

7.D.R., Miss Mosenthal, Teddy

Two future Assistant Secretaries of the Navy and friend in the Harz Mountains near Bad Nauheim.

The first Campobello house, erected in 1885.

*In Fairhaven, Massachusetts, F.D.R.'s great-grandfather
Delano, a New Bedford sea captain, built "The Homestead," which sheltered four generations of the family
until, in 1942, it was sold and subsequently demolished.*

Confined to a wheelchair after paralysis overtook him in 1892, Warren Delano II posed for this picture with his grandchildren not long before his death in January 1898.

Photographs of F.D.R. at the water's edge or at sea almost always caught him in a happy mood.

Home from Groton for the summer, he posed for this picture with his Newfoundland, "Monk."

"I have just proved four diffi-
cult new propositions . . ."

Dear Papa and Mama

I received your letter today and I am thinking that I will not get many more this term written on this side of the ocean.

I have passed my Geometry Exam and I am not going to be examined in Latin.

I have just proved four difficult new propositions and I got on splendidly in class today.

We have had service in the chapel both yesterday and today which I attended.

Tomorrow we have no lessons except evening school, and we go to Church as on Sunday.

Friday—

We have had two services today, and the choir wore their cassocks but no surplices.

After the afternoon service I played golf with Goodwin, & I find that I am beginning to play much better.

My place at table has been changed and I now sit two places from Mr. Woods, on his left.

We are to play the first baseball game of the season tomorrow, with the Boston Latin School.

Canoeing is very good now and I am daily waiting permission to go on the river. Please tell me when you write Mr. Peabody so that I can find out from him.

I will write you Sunday and to the Teutonic on Monday.

With loads of love   affectionately

FRANKLIN D. ROOSEVELT

Groton was certainly one of the very first institutions of learning in this country to boast its own golf links, but praise must stop with this statement. It was a short, nine-hole course, and the fairways were very similar in appearance to a cow pasture—not an unreasonable resemblance, inasmuch as cows continually grazed on them. Mr. Arthur Woods was a master at Groton from 1893 to 1909; he left, later to make a notable reputation as police commissioner of New York City during the four years of the First World War. At this time F.D.R.'s parents were scheduled to sail on the *Teutonic* for the annual cure.

∽

"We had a splendid time and caught a turtle . . ."

[GROTON]
APRIL 18, 1897,
SUNDAY.

Dear Papa and Mama,

We have had a very quiet Easter here, and the sky has been cloudless today. The services were lovely, although the choir did not distinguish themselves. Yesterday afternoon I went on the river with Taddy; we had a splendid time and caught a turtle. The river is not as pretty now as it will be later, as the leaves are not out yet. The water is still too cold for swimming, but we shall probably begin in about three weeks. I have put my name down for playing baseball, and I expect to be put on a junior team, as I do not play well.

Mr. Gardiner appeared today in a tail coat, spats, orange shoes and a green westcoat; he was greatly admired!

As it rained yesterday morning, we did not play the Boston Latin, but we are to play them tomorrow afternoon, and study more in the morning than usual.

I have put the Easter-card on my bureau, & I shall think of you whenever I see it.

Please don't forget to tell Aunt Annie to send me the news of your arrival in England and I shall be impatient to get your letters when you are abroad. I shall try to do some good reading this term in spare moments but I shall keep outdoors as much as possible. I shall write you to the Steamer tomorrow and with lots of love kisses & hugs affectionately

FRANKLIN D. ROOSEVELT

P.S. Be sure you keep me informed where to send my letters to you while you are abroad.

F.D.R.

∽

"Mr Peabody played . . . but he
did not distinguish himself . . ."

[GROTON]
APRIL 19, 1897,
MONDAY.

Darling Papa and Mama

We have just played a game with the Boston Latins in which we won by a score of 8-4. It was very good considering that it was the first game. Mr Peabody played in the latter part, but he did not distinguish himself.

Today has been a half holiday in honour of graduates taking honours at college and also as it is Patriots Day.

We have had a small shower here today, but otherwise the weather has been fine, so I trust you will have a smooth and short trip across the ocean.

I am getting on much better in my studies this term, although as more boys have come who were not here last term, I may not get a better place in my form. I am much improved in Geometry, and I seem to have the knack of it now.

This term is the nicest one of the whole year, and the buds are coming out nicely, although they are not much further advanced than they were two weeks ago at H. Park. I shall write you to London by the Saturdays steamer.

I will be thinking of you for the next two months constantly, and it makes me very sad to think that the ocean will be between us

With tons of love & kisses dear Papa and Mama   Ever affectionately

FRANKLIN D ROOSEVELT

83

Groton graduates winning scholarships and other honors at Harvard and Yale did their followers at the school a service; if the showing was, in the Rector's judgment, creditable, the school gained a half-holiday. "Patriots' Day" is a legal holiday in Maine and Massachusetts, commemorating Paul Revere's ride and the defense of the Minutemen at Lexington and Concord.

∽∽

"I play centre-field on Hugh Minturn's nine . . ."

[GROTON]
APRIL 22, 1897,
THURSDAY.

Dear Papa and Mama,

I am thinking of you as sitting in your chairs on deck enjoying this lovely weather. You must be glad not to have a lady continually calling for brandy and champagne opposite your state-room. Do you remember the one you once had bothering you?

We played the Harvard 2nd 'Varsity yesterday and were beaten 12-2 I am sorry to say, but as it is Harvard's second best team we could not expect anything better.

I play centre-field on Hugh Minturn's nine, on which Taddy plays left field also.

We played Charley Lawrance's nine today for the first time and we were victorious, we a score of 15-3!

I have just received the bill of shipment of my canoe, so I suppose it will be at Groton in a day or so. I shall have Johnson get it and bring it to the river. I expect it will last me for many years, as I intend to be very careful with it.

Taddy has had his for over two years and it is today as good as the day he got it.

I do not expect to do very much canoeing till the end of

May, as baseball takes up most of the time till the St. Marks game, which is to be played at Southboro' on the 29th of May.

I go to bed early on Saturday, Sunday, Monday and Tuesday, but I have to sit up on other days to get my lessons done, and choir-practice takes about 1½ hours every week out of my lessons.

The choir-festival is to be held on the 8th of June and we have been practicing for it ever since Xmas. and we don't half sing it yet.

With tons of love & hoping the journey has been comfortable

FRANKLIN D. ROOSEVELT

Charles Lanier Lawrance, Groton 1901, later achieved fame as the designer of the Wright Whirlwind airplane engine. He was even then exhibiting inventive tendencies, as witness two stanzas in Mr. Gardner's School Birthday poem of 1896: "When Charlie Lawrance *seems* to work / With singular devotion, / It's not his Latin nor his French, / Oh, no, he's got a notion. // He's busy with the last details / For crossing land and ocean / On his new patent flying car / Run by perpetual motion." The mention of "Johnson" refers to the owner of the Groton livery stable. Concerning the "choir-festival," Dr. Edwin J. van Etten, dean of the Cathedral Church of St. Paul in Boston, writes: "Each year, in those days, they [the Cathedral] had an annual choir festival with some six or eight choirs of the Diocese taking part. We find that Groton School joined in three of these occasions, namely, June 1896, 1897 and 1898. The services consisted of well-known hymns and a musical setting for the order of evening prayer. They also sang two or three anthems which were given out to the choirs ahead of time and practiced by each choir separately. Then, once before the festival, they all sang together in one grand final rehearsal."

Dear Papa and Mama

I am going to try to keep a sort of diary, writing a little each day and posting it to you on Mondays and Thursdays. I think you will like it better than writing all at once, as I am very likely to forget things that happened several days before.

It is very warm here today and I played golf in the a.m. with Louis De Koven and beat him by one hole. I find that my driver is cracked through and through and as it has only been used a few times I shall send it to Schläzenger's to have a new head put on. He ought to do it for nothing, as it was a bad piece of wood, and has not had any rough use.

Saturday 24th

I went canoeing with Taddy in the a.m. and the river was lovely. We went down to the Lawrences bridge and met the crews practicing. They do not row well yet, but under Mr. Abbott's coaching they ought to row splendidly in the races which take place early in June.

In the afternoon we watched an interesting game with the English High School. In the first five innings E.H.S. was ahead of us, but we braced up afterwards and finally beat them by a score of 8-5. Mr. Peabody played very well today and he was greatly applauded when he made a two base hit. It is very warm here and I shall leave off my westcoat tomorrow as I have been roasting today. I had a nice letter from Aunt Doe today which I shall answer tomorrow. I shall try to write to someone at Algonac once a week, as by writing to you every day I have more time on Sunday.

Sunday. 25th.

I answered Aunt Dodo's letter in the morning and after church Edmund and I went to lunch at the Wharton's. We had roast-beef cooked to a turn, and I think it is the first good meal I have had since April 13th. After lunch we talked as it was too hot to walk.

After afternoon service Mr. Gardiner gave us "google"; it is the first time this year as we have had tea through the win-

Monday. 26th

We had .six periods in the morning today and none in the P.M., as Mr. Lehmann the great English rowing coach came up to coach our crews. In the afternoon Taddy and I went out in the canoe, and were gone over three hours. We went about 8 miles, far up the Squannacook and up a great many rapids which were very exciting to shoot, and we were almost upset once, as the canoe was carried broadside on the current.

We went out after supper for the first time tonight and it is very warm now.

With loads of love & kisses.

FRANKLIN D. R.

Louis B. de Koven, Groton 1900, was a cousin of the composer, Reginald de Koven. "Schläzenger's" was the New York sporting-goods store of Slazenger & Sons, at that time located at 6 East 15th St. The "great English rowing coach" was Mr. Rudolph Chambers Lehmann, coach of the Oxford crews and exponent of the "Lehmann stroke." He was invited to Harvard at a time when that university's rowing had sunk to a low ebb, and taught crew there from 1896 to 1898.

〜〜

*"Last night we had a lecture on
the amusements of the Romans . . ."*

[GROTON]
APRIL 27, 1897,
TUESDAY.

Dear Papa and Mama,

Last night Mr. Lehmann the English coach, gave us an informal talk on rowing. He went to Cambridge with Mr. Pea-

87

body and as you probably know, he is about the greatest authority on rowing in the world. The talk was in Mr. Peabody's study and was very interesting; he told us all about the training of the Oxford and Cambridge crews. This morning I helped roll the tennis-courts, which are being made ready for use, by all the boys who intend playing on them.

Wednesday. 28th

I am thinking of you today as arriving in dirty Liverpool and getting to London in the evening.

I wonder what hotel you are staying at?

Last night we had a lecture by a Mr. Spalding on the amusements of the Romans. It was very interesting, and he gave us some very interesting pictures and descriptions of their amphitheatres, chariot races, gladatorial combats, etc. It did not end till ten o'clock, so I am rather sleepy tonight. This morning we were all in our seats at 7.20 a.m. & ready for breakfast, but as some mistake was made, we did not get breakfast till nearly 8, so we had a nice play for half an hour.

This afternoon we had a good game of ball with the Technology Sophomores. In the first inning by a great many errors we let them get six runs, which they increased to 12 before the 7th inning, while we only made six. But in the last inning we did much better and made four more runs but the game ended with a score of 12-10 in their favour.

I am reading "Phroso," the new book by Anthony Hope It is awfully exciting and I cannot leave it for one moment. Have you read it?

Thursday.

I have been doing the usual things today and this p.m. we had a baseball-ball in which my side was beaten.

It is time for the mail so goodbye

With lots of love

FDR.

Henry George Spaulding, then in his sixtieth year, was a prominent Unitarian clergyman turned lecturer. He toured the United States and Europe for years, speaking on such varied subjects as "Christian Art," "Famous Books and Famous Places," and "The Poetry of Robert Browning." The "Technology Sophomores" were from Massachusetts Institute of Technology in Cambridge. The American publication of Hope's *Phroso* in 1897 followed by three years that English nobleman's fabulously popular *The Prisoner of Zenda*.

◇◇

"It was a sort of prayer-meeting . . ."

[GROTON]
APRIL 30, 1897,
FRIDAY.

Dear Papa and Mama,

This morning I practiced baseball on Hugh Minturn's team and I think I am improving. This afternoon was a choir half-holiday, the first this term. Edmund and Ben Joy went out on the river with me, and we had great fun, although it was rather hot to do much paddling. We came home about 4, and I kept score in a baseball game between two of the cup teams.

In the evening after tea I had a game of tennis with Goodwin.

I received a letter from Aunt Annie yesterday from Fairhaven She was to have come up here tomorrow, but as some friends are going to visit her, she will not come till some time in May. I was also delighted to get a clipping from Aunt Doe, saying the "Teutonic" had been seen off Crookshaven.

Saturday May 1st

I practiced baseball all morning, and this afternoon we had a game with Phillip's Andover Academy. I am sorry to say that our team did not distinguish itself and we were beaten 16-0. As Andover is almost like a college and very big, we did not expect to beat her, but we did not play well.

Sunday, May 2nd.

It is pouring here today and as we are to go to Groton for

89

the first of the May services, after supper tonight, I am not looking forward to a long tramp in the rain. We had the usual service in the morning, and evening school at 4 p.m. after which we went for afternoon tea to Mr. Gardiner's. We are to go to Groton in a barge, but we must walk back.

Monday. May 3rd

We all went to Groton last night in the barges and at 7.30 the service began in the town-hall. We sang several hymns and a Mr. Brent of St. Stephens Church Boston gave us a splendid address, on "How to Pray," from the theatre-stage. It was a sort of prayer-meeting, and the house was full. It ended at 8.30 and we all walked back in the mud and dark. We are to go there every Sunday in May, & it will be very pleasant when the weather is warmer.

It is misty and muggy today and I shall stay in the house most of the time unless it clears up. I am afraid you will shiver in damp rooms for a few weeks at Nauheim & I hope you will not get cold. I have just had a nice letter from Aunt Kassie & am glad to hear that the baby has gained since we saw her.

With lots of love

                                                            F.D.R.

If you see any German colors which could be turned upside down into Groton colors, you will know what to do with them!

                                                            F.D.R.

"Crookshaven" was the German port of Cuxhaven, downriver from Hamburg at the mouth of the Elbe. A word about "the May services": Every year the school sponsored Sunday evening services at the Groton Town Hall; interdenominational, they were held each Sunday in May with the school attending; a good preacher was invited; and, in place of Episcopal hymns, *Pull For The Shore, Sailor* and the rest of the Moody and Sankey collection rolled out. The "barges" were wagons drawn by two-horse teams; two long parallel benches were set in the back, and each barge carried about sixteen boys. The preacher mentioned here was Charles H. Brent; subsequent to his service at St. Stephen's Church he was consecrated Missionary Bishop of the Philippine Islands, and later headed Pershing's staff of chaplains in the First World War. Aunt Kassie's baby was Sara R. P. Collier, now Mrs. F. C. Fellowes-Gordon; F.D.R. was her godfather. As for the rather obscure remark about the "Groton colors" (which were red, white, and black), they appeared to have had a similarity to the German merchant marine flag of that era.

$\sim$

"The hat was $2.50 . . ."

[GROTON]
MAY 4, 1897,
TUESDAY.

Dear Papa and Mama,

There is not much going on just now, and I have been loafing for some time. The weather is very warm, and a few duck trousers have appeared, but I shall not go into mine for some time yet.

Collins & Fairbanks the Boston hatters came up here today, with a large assortment of straw hats, cravats, etc. I bought a nice light hat, two Groton hat-ribbons and a Groton bow-tie. The hat was $2.50.

Wednesday May 5th.

I played ball with Goodwin in the a.m. and this afternoon watched a ball game with The Institute of Technology Freshmen in the afternoon. They had a very strong team and although we led in the beginning, they finally beat us 15-10. The nine is quite discouraged as it is our fourth defeat while we have only won twice. At this rate, I am afraid we shall be beaten on the 29th when the eventful game is to be played with St. Marks. I have had a boy develop my plates and some of them are very successful. I am printing them myself, and will send you the best.

Lathrop Brown, the boy who dislocated his knee while boxing last term came back tonight and he still limps a little.

My arm is better, but it still hurts me at times and I suppose it will continue for several months. Russell Sturgis came up for two days to visit his uncle; he has grown a good deal, but is still as shy and queer as usual. The Sturgis family are going to Camp. about the 7th of July, so we shall find them there when we go.

Thursday May 6th

I practiced ball in the a.m and am printing some pictures from plates. They are very successful.

I hope none of the Forbes were in the awful catastrophe at Paris. Everyone here is talking about it. America is not the only place for big accidents

Yours with loads of love, and expecting a letter from you soon,

Franklin D. Roosevelt

The Russell Sturgis mentioned here was a brother of Beatrice *(vide supra)*; he was two years older than F.D.R. Edward Sturgis, a master at Groton from 1894 to 1897, and S. Warren Sturgis, master from 1891 to 1935, were his half-uncles. The "awful catastrophe" occurred in early May; it was a fire in a charity bazaar held in a building on the Rue Jean Goujon, and over one hundred and fifty people were killed. His Aunt Dora, with her late husband's two sisters, lived on the Avenue de l'Alma in Paris at this time.

"It has no captain but is a re-public . . ."

[GROTON]
MAY 7, 1897,
FRIDAY.

My dear Papa and Mama

I received my first letters from you by tonight's mail. I was very glad to hear that you had a smooth passage and that you knew so many of the people on board. You must have taken a very southerly course for this time of the year, & I suppose it made the voyage a little longer, but as long as you got to London on Wednesday night it did not matter much.

I have been playing baseball all day, and I am on a new team which is called the BBBB or Bum Base Ball Boys. It has no captain but is a republic & is made up of about the worst players in the school.

Saturday May 8th

We played the Brookline High School this afternoon, and I am glad to say we beat them 11-0. It quite cheered us up, as we have not won for some time. We played very well, and as B.H.S. was the champion in the School League last spring we think it very creditable to have beaten them so badly.

I went to the river to see my canoe which came two days ago, and I think it is lovely. The colour is olive-green not dark-red as you ordered, but I like it almost better, & my name is painted in gold on each side of the bow. I have not used it yet, as baseball takes up all the time, but I expect to use it a great deal as soon as swimming begins, and it is likely to begin in a few days.

Sunday May 9th.

I walked to the river this morning with Goodwin and saw the canoe, which is lying bottom up with the other canoes, on the grass by the boat-house.

The four paddles are very nice

Monday May 10th

We went to Groton last night for the second of the May services. We had a very good service from a Mr. Floyd Tompkins of Providence R.I. The walk was lovely and it was not too hot to be uncomfortable. I have just got your London letters, and was delighted to hear that Dr. Weber gave a good account of Papa. I suppose you did a great deal of shopping with Mrs. Neale, but I was sorry to hear that Mrs. Berkeley was not so well. I wonder if she is going to Nauheim? It is too bad that

Cousin Bammie has stolen Toutou for the summer, but I suppose it is too late to recover her!

We are having the first thunder-storm of the year & as we have not had rain for some time, it is most welcome. It is coming down in buckets and I do not think we will be able to play a base-ball game after school, between our team and C. Lawrance's (I am writing this in P.M. School instead of studying English)

The monthly marks are to come out on Saturday & I think I may get second. It was a great surprise to me to hear that you are going to Paris. I have wanted to go there every year but this year you are going & I shall not be with you! Who carries the bags when I am not there!

I have a photo which was taken at Easter in which I am on the piazza in a group. If it is good when developed I will send to you.

    lovingly

FDR

We are just off for our first swim

The preacher at the second of the May services was Dr. Floyd Tomkins, rector of Grace Church in Providence, who later ascended Phillips Brooks's old pulpit at Holy Trinity in Philadelphia. Dr. Leonard Weber, then president and consulting physician of St. Mark's Hospital in New York, is known to have been consulted about James Roosevelt's heart condition; but whether this reference is to him or to some London specialist, is not clear. "Mrs. Neale and Mrs. Berkeley" were English friends of the James Roosevelts, but no further information is available. They later (Letter of April 19, 1898) appear as "Mrs. O'Neil and Mrs. Barclay." Anna Roosevelt, mentioned in the early Hyde Park "news journal," was "Cousin Bammie."

"We had to hold him up by the
hair until a canoe came..."

Dear Papa and Mama,

Yesterday afternoon we went swimming for the first time.
The water is quite warm but we were not allowed to stay in
more than three minutes. I just had time to pass my swimming
exam, which is across the river and back again. I found it very
easy, and several other boys passed at the same time.

This a.m. I rolled the tennis courts and Mr. Cushing invited
us to his house to have some root-beer. My!, it tasted good!

After lunch the choir took it's second half-holiday. I went
out canoeing with A. J. Drexel Paul; we used my canoe for the
first time, and it went splendidly. The four paddles were not
marked, but I have cut my name in them. We came back to
the boat-house in time to go in swimming. One of the new boys
got half way across the river and got very tired, and we had to
hold him up by the hair until a canoe came to the rescue. He
was rather frightened and struggled a little, but we managed
to keep him up till the canoe came.

Wednesday May 12th

It has rained all morning until 12, and I then went out and
helped roll the tennis courts.

After lunch a semi-professional team came up from Ayer
and we beat them 7-2.

I intended to go out canoeing with Taddy but as the team
came up from Ayer we could not go.

Thursday May 13th

Eugene V. R. Thayer has taken my plates and will develop
them by Sunday, so I hope to be able to send you some by my
next letter, but they may not turn out to be good, and if they
are bad, I will have some boy take me.

I am hoping to get letters from you by tonight's mail from

Paris and I am very anxious to hear how many new dresses you have bought there! It is pouring here today, and as I having a gumboil which feels about three feet in diameter, and as I had too much pudding at dinner, I do not feel very cheerful.

I hope you won't go to any flimsy bazaars in Paris, as they are apt to burn up!

We are thinking the chances for winning the St. Marks game are better and as it is only two weeks off we will not have much time to improve in.

I wrote to Aunt Annie today & shall write to Grandpapa on Sunday.

With lots of love & kisses, Ever   F.D.R.

"Mr. Cushing" was Grafton D. Cushing, master at Groton during 1888-9 and 1892-1906; he left the school to go into politics, and in 1915 was elected lieutenant governor of Massachusetts on the Republican ticket. He was habitually referred to as "The General."

∽∽

*"The Negro lawyer told us of
what good Hampton is doing . . ."*

[GROTON]
MAY 14, 1897,
FRIDAY.

Dear Mama and Papa,

This is the first day this week that it has not rained, and the B.B.B.B. team took advantage of it to play the Carter's Little Liver Fills, another team which has just been born. As the C.L.L.P.s got ahead of us at first, our captain, (who is 6 ft 4 inches in his stockings) tore up the score-card and afterwards claimed to have won! The only ball that I received, I nobly missed, and it landed biff! on my stomach, to the great annoyance of that intricate organ, and to the great delight of all present. The walls of my tummy caved in and a great panic ensued inside, similar to the Paris bonfire, only that a thunderbolt caused my catastrophe. Excuse all this tummy rot, but I have no larger change.

By the way, last night we had a great shindy. A quartet of negroes, & a negro lawyer, & an Indian soldier, and one paleface, all came up from Hampton Institute, which you have probably heard of. It is for the Education of Negro and Indian young men & women at Hampton, Virginia.

The negro quartet sang splendidly, and all had really fine voices. They gave us some fine old negro hymns, and a few funny songs. The Indian soldier gave us a fine speech which he had learned by heart, but he got stuck in the middle of it. The Negro lawyer next told us of what good Hampton is doing among the negroes. He has argued before the Court of Appeals at Washington, and is very prominent in his own state.

Saturday May 15th

I have served off my first black-mark today, and I am very glad I got it, as I was thought to have no school-spirit before. Old Nutter Barbarossa gave it to me for talking in the schoolroom.

We played Hopkinson this P.M. and we had a splendid victory with a score of 17-8. As Hoppy is about the best team in the School League about Boston, we may be said to have about the best school team in Mass. and if we were in the league we would probably win.

Sunday May 16th

I wrote to Toutou and Grandpapa today, but I have not heard from Algonac for two weeks. Will you let me take 50 cents out of your money to help the negroes at Hampton? We got up a subscription for them & I have already given 50 cents.

Toutou wrote Taddy that she may come up here for a few days this term, and Taddy hopes to be able to stay over a steamer so as to see her a few days.

Monday, May 17th

As Mr. Gardner's servants were busy yesterday afternoon, we did not go over to his house for google. In the evening we went to the town-hall for the 3rd May service. A Mr. Parks, of Emmanuel Church Boston gave us a very good sermon. I walked both ways with Taddy, and as it was cool we found it very pleasant.

The new boys were drilled today for the parade on Decoration Day, and it is quite difficult.

We went in swimming today and it was great fun, as we were allowed to stay in longer as the water is a good deal warmer, I had a nice swim across the river and back.

I have just received your second Paris letter, and you must be having a lovely time there.

I am afraid you will find it rather cold at Nauheim for the next few weeks, as even here we have not had any very warm weather.

With lots of love

F. D. ROOSEVELT

The captain of the BBBB's—which had apparently ceased to be a republic—was Francis B. Riggs, Groton 1899, the founder of Indian Mountain School in Lakeville, Conn. According to Mr. Gardner, he was actually 6 ft. 6 in. while at school. The Negro lawyer who spoke was, according to the *Grotonian*, a "Mr. Walker"; following his visit a subscription of $124 was raised. (Booker T. Washington was also a frequent speaker at the school.) Donor of the black-mark which preserved F.D.R.'s school spirit was Charles R. Nutter, a master from 1894 to 1900. He was the organist, trained the choir, and had a sharp manner. His nickname was descriptive, for he boasted a very prominent red beard. Dr. Leighton Parks of Emmanuel Church was one of the early trustees of the school; Peabody, while still a theological student, had assisted him at his church. On Decoration Day the boys marched in formation in the town parade, their costume being blue coats, white ducks, and straw hats.

"I tried upsetting my canoe and found it great fun . . ."

Dear Papa and Mama,

The monthly marks were read out today, and I got 3rd in the form. My mark was 7.98, the next highest I have ever had. Krumbhaar as usual was first and Laurie Rainsford was second, and I was only 3 points below him.

Dan Draper tells me that Aunt Nelly is coming up here on Friday with his mother, and Aunt Annie is coming up on Saturday. Also Mr. Gladwin has had a letter from Cousin Bammie, saying that she is coming up on the 4th of June with Helen, so you see I shall have plenty to do, as the St. Marks game comes on the 29th and the choir festival on the 8th.

I went swimming in the P.M with Taddy and we had great fun, as the water is a good deal warmer and we were allowed to stay in a little longer.

Wednesday May 19th

We played the team from Ayer again today, as the New Hampshire College team, which we intended to play today could not come.

The game was uninteresting and we beat them easily. I left before the end and went swimming; I tried jumping from my canoe and upsetting it, and I found it great fun, although the strong current made it hard work to get back to the float.

We had drill after supper on Monday & Tuesday, but we did not have it today. I am in Company B and just in front of Edmund. We have to wear duck trousers, blue coats, and straw hats on Decoration Day and I am afraid it will be pretty hot walking down to Groton in the heat of the afternoon, and as it has been very cool so far during May, I suppose it will be piping later on.

Thursday May 20th

It is still cool today, and we are having the usual routine.
Aunt Nelly comes tomorrow evening but as she arrives late I will not see her till saturday. I wrote to Aunt Dodo today & I had a nice letter from her yesterday and one today from Ellie Roosevelt who says all are well at Hyde Park & the dogs are clipped like lions   Aunt Doe sent me my grey suit, & I have received the lovely night-cloths from Elsie   I think them very pretty & nice & shall begin wearing them in a few weeks
With love & haste,

F.D.R.

The report for May 15, 1897, placed him third in a class of sixteen with an average mark of 7.98, as noted. His best subjects were French, with a grade of 9., and Latin with 8.98. Punctuality and Neatness were noted for a 10. and a 9.33, respectively. That one black-mark was registered opposite the heading Decorum. "Very good," remarked the Rector. "Dan Draper" was George Draper, Groton 1899, a son of the Mrs. William Draper mentioned earlier. He became an expert on infantile paralysis, and was F.D.R.'s doctor during the years when the latter was recovering from that disease. His former wife is the well-known interior decorator, Dorothy Tuckerman Draper. At "Rosedale," the family home not far from Hyde Park, lived Ellen ("Ellie") Roosevelt, daughter of F.D.R.'s paternal uncle, John Aspinwall Roosevelt. She was Ladies' National Singles tennis champion in 1890 (at a time when the game was both geographically confined and physically restrained), and with her sister Grace won the Doubles championship that same year.

〜〜

"It was the last square meal I will get . . ."

Dear Papa and Mama,
I received your lovely letter from Nauheim today and I am so glad you find it warm & pleasant there. It must seem rather

queer to you not having the big sitting-room but you do not need it at all, as you will be out all the time. I thinks Frau Juggernaut must have reformed, as you say the same Gretchen is there again.

Poor baby Theodore, I pity him if he has just his popper's ears, but I hope he won't inherit his pa's manners! (Don't tell our worthy humbug I said so!) Tell him "I go not to Nauheim nex yeear weder he permit me or no!" (Don't show this to Papa as he may get rebellious and leave at once!) The Graphics & Punch are a great delight to the whole school and they are engaged for weeks ahead. If I charged .05$ a copy I would make my fortune.

Aunt Nelly & Mrs. Draper get here at 7 p.m & I hope they will come to the parlor. I went canoeing this p.m with Taddy and it was too cold for swimming, so we went quite far.

Saturday May 22nd

I have a lot to tell you today so I will begin with last night. Aunt Nelly & Mrs. Draper came to parlor and I went in to parlor with both the younger & the older boys and had a long chat with Aunt Nelly. She is to stay till Monday and did not know that Aunt Annie was coming today. After morning school today, I went over to the Powell cottage & met Aunt Annie there at 12.30 I then took her all over the school and showed everything & at 1:30 I lunched with her. Afterwards I showed her the chapel & we walked about till 3 p.m. when had to leave. She expected to get to Fairhaven at 7. & meet Uncle Fred there. They had been buying furniture for the little house, in Boston & are very busy getting it ready. I then went to the Whitney cottage and went for a long drive with Aunt Nelly, Mrs. Draper & George, we went about 15 miles and were gone nearly 3 hours. We passed through a village, whose streets were lined with horse-chestnuts trees in blossom and they reminded me of Nauheim.

Aunt Nelly brought Edmund & me each a two lb. box of

candy, and mine has almost disappeared between the dormitory
& my appetite (which is not small).

We did not play any game today and most of the team are
laid up and are saving up for St. Marks on Saturday next.

Sunday May 23rd

Mr. & Mrs Bowditch are up here and Mr. B. sang a very
fine anthem in church this morning. The altar was covered
with beautiful lilacs and looked lovely.

I lunched with Aunt Nelly & Edmund & Edwin Corning
were there also. We had real spring chicken & strawberries,
& you may imagine that I gorged every moment I was there,
as it was the last square meal I will get till Cousin Bammie
comes on the 4th. At 5 p.m I drank several barrels of Google
& Root-beer at Mr. G's so I am full to overflowing now.

Monday. May 24th

We went to the 4th May Service at Groton yesterday, and
the service was given by Rev. Arthur Lawrence of Boston.
I walked both ways with Taddy, & although Aunt Nelly &
Mrs. Draper were there we did not see them, as the crowd was
great.

I enclose a letter for Mrs. Astor which Taddy asks you to
send her as he does not know the address.

I went over to the Whitney's after breakfast today to say
goodbye to Aunt Nelly, and I persuaded Taddy to go too,
although it was a struggle.

It is showery here today, but we had splendid weather before
of which I was glad, as Aunts Annie & Nelly were here.

I have been trying hard to have the photo developped, but so
far Thayer has not had time, but he is going to show me how
tomorrow & I hope to be able to send you one by the next mail.

I have worn my duck-trousers several times already, but I
have not gone into summer flannels yet, as so far we have not
had any really warm weather.

The BBBB team was not a success & bust, so I am back in
my old place on Minturn's, but as the races come on Friday

there is not more baseball as the river is the great attraction in June.

I have not heard what steamer you are coming home by, whether the 23rd or the 30th or when you leave Nauheim, so I shall address my next letter Baring's in case you leave early.

With loads of love

FDR

"Frau Juggernaut," "Gretchen," and "Theodore" were Nauheim folk now swallowed up in the past, along with the highly personal allusions made here. The Bowditches who sang were the parents of Edward Bowditch, Jr., Groton 1899; they were an Albany family, "very musical," and frequently sang at the school. The Reverend Arthur Lawrence, a first cousin of Bishop Lawrence's, was rector of the Episcopal church in Stockbridge. Concerning the letter for Mrs. Astor, it may be noted that this was Mrs. William B. Astor, at that period known simply as *the* Mrs. Astor." She was Taddy's grandmother; her daughter, Helen Schermerhorn Astor (who had died four years earlier), had been James Roosevelt Roosevelt's first wife and an aunt of Vincent Astor, on whose yacht *Nourmahal* F.D.R. vacationed after his election in 1932.

〜〜

"All expected a big talking to . . ."

[GROTON]
MAY 25, 1897,
TUESDAY.

Dear Papa and Mama,

I received a letter today from Mr. Dumper, who says he is very well & getting on nicely at St. Paul's. He sent you his kind regards.

The second crew races were held today, and I am glad to say the Hemenway's beat the Squannacooks' by almost four lengths. The crew rowed very well and the time was about the lowest ever made by a second crew. It was 6 min. 30 seconds over a mile and 1/4 course.

After dinner today Mr. Peabody called the choir into his study and all expected a big talking to, but he surprised and delighted us by saying that he had decided to let the choir go to Southboro' for the game next Saturday. As only the 5th & 6th forms & the leaders of the lower forms are allowed to go generally, we were very much pleased.

After the race we had a lovely swim and the water is much warmer than it was two weeks ago.

Wednesday May 26th

We played baseball this a.m. and beat Charley Lawrance's team quite badly.

This p. m. we played Cushing Academy which we were to have played last Saturday and we had a splendid victory with a score of 5-1. As Cushing Acamedy beat St. Marks 7-4, we have hopes of winning next Saturday's game.

Thursday May 27th

I developped the photo's this morning and the one of me is pretty good, but as the sun is not out today I cannot print any pictures for this mail. The one of our house is splendid, & I will send you all the good ones by next mail.

Aunt Annie sent me a regular feast yesterday from New Bedford. It is composed of a lb. of figs, 2 lbs of dates 1 doz. oranges and a box of ginger-snaps. You may imagine that Taddy is delighted to have something to eat, but I am almost as bad.

It is pouring here today and I am spending the time filling an empty void with Aunt Annie's supplies; I do not know what I should do without them.

We have just begun the 2nd book of Geometry & are way ahead of last year's 3rd form. Tomorrow are to be the races, on Saturday the big game & on Monday the Decoration Day parade & possibly Helen & Cousin Bammie come on Wednesday, so I shall have plenty to tell you in my next letter.

With lots of love & kisses

F. D. Roosevelt

The Hemenways and the Squannacooks were the two Groton club crews, the former named in honor of Augustus Hemenway, the latter adopting a regional Indian name.

∽∽

"Please don't make any more arrangements for my future happiness . . ."

[GROTON]
MAY 28, 1897,
FRIDAY.

Dear Papa and Mama,

This a.m. the nine had it's final practice before the game, and the whole school assembled and cheered each player. The catcher, Harry Markoe is in our form and as he is very good, you may imagine that we are proud of him.

I am very sorry to hear that you refused Cousin Bammie's invitation for the 4th and as you told me I c^d make my own plans and as Helen writes me there is to be a large party & lots of fun on the 4th, I shall try to arrange it with Cousin B. next Wednesday. Please don't make any more arrangements for my future happiness.

The races were held this p.m and I went to the finish with Taddy in my canoe. Amid shouts & cheers the crews came round the last turn with the Squannacooks leading by about half a length. They rowed beautifully and they crossed the line with the Squanny's about 6 feet ahead of the Hemenways. The latter made a splendid spurt near the end and if the race had been a hundred feet longer they w^d surely have won.

Groton 5	St. Marks 7

Saturday May 29th

We left here at 10.30 in barges & went to Ayer, where we took train to Marlborough and had lunch there. We then drove over to Southboro, about 2 miles and got there about 5 minutes after the game had begun. We played splendidly & at the end of the 2nd inning the score was Groton 2 St.M. 1 & at the end of the 4th it was Groton 5 St.M. 1. In the next 2 innings they made 2 runs, & in the 8th inning by a few good hits & some errors on our side they managed to make 4 runs, while in the last inning no runs were made by either side. We were sure of winning in the beginning, but a few unlucky chances decided it. Even the St. Markers were obliged to acknowledge that we played a better game than they did & that they won by pure luck. It is too bad for George Clark that we were beaten as this is the second year he has been captain & been beaten. We do not feel very badly about it as it was so close & nothing can wipe out 46-0 last autumn.

After the game I found Lyman & he showed me over the school, which I don't like half as much as ours. It is dark & damp & dirty inside with bare stone walls & I think the cubicles are horrid. We came back by way of Clinton where we waited half an hour & I got a soda & some maple-sugar. We arrived at the school at 8.15 & had supper & went to bed right afterwards.

Sunday May 30th

Everyone is hoarse here today from yesterday's cheering, so you may imagine that the singing was not A.1. today.

I am sending you 3 photos by this mail, & you will notice that the one of Lyman & me is cut short. It was taken with Taddy in the group with us, but I suppose that he had such a halo round his head that it *scared* the plate; but the result is not edifying as there is one large blank above his waist, & it is not pleasant to see pair of long legs ambulating alone in the photo. It is a lovely day here & not too warm & I am taking life easy & I do not intend to strain my brain. There is some talk of getting up two crews from the second & third forms & if they do I shall try for the Hemenway one.

Tomorrow we are to go to Groton to help decorate the soldier's graves.

Monday May 31st

We went to the last of the May services & had a good sermon from a Mr. Rev. Hodges of Boston & I had a pleasant walk both ways with Taddy, who is very well.

Owing to pouring rain this a.m we did not take the holidy but shall have it the first fine morning.

This p.m we went down to Groton in barges, and formed in front of the town-hall. The veterans then came out and we marched past them and out to the cemetery which is about half a mile from the village. There we disbanded & had lemonade & oranges while the graves were being decorated. We then marched back to the village & disbanded. The effect was very fine, as the whole school was divided into two companies & everyone wore duck trousers, blue coats, straw-hats, and Groton ties.

After disbanding, Taddy & I bought some maple-sugar & got some soda & then walked home together.

This evening Ex. Gov. Boutwell who was Sect. of Treasury under Grant gave us a long talk on Gen. Grant, which was very interesting and also spouted a long piece of prose by some creature by the name of Rufus Choate.

If tomorrow is fine we will not have lessons in the a.m

[no signature]

The Groton-St. Mark's score is framed in a heavy ink border. "Lyman" was his cousin Lyman Delano, previously noted. Like most of the ministers who were invited to Groton, Dr. George Hodges was a close acquaintance of Peabody. After a period as rector of Calvary Church in Pittsburgh, he returned to become dean of Cambridge Theological School, where he remained for twenty-five years. George Sewall Boutwell, who gave the school the "long talk on Gen. Grant," was a native son, having begun his career in Groton village. He studied law there, and was elected governor of Massachusetts in 1851.

Subsequently he bolted the Democrats and became one of the founders of the Republican Party. He represented Massachusetts in Congress during and after the Civil War, served as Grant's Secretary of the Treasury from 1869 to 1873, and for four years thereafter was United States Senator from Massachusetts. He returned to Groton, full of years and honors, and died there in 1905. One of Boutwell's great idols was the famous lawyer, Rufus Choate, who had been Daniel Webster's successor in the United States Senate.

∽

"We got out on a mossy bank,
and had a delicious feast . . ."

[GROTON]
JUNE 1, 1897,
TUESDAY.

Dear Papa and Mama

We studied only two periods this a.m to make up for not having our holiday yesterday morning, and I played baseball before lunch. This p.m as we had no school, I went out canoeing with Taddy and we got out on a mossy bank, and had a delicious feast, composed of dates, maple sugar and google which Taddy got in the village yesterday. I had to return at 4.45 as a man came up from Boston to rehearse for the choir-festival on the 9th. We did about half the work before tea & finished it afterwards. He thought we did very well and were about the best choir he had heard this year.

Wednesday. June 2nd

I played base-ball all morning and find that I am getting better, than was at first.

I was surprised not to get your letter by Saturday's steamer and I suppose it missed the mail.

Cousin Bammie & Helen got here at 4 p.m. and we showed them all over the school, and took them to see Mr. Peabody. Mr. Gladwin was very attentive and Mr. Griswold went to

St. Pauls School today & does not get back till tonight. We had tea with them & went into the parlor alone to see them after prayers.

Thursday June 3rd

We breakfasted with Cousin Bammie at 7.30 and left them at 8.15 for school. They go to St. Paul's today for Commemoration Day & Cousin Theodore is to speak there today & here tomorrow.

They go to Boston from Concord & thence to Oyster Bay. I have arranged to go to them for two days, probably the 3rd & 4th of July.

We had the June system of study begun today. We have three periods, from 8.30 to 11.15, & then 15 minutes recess in which we have crackers to eat. Then 3 more periods from 11.30 to 1.20 & lunch right after. In this way we get the whole afternoon free which is splendid, as it gives a good chance for canoeing and swimming. Cousin B. brought us each a 2 lb. box of candy so we are well off in the line of victuals!

I am afraid Warren cannot get in this year, & there seems to have been some mistake, as Mr. Jefferson now says he stands about 65th! instead of 37th so he will stand very little show even for next year.

Your letter has not come yet but I shall expect to get one tomorrow by Wednesday's steamer.

Ever with lots of love

F.D.R.

"Mr. Griswold" was Clifford S. Griswold, a master at the school from 1892 to 1936. He was extremely aggressive in manner, played a violent game of football, and was generally known as "Push." "Cousin Theodore" was, of course, Theodore Roosevelt. The mention of his cousin Warren Delano Robbins' difficulty in getting into Groton brings up the question of the Groton waiting lists. By this time the school had become popular and each successive class had ever-larger numbers of boys entered; since the forms were strictly limited in size, this meant that only those well up on the list were taken. Priority of enrollment was what counted, and as time went on it became customary for Groton fathers to rush to the telegraph office and enter their sons immediately after birth.

〜〜

"Cousin Theodore gave us a
splendid talk on his adventures . . ."

[GROTON]
JUNE 4, 1897,
FRIDAY.

Dear Papa and Mama

Cousin Theodore came today and wants me to stay with him for July 4th, so I have decided to divide my time at Oyster Bay between him and Cousin Bammie.

I went canoeing with Taddy this p.m. and we had another maple-sugar feast about two miles from home.

After supper tonight Cousin Theodore gave us a splendid talk on his adventures when he was on the Police Board. He kept the whole room in an uproar for over an hour, by telling us killing stories about policemen and their doings in New York.

My plans so far are to spend Tuesday the 29th at Fairhaven & to take the Fall River boat to New York & go to Algonac for Wednesday & Thursday; to Hyde Park on Friday & Oyster Bay on Saturday. Then to Barrytown on Monday and to meet you in N.Y on Wednesday. I have to go to so many places that I will not have long at any one of them, but if necessary I can shorten my visit to Barrytown & go there after you come back for the day as it is so near us.

Saturday June 5th

This a.m after school the pictures of the school were taken. First came the large photo of the whole school assembled in front of the new building on the steps of the left door. After that came the one of the graduating class, then of the base-ball nine & finally one of the editors of the Grotonian.

This p.m. I went bird-nesting with Laurie Rainsford in the swamp near the pond. We were fortunate enough to find a nest of the Summer Warbler with 4 eggs. We each to [took] one and as the nests are quite rare we were very much pleased.

When I got back Mrs. Goodwin invited me out to tea & I had a very good meal!!

(I am quite full now)

Sunday June 6th

Last night Dr Rainsford gave the older boys a very interesting talk on tramps and today he preached a splendid sermon. The singing was very weak but we have not done much practicing for Sundays as all our time has been taken up preparing for the festival next Wednesday.

Edmund & I lunched with Mrs. Goodwin & filled up again. Afternoon service was again held in the chapel and we are all very glad, as it is a rather long walk to Groton in June.

Monday June 7th

It is cloudy & cool here today but I went into my summer flannels yesterday & I do not feel much difference today. I played ball this p.m & it is very nice having every afternoon free, although it is a pretty long pull in the morning

Thank you so much for the Paris Herald it is always most welcome.

Ever with lots of love

F.D.R.

Barrytown was the Hudson village a few miles north of Hyde Park where "Steen Valetje," the home of his Great-uncle Franklin Hughes Delano, was located. The estate had come to the latter as a gift from his father-in-law, William B. Astor, and passed in turn to Warren Delano III. The father of F.D.R.'s classmates Laurence and Kerr Rainsford was Dr. William S. Rainsford, rector of St. George's Church on Stuyvesant Square in New York City. During his twenty-three-year ministry at St. George's, Dr. Rainsford put that church back on its feet, and built himself a notable reputation as a leader not only in religious but in civic reform circles. He was an honest and outspoken critic. Among the many projects which he instituted was a mission for the down-and-out on Avenue A in New York. The "Paris Herald" was the English-language newspaper founded not long after the Civil War by that genius of American journalism, James Gordon Bennett.

〜〜

"I was the last of the Sopranos . . ."   [GROTON]
                                              JUNE 8, 1897,
Dear Papa and Mama,   TUESDAY.
   This p.m. after lunch Mr. Nutter gave the choir it's final intructions for the Festival. We are to be the last choir in the procession and as we sit next the congregation it is quite a post of honour.
   I went out on the river with Taddy for an hour and then came back and had an exciting game of tennis with Goodwin. I succeeded in beating him and I think I am playing [? well]. I am going to Oyster Bay to stay with the Theodore Roosevelt's on Friday July 2nd & shall stay there all Monday. I go to Hyde Park for 1 ½ hours (!) on Friday Morning, but as I have to catch the 4.15 train for Oyster Bay I shall not see the boat-race in the p.m.
   Wednesday June 9th
   We leave via Ayer at 3. p.m. & I shall tell you all about it tomorrow as we do not get back till after midnight & I shall be too sleepy to write then!
   Thursday June 10th
   We got to Boston yesterday at 4 p.m and I have never seen anything like the way it poured. We walked in the rain to the Shaw Monument, which as you probably know was unveiled the other day. We thought it very fine & after that we got a soda and some candy, most of which I succeeded in upsetting in the street-car   We then went to the Chadwick's house (their boy is here & in my form) & had a delicious repast. We got to St. Paul's Church at 7 & the service began at 7.30. We all

wore school badges on our surplices & the plan of the church was this:

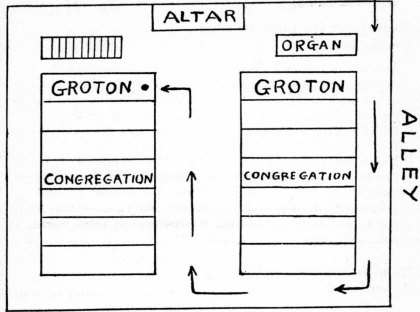

STREET

We came in from a little chapel through the door in the upper righthand corner & followed the arrowed aisle. I was the last of the Sopranos & had the seat next the aisle, with Howard Cary on the opposite side of the aisle. My seat is dotted & Edmund sat next me on the left. The congregation was just back of me & we were told that we were the second best choir there. There were some splendid solos & altogether it went off very well. It ended at 9 p.m. & we took the trolley to the station where we waited till 10.20. We had sandwiches & milk from the school in the train & got to Ayer at 11.30 p.m. where we found it still pouring & we got to the school at 12.15 *Thursday!* We had ginger-bread & milk & tumbled into bed at 12.30 We had to get up at 6.50 as usual & I am more dead than alive today.

It is still raining today and everything is soaking wet but I suppose it is good for the crops

With lots of love

FDR.

Excuse paper but I have no other
4 weeks more!

Showing an equestrian figure surrounded by troops, the Shaw Memorial on Boston Common is one of the finest examples of the work of Augustus Saint-Gaudens. The monument was erected in memory of Colonel Robert Gould Shaw, who was killed in the Civil War while leading the 54th Massachusetts Regiment—notable because it was the first state regiment of Negro soldiers to fight in the war. F.D.R.'s classmate, E. Gerry Chadwick, was a descendant of Elbridge Gerry, the notable Revolutionary figure, signer of the Declaration of Independence, governor of Massachusetts, and vice-president of the United States. This letter was written on ruled school notebook paper.

〰〰

"June is not very encouraging
for hard work . . ."

GROTON SCHOOL
JUNE 11, 1897,
FRIDAY.

Dear Papa and Mama,

It is quite warm today and everything is soaking from the hard rains of the last few days. I played tennis this p.m. with Goodwin and succeeded in beating him. Two boys went out in a very wide rowboat and the river was so high that they upset, and the boat got jammed under a fallen tree. They could not get it out so had to walk home about 3 miles. The rector on hearing of it forbade the boys in the 3 lower forms from going on the river till it went down, without a master.

Saturday June 12th

I played tennis in both the a.m. & p.m. and I had 1 Black Mark to serve off which "Old Six Black Marks" (Mr. Abbott) gave me.

I shall send next Sunday's letter to Queenstown & I hope you will get it before leaving there.

Sunday June 13th

For a wonder the singing was very good today, and a Mr. Codman gave us a splendid solo. When we went to church there was not a cloud in the sky but when we came out it was pouring. I waited till it stopped & got home perfectly dry. Exams begin a week from next Thursday and I shall begin tomorrow to work for them. June is not very encouraging for hard work as there is so much to do out of doors. I am sorry you didn't want me to go to Oyster Bay for the 4th but I had already accepted Cousin Theodore's invitation & I shall enjoy it very much, and shall go to Steen Valetje on Monday the 5th. I shall expect to get some money by cheque from you to defray the expenses of my varied travels (!) as I have only 35 cents to my name!

It rained again this p.m, and we have now had nearly a week of rainy weather. I have developped another picture of our house taken from the Southern end of the lawn. It is very good with puppy & my bicycle in the foreground.

Monday June 14th

We had two thunderstorms again today, and this p.m. I ordered the pictures of the school. They are very good and quite cheap.

Last night Mr. Codman & a Mrs. Keene sang in the schoolroom. It was very good and they both had very fine voices.

I am so sorry you have refused Cousin Bammie's invitation and I wish you had let me make my own plans as you said. As it is, I have accepted the Theodore's invitation and I hope you will not refuse that too.

With lots of love & kisses

FRANKLIN D R.

This was the first of many letters using a regular "Groton School" letterhead, printed in blue and also in red. Mr. John Codman of Boston, an acquaintance recently reported, "will sing for you today if you ask him."

[GROTON]
JUNE 15, 1897,
TUESDAY.

Dear Mama and Papa,

I am thinking of you as soon leaving 3t. Blasien, and I hope you have had good weather there as other years we had a good deal of rain, and it is a place where one wants to be out all the time.

We had another thunderstorm today and I think this spring has been very good for the crops as we have had a good deal of rain and no frost late in the season.

I went out canoeing with Taddy in the p.m. and we took some google and figs with us.

Wednesday June 16.

I studied a little in the p.m and then went out to observe birds with Kerr & Laurie Rainsford. We did not see many birds, but it is rather late in the season to see many; we ended up at the river and had a delightful swim. The current is still quite swift from the recent rains, and it is all one can do to swim against it. You need not worry about my getting drowned, as there is always a master there in a canoe who watches us.

Thursday June 17th

I shall see you in 3 weeks more and shall come down the river by the 5 a.m train, so as to meet you on the wharf.

Yesterday and today have been the hottest days we have had, and it begins to be quite like June. I went swimming in the p.m and had great fun.

I have not received any money from you yet, but I hope to soon, as I should be in a nice fix without any cash and should have to borrow some from Aunt Annie. I am afraid the holidays will be rather muddled up as you have written one thing & I another; but I suppose it will all come straight in the end.

I will only be able to send you one more letter to Queenstown.

Ever with loads of love & kisses & hugs

F.D.R.

～～

*"Exams begin on Thursday & I
do not feel at all confident . . ."*

My dear Mama and Papa,

I forgot to tell you in my last letter about my trying for the reading-prize. The four or five best readers in each of the 3 lower forms met in the music-room to have a trial to choose the 2 best readers in each form, who compete later. I, like a donkey, after being chosen to try as one of the four, read a piece of poetry from "Romeo and Juliet" which was fearfully hard; as a consequence I was not chosen to compete.

I have been playing tennis all afternoon till 5 o'clock when I had a delightful dip in the river.

Saturday June 19th.

A man came round today with delicious strawberries and I indulged in a box for $.15. It seemed quite like home getting good grub again, but next Monday being prize-Day we shall have a real feast.

I had a good swim in the p.m and played tennis the rest of the time.

Sunday June 20th

After church today Edmund & I went to lunch with Mr. Amory Lawrence. We had great fun, and I managed to stow away 3 good helps of real roast-beef, two huge chunks of strawberry-shortcake and 1 ½ bottles of ginger-ale besides a ton or so of other other [*sic*] odds & ends. We stayed till time for afternoon service & then walked home. We had several showers during the morning but it was fine afterwards. I wrote to Elsie & Aunt Jennie & I will only have 2 hours at H.P. on Friday before going to Oyster Bay & then to Steen Valetje on Monday early.

Monday June 21st

Only one week to Prize Day! I hope to get the *lateness* prize and the high-kick medal. Exams begin on Thursday & I do not feel at all confident. I am afraid I shall fail in Greek & Geometry, but lots of fellows are going to fail Greek as "old Abbott" has given us an awful lot more than we can possibly do in the last 2 weeks. I do hope you will have a good passage & you may expect me on the dock early Wednesday morning. I am afraid you will not get this letter as it goes by the Britannic I think & if so you will get to Queenstown before she does. The monthly marks come out tomorrow & I think I shall be 4th or 5th as I have not done so well this month. With tons of love & kisses & looking forward to the 7th

Affectionately

F.D.R.

The crowning event of the Groton year was "Prize Day," the graduation. It involved an assembly of the whole school in the gymnasium, with remarks from the trustees and other notables, and one long address, followed by luncheon in the dining room, at which time the various prizes were awarded. No diplomas were given in F.D.R.'s day. Amory Lawrence was a brother of Bishop Lawrence; he had a "between season" place at Groton which was later purchased by the Whartons. "Aunt Jennie," who married Warren Delano III, was the daughter of a very prominent and propertied Baltimorean, Henry Walters, founder of the Walters Art Gallery. After the death of his wife, he became accustomed to having his daughter around to act as hostess and companion in her place, and received with considerable displeasure the news that Jennie was contemplating marriage. This displeasure became very considerable after the engagement became a fact: Jennie was

118

asked to leave her father's home and not return to it until she had altered her plans; and since she did not choose to do so, she was disinherited upon his death. Her brother Harry Walters, however, shared the inheritance with her later. This was the last letter written during F.D.R.'s first year at Groton. His final report, dated June 19, 1897, placed him fourth in a class of seventeen with an average of 7.86, which the Rector termed "Very satisfactory." He failed in only one examination, Greek; the Geometry mark was 65. His summer was spent at Hyde Park and Campobello; in September he entered the fourth form at Groton.

∽

*"I took him to the nurse to be
rubbed . . ."*

[GROTON]
SEPT. 23, 1897,
THURSDAY.

Dearest Papa and Mama

Just a line to say that Warren is getting on splendidly here and I think he likes it immensely. Yesterday afternoon he went out to play foot-ball while I took my Greek exam, and when I finished I found that he had quite covered himself with glory as he had been stepped on in the small of his back and had a bruised eye. He was very plucky about it, and I took him to the nurse to be rubbed.

He got on very well with his lessons, and also knows a number of the boys already.

All the new boys went into Mr. Peabody's study last night, but I have not yet heard the result of the interview, as I have not seen Warren yet.

I don't think there is a chance of Warren's being homesick until after Thanksgiving anyway, & I don't think he will be at all. All (G. Low & a few others excepted) of the new kids seem to be exceptionally decent. Two horribly clever boys have

119

entered my form, so they will put me a few places lower, as one of them led his form at St. Marks for two years.

I took my Greek exam & altho' it was a rotten paper I am almost sure I passed. I sit two places from Mr. Griswold at table, and my cubicle is the one Taddy had last year (worse luck)! Taddy had lessons with us yesterday, but he thinks he passed his exams, so he may get to the V Form after all

With a great deal of love to you both & hoping your cold is alright now

Franklin D. Roosevelt

His cousin Warren Delano Robbins, despite the dire predictions of a previous letter, had managed to get into Groton. The failure in Greek the previous June had to be made up in order for F.D.R. to remain with his class. An interesting further note to the corrections and additions which his mother made to this collection of letters: the word "there" in the first line of the fourth paragraph had originally been written by F.D.R. as "their"; his mother crossed it out and added the correct word above the line. George C. W. Low, Groton 1902, was a cousin of F.D.R.'s—and the object, in this letter, of an amusing judicial review by an "old boy" surveying youthful new arrivals.

∞

"But it tasted like home . . ."

[GROTON]
SEPT. 26, 1897,
SUNDAY.

Dear Papa and Mama

It seems as if we had been here a month at least, altho' it is really less than a week. Warren is getting on very well and I am glad to say is in the choir. He has played foot-ball several times but as he is rather small and knows nothing about it he does not have much of a chance of making any team, which is just as well this year. I am not in the choir this year, as my

120

voice is not high enough for soprano, but as there are a number of good altos, I was not needed. Warren sang splendidly today and better than any of the other new boys. He was quite surprised at not being asked whether he wished to join or not, as he was calmly told that he was in it.

Our mackintoshes have not come yet but I suppose Papa has not been in New York yet, long enough to have got them We have had such cold nights here that I have worn my heavy pyjamas and I find them none too hot.

I still wear my thin flannels as the days are quite warm. We have not played foot-ball yet, (except the kid team) as the 1st & 2nd elevens are not yet made up.

We had a new delicacy for tea today in the shape of raspberry jam but if we took it we could have no preserved peaches, & even then we could only have one teaspoonful! But it tasted like home so I enjoyed it.

I think James will get into the 5th Form as he is working conscienciously & seems to have taken a new start in every way.

Monday p.m.

I forgot to send this off this a.m. so I finish it now. It seems awfully queer to have a lot of new kids here, there are about 24, but on the whole they are quite nice.

Thank you so much for your lovely letter & the tie & nail-stick. They are just what I needed.

I am afraid you won't shake off your horrid cold quickly unless you are careful, as you had a cold last year from Easter till July, & you might not shake it off so quickly this time.

We have old Nutter in English this year & you must not be surprised if I get a very low mark this month in English as the highest mark anyone got last year the first month in English was 3.50!

With a great deal of love & kisses to you both.   Yours

F.D.R.

∽∽

" . . . exceptionally kiddish and trivial . . ."

My dear Papa and Mama,

I have had a cold for two days, but today I am much better as a result of playing foot-ball violently. I am on the 3rd 22 and my usual position is tackle altho' today I played full-back, as the regular full-back was hurt. Taddy has a position on the same team, but as he has gone to Boston the last two days, he has been unable to play. His teeth were in a horrible condition, all rotten, and he had to have arsenic put in one tooth to kill the nerve! He is getting on splendidly with his lessons, and quite seems to have waked up.

Warren plays on the 5th twenty-two and gets along nicely altho' of course he is one of the smallest and has never played before in his life. He has escaped all black-marks and latenesses so far and gets on very well in his lessons, I think.

There are two new masters this year; one, Mr. Cooledge teaches the lower forms, and the other is a gymnazium instructor a Swede, by name Skarstrom (nicknamed "Cigar-stump") He is to give us all physical examinations and tell us where we most need development. I have purchased a share in a dark-room for Warren and myself but as no one has a key to it & it is locked it cannot be of much use to us until we can get a new lock put on.

Le Grand Cannon Griswold (!) and Jack Minturn have dropped into our form but Jack doesn't care a fig where he is!

I do hope you have got rid of your cold by this time and I shall be terribly angry if you don't.

Please tell Helen I shall answer her letter soon, but as the numerous questions contained in it were exceptionally kiddish & trivial I have taken my leisure about it, and when I do write it will be a stinger.

With a great deal of love to you both   Yours,

FRANKLIN D. ROOSEVELT

"Mr. Cooledge" was Julian L. Coolidge, a master at the school from 1897 to 1899; he left to become one of Harvard's leading mathematicians, and master of Lowell House at that university. Of Dr. William Skarstrom, who was in charge of physical education until 1900, Mr. Gardner versified in his Christmas poem for 1897: "Addie Humps! Addie Humps! a continual shriek, / These days at the School we must mention. / It isn't Choctaw and I know it's not Greek, / Mr. Skarstrom's new call to attention. // You should see his gymnasium classes some day / When there's kicking and jumping Buck. / Not a bit of allowance is made for your age, / But you somehow get through with good luck."

∽∾

*"Not only was the paper unfair
but the marking was atrocious . . ."*

[GROTON]
OCT. 3, 1897,
SUNDAY.

My dear Papa and Mama,

I forgot to mention in my last letter, that I, together with many others had had the great pleasure of failing the most outrageous Greek exam. which has ever been known in the history of education. Not only was the paper unfair but the marking was atrocious, and altho' I got about .50 the old idiot Abbott refused to pass me as is customary when one almost passes.

Another week has passed & everything is going on as usual.

Yesterday afternoon we had the first foot-ball game of the season with English High School, and it resulted in a splendid victory for us of 10-0   Last year the score was 0-0 and as E.H.S. has one of the strongest teams around Boston, we feel very proud of our first game.

I got a rather nasty kick on my shin the other day while playing foot-ball & was lame for a day or so, but I had it rubbed & it is much better today.

Warren gets on very well & this is his second Sunday in the

choir, and I I [*sic*] think he enjoys it much more than he expected.

I take my Greek exam again next Saturday & I am working hard for it.

We have the Rector in Sacred Studies this year which is very nice. Mr. Gardner came back today and we went to his house after chapel for google as usual. I am not sure what division of Greek I will be in yet as we have been working under Mr. Higley (popularly called the "old growler") so far.

Many thanks for the lovely mackintosh which is a perfect beauty and which I am sure will last me a long time. I intend to assasinate old Abbott if he does not pass me in my Greek this time, as I know the whole book by heart. You will be pleased to hear that George Cabot Ward Low (O! law!) has been pumped, & a pretty sight he was! He left off swaggering immediately!

Warren has been pronounced to be "the nicest of all the new kids" by several fellows and he is generally liked.

With a great deal of love to both of you & hugs & kisses
F. D ROOSEVELT

Major Edwin Hall Higley came to Groton from Middlebury College in Vermont. He was a veteran of the Civil War, sported a long yellow mustache, and was known variously as "The Walrus," "The Growler," and "Tuskers." A fine scholar, he remained at Groton from 1885 until his death in 1916.

〜

"Mr. Skarström said I was well
developed & proportioned . . ."

[GROTON]

OCT. 7, 1897,

THURSDAY.

My dear Papa and Mama,

Many thanks for your Sunday letter which enclosed the photos both of which I think are excellent, and I am very sorry yours were not a success, and I wish you would keep the proofs for me to see at Xmas. As I find a number of boys wish to have one of me, I wish you could send me ½ dozen of each kind as I think they are equally good.

I am sorry I did not let you know about my Greek sooner, but the first Sunday it was not corrected and I entirely forgot it in my next letter.

I have been playing violently every day and today I managed to get my hand smashed and my shin broken.

Warren's team has only played once or twice, so there is not much danger of his being hurt.

I was measured two days ago, by Herr Cigar Stump, & it was a very interesting process. I was done all over & in every conceivable position, lying down, standing up & kneeling Mr. Skarström said I was well developed & proportioned & that I did not need special exercises, only general developement (you see even I (!) get stuck sometimes in spelling). Everything was put down, to be compared with one next year.

Warren has six black-marks this week and is terribly cut up about it & I must say that 2 were given unjustly by Mr. Coolidge the new duck! I believe he is a brother or something of Mrs. T. Newbold. He talks just like a baby pronouncing all his "r's" like "w" & "th" like "z."

Warren went to Groton the other day & bought a cheese & some crackers which he has since demolished! He has also bought a camera from another boy for $5.00. which he is very proud of.

Several boys have been pumped but Warren stands no chance of it as he is universally liked.

I have found a box of your note-paper which was packed by mistake & I shall keep it for you till you come.

With loads of love & kisses

F. D ROOSEVELT

Mrs. Thomas Newbold of Hyde Park, the mother of his childhood playmate Mary Newbold, was the former Mary Coolidge.

In paragraph five there was a merry mixup over spelling. He wrote "developped," which his mother corrected for posterity; then, in the next line, he wrote "developpment" and corrected it himself (with a comment) to "developement," gaining no ground whatever, or very little.

〰〰

*"I am bound to say that the food
is much better this year . . ."*

[GROTON]
OCT. 10, 1897,
SUNDAY.

My dear Papa and Mama,

We had a very successful game yesterday afternoon with the Boston Latin School, and outplayed them on every point, the score at the finish being 28-0, a splendid performance for our team as it was only the second game of the season.

I took my Greek examination before the game in the afternoon, and I passed with a very good mark—about 90 I think. I was given two hours to do it in but it only took me an hour as it was not very hard and I answered all the questions immediately.

Poor Warren had nine blackmarks last week, and he is very much cut up about it, and intends never to get another. In his dormitory they are much more strict than in the others & he got most of them there.

Last night I went out to supper with Goodwin, whose brother is up here for a few days for his birthday. I went there again today to lunch, & Charlie Brown who is a cousin of the Goodwins' was there also. We had some delicious roast-beef, and real cauliflower, which I greatly appreciated. I am bound to say that the food is much better here this year, and we not only have better old dishes, but several new ones have been added to the men*oo*.

Warren is a great friend of a little fellow by the name of

Woolsey, the son of a Prof. at Yale & also a grandson of an even more celebrated Prof. Woolsey of Yale. Are they any relations of the Woolseys who are our cousins? Warren & he are going to build a canoe of wood and canvas down at the river after the St. Marks game which is to take place on Nov. 6th. They will have plenty of time then as there is not much to do after football is over and before there is skating.

Bishop Lawrence is up here and he preached a good sermon today.

I hope you ordered the photos as I have not heard anything more about them. On Sunday evenings the Rector is reading a story of a man who worked his way from N.Y. to San Francisco! & on the other nights he reads "Put yourself in his place" by Reide.

With a great deal of love   Yours always

F.D.R.

James L. Goodwin's younger brother was Philip L. Goodwin, Groton 1903. The "Charlie Brown" of the reference here was Charles Tracy Brown; he was not actually a cousin of J. L. Goodwin, but a connection by marriage. The "little fellow by the name of Woolsey" was Heathcote M. Woolsey, Groton 1903; his father was T. S. Woolsey, professor of International Law at Yale; and his grandfather was Theodore Dwight Woolsey, president of Yale from 1846 to 1871. James Roosevelt had a cousin named Charles Woolsey, but there was no close connection between the two families. The author of *Put Yourself in His Place* was Charles Reade, more noted for his *The Cloister and the Hearth*.

〰〰

"I weighed today 116 lbs. with
my clothes on . . ."

[GROTON]
OCT. 14, 1897,
THURSDAY.

Dear Papa and Mama

Many thanks for the Graphics which I forgot in my last letter to mention. Also for the photos, which were all snapped up, almost before I could open them; do you think you could send me just 3 more, which I had already promised to Howard Cary, Edmund, & Jack Minturn. Jack sits behind me in the school-room, & we have terrible scraps in evening school. He tries to kick me, but I have several times succeeded in seizing his feet & removing his shoes (!) for which we have narrowly escaped black-marks several times.

Yesterday afternoon Warren and I walked to the village & bought some towels, matches & candles for our dark-room, which I procured from Dick Derby for $2.00. We also bought a basket of delicious grapes for 15 cents.

Today I have played football violently and escaped serious injury altho' I am rather sore. You will be pleased to hear that I weighed today 116 lbs. with my clothes on, or about 112 without, which is a considerable gain since I was last weighed, I think.

Tomorrow is the School's birthday and consequently a half-holiday. We all expect to have great fun and we have a regular feast in the evening. On Saturday we play Hopkinson & it promises to be an exciting game as Hoppy has a very strong team.

Taddy is terribly cut up & anxious because his friend Alice has smashed her head & he had just received a letter from her a little while before!!!!!!!!

With loads of love

F D.R.

Dr. Richard Derby graduated from Groton in 1899. He was one of F.D.R.'s early Hudson Valley friends, and later married Theodore Roosevelt's daughter Ethel. Another of T.R.'s daughters, the only child of his short-lived first marriage, was the renowned Alice, later wife of the Speaker of the House of Representatives, Nicholas Longworth; it is she who was the injured young lady mentioned in the final paragraph of this letter.

〜

[GROTON]
OCT. 17, 1897,
SUNDAY.

My dear Papa and Mama,

I will begin by telling you about last Friday, the School's Birthday.

In the afternoon, as it was a half-holiday, there was a football game between the 2nd Eleven and the Graduates, many of whom were here. The graduates won amid tremendous cheers, and we then went to a tea consisting of bread & butter only as the grand feast came at 8 o'clock. At 6.30 we had evening school for an hour & when supper was ready we all marched round the school-room, headed by the graduates & masters, & walking two by two, singing "John Brown's Body" at the top of our lungs. We then went in to the dining-room and "fell to." The first course was oyster-stew, the second delicious chicken-salad, then ice-cream & all kinds of cake. The 5th and 6th form tables sang songs & after the fruit we all went to the library for the entertainment. First we had a very good song from the Glee Club, in which Warren took part. Then Mr. Griswold gave us a piece on his violin & Mr. Jefferson sang several songs and the musical part then ended with another song from the Glee Club. Then Mr. Gardner gave his poem, which as usual was excellent, bringing in many jokes on the boys & masters also. After that we sang the School Hymn & had prayers.

Yesterday afternoon we played Hopkinson & the result was a splendidly contested game in which neither side scored. They are easily the strongest team around Boston with exception of Harvard, so we are quite pleased that they did not beat us.

I do not think there is much chance of my going to Southboro' on Nov. 6, unless the whole IV Form is taken I don't believe even the choir will go this year, as they have not sung long enough to deserve it.

It is a beautiful day here & the last few days have been really hot.

I think I forgot to tell you that since Mr. Gardner came back he has the whole form in Greek, which is delightful, as I can learn better & quicker with him than with anyone else

Taddy is getting on really very well, and takes an interest in everything & gets on well in football, playing half-back on the same team I play on.

With loads of love to you both   Ever

F.D.R.

The Groton School hymn was written by Phillips Brooks (also the author of *O Little Town of Bethlehem*) in 1887 at the request of Mrs. Peabody, to music by her great-uncle, George Peabody. Its opening words are: "Father of all, below, above. . . ."

∽

"Then paper & ink & nutshells
flew thick & fast . . ."

[GROTON]
OCT. 21, 1897,
THURSDAY.

Dear Papa & Mama,

There is not much to write about this week, as nothing has happened. We have had fine weather & played football every day. This afternoon I went out walking with Goodwin & we got a lot of splendid hickory nuts, which are now reposing in our rubber boots.

We had an audience today in our geometry class in the person of Miss Chamberlain, the daughter of Joe Chamberlain. She is staying here for a few days & is evidently horribly learned, as she understood geometry!

I have managed to get 3 or 4 black-marks this week, but I had good fun, quite worth them! Poor Warren has five more this week, and I know how hard it is for him to keep from getting them   The new kids are up to all sorts of mischief so the masters are doubly watchful, and give a good many at a time. He has had them all from Mr. Coolidge, the new duck, who, I am bound to say, does not at all understand how to give black-marks. The other day when he had charge of the school-room, the 3rd & 4th forms were studying, and I wish you could have heard the noise we made

Some musical gentlemen in the far end of the room had a whistling concert, while I amused myself by singing Yankee Doodle in a high falsetto key. Old Coolidge made the whole form stand up. That did not do much good, & we all sat down again & the 3rd Form stood up. Then paper & ink & nutshells flew thick & fast, and the old man got perfectly wild. He called up the wrong boys & for ten minutes he yelled at a boy who really was not in the room, while he really wanted me, but the end of the period came just in time to save me from a large number of Black-marks.

I have been playing golf in all my spare time and we are getting really quite good links now.

With a great deal of love & kisses   Ever

F.D.R.

The object of concealing hickory nuts, candy, and similar acquisitions in one's dormitory boot-locker was not so much a rule against having them at the school, as a desire to prevent any pillage of the treasure by one's schoolmates. On summer vacations in England, the Rector frequently stayed with that noted British statesman, Joseph Chamberlain, whose wife was the former Mary Endicott of Salem, a cousin of Peabody's. Miss Chamberlain was repaying a visit while her father, as Colonial Secretary in Salisbury's cabinet, wrestled with the grave problems which were shortly to result in the Boer War. In this letter it is amusing to note the change in F.D.R.'s attitude toward black-marks, presumably due to an access of school spirit.

∞

*"It was found that one of their
men had run away . . ."*

My dear Papa & Mama,

We had the most absurd game yesterday which I ever saw.
It was with the Brookline High School. The game was divided into two 20 minute halfs, and before we had been playing 20 seconds we had scored a touch-down.

On an average of every 2 minutes we made touchdowns, so
that before the half was over we had scored 50 to their 0! At
the beginning of the second half it was found that one of
their men had run away, so we could not play any more

If we had gone on we should have easily reached the 100
mark and so beaten all previous records of big scoring. The
missing guard was found in the gymnasium, and of course we
suppose he was sent away so that we should not do any more
scoring. 2 of the touch-downs were made within 50 seconds
of eachother. At St. Marks yesterday, St Marks was beaten
30-0 in a game with Hopkinson, whom we tied last Saturday,
so we are all hoping to beat them badly.

The choir are to be taken to Southboro' so Warren will see
the game, and I only wish the 4th form could be taken, but
there is no chance of it at all.

I was greatly surprised to hear that you are going to West
Superior this week. I wonder what day you leave & if it is in
the D & H car. I wonder if Mr. Gilbert has "busted" that you
are going out on such short notice.

I was much amused at Captain Mitchell's letter, and as usual
very pleased to get the Graphic.

Warren gets on well & both he & I had 4 black-marks last
week. The monthly marks come out next Wednesday, and I
hope to get a good B.

Warren has a slight sore-throat and is sleeping in the infirmary tonight, but I think he will be out tomorrow.

I enclose our English Exam which comes monthly & we took it last Thursday. It is perfectly horrible as you may see, & the last part are questions on a book the "Sir Roger De Coverley Papers" which we had to read out of school in 3 weeks! I have very little extra time but in odd moments I try to read "Foul Play" by Charles Rede.

With lots of love   Yours ever   F.D ROOSEVELT

James Roosevelt had mining interests at West Superior, Wisconsin, near Duluth; "Mr. Gilbert" was his manager. The Delaware and Hudson Railroad provided a private car, the *Monon*, for its vice-president. "Captain Mitchell" was the skipper of the Roosevelt boat *Half-Moon*. The second reference to Charles Reade again does that gentleman a spelling injustice.

∽∾

The following is the text of the
English examination mentioned
in the letter of Oct. 24, 1897;
it is included here as typical:

IV English, Oct. '97

A.

Explain:
  1. Till that Bellona's bridegroom, lapp'd in . . .
  2. You greet with present grace and great prediction of noble bearing and of royal hope.
  3. Time and the hour runs through the roughest day.
  4. The rest is labour which is not used for you.
  5. Wherever in your sightless substances.
  6. Has made his pendent bed and procreant cradle.
  7. If it were done when it is done, then 'twere well it were done quickly.

8. The love that follows us sometime is our trouble, which still we thank as love. Herein I teach you how you shall bid God 'ield us for your pains and thank us for your trouble.

B.

1. Who was Sir Andrew Freeport? Will Wimble?
2. Explain fully, the Mohocks, Coffee Houses, The Pope's Procession.
3. Describe either (a) The Widow and Sir Roger, or (b) The death of Sir Roger.
4. Write, from memory, six lines beginning, "And pity, like a naked new born babe."

∽∽

"The house was so tiny we could only go in 40 at a time . . ."

[GROTON]
OCT. 28, 1897,
THURSDAY.

[No salutation]

The marks were read out today, and as I expected, I got B. I think I got a good B as I led the form in French, and also received A in several other studies.

Last Tuesday we had a half holiday in honor of Mr. Abbott's wedding. He & Mrs. A. (who looks just like a wax doll) have fittted up the little house just opposite the Whitney còttage. In the afternoon we played a very exciting game with with [*sic*] the Harvard Juniors and were beaten by the close score of 4-0. After the game the whole school went to Mrs Abbotts house for afternoon tea and cake, but as the house was so tiny we could only go in about 40 at a time.

Yesterday was again a half-holiday, so I played golf all afternoon with Goodwin & altho' I played very badly I was able to give him 2 strokes a hole & beat him.

I suppose you have had a lovely journey in the car, and you must be pleased to see Uncle Fred. I was [wish] I were with you, as I enjoyed my last trip to West Superior immensely, & you remember I smashed my head open that trip on the way home.

Please do not show this scrawl to anyone as I am in a terrible hurry to catch the mail before the gong rings

Please give my love to Uncle Fred, Aunt Tilly & all the children

I hope you will find things booming in West Superior & that you will come here when you get back

Mrs. Rogers arrives tomorrow, Edmund tells me.

With loads of love

                                        F D ROOSEVELT

Mather Abbott married a boyhood neighbor, Elsie Twining. In the first report of F.D.R.'s fourth-form year, dated Oct. 23, the system of grading by letters was used, an "A" equaling 85 or above, a "B," 70 to 85, a "C," 55 to 70, and a "D," below 55 or failing. No relative position in the class was given, as previously. To get his B average, F.D.R. had four A's, three B's, one C, and a D in English Composition. "Very fair," from the Rector.

〜〜

"He talked in pretty strong language against . . . Tammany . . ."

                                        [GROTON]
                                        OCT. 31, 1897,
                                        SUNDAY.

My dear Mama and Papa,

It is very gay up here at present, as there are about 20 people staying at the Powell's & Whitneys. First Mrs. Rogers, Mr. Conover & Coleman arrived Friday Night & the same day Mr. & Mrs. Henry Rogers came. Yesterday Dr. & Mrs. Rainsford, Cousin Marion Low, & Mr. & Mrs Goodwin.

On Thursday night, to go back, we had a lecture on Rome by Mr. Spaulding, who lectured last year on the Roman sports. It was quite good tho' much like the other.

Last night Dr. Rainsford gave the upper school an informal talk in the study on the present political crisis in New York. It was extremely interesting, and he talked in pretty strong language against the Platt & Tammany machines & especially against the *former*

Yesterday afternoon I played golf with Wendell Blagden & then watched a game between the 1st & 2nd elevens as there was no outside game yesterday. Mrs. Rogers invited me to lunch but as there is a new rule that only 2 boys can go to lunch with one family at a time & as Warren & another boy were invited before me I was unable to go. Today I went to lunch with the Goodwins & had a delightful time & devoured all the good things. Mrs. Powell's new addition is just opened and is really very nice. There is a splendid hall and public parlor, very swell, and a private dining besides the enlarged old one.

Cousin Marion Low invited me to supper, but as there is another new rule this year, that boys can only go out [to] supper with their parents, I was unable to go.

Mrs. Rogers says you will probably come here direct from West Superior, so I suppose you will arrive on Friday or Saturday, altho' I have not heard anything about it from you.

I send you a few of the pictures I took at Campobello; so far I have been altogether too busy to do any developing but I expect to have a good deal of time later on. I have finished Foul Play, and am now reading the "Vicar of Wakefield", which is part of our English course this year. Next year we have to write daily themes, & in our preliminaries, a year from next spring, we are supposed to have read all the standard books & must answer questions on them.

Warren stood 9th in his form last month, with a mark of 6.00. There are [space left blank] in his form and I do not

consider his standing bad, as he has never been to school before
and the first form is a good deal harder than the 2nd in comparison. I hope you are having a nice trip, & that you will find
Mr. Gilbert with his head above water, & please give my kind
regards to William Yap, who is with you, I suppose

With loads of love to you both   Ever

FDR

P.S. I was thunderstruck by the original idea of the Ashton's
& I have been hunting in vain for a motto, I can only think of
Much meat, much malady!

Another son of Mrs. Archibald Rogers was W. Coleman
Rogers, Groton 1906 *ex;* "Mr. Conover" was his tutor. The
cousin mentioned in this letter was Marian Ward Low, wife
of Abbot A. Low and mother of the George Low referred to
earlier. It is interesting to note, in the family connection, that
the owners of the clipper *Surprise* in which Sara Delano sailed
to Hong Kong in 1862 were A. A. Low & Brother. The elder
Abbot Low, father of that eminent public figure, Seth Low,
leased Algonac during 1862-1869 from Warren Delano, to
assist the latter while he recouped his fortunes. Thomas C.
Platt was the leader of the Republican political machine in
New York State. He had come into his greatest power with
the election of Levi Morton (*vide supra;* a Roosevelt family
friend) as governor in 1894; had played an important part
with Mark Hanna in the nomination and election of Mc-
Kinley in 1896; and at this writing had just entered the United
States Senate for the second time. Tammany Hall had in 1897
wrested control of New York City from a reform administration by electing Robert A. Van Wyck mayor. The "Ash-
tons" mentioned in the postscript were the family of the
rector of St. James Episcopal Church in Hyde Park, the
Roosevelts' church.

~~~

"... the remodelling that is
going on all over the East ..."

Dear Papa and Mama

Last Monday evening Mr. Cary gave us an informal talk on China. It was very interesting & he seemed to know a great deal about the remodelling that is going on all over the East. I was to have had my strength test yesterday but in playing foot-ball in the morning I had my hand stepped on so that my wrist and fingers are slightly strained. I find it very hard to write as it hurts whenever my hand is contracted, so you must excuse this scrawl

As Warren had detention we could not go to the Lawrence's yesterday p.m. but we shall go the first opportunity.

Many thanks for the Graphics & your letters which I got all right; also for the valise which came tonight but which I have not yet opened, but shall do so when I go to bed.

I hope your *musicaly* on Wednesday was a success and the prodigal son—no, I mean the infant prodigy Padyrewsyky No. 2 did not make an ass of himself & that our piano is still intact. (it stood a good deal from me, but it might not stand the fine touch of a long-haired Polish Jew).

As it pains me a good deal to write I will close & write a better letter on Sunday.

With loads of love   Ever

                                                    FDR
P.S. Sorry to hear that Aunt Kassie can't come here on Thanksgiving day. Shall order a horse & wagon & try to get Warren invited to the Lawrence's in the evening with me.

                                                    FDR.

Guy and Howard Cary's father was Clarence Cary, who had been in the Confederate Navy as a boy, and later moved to New York to practice law in the firm of Cary & Whitridge.

Mr. Cary had made two long trips to China representing a group of businessmen who secured the concession for the Peking-Hankow Railway, and the talk mentioned in this letter was doubtless based upon his experiences then.

〰️

*"Please don't forget to send me
the dollar you borrowed . . ."*

[GROTON]
NOV. 14, 1897,
SUNDAY.

My dear Mama and Papa,

It seems as if you had left here only yesterday, and yet it is nearly a week. We were all much excited yesterday over the Harvard-Yale game which resulted in a tie. The eleven and upper VI Form went to Cambridge for it and I [it] must have been very exciting, and free from all rough play.

I think some mistake must have been made about my heavy yellow shoes, for they fitted me perfectly, and it was the old square-toed ones that were too short for me. I am glad you found my watch-chain; how did you get into my top-drawer. I think it was a great joke my having it all the time. You had better keep it till Xmas as I shall not need it till then

Many thanks for paying the A.O.U. bill & for the receipt you enclosed. I shall write to M.A. Frazar to send my birds to you.

Please don't forget to send me the dollar you borrowed as I shall need it on Thanksgiving Day.

We had quite a snowstorm on Friday which later turned into slush; about 2 inches fell and the board-walk between the two buildings was promptly laid down. You talk of double-windows; what a luxury! we have to put up with thin panes and not much furnace heat.

My wrist is much better now although it still hurts to write & shake hands.

We are to play the Harvard Freshmen on Wednesday, and

it is the last game of the season and promises to be very exciting & close.

Today it is quite cold here and I wore my covert-coat to church, although my cough has almost entirely disappeared.

I wrote to Johnson today for wagon & pair for Thanksgiving Day, but as several boys wrote ahead of me it is doubtful if we can get one, but if we can't I shall try to get one from Willis.

I have not yet had a chance to take Warren to Mrs Lawrence's, but fondly hope to some time this week if possible!

I have finished the "Vicar of Wakefield" and must now read the "Flight of the Tartar Tribes" by Quincy. Next week will be the end of the 2nd month here and Warren hopes to have a better place in his form & he has had very few black-marks this month in fact none this last week

With loads of love & kisses Ever,   F.D.R.

M. Abbott Frazar Co. were taxidermists in Sudbury, Mass., about twenty miles south of Groton. "Willis" was a story-telling New Englander who ran a livery stable in Ayer that competed with Henry Johnson's Groton stable. The author who followed Goldsmith as supplementary reading to F.D.R.'s English course was Thomas de Quincey; *Revolt of the Tartars* was the book.

∽

"Then followed pullings & squeez-
ings in every possible way . . ."

[GROTON]
NOV. 18, 1897,
THURSDAY.

Dear Papa and Mama,

Yesterday afternoon we had a magnificent game with the Harvard Freshmen. From beginning to end it was terribly exciting and although the result was a tie, 0-0, we consider it as a victory as we fully expected to be beaten at least 15-0. The Freshmen are the strongest team at Harvard next to the 'Varsity & even they were beaten by the Freshmen in one game, so we feel very proud especially as they were at least 20 lbs. heavier to the man.

Warren had quite a bad tooth-ache Tuesday night so he went to Boston yesterday. I was to have taken him in but as Taddy had to go in anyway for his own teeth he took charge of him. His tooth was filled & he is all right now. Tuesday was like summer weather here but yesterday was much colder. My hand is much better, although I can not yet take my strength test, as every day when I play football, I hurt it again. I saw Mrs. Nat. Thayer yesterday at the game & had quite a conversation with her. She said she had seen you about two weeks ago at Staatsburg.

The Xmas holidays do begin on Dec. 18th & last I think till Jan. 4th

Foot-ball is about over but we may play a few dormitory games.

The IV, V, & VI Forms may be taken to Ayer on Saturday to see a foot-ball game but it is yet doubtful.

Warren and I went to Mrs. Lawrence's this a.m. but she was upstairs with a head-ache & so we could not see her; I shall take Warren down some day next week as I want him to be invited there on Thanksgiving Day.

I was given a black-mark yesterday which was not deserved. Some boys had been in the lavatory & had cracked an electric globe & had then screwed it half on again. When I came into the lavatory I touched the globe which fell in a thousand pieces & Mr. Ayrault on my reporting gave me a black-mark.

This evening my hand was a little better so I took my strength test & my average was 350 somethings, I am not sure, but I think it was *kilometers!*

It was very interesting & the first thing I did was to blow down a tube to see the capacity of my lungs. Then followed pullings & squeezings in every possible way.

With loads of love & kisses   Ever yours

FDR

Mrs. Nathaniel Thayer was a Boston lady with the eminently Revolutionary maiden name of Pauline Revere. She was a cousin of the Delanos through Catherine Lyman. Guy Ayrault was a master at Groton from 1886 to 1927; he was an excellent football coach, with very advanced theories, and also furnished most of the enthusiasm behind the golf course.

〜〜

*"I shall get you to buy all my
shoes in the future . . ."*

[GROTON]
NOV. 21, 1897,
SUNDAY.

My dear Papa and Mama

On Friday evening and nearly all day yesterday it snowed lightly and last night about 2 inches had fallen.

This morning it melted into horrid mud and slush.

The month ended yesterday and the marks are to come out next week. Warren had seven black-marks only, last month which is much better than the one before. I had none, as Mr. Ayrault took off the one he gave me. Warren hopes to stand a little better in his form and I hope to get a good B.

We are now reading the "House of the Seven Gables" and it is more interesting although longer than the others we have read.

I shall take Warren down to the Lawrences' tomorrow or next day, as it would be too bad if he could not go there on Thanksgiving Day evening.

The shoes came last night & I am glad to say fit perfectly. I think I shall get you to buy all my shoes in future as they fit so well and are so nice!

Many thanks for the two Graphics, which are always acceptable, and they are now being devoured by a large crowd on a neighboring desk.

This afternoon I went to Mr. Gardner's and listened to some new songs on his Graphophone.

142

There is nothing to do out of doors now as everything is wet & it is too early for skating.

I hope we shall have good weather & good roads Thanksgiving Day, as it would be dismal if we had to stay in the house all day.

There is very little to write about so I will close
Ever with loads of love.

FRANKLIN D ROOSEVELT

Less than a month more!

The November report confirmed the guess that he would get an average mark of B. Individual grades showed five A's, three B's, and two C's, both in English. "Good," stated the Rector.

∽∽

". . . the water is only up to
their knees so no one was
drowned . . ."

[GROTON]
NOV. 26, 1897,
FRIDAY.

Dear Papa and Mama

Please excuse my not writing yesterday but I was busy from 6 a m to 11 p.m.

We had breakfast at 6.30 [on Thursday] and the Boston boys left soon after. I went down to the pond and skated hard until 11. By the way we had the first skating on Wednesday Morning, on the little pond; several boys went through but the water is only up to their knees so no one was drowned.

I am terribly tired and as we have a hard lesson in Mathematics, I will not write more now but will tell you all about [Thanksgiving] on Sunday.

It is pouring now & all the ice has disappeared
With lots of love

F.D.R.

Groton boys who lived in or near Boston were allowed to return home for Thanksgiving Day; the rest stayed at the school.

This letter was written on paper with a fancy blue mono-grammed "F."

∽∽

*"I have quite recovered from my
late dissipation . . ."*

My dear Papa and Mama,

I have quite recovered from my late dissipation so I will begin to tell you about it. As I wrote before I skated till 11 a m. and had an exciting game of hockey. As the ice became soft we had to leave.

Lunch was at one and as only 35 boys were left three tables were put together lengthwise in the room and we all assembled for the feast. First came oyster soup in which I found two good-sized pearls. Then came turkey and ham, cranberry sauce, celery, potatoes (inevitable), corn & sauce. I managed to make way with two helps, and then came mince & apple pies. Then ice-cream & cake and lastly fruit of various kinds and nuts. I just managed to waddle away from table!

At 3 o'clock the team came and Lathrop Brown & I got into the front seat with Warren and Julian Hinckley behind. We first drove down to Ayer and for about 30 minutes watched a foot-ball game between Ayer and Worcester. We then drove to a peanut-stand & got some peanuts etc! & then drove about 2 miles beyond Ayer & tried to get some cider but unhappily failed. We then drove back to Ayer & got some Birch Beer and Sarsaparilla at the station as it was the only place open. We then drove home arriving at about 5. At about 6.30 I dressed for the dinner, but as none of the .other boys going there [*i.e.,* to Mrs. James Lawrence's] were to wear dress-suits and as Mr. Ayrault rather frowned on it I wore my Sunday suit. At 7. we left here in a 3 seated wagon. Mr. Billings & Mr. Griswold, Richard & Roger Derby, Alex. Craighead, Jack

Waterbury, Horatio Whitredge & Polly Wharton with his Ma & Pa, Mrs. & Miss Sears & a Mr. Greenough were there, 19 in all. The table was very pretty & we had a tremendous dinner which I have not yet got over. After dinner we talked and wrote our names in the visitor's book, leaving at 9.30 in a closed carriage as it was raining. On our way home we saw the flames of a big barn which burned down back of Groton. Rosey, Jack Minturn & 2 other boys went down to it after supper. Jack was found out and is on bounds now, not able to leave the School grounds. I hope Rosey will not be found out, as it is not pleasant to stay near the buildings all day.

We slept till 8 o'clock on Friday and school did not begin until the return of the Boston boys at 10.45. Yesterday I played golf with Mr. Coolidge in the afternoon and managed to beat him by one hole.

Today it is much colder than yesterday and we may have more skating tomorrow. This afternoon we had the Thanksgiving Service and a long Harvest Cantata by the choir and Mr. Bowditch which lasted about 40 minutes. It was very good but I think Mr. Bowditch is beginning to lose his voice. Please write to Mr. Dumper to ask him to Hyde Park some time during the Xmas holiday I have not yet decided who I want, but I think we ought to ask Goodwin as I have been invited to stay with him several times.

I am beginning to work for the exams, which begin in two weeks and I hope to pass most of them altho' they are all much harder this year.

With loads of love   Ever

FRANKLIN D. ROOSEVELT

Alexander Craighead, John C. Waterbury, and Horatio L. Whitridge were all in the form ahead of F.D.R. "Mrs. & Miss Sears" were Mrs. Knyvet W. Sears (a cousin of the Rector) and her daughter, Clara Endicott Sears; the latter now lives in Harvard, Mass., and is reputed to have a very fine collection of early Americana, especially Grotoniana (ante-school).

*"Most of the buttons were off,
my other suit . . ."*

My dear Papa and Mama,

We have had another fall of about two inches of snow and since then the ponds have frozen with good black ice, which we hope will bear tomorrow on the big pond. Yesterday afternoon we had about an hour's skating on one of the little ponds, but some boy went through so we had to stop.

This morning the eleven put on their foot-ball clothes and several fellows took their pictures on the steps. I developped mine before lunch and I don't think it was much good, so I shall take another when the regular professional photos are taken. In running up the slippery steps this afternoon I fell on the doormat which is made of wire and cut my knee, so that now it is bandaged and it is not very easy to walk; you see that bad knees certainly run in the family!

I think I forgot to tell you in my last letter that Warren got 6th place in his form last month with a good deal higher average than last time. He also got only 7 black-marks I think. I got B. & a good one I think, with several As.

I think yours plans for the holidays are very nice and I shall be glad to have ten days at Hyde Park. I think I had better keep the coat-case and bring it home with me as I shall be very crowded then & the trunk will not hold everything & my brown & dress-suits would not fill the valise. I have not had any more black-marks since you were here & I hope not to get any more this term. Warren has had 6 again this week but I have threatened or rather hinted that he may be put under the pump if he gets any more, so he has quieted down a little.

I wonder if my birds have come from Frazar's yet? If they have not please write me & I will have him send them.

I have put on my heavy flannels and winter-suit now and

146

find them very comfortable, as most of the buttons were off my other suit

With much love Ever

F.DR.

At this time Mrs. James Roosevelt was having some minor trouble with her knee, a temporary and not a permanent annoyance. Here, and in the two letters following, can be noticed a certain quickening of interest in the social aspects of his holidays—dances and the like, beyond the mere prospect of a stay at home.

∽∽

*"Mrs. Peabody has a new baby
. . . we shall have a half-holiday . . ."*

My dear Papa and Mama,

Only two weeks more and I shall be at home once more! I really have no idea what I would like for Xmas. The only thing I can think of at present is a subscription to the "Scientific American" but I think that if both of you were to send me your wishes I might be able to scrape up some more.

Mrs. Peabody has a new baby, a little girl, born yesterday & I suppose we shall have a half-holiday in consequence, which will be very welcome, as it is hard to study when the holidays are so near.

I do hope Grandpapa is better now and I shall write to him today.

Yesterday afternoon I helped clear off the pond, which had about one inch of snow on it, & then had an exciting game of hockey. Today everything is melting & during the night it rained quite hard, so I fear we shall not have more skating for several days.

Warren had two black-marks last week, but I hope he will not get as many this month as the first.

It is growing colder this evening so the prospects of skating are brighter for tomorrow.

Taddy is delighted at the prospect of the Dodsworth dance & I think that in the bottom of his heart he hopes to get a certain *horrid* partner!

I think we ought to have an Xmas tree or something of that sort this year, don't you?

The exams begin on Monday a week from tomorrow and on that day we only have Sacred Studies. The hard ones this year will be English, Mathematics & Greek, and there is very little chance of my passing English, as in last year's IV Form only 4 boys passed! Mathematics is a great deal luck, whether one can do the problems or not, and Greek is I think a little easier this year than last, as Mr. Gardner, altho' he gives hard exams, marks quite easily.

I hope I shall not get any dread desease during the holidays as last year, but I do not want to miss any lessons this year or get an unenviable reputation for bringing back diseases

With lots of lots etc.

FDR.

His mother wielded the editorial pen twice in this letter, adding the word "at" in the opening sentence, and correcting the second misspelling of "deseases" in the closing one. The new Peabody baby was Margery; she later took up a nursing career in Boston, and has always remained closely associated with school affairs. Mr. Thomas George Dodworth ran a dancing school at 12 East 49th Street in New York; during the Christmas and Easter holidays a formal dance was held there. Anna Eleanor Roosevelt, in her book *This Is My Story* (New York, 1937), recalls: "I joined a dancing class at Mr. Dodworth's. These classes were an institution for many years, and many boys and girls learned the polka and the waltz standing carefully on the diamond squares of the polished hardwood floor. Mr. Dodworth was dapper and very slim and very correct and kept us in order with what looked like a pair of castanets. Mrs. Dodworth, always in evening dress, had a sweet face, and tried to make us feel at ease and consoled us if Mr. Dodworth was too severe."

∽∽

"I have received my anthropo-metric chart from Mr. Skarstrom . . ."

[GROTON]
DEC. 9, 1897,
THURSDAY.

Dear Mama & Papa

Many thanks for your letters & instructions for coming home. I am so glad I get home so early, almost as soon as the New York boys. Do I understand that the train on the N.Y. Central will have to wait anyway even if I am on time at Troy, as there is only 10 minutes between my arrival at Troy & departure from Albany?

I have received the enclosed invitation and don't know what to do! Is it another extra one & shall I answer it & if so what is Mrs. B. Tuckerman's address? Please answer it for me if possible as I am not extra at that kind of work!

The weather for the last two days has been warm & all the snow & most of the ice has disappeared.

We have not had the half-holiday yet as the weather has not permitted.

I am sorry Uncle Warren's children could not come, but I am glad you asked Russell, although I think the other wild indians will be rather a nuisance.

I am sorry to hear Grandpapa is not better, but I trust he got my letter & will be better by Xmas.

The marks for the last 3 weeks end tomorrow as we are not marked during examinations, and I suppose you have got my last report although they have been very slow in sending them.

I have received my anthropometric chart from Mr. Skarstrom & he has given me a series of exercises especially adapted to me, such as exercises for the neck and wrists. I got 335 as a total which Mr. S. said was very fair.

I have no more time to write now.

Ever with love.

FRANKLIN D ROOSEVELT

Mrs. Bayard Tuckerman of New York was a family friend, and the mother of one of his young lady acquaintances, Elizabeth Tuckerman (see Letter of June 25, 1900).

<div align="center">~~~</div>

"I hope you have been thinking
of your Christmas wishes . . ."

[GROTON]
DEC. 12, 1897,
SUNDAY.

My dear Mama and Papa,

It has continued to be warm up here and today it is raining. Last night Mr. Peabody's father began reading the "Christmas Carol" which he reads every year. He read for an hour and he will finish it this afternoon & tonight.

On Friday we had the half-holiday for the baby & of course we cheered the kid! In the afternoon I went out on the river with Lathrop Brown as the day was very warm. We had to get special permission from the Rector as we are not allowed on the river now without permission.

We paddled up the Squannacook, and the rapids were very swift owing to the thaw. It was very exciting and some of the rapids were so swift that we had to pull up by the bushes along the bank & several times we came close to upsetting, but the water is only a couple of feet deep.

We were gone from 2.30 to 6 so felt quite tired when we got back.

Yesterday morning I played golf but spent the whole of the afternoon in the house studying for the exams.

We have Sacred Studies tomorrow & nothing on Tuesday; two on Wednesday & 3 on both Thursday & two on Friday.

Warren I am sorry to say has had 12 black-marks this month but I have told him he may be kept over if he gets any more & I think he will try not to get any more.

He wanted to go on the river on Friday but as it was swift & full I did not let him.

I am counting the days now before coming home & I shall try to drop you a line Wednesday Night or Thursday Morning which you ought to get Friday evening.

I hope you have been thinking of your Christmas wishes as I shall not have any unless you do.

I think I may have to go to New York for one day before Christmas to get a few presents, as Poughkeepsie does not have a great variety of things.

As you have probably heard Taddy has been moved over to the Old Building and is now in a room with two other boys. I hope he will pass his exams all right although he has not done much studying for them.

With a great deal of love & looking forward to seeing you in five days   Ever

F.D.R.

〜〜

"I think Old Nuts will flunk me . . ."

[GROTON]
DEC. 15, 1897,
WEDNESDAY.

Dear Papa and Mama

Many thanks for your letters & am sorry will only have time for a line. I passed Sacred Studies on Monday all right & today took English & French. The latter I am sure I passed but in English I think Old Nuts will flunk me altho' any other master would give me 70 or so! This afternoon I studied until 5 p.m. & then went over to Mr. Gardner's and had afternoon tea & cake. It has rained here both yesterday & today but is clearing now.

It is too bad Russell cannot come & it will be a horrible
nuisance having those *squaws* on our hands for such a long
time!

Now [no] more time as I must grub.

With lots of love

FDR

"Old Nuts" was the aforementioned Mr. Nutter. In the report
dated Dec. 18, F.D.R.'s exam mark in English was a C, so the
worst was not realized. All subjects other than English showed
A's and B's; his average mark was a B. "Good," commented
Mr. Peabody. And the Christmas vacation ensued.

∞

"I shall take my Castoria to-
night . . ."

[GROTON]
JAN. 4, 1898,
TUESDAY.

My dear Papa & Mama,

Our train was half an hour late on arrival at Worcester,
owing to a hot-box in our car and the snow. We consequently
missed our connection and could not leave W. until 6.30. We
got here at 8.00 and have just had supper.

The sandwiches were delicious and you may be sure there
were no doughnuts left over. At W. I had a cup of hot coffee
and some rolls, so I faired pretty well.

I feel a little tired after the long journey but I think my
cold is better, altho' I cannot tell much about it until morning.

I shall take my Castoria tonight & hope to be all right tomorrow but shall telegraph you anyway in the afternoon.

Warren is all right & Taddy came in the drawing-room car
in order to study. He has not got his health certificate but
telegraphed for it at New Haven!!!

No more now; I shall write tomorrow or next day,

With a great deal of love to you both

FRANKLIN.

The great bane of Groton's existence (as of any boarding school's) was contagious disease, which required getting in extra nurses, turning school buildings into temporary infirmaries, loss of class time and makeup work, and even on occasion the closing of the school. Every boy was therefore required to produce a health certificate in proper order on return from vacation.

〰〰

"I shall keep the Calisaya Bark
in my cubicle . . ."

[GROTON]
JAN. 5, 1898,
WEDNESDAY.

My dear Mama & Papa,

I feel really better today and my cold has almost disappeared.

We had breakfast this a.m. at 8 o'clock and so had only three periods for lessons.

I unpacked this a.m. and found everything all right.

I have been moved up one table and now sit at Mr. Ayrault's about three places from Mr. Gardner's end.

Three new boys have come, Webb, another Greenough (his cousin) & Star's younger brother.

I enclose the bill for Thurston which is $1.00 less than I thought and I think it is awfully good of you to pay it for me as you have given me so much already.

I shall keep the Calisaya Bark in my cubicle & take it myself before meals, as it is such a small bottle.

Some of the boys are going to clear of[f] a hockey-space on the river this p.m but I shall not go as I want to be careful for a few days. Please tell Edmund he has been moved up to Mr. Griswold's table where I was last term.

I shall send this to N.Y. as you said in your letter which came this a.m.

With a great deal of love to you both & looking forward to seeing you in February   Affect.

FDR.

The new Webb arrival was J. Watson Webb, a grandson of William H. Vanderbilt of the immortal dictum. Charles P. Greenough, Groton 1902, was a cousin of Carroll Greenough in F.D.R.'s form. Dillwyn P. Starr was the younger brother of Louis Starr, Jr., who was three years behind F.D.R.

∽∽

*"I am absolutely well now and
my digestion is perfect . . ."*

[GROTON]
JAN. 6, 1898,
THURSDAY.

My dear Mama and Papa,

Doctor Coit came up here today and I had a conversation with him after lunch. He wants you to pay him a visit when you come to see me in February, so I suppose you will hear from him soon.

We have about a foot of snow on the ground here, but the hockey squads have cleared spaces on the river and this a.m. we (the 3rd) had a good game.

I am absolutely well now and my digestion is perfect.

The calisthenics began again this afternoon and I shall like it very much more than last winter, I am sure.

I shall try to go to Boston to have my tooth pulled next Wednesday, and it will be a comfort to have it over with.

Friday Jan. 7th.

Last night it rained & today there are only a few inches of snow left, and everything is slush.

It seems as if we had been here a month instead of three days, but the time will soon begin to pass quickly enough.

I wish you could send me a small bottle of good ink for my fountain-pen as the school ink is two-thirds water.

I have just received your letter of Thursday and shall return the flannels if I can wear a larger size.

Warren failed his exam in Physiology again, and takes it for the 3rd time next Wednesday. I do hope he will pass it

154

then, as he may have to go home for a while as he cannot drop into a lower form.

With a great deal of love to you both I am you affec. son
FDR.

∽

*"I forgot to tell you I had arranged
to take boxing lessons . . ."*

[GROTON]
JAN. 9, 1898,
SUNDAY.

My dear Mama and Papa,

I forgot to tell you last Friday that I had arranged to take boxing lessons. Papa wanted me to take them last year but as the measles prevented it, I was sure he would not mind my taking them this year.

I had the first yesterday afternoon for 15 minutes from 4.45 to 5 p.m. It was very nice and the man, who is to come from Boston every Wednesday and Saturday, taught me several movements.

Right after lunch I walked to the village with Warren Motley chiefly for the sake of the walk as it was slushy & there was nothing else to do. Last night it froze a little but I am afraid the sun will melt it all again today.

Jack Peabody & one or two other fellows have gone to the infirmary, so we are momentarily expecting an outbreak of some dire plague.

Tomorrow if the weather is fine we are to have a half holiday in honour of one of our graduates taking the John Harvard Scholarship Prize.

I did not go to Mr. Gardner's this afternoon as I wanted to finish "St. Ives" so I could begin one of the Waverley Novels, I have not yet decided which one.

It is freezing this p.m in spite of the sun so I think we shall have skating & a half-holiday tomorrow

With a great deal of love & haste
FRANKLIN.

John D. Peabody was two forms behind F.D.R.; he was no relation to the Rector. The graduate who took the John Harvard scholarship was W. Bayard Cutting, Jr., Groton 1895. Robert Louis Stevenson's *St. Ives* had been published just the year before in New York.

∽∽

" 'Resolved, that Hawaii be
promptly annexed.' . . . we are
Con . . ."

GROTON
JAN. 12, 1898,
WEDNESDAY.

My dear Mama and Papa

I was much excited when I got your letter telling of the runaway and I am only too thankful that neither you nor Papa were in it, and that no one was hurt.

I am so glad you have got new horses as I was heartily tired of the old pair! I only hope you (I mean McFarland) will not let them lose their "fast trotting" speed!

I think the names are very good and I am very anxious to see them, especially "Top Mast" the prize-winner.

You will be surprised to hear that I am to debate next Wednesday the 19th. We are not to debate alphabetically this year but by lot & I fell in the first debate with Blagden, Harold Peabody and Krumbhaar. I debate with Blagden against the other two. We have chosen for our subject: "Resolved, that Hawaii be promptly annexed." Krumbhaar & Peabody are for it, Pro, & we are Con.

On Monday we had the half-holiday and we all played hockey on the river.

Yesterday it began to melt and today it has been drizzling at intervals but this a.m. we managed to go down to the pond and flood the ice. This p.m I worked on my debate and took my second boxing lesson I am afraid you will think it very expensive, $5.00 for six lessons, but I try to learn all I can and so far he says I have got on very well. Warren has been on bounds since he came back and tomorrow he takes his exam. again. I hope he will pass this time.

I was surprised not to see Edmund last night but suppose ice-boating etc. have proved to be not very good for him. I got the lovely skis and mocassins tonight and think you were awfully good to give me so much more than I deserved this Xmas. I have given my old skis to Warren. They will do him to potter round on this winter but are too much damaged to be of any real use. If you see any articles in the papers or the Spectator against the annexation of Hawaii I wish you could send them to me.

With a great deal of love to you both   I am your affec son
                                          FD.R.

"McFarland" was coachman for the James Roosevelts, who had recently acquired a beautiful matched pair of horses, called "Top Mast" and "Top Royal." James Roosevelt took something more than an amateur's interest in his horses; one of them, "Gloucester," set a world's trotting record. When this latter animal died, its tail was preserved, and (testimony of F.D.R.'s insatiable habit of collecting and keeping anything and everything) eventually turned up in his White House bedroom when the Roosevelt possessions were moved back to Hyde Park. Harold Peabody, in F.D.R.'s form, was a son of the Rector's brother, John E. Peabody. Typical of the inter-weaving of the Lawrence and Peabody families, his mother was a sister of James Lawrence, and his future wife a daughter of Bishop Lawrence. Queen Liliuokalani of Hawaii had been deposed in 1893 and a provisional government established, with annexation to the United States as its object; at this time disagreement was raging in Congress and throughout the country, but the annexation was formally accomplished in August of 1898.

〰〰

*"I thought it might interfere
with my speaking . . ."*

Dear Papa and Mama

Just a line to say that I forgot to last [?] you in Wednesday's letter. As my debate comes on Wednesday I have put off having my tooth pulled until Saturday Jan. 22nd. I thought it might interfere with my speaking for a while and I wanted to be all right for the debate.

For the last three days it has melted but today it froze again and this a.m. we had a little skate.

Taddy is in the infirmary today but I think he only has a cold.

Warren's exam has been off till Saturday and I have made him work every day, so I think he ought to pass.

The cod liver oil & ink came last night and many thanks for the ink! (not the other)

The night-clothes came also but I have not yet tried them but shall do so tonight

With much love   Ever

F.D.R.

∽∽

*"Please don't be alarmed if I
get the pink-eye . . ."*

My dear Mama and Papa,

I cannot tell you how sorry I was to hear of dear Grandpapas illness. As I have heard nothing since Papa's letter of Friday, I trust he is holding his own.

I fear the time of the year is not good for pneumonia and I only trust his great vitality will carry him through

Nothing much has been going on here, except that yesterday we played a game of ice-polo against the Myopia Hunt Club and beat them 5—⅓ They made a third of goal by a foul of one of our men but we outplayed them in every way.

Many thanks for the newspaper article & the Graphic. I am working every moment on my debate, and expect it to be quite close but with Krumbhaar on their side they stand a little more chance of winning than we do.

Please don't be alarmed if I get the pink-eye. The boy who sits next me in both school-rooms & the boy I sit next to at table have both got it besides about six others. Some of them have been sent home, so do not be alarmed if I appear at Hyde Park before the week is up.

We are having quite a time up here over a translation of Virgil which has been found. As no one is of course allowed to have one, the Rector is vainly trying to discover who it belongs to. One fellow is in the secret but he won't tell.

As I am terribly busy with my debate I will write no more now.

As I have not heard anything more about dear Grandpapa I only hope that "no news is good news" but I suppose I (or Warren) shall get a letter tomorrow.

Ever with much love

F.D.R.

His grandfather, Warren Delano II, died the day after this letter was written, at nearly ninety years of age. He was buried in Fairhaven. Enclosed in the letter was a pressed flower.

∽∽

*"We must remember that he has
gone to a better place . . ."*

GROTON SCHOOL
JAN. 17, 1898,
MONDAY.

My darling Mama,

You can never imagine how deeply grieved I was to hear that my darling Grandfather had passed away. I know you are heartbroken, but we must remember that he has gone to a better place than this earth, and will be far happier there.

159

I suppose Warren and I are to meet you at Fairhaven, at least we both wish to, and feel we ought.

Warren is much distressed, and the more so, because he fears the great shock will make Aunt Kassie very ill.

I shall telegraph you early tomorrow, asking when I am to go to Fair Haven

I only wish I could have been near you in our great trouble.

Ever your own loving son

FRANKLIN.

∽

"Mr. Peabody has told us that our country cannot be safe without Hawaii. I shall try to disprove this . . ."

The following is the text of the address which F.D.R. delivered on Jan. 19, 1898, upholding the negative in the debate: "Resolved, that Hawaii be promptly annexed." This was a rough pencil copy of his speech, with marginal eye-catchers, which served him for notes.

Mr. President, Lady and Gentlemen.

Of all the great powers of the world the United States and Russia are the only ones which have no colonies to defend. All our territory is on this continent and all of it except Alaska is continuous.

Therefore the United States and Russia are the only two countries no part of whose territory can be cut off by a naval enemy. At present we have no really vulnerable point. Now, the annexation of Hawaii by us would affect the feelings of the European powers in two ways: first it would anger them because Hawaii is a common stopping point, secondly it would embolden them because we should for the first time in our history have a vulnerable point.

1

Mr. President, Lady and Gentlemen.

Of all the great powers of the world the United States and Russia are the only ones which have no colonies to defend. All our territory is on this continent and all of it except Alaska is continuous.

* Therefore the United States and Russia are the only two countries no part of whose territory can be cut off by a naval enemy. At present we have no really vulnerable point. Now the annexation of Hawaii by us would affect the feelings of the European powers in two ways: first it would anger them because Hawaii is a common stopping point, secondly it would embolden them to because we should for the first time in our history have a vulnerable point. Mr Peabody has told us that our country cannot be safe without Hawaii. I shall try to disprove this. Now if we own the islands it means that we must protect them, and to do that we should

"Mr. Peabody has told us that our country cannot be safe without Hawaii. I shall try to disprove this...."

have not only to fortify the Islands
themselves but also maintain a much
larger navy. Now to do this we should
have to spend at least $100,000,000, every
year on our navy besides a large sum
on erecting forts and maintaining soldiers
on the Islands. Let us remember that
the islands are over 2,000 miles from
the nearest point of the U.S. and so
are too far away to be of any service
to our Western coast in time of war
For the same reason they would not
help to defend the Nicaraguan canal
should we ever built it, and also,
as California is nearer Nicaragua than
Hawaii it would be quicker to send
warships from the former place.

Another argument of Mr Peabody's
that we need a coaling-station for
our ships. Now it is not generally
known that Pearl Harbor, a port in one of the
islands belongs to the United States
All that is needed is a little inexpensive
dredging and we shall have a coaling-
station without annexation.

margin note: 100 million

margin note: another argument ☆

3

If we must have another coaling-
station in mid-Pacific why not fit
up one of the Aleutian Islands in the
North.

But before we bother about foreign
coaling-stations and fortifications we
should look to the defense of our
own coasts. New York, Boston, and
S. Francisco are still at the mercy of an
enemy and why should we spend the millions needed to fortify these cities on those
worthless Islands in the middle of the
Pacific. Captain Mahan himself says
it is nonsense to think of annexation
unless we decide to spend an enormous
sum for fortifications. Now is it worth
while to do this? In what way will it
advantage us?

Mr Reuhot Says that, if we do
not take the islands, some other power
will, but let us look at the question.
England to begin with has disclaimed
any intention of taking Hawaii, but
supposing doested In what way would
it harm us? We should have free

4

Trade with the Islands, for England
stands for free trade. England
would not use the group as a base of
supplies against us in case of war,
for she has a veritable Gibraltar at
Esquimault a port in British Columbia
within sight of our own shores.

Japan interfering Now about Japan's interfering. She
also has disclaimed any intention of
seizing the Islands, and it would be
indeed a foolish enterprise for her,
for any armies on Hawaii would be as
lonely as Robinson Crusoe. Besides all
this Hawaii is entirely out of the Japan
America sailing-route. No country
outside of the U.S wants to have Hawaii
and.

Abandon Isles Some foolish Senator has argued that
if after annexation for any reason we
should wish to abandon the Islands we
could easily turn them over to Japan,
England or Germany. Now the United
States has never been in the habit of
giving up territory once acquired, and
I am sure the people of this country

would never consent to have the
Stars and Stripes hauled down from
a country over which they had once
waved. Therefore if we once annex
Hawaii we shall always be obliged
to keep the wretched Islands whether
we wish to or no.

Nicaragua There is no more reason for the U.S
to annex Hawaii than to annex
Nicaragua and it is ridiculous to say
we could hand over that country to a
foreign power for that would be
contrary to the Monroe Doctrine. We
do not want to own any of these
tropical countries or to go there our
selves. By the Monroe Doctrine we

Monroe are only supposed to keep foreign
Doctrine powers from these countries but not
to govern them or own them. Now if
we once go in for foreign colonies we
must stick to that policy and not only
are foreign colonies expensive, but they
are dangerous children and may
bring political difficulties upon the
mother country at any moment.

6.

Trade Treaty

What we want is a favorable
trade treaty with the Islands, and this
we have already, for everything of commercial value is provided for in it.

The Bill for annexation before
the Senate now comes straight from the
White House. It is significant to
note that if the treaty were not pressed
by McKinley himself there is no doubt
that it would be beaten, for not one
of the older Republican Senators are
in favor of it. All the goods Democrats
in both the House and Senate are
against the treaty, while the only support comes from the White House and
McKinley is only trying to make his
administration popular with the masses.

Why can we not leave Hawaii
alone, or else establish a sound
Republic in which all of Hawaii's shall
be represented not a government such
as they have at present, under the influence
of Americans. As I have shown no
power would take Hawaii now as a gift, and
supposing some Power should in the

McKinley
only support

remote future should wish to Have it. They the
expression of the feelings of the United
States would be enough to stop it, just
as the feeling of America led Louis
Napoleon to withdraw his troops from
Mexico, a number of years ago.

Several nations of modern times
ruled upon the monarchic plan, have
seized territory for commercial reasons
and because of sympathy with the people
residents, but as a Republic we should
not follow in this plan and nothing
can justify us in so doing. Why should
we soil our hands with colonies? See how
Italy's colonial system has utterly failed,
then ask yourself what good France's
colonies do her

As Mr — has so ably shown
the inhabitants are not ignorant folk.
Why then does the Government shrink
from submitting the treaty to a general
vote of the inhabitants. The answer is
obvious: they would vote against it to
a man. Why then annex them without
their consent? Why take away to

nationality of a free people? Why
meddle with this land thousands of
miles away whose inhabitants are so
different from us in every way? Why
weaken our strategical position and
why spend millions in a foolish cause?
I appeal to your American
common-sense, that common sense
which has never yet made a mistake
and which let us pray never will.

Mr. P. says our trade will double in ten
years, I do not see why this should be so
as he has not proved it

This rough copy of his speech, with marginal eye-
catchers, served F.D.R. for notes. The debaters
were not allowed to read their speeches verbatim.

Mr. Peabody has told us that our country cannot be safe without Hawaii. I shall try to disprove this: now if we own the islands it means that we must protect them, and to do that we should have not only to fortify the Islands themselves but also maintain a much larger navy. Now to do this we should have

100 million

to spend at least $100,000,000., every year on our navy besides a large sum on erecting forts and maintaining soldiers on the Islands. Let us remember that the islands are over 2,000 miles from the nearest point of the U.S. and so are too far away to be of any service to our Western coast in time of war. For the same reason they would not help to defend the Nicaraguan canal should we ever built it, and also, as California is nearer Nicaragua than Hawaii it would be quicker to send warships from the former place.

Another argument

Another argument of Mr Peabody's that we need a coaling-station for our ships. Now it is not generally known that Pearl Harbor, a port in one of the islands belongs to the United States. All that is needed is a little inexpensive dredging and we shall have a coaling-station without annexation.

If we must have another coaling-station in mid-Pacific why not fit up one of the Aleutian Islands in the North.

Before bothering

But before we bother about foreign coaling-stations and fortifications we should look to the defense of our own coasts. New York, Boston, and S. Francisco are still at the mercy of an enemy and why should we spend the millions needed to fortify these cities on those worthless Islands in the middle of the Pacific. Captain Mahan himself says it is nonsense to think of annexation unless we decide to spend an enormous sum for fortifications. Now is it worth while to do this? In what way will it advantage us?

Mr. Peabody says that if we do not take the islands, some other power will, but let us look at the question. England might have had Hawaii years & years ago if she had wanted it. She has also disclaimed any intention of taking Hawaii, but supposing [she] does take it. In what way would it harm us? We should have free trade with the Islands, for England stands for free trade. England would not use the group as a base of supplies against us in case of war, for she has a veritable Gibraltar at Esquimault a port in British Columbia within sight of our own shores.

Now about Japan's interfering. She also has disclaimed any intention of seizing the Islands, and it would be indeed a foolish enterprise for her, for any armies in Hawaii would be as lonely as Robinson Crusoe. Besides all this Hawaii is entirely out of the Japan-America sailing-route. No country outside of the U.S. wants to have Hawaii and . . .

Some foolish Senator has argued that if after annexation for any reason we should wish to abandon the Islands, we could easily turn them over to Japan, England or Germany. Now the United States has never been in the habit of giving up territory once acquired, and I am sure the people of this country would never consent to have the Stars and Stripes hauled down from a country over which they had once waved. Therefore if we once annex Hawaii we shall always be obliged to keep the wretched *Islands whether we wish to or no.*

There is no more reason for the U.S. to annex Hawaii than to annex Nicaragua and it is ridiculous to say we could hand over that country to a foreign power for that would be contrary to the Monroe Doctrine. We do not want to own any of these tropical countries or to go there ourselves. By the Monroe Doctrine we are only supposed to keep foreign powers from these countries but not to govern them or own them. Now if we once go in for foreign colonies we must stick to that policy and not only are foreign colonies expensive, but they are dangerous children and may bring political difficulties upon the mother country at any moment.

What we want is a favorable trade treaty with the Islands, and this we have already, for everything of commercial value is provided for in it.

The Bill for annexation before the Senate now comes straight from the White House. It is significant to note that if the treaty were not pressed by Mc.Kinley himself there is no doubt that it would be beaten, for not one of the older Republican Senators are in favor of it. All the goods Democrats in both the House and Senate are against the treaty, while the only support comes from the White House and McKinley is only trying to make his administration popular with the masses.

Why can we not leave Hawaii alone, or else establish a sound Republic in which all Hawaiians shall be represented not a government such as they have at present, under the influence of Americans. As I have shown no power would take Hawaii now as a gift, but supposing some Power should in the remote future should wish to have it. Then the expression of the feelings of the United States would be enough to stop it, just as the feeling of America led Louis Napoleon to withdraw his troops from Mexico, a number of years ago.

Several nations of modern times ruled upon the monarchic plan, have seized territory for commercial reasons and because of sympathy with the people residents, but we have no such plea for seizing

Hawaii as W [Wendell Blagden] shows. Why should we soil our hands with colonies? See how Italy's colonial system has utterly failed, then ask yourself what good France's colonies do her.

As Mr —— has so ably shown the inhabitants are not ignorant folk. Why then does the Government shrink from submitting the treaty to a general vote of the inhabitants. The answer is obvious: they would vote against it to a man. Why then annex them without their consent? Why take away the nationality of a free people? Why meddle with this land thousands of miles away whose inhabitants are so different from us in every way? Why weaken our strategical position and why spend millions in a foolish cause?

I appeal to your American common-sense, that common-sense which has never yet made a mistake and which let us pray never will. [In the manuscript this sentence was crossed out and the following conclusion substituted:]

Mr. P. says our trade will double in ten years, I do not see why this should be so as he has not proved it.

Captain Alfred Thayer Mahan, cited as an authority in this speech, had retired from the Navy in 1896. Earlier, in 1890, lectures he gave at the War College in Newport had been collected and published as *The Influence of Sea Power Upon History, 1660-1773*, a book at this time just beginning to receive prominent attention. After his retirement Mahan wrote numerous magazine articles, furthering his international reputation, and influencing such men as Theodore Roosevelt and Henry Cabot Lodge, who were then engaged in an active effort to enlarge and improve the Navy. Shortly after the time of this debate, when the Spanish-American War broke out, Mahan was recalled from retirement to serve on the board of strategy directing naval operations. He died in 1914; with the outbreak of the Second World War, and especially after the

Japanese attack on that "not generally known" United States port, Pearl Harbor, his name and work again became front-page news. An article in the *New York Tribune,* datelined Washington, January 11, 1898, commented on the majority committee opinion which Senator Cushman Kellogg Davis of Minnesota, chairman of the Committee on Foreign Relations, presented before the Senate. He was quoted in part: " 'We should take the islands while we have the opportunity, and if we do not want them it will be a very easy matter to get rid of them on our own terms.' " The *Tribune* then went on to state that the Senator "showed that they [the islands] would be a very important territorial acquisition to either Japan, England or Russia, and expressed the opinion that either of those powers would take the islands off our hands at any time we might make known our desire to be rid of them." The report concluded: "It would be easy enough to turn them over to some other country . . . but who, the Senator asked, will say that it will be so easy for us to take them at some future time, in case we voluntarily deprive ourselves of the present opportunity?" Since Davis' speech would have appeared in all the newspapers the morning of F.D.R.'s debate, undoubtedly he was the "foolish Senator" mentioned.

∾

"I am hoping to get the pink-eye
so I can come home . . ."

[GROTON]
JAN. 21, 1898,
FRIDAY.

My dearest Mama,

After leaving you this morning Warren and I settled ourselves in the train. As we had both forgotten to wind our watches last night we asked the conductor for the right time. He told us 8.30 so we set our watches. On arrival at Boston we went straight to the Union Station & left our coats & parcels, intending to take a walk, for we had two hours on our hands

After looking into various shops we returned to the Station at 10.30 but to our dismay we found our watches were 1 hour slow and that it was 11.30 *not 10.30!* We had therefore missed the 11 o'clock train & had to wait till 3 p.m.! We then had lunch in the station & as we had loads of time I looked up Dr. Niles address 561 [? 361] Boylston St. and went there in a trolley with Warren. When I told him I wanted my tooth out he held up his hands with horror. He said that no decent Dr. in Boston would recommend doing it & I think he is right. He said the cavity would never entirely fill up and that the difference in size of the two teeth would always be disfigurement. He advised having a porcelain tooth (which can be made an exact match of the other) screwed on the root and he said it would be absolutely permanent. He says my jaw should not have any teeth pulled at present as it will continue to widen till I am 30 yrs. old. He said every dentist in Boston would say the same & was quite surprised at Durand. I have therefore given up my appointment tomorrow.

As Warren's teeth still had a good many holes, he took my appointment but I am afraid he will not be able to go, as he complained of a sore-throat this p.m & is spending the night in the infirmary.

After leaving the Dentist we took a ride through the subway. We left at 3.00 & got to Ayer at 4.00 & at the School at 4.30

There is hardly any snow left here & all is slush, so I am hoping to get the pink-eye so I can come home

With much love & hoping you had a comfortable journey home, & found Papa all well

My cold is about the same but I shall take a dose of Cas—— tonight

Ever

F.D.R.

This letter was written after returning from his grandfather's funeral at Fairhaven. "Durand" was the Roosevelt family dentist in New York. F.D.R. had injured his tooth at Campobello the summer before; the eventual result was to be the well-known denture which had always to be screwed into place before he gave a speech.

~~

"I am almost sorry this has not turned into pink-eye . . ."

GROTON SCHOOL
THE INFIRMARY,
JAN. 25, 1898,
TUESDAY.

My dear Mama and Papa,

I have been up here since Saturday Night, with a sore-throat, but it is not at all serious. I was in bed on Sunday & yesterday so could not write you, but today I am up in the convalescent room.

Warren is here too; he came in on Friday night with the same complaint, and yesterday we were in the same little room together. Today Warren has taken his meals down stairs, but still stays in the convalescent room with me and several others, who are getting over colds. I am almost sorry this has not turned into pink-eye, as I should have come home in that case, but should have lost a lot of lessons. As it is I shall have to work hard for I [a] few weeks as I have missed almost a week.

Since I saw you at Fair Haven we have had a regular January thaw here so I have not missed any winter sports. I have been playing games violently & studied the rest of the time.

Many thanks for the ties & your letter which came this morning. I think the ties are awfully nice & have one on at present.

As usual this Infirmary is terribly hot the thermometer being 78° in this room at the present moment. I am sure it must be

167

bad to have such heat and I feel like a fading flower already, & am sure I will have entirely wilted by tomorrow.

I have begun taking my Cod Liver Oil regularly now and I think it must have some peculiar qualities for it makes me sneeze every time after taking it.

I am wondering when Edmund is coming back for he is the only boy who has not returned since the Christmas holidays.

I was really pleased to hear that dear Grandpapa had left Algonac to Uncle Fred A. and I think Aunt Tilly will grow to love the old place if she lives there any time. I was also glad to hear that a legacy has been left to Kitty Crummy & the old servants, but I am wondering what Aunt Annie & Uncle Fred will do, & if they will continue at Algonac

Ever with dear love

F.D.R.

This letter was written in pencil, and is badly smudged. Though Algonac passed to Frederic Delano, he only used it in the summer months; it was the Hitches who lived in it, and Aunt Annie who presided over and became identified with it, for the next thirty-odd years. After her death, Frederic Delano and his wife made it their permanent home. Kitty Crummie was the family seamstress at Algonac.

∽

"Warren got a bloody nose, but he gave Farr a black eye . . ."

[GROTON]
JAN. 27, 1898,
THURSDAY.

My dear Mama & Papa

This morning I came out of the infirmary for good and although still a little weak and shaky I feel almost well. Yesterday I took dinner and supper down stairs but had to spend the rest of the time in the convalescent room.

168

Warren left the infirmary yesterday and seems to be perfectly well today. He had exactly the same trouble I had, and we were both in the infirmary the same length of time.

I am so glad Brother Rosy is coming up here next Saturday as it will break the tedium of the term very nicely and he will be here on my birthday besides. I do hope he won't stay at the Lawrence's as that would be an awful nuisance, especially now when the roads are in very bad condition for walking.

We have about 10 inches of snow here now and consequently there is no skating, but the tobogganing is not good as there is no crust and the snow flies and drifts all over.

I have really missed a whole week of lessons as it was a week ago today that I went to Fair Haven.

Warren had a fight in the gymnasium with Mr. Thomas H.P. Farr Jr. Esq. the son of one of Aunt Jenny's bosom friends at Orange I think. Warren got a bloody nose, but he gave Farr a black eye & cut lip and on the whole got a little the better of him I think.

There is very little to write about now and everything will be dull until Washington's B. I hope Papa went to the meeting of the parents on Monday as I hear it was interesting and that 68,000$ was raised for the endowment fund and the new building and chapel; they have $135,000 already I heard and want $200,000.

With loads of love   Ever your own son

> FDR

∽∽

"What a surprise and delight . . ."

[GROTON]
JAN. 30, 1898,
SUNDAY.

My dearest Mama and Papa,

You have no idea what a surprise and delight the Birthday hamper was to me.

Everything I like best was in it and I shall be able to feast for weeks to come with my friends.

It seems indeed strange to be away from home for my birthday, but as I saw you only a week ago it does not seem so bad.

You are altogether too good to me, giving me a much needed key-ring, on top of so many other presents. But of course since you insist on giving it to me, I cannot but accept! I think you had better keep the key-ring until I see you again as I never use my keys up here. Many thanks for your telegram which I got late last night. It quite made me feel as if I was with you.

I was so sorry to hear about Edmund's voice and hope he will be back soon, as he is missing a lot of lessons

Poor James is in the infirmary and so I suppose prevented his father from coming up yesterday. He is better today and may get up and go to the convalescent room.

Yesterday afternoon I went with skiing with two other boys, and had a very exciting time on some hills near the pond.

The month for marks ended yesterday and the marks will be read out in a day or so. I do not expect to get a high mark as I have missed so much. I have only had one black-mark and no latenesses so I am one month nearer the prize.

This morning we had morning service in the School-room as the chapel was very cold and could not be heated.

Mrs Low is up here and I saw her this morning after service

This morning I got a telegram from Aunt Annie and Uncle Fred saying: "Loving wishes for many happy returns of the day." I think it was awfully good of them to think of me and I shall of course write them immediately.

We had afternoon service again in the school-room this p.m and after that I went to Mr. Gardner's.

I sent you my debate in rough last night and I hope you got it. Many thanks for the two Graphics you sent last week. I got them when I was in the infirmary, so they helped to pass away the time up there very well

Ever with dear love to you both   Your affec. son

FRANKLIN D. ROOSEVELT

As for the monthly report of Jan. 29, 1898, it showed a B average—probably the expected "low B," as there were three C's and only one A, the latter in Sacred Studies. "Good," said the Rector.

〰〰

"I have wanted Audubon's Journal ever since it came out . . ."

My dearest Mama and Papa,

Your dear letters of Sunday came last night bearing news of more presents. You *must* really stop giving me so many lovely things, as I am sure I do not deserve them. You have both been far too good to me already and I feel as if I had been getting presents every day since Christmas. I have wanted Audubon's Journal ever since it came out and it is the nicest present you could possibly give me. I shall spend every moment on it, but I dont really think I could give such a lovely book to the Library as I should very much like to have it at home on my own ornithological book-shelf!

The confirmation lectures begin tonight and are to be held every Tuesday. The Bishop is coming up on March 16th for the confirmation, so if you decide to come up I will get a room for you at Powell's.

Yesterday afternoon it began to snow and during the night it increased to a gale. My transom blew open and the snow poured in. I was awakened by a boy who felt the snow fall on him and I found a quarter of an inch on the floor and everything was wet   Luckily I was fairly dry, as the snow blew right *over* me.

I managed to shut the transom with great difficulty and then pulled my bed out into the middle of the dormitory and went to sleep. In the morning I found my clothes all wet but I dried them over the register and for a wonder have had no cold since; I am absolutely well now and take my Cod Liver Oil regularly.

You have never told me what became of the vase I gave you at Xmas and whether you got a new one. I wish you would tell me about it when you write next.

Many thanks for the 16 kisses and spanks you sent. I received them yesterday and the latter are especially welcome!

Wednesday. This morning I went skiing over the drifts which are in some places 15 feet deep. I think skiing is great fun, and am sure you would like it very much yourself as it is not nearly as tiring as snow-shoeing and is much more easily learned.

James is still in the infirmary but will be out tomorrow or next day as he is up in the convalescent room today. I hear that *Rosy* is coming up on Saturday & I hope Taddy will be entirely well by that time

Warren is going to ski to Groton this afternoon and I am to take my boxing lesson at 4.

I shall take a few pictures in the snow this year and bring my camera home at Easter as I want very much to take the new horses. They must be beauties and I am dying to see them

With a great deal of love and kisses to you both   I am ever your own son

FRANKLIN D. ROOSEVELT

Another maternal correction: the word "dieing" in the final paragraph was altered to read "dying."

⌘

"Some one has stolen the ginger-
snaps out of my left rubber boot . . ."

[GROTON]
FEB. 4, 1898,
FRIDAY.

My dear Mama and Papa

Just a line to say that the marks came out today and that I got a B as usual. I am afraid I was not as good as last term but

172

I missed nearly a week and had my debate on hand besides. Taddy got a C. and Warren I am sorry to say stood 12 in his form of 16. His mark was 5.92 He is rather ashamed I think and I have asked him to take a regular time every day to study out of school.

Yesterday the lovely "Aududon; and his Journals" came and I am perfectly delighted with it. I have already read quite a lot and am sure I shall spend every spare moment on it until it is finished.

Taddy came out of the infirmary today, so I hope he will be all right when his father comes tomorrow. I hear that they will not get here till 7 o'clock so suppose I shall not see them until Sunday.

I suppose you will have given up all idea of coming up this month if you come up on March 16th for the confirmation

I still continue to delight in the "goodies" although some one has deliberately stolen one of the tins of the ginger-snaps out of my left rubber boot. I have vowed vengeance and will not bury the hatchet until I recover it.

Ever with dear love Your own son,

FRANKLIN D. ROOSEVELT

The word "moment" in the second paragraph was added by his mother.

~~~

*"He showed us some of their
money which is tin . . ."*

[GROTON]
FEB. 6, 1898,
SUNDAY.

My dear Mama and Papa,

Brother Rosy and Helen came last night but as it was so late I did not see them till this morning.

Yesterday afternoon I went to Groton on skis with Warren Motley. We had a splendid time and as there were several good sized hills it was quite exciting

Just before we got to the village we took off our skis and buried them in the snow and went into the village to buy crackers on foot.

I went to lunch with Brother Rosy and spent most of the afternoon going over the school with them.

I will find out whether the confirmation service is to be in the morning or the afternoon, but will take the two rooms for the evening of the 15th anyway, as I will be able to change in case you decide to come Wednesday morning.

This evening there is to be a talk in the study by Mr. George about the George Junior Republic which you have of course heard of.

It has been melting today so if it freezes tonight we shall have good tobogganing and skiing on the crust.

Monday a.m.

Last night Mr. George gave the talk which was extremely interesting. Brother Rosy and Helen were there and I think enjoyed it very much, but strange to say they went back right afterwards and did not stay for prayers. Mr. George told how the Junior Rep. was an almost exact model of our own on a small scale (indeed they had only one policeman!) He showed us some of their money which is tin with George Junior Rep. & the value stamped on it.

Ever with a great deal of love   Your own son

FDR.

In 1890 William Reuben George established a camp on a farm at Freeville, N. Y., near Ithaca; it was known as the "Freeville Fresh Air Camp" and the boys and girls who went there were sent through the *N. Y. Tribune* Fresh Air Fund. Over a period of a few years the camp underwent a curious change. It instituted trials of those who misbehaved, by juries composed of other boys and girls. In payment for the work done, token money was issued which was good for purchases within the camp. A regular government was established, modeled on that of the United States, with three branches; farm buildings were named the "Court House," the "Government Building," and so on. By 1895, the camp had come to be officially known as the George Junior Republic. It operated like a town, observing the laws of New York State and adding its own local ordinances. At the time that its founder spoke to Groton School, the movement was spreading, with Junior Republics starting in other states; shortly the National Association of Junior Republics was established, with George's great friend and supporter, Thomas Mott Osborne, as president.

∽∼

"He wore no tie, had no teeth
and had a white beard . . ."

[GROTON]
FEB. 9, 1898,
WEDNESDAY.

My dear Mama & Papa
I was perfectly delighted to hear you are coming up next Saturday to spend Sunday.

I went to Mrs Powell's this morning and have engaged a room and dressing-room for Saturday afternoon. I had no difficulty in getting the rooms so I suppose you will be there alone, which will be much nicer than if there were a crowd.

It is melting here hard today and the snow had already perceptibly decreased, and as it is too sticky for snowshoeing or skiing there is not much to do.

Warren had another tooth ache last night so he has gone to the dentist in Boston today to have it attended to.

I think [I] forgot to tell you in my last letter that we had had a lecture last Friday on Memory; it was by a Dr. Pick who looked as if he had come out of the ark! He wore no tie, had no teeth and had a white beard nearly two feet long! His lecture was very good & he showed us how to remember a long list of words in a very short time.

I must close now and go to my boxing-lesson which is at 4.45.
Ever with dear love

F.D.R.

175

P.S. I shall try to meet you at Powell Cottage on Saturday night but as school begins at 7 p.m I will not be able to if you are late, but I shall see you early Sunday morning anyway.

The archetype Dr. Edward Pick was the author of *On Memory and the Rational Means of Improving It,* published some thirty years before; he was a noted authority in his field and looked, schoolmates recall, much as F.D.R. describes him. There was considerable dispute as to whether he did or didn't wear a necktie; boys would stand on either side of him and alternately ask questions, causing his head to turn sharply and his beard to flutter, but never enough to decide the matter. There were two emendations by Mrs. James Roosevelt in this letter: in the fifth paragraph she changed "forget" to "forgot" but neglected to add the necessary "I"; and, in the final sentence of this same paragraph, she added an "s" to "word."

∽

*"A little bird whispers to me
that they were Hyde Park donkeys . . ."*

[GROTON]
FEB. 15, 1898,
TUESDAY.

My dear Mama and Papa,

After school yesterday I went to Mrs Powell's and got the garment you mended for me. At noon the mail came at [and] it took several boys to carry it as there were so many Valentines. I got two from Tuxedo, in the morning and another in the evening from Orange

As two of them were alike I enclose one of them which I think you will find very amusing.

I was much surprised and pleased to get your letter from Worcester last night. The delightful surprise Warren and I got the other day we forget to tell you about. We very naturally thought they were from Muriel, in fact I had begun a letter to her thanking her for them! Of course I shall not write her now, as a little bird whispers to me that they were Hyde Park donkeys, & fine specimens at that.

The asses are indeed symbolical of their owners and I am sure you will agree with me in this!

I shall be very careful in taking the pills not to take too much, but I do not expect to need them long as I have not coughed yesterday as much as I did the day before, and if the weather continues fine I hope to shake it off entirely

It was too delightful having you up here and I only wish you could have stayed a week. You will be pleased to hear that little Hollister is really improving and is practically out of danger now. I hope you had a comfortable journey on and that Papa did not have to be in N.Y. much this week.

Ever with dear love to you both

FDR

P.S. Warren is still in bed from some unaccountable reason but the nurse says he will get up at noon & will be out to-morrow.

FDR

∽∾

"We heard the news of the 'Maine' yesterday . . ."
[GROTON]
FEB. 17, 1898,
THURSDAY.

My dear Mama and Papa,

Many thanks for your letters and the Bromo-Quinine and Gum-Arabic. I have taken the B-Q two or three times a day and I think my cold is much better

Yesterday it snowed and blew very hard so the half-holiday was postponed till this afternoon

Taddy has asked me to go to Groton with him on skis and as it is the best exercise I can take I shall go but I do not intend to buy much food.

You will be surprised to hear that poor Warren is still in the infirmary The nurse says he may be out tomorrow, but his cough has not got much better.

Hollister is rapidly improving and is entirely out of danger now. His father & mother dined at the school yesterday and may go home soon.

We heard the news of the "Maine" yesterday & everyone is much excited

If the accident turns out to have been done by Spaniards, I think the whole school [will] take up arms and sail to Spain!

Friday 8. a.m.

Yesterday afternoon I went to Groton with Taddy on skis. We had great fun and Taddy was too funny trying to carry home a lot of oranges a pot of jam & some biscuits. We missed the oranges when we got half way home & found a hole in the bottom of the bag. We turned back and found an orange every hundred feet & finally recovered them all.

Many thanks for the photos. Two have already gone, but I think I shall give the other to Mr. Billings. The weather is fine and I hardly coughed at all yesterday. The stage is being put up in the gym. & we are all looking forward to Tuesday.

Ever with dear love

FDR.

The *Maine* was blown up in Havana harbor on February 15. Slightly more than a month later the Navy Department announced that the explosion had been caused by an exterior bomb.

∽∽

"People have already begun to arrive for the play . . ."

[GROTON]
FEB. 20, 1898,
SUNDAY.

My dear Mama and Papa.

I received a dollar from Aunt Jennie the other day for the Grotonian and as you gave me the money for her subscription, I enclose the dollar to you.

Warren came out of the infirmary yesterday for his meals, and today will be out a little longer, but I think he will come out for good tomorrow.

We have tickets for the play on Tuesday, & I have a ticket also for the play at Groton on Saturday the 26th as the IV Form is allowed to go.

Yesterday afternoon I went skiing on a very steep hill above the pond. We shot nearly half way across *if* we got safely down the hill. Once I fell right on the edge of the ice and it gave way under me so I got one leg nicely soaked. You can judge from this that my cold is absolutely gone, & tomorrow I shall begin calisthenics again.

People have already begun to arrive for the play, among others Mr. & Mrs. Farr, Aunt Jennie's friends.

I hear that Aunt Kassie is coming up here next Saturday, & Warren is delighted as it is the first time she has been up since he has been here.

It has half-snowed, half-rained here all day so we have not been able to go out except to church. The Lenten services begin next Thursday & are to be held every Thursday till we go home.

Monday a.m. It is still sleeting here today. Warren is to come out of the infirmary for the whole day, so I think he will be all right for the play tomorrow. Your letter of Friday just received. Too bad about Lyman and the measles, Aunt Jennie thought he would escape them this time as he has had them before. Buell Hollister is fast improving, and is entirely out of danger now

Ever with love

F.D.R.

The *Grotonian* was the school magazine, which published a miscellany of literary efforts, school news, and reports on athletic events; F.D.R. later "heeled" it.

"I should think he would stick
to a good job when he has it! . . ."

My dear Mama and Papa

It rained and snowed all day on Monday and Tuesday so the visitors did not have good weather. About sixty people came up, including Mrs. Goodwin & the little kid Goodwin.

I went to lunch with them on Tuesday and in the afternoon when the rain stopped for a moment we went out driving, but had to come back when it began again.

Supper was at 5.45 and we only had ¾ of an hour evening school. The play began at about 8 o'clock and was really splendid, the best they have ever had. I send you the programme, which please keep as I would like to have it.

The play is to be given again in the Town Hall on Saturday & I have a very good seat. Warren & I have also got three seats for Aunt Kassie, Mr Collier & Muriel, as I think the last two would like to see it even if Aunt Kassie is unable to.

Warren will not go to the Village as only the three upper forms are allowed to but my seat is only a short distance from the others. Yesterday afternoon I worked in the gymnasium & boxed as it was wet outside & today I am very stiff as a result. The monthly marks end on Saturday so they will come out some [time] next week. This afternoon we had the first of the Lenten services. The sermon was by Mr. Sprague of Charlestown and was very good.

I got a nice letter from Mr. Dumper today & you will be surprised to hear that he expects to go back to Kenyon College next autumn. I should think he would stick to a good job when he has it!

Ever with loads of love

FDR

The minister mentioned here was Philo Woodruff Sprague of St. John's Episcopal Church, Charlestown, Mass.

∾

*"No one was hurt and the horses
were quiet . . ."*

My dear Mama and Papa,

Yesterday morning at 12.30 Aunt Kassie Muriel & Mr. Collier got here. Warren and I met them at the Whitney cottage and stayed to lunch. After lunch we went out for a sleigh-ride, thro' the village and over the Lawrence's bridge towards West Groton. When we tried to turn the sleigh the runner, catching in the hard crust broke & the sleigh upset. No one was hurt & the horses were quiet, but the sleigh would not run as the broken runner turned under. We borrowed an old board at a farmer's and wedged the two runners apart, & so managed to get home. I then had a boxing lesson and went over to supper with Aunt Kassie. At 7 o'clock Warren went back to school and Mr. Collier Muriel and I drove with several other visitors at the cottages, to the town-hall for the play; it was very good, as before, and Muriel was perfectly delighted with it. I sat with them and drove back with them but it was too bad that Warren could not come with us.

This morning after breakfast I went over to Whitney's to tell Aunt Kassie that Warren could not come till later on account of Choir-practice. At ten o'clock the Peabody baby was christened in the study by her father. She was named Marjorie and her God-parents were Mr. Billings, Mrs. John Lawrence and Mrs. Peabody

I went to lunch with Aunt Kassie and afterwards we took a walk about the grounds. In the evening they came over to early parlor but did not stay for late as they left so early tomorrow.

181

Monday. a.m

I went to say good-bye at Whitney's just after breakfast as they left at 8.30. After school I went skiing on the fine crust and had a very exciting time. The exams begin in two weeks so I shall begin studying pretty soon. Many thanks for the Graphic which came on Saturday

Ever with love to you both

FRANKLIN D ROOSEVELT

〜

*"You will be surprised to see
what good girls boys make! . . ."*

[GROTON]
MARCH 2, 1898,
WEDNESDAY.

My dear Mama and Papa.

I have asked Mr. Peabody about the confirmation and find the Bishop is coming on Wednesday March 16th and the service is to be in the *afternoon.* Please tell me if you wish me to get rooms or if you have got them already.

Yesterday morning I went skiing and in the afternoon the marks for last month came out. I, as usual, got a B, a pretty good one I think, and I got an A in Latin for the first time this year. This morning I got an invitation for Warren and me to lunch with the Reynolds We went there at 1.30 and had a very nice time, staying a short time after lunch. I then went skiing until supper time and had a very good time as Mr. Ayrault and several other boys made record breaking very exciting.

The winter Sports begin on Saturday, and I have entered several events among which are boxing and high-kicking. I think you will be sorry I have entered the high-kick, but I do not think I shall hurt myself much this time. I do not expect to win this time as I am in the 2nd class instead of the 3rd and several boys in it are better kickers than I am.

182

Thursday.

The examinations begin two weeks from today so I shall begin studying next Monday.

We are to have the 2nd Lenten service this afternoon and the sermon is to be from a Professor Natch of Theological Seminary.

Warren stood better in his form last month than the month before His place was 9th I think and his mark 6.25 about.

I have ordered a few pictures of the actors in the play and I am sure you will be surprised to see what good girls boys make! The Fives Tournament is in progress and what with practising for the Sports we are all kept very busy now. I was so sorry to be away when the babies were at Hyde Park, as I am sure you must have enjoyed having them very much

Ever with dear love to you both

FDR

"Natch" was a misspelling of the last name of Dr. Henry S. Nash, of the Episcopal Theological Seminary. He was one of the Rector's very closest friends. His son, Dr. Norman Nash, became Bishop of Massachusetts in 1947.

∽

"I got on very well until one of
my potatoes fell out . . ."

[GROTON]
MARCH 6, 1898,
SUNDAY.

My dear Mama and Papa,

The winter Sports meeting began yesterday morning with the ten yards dash. I came in second in my heat, and so lose all chance for the cup. In the afternoon we began with Potato Race which is always very amusing I got on very well until one of my potatoes fell out of the bucket, and in my haste to put it in I fell down, and my potato rolled away!

After the Potato Race we had Featherweight Boxing, several

good matches between kids. After that came Light-weight Boxing in which I had two three minute rounds with Fuller Potter. We both came out with bloody noses and cut lips, but the match was decided in his favor. I did not much expect to win as this is the third year he has boxed and even then we were quite close.

It is too lovely to think of coming home in two weeks, even though a week of exams comes first. I think I shall pass nearly all, but I may fail one or two as I am so very busy now, and am not going to grub much for them.

Last Thursday we had the second Lenten service and the sermon was from Prof. Natch of the Divinity School, and was very good.

I can hardly realize that you sail next month and I think that in some ways it would be nicer if we could all go together later, but in that case we should have to give up Campobello.

I have not yet received the plans for my boat but expect them every day, and shall send them to you when they come. Please don't forget to bring up something to take my ulster and extra clothes home in when you come on the 16th. Poor Edmund has been in the infirmary several days with a cold, but he may be out tomorrow. This evening we had a new dish added to our supper in the shape of cheese. Our Sunday supper is very good now, as we have hot rolls, raspberry jam, cheese and cake.

I have written to Arthur Dumper asking him to come to Hyde Park for a day or so during the holidays   I was sure you would not mind having him for a day or so, and it is not as if he were at all a stranger.

Ever with dear love to you both

F.D.R.

"The plans for my boat" is a reference to the knockabout *New Moon;* when it was built he sailed it summers at Campobello, and also had it brought to Hyde Park for use on the Hudson.

". . . as far from the Good Path
as ever . . ."

My dear Mama and Papa

You will be surprised to hear that that [*sic*] we have a new boy here, in the place of Billy Rogers. He is Duane Humphreys whom you doubtless remember at Hyde Park. He has entered the 3rd form and seems to get on well

Buell Hollister has gone home to recuperate and his recovery has been very quick and satisfactory. Edmund has been in the infirmary nearly a week but is much better now and expects to be out tomorrow. Warren also had a little cold and went to the infirmary on Monday evening, but he may be out tomorrow.

The Sports are still going on and I think my high kick will come on Friday or Saturday. I am not sure when the confirmation comes on Wednesday, but I rather think it comes soon after lunch, but if it comes after 4 p.m I shall telegraph you. I do hope Papa will be able to come, and am very glad there is a chance of Aunt Dora's coming.

Mrs & Miss Reynolds have left and Mrs Reynolds seemed very well, and she came to church several times before she left.

Thursday

Warren came out of the infirmary this morning, but Edmund is still there only coming down for meals.

I found this morning that the confirmation service will be at 3 o'clock so you can not possibly be in time by coming on Wednesday. My high kick comes tomorrow morning after school, so you may find me on crutches as I have made up my mind to get the 2nd prize, altho' I shall have to beat three boys who kicked higher than I did last year.

We are to have a confirmation lecture on Saturday night and the last one on Monday, and on Tuesday evening there is one for the boys who are to be confirmed—only about 20 I think.

You ask if Taddy is to be confirmed. No such happy thing, and altho' he went into one lecture, he has not been in since, & is as far from the Good Path as ever

With a great deal of love to you both & excuse for this hasty scrawl   Ever

FRANKLIN D ROOSEVELT

William Beverley Rogers, who dropped out of the class of 1899, lived at Garrison, not far from Hyde Park. He was distantly related to Edmund Rogers.

∽

"I have heard several Bluebirds and seen one Robin . . ."

[GROTON]
MARCH 13, 1898,
SUNDAY.

My dear Mama and Papa,

Last Friday morning after school the II class High Kick took place. I got second with Louis De Koven first. His kick was 8 ft ¼ in. and mine was 7 ft. 11 ¼ in, just one inch lower, but my kick was 8 inches higher than I did last year. I hurt my elbow the same way as last year, but I do not think I will have any trouble with it, as I rub it and put vaseline on every day.

I am so sorry that Papa has a meeting on Wednesday and cannot come up here, but I am glad Aunt Dora is coming. I wonder if you are going to spend Tuesday night in Boston or if you come straight here on Tuesday.

We are having really hot weather here and the snow is rapidly disappearing. The lovely birds are beginning to arrive. So far Song Sparrows have come in full force and I have heard several Bluebirds and seen one Robin. It is too bad the holidays come so early this year as only a few birds will have arrived, and very few things will be out.

Yesterday afternoon the finals of the Fives Tournament were played by Devens and Birckhead. It was a splendid and very close game and finally Birckhead won by a close margin. The Sports are all over with the exception of the final Heavy-weight boxing and that is to be decided tomorrow morning.

Last night Mrs. Robeson who has a boy here in our form, read to us in the study. She read several very amusing short stories and some good poems.

Edmund still stays in the infirmary only coming down for meals, but he hopes to come out tomorrow.

It is lovely to think of seeing you so soon and then in less than a week I shall be home.

I shall let you take home with you my wrapper, ulster, rubber boots, red sweater, blue suit, camera, tripod, and perhaps my waterproof so bring up plenty of room for them please.

If Warren gets 5 more black-marks this term he will have to stay over a day, as he has 7 or 8 carried over to Saturday, but he expects to be very good and is rather frightened I think.

I do not understand why I did not have an A in Latin on my report as Mr. Abbott told me himself that I had an A. I intend to speak about it as I do not wish to be cheated out of it if I really deserved it.

Ever with dear love to you both

F.D.R.

His mother and his **Aunt Dora Forbes** came up to see him confirmed in the chapel at Groton by Bishop Lawrence, on March 16. His February report did, indeed, make no mention of an A in Latin, but he got A's in Algebra, French, and **Sacred Studies.**

"Today is perfectly lovely . . .
but we had calisthenics . . ."

My dear Mama and Papa,

I hope you had a pleasant journey on with Aunt Dora, and found Papa well.

Yesterday afternoon we had a Latin Composition Exam. and I passed all right.

This morning we had a very hard Mathematics exam and you will be pleased to hear that I got a good B. We then had a Greek and Greek Composition Exam and I got through it all right

This afternoon I had a French Exam which I am sure I passed easily. Tomorrow a.m we have English and Latin. I rather expect to fail my English as I have had very little chance to study it, but I hope to get through my Latin. On Monday a.m we have Sacred Studies & History both of which I expect to pass.

I am terribly busy so please excuse this hasty scrawl. I am looking forward to seeing you at 3.30 on Tuesday

Today is perfectly lovely without a cloud in the sky, but we had calisthenics for the last time after school so we could not go out.

Ever with dear love to you both

FRANKLIN D. ROOSEVELT

His final mid-term report, dated March 21, showed that the expected failure in English did not materialize, for he got a B in that examination, also in the Latin test. His average mark was a B, and the Rector jotted down: "Very good." And Easter vacation intervened.

〜〜

*"It seems very familiar to be
back here, and rather sickening . . ."*

My dearest Mama and Papa,

It seems very familiar to be back here, and rather sickening
to think of twelve longs weeks here, before getting home again.
On account of the snow and sleet our train was nearly an hour
late when we got to Worcester, & we therefore missed the regular train on here; we however left again at 6.30 and got to the
School at 8.15 instead of 6.45 We immediately had Supper
and we are now in the School-room writing home.

I eat my little lunch at 2. o'clock and drank a bottle of
Sarsaparilla.

As we were so late getting to Worcester, I took there a cup
of Coffee and some rolls. We found it snowing here and everything sopping. I was only too thankful to have my water-proof,
as the snow poured through the front of the barge altho' it was
closed on the sides.

My dormitory is unchanged much to my disappointment
although it will be nicer in some ways in summer, as it is so
airy. I do not yet know what my seat at table is, but I am
hoping to be near Mr Gardner.

I hope Papa will see Fred. Tams about the knockabout and
if he can only get good plans, I will see about having Richardson build her.

I am of course hoping to see you before you sail but I do
not want you to come on if it is at all inconvenient, and you
must not be worn out before you sail

It is time to close & I hope will excuse this scratch, written
with a very pointed pen & with a great deal of love to you both
and lots of kisses

Ever your own son

F.D.R.

J. Frederic Tams and Ashton Lemoine were partners in the firm of Tams & Lemoine, yacht brokers in New York City.

~~

"War seems to be less likely today . . ."

My dearest Mama & Papa,

This morning breakfast was at 8 o'clock, so we did not have to get up till 7.30. School began at 9 and lasted till 11.45. We then handed in our money and went up to unpack. I found my things all right, and everything is in its right place now. I feel as if I had been here quite a week instead a few hours, and everything is running as smoothly as if we had never left.

I hope you did not forget to write to Thomas Rowland, & that Anderson sent the bird all right.

There is to be a service & address in the chapel this afternoon and services every day this week.

My seat at table has been changed and I now sit next to Lathrop Brown and 2nd from Mr. Ayrault. There are about 2 inches of snow here, but the sun is shining brightly now and we hope it will soon disappear.

War seems to be less likely today, so I think you will leave all right on the 20th.

Several boys have not come back on account of colds and I hope neither you nor Papa will get cold in this bad weather.

Mr. Coolidge had a mild case of Diphtheria in the holidays, and will not return until May, so we must continue our Mathematics with Mr. Ayrault until he returns.

I have read some more in "Pendennis" and expect to finish it by Saturday all right.

Tomorrow there will be a service in the afternoon and Friday with [will] be just like Sunday and [with] Church twice. This p.m. we had a short service & address from the rector.

The shoes came tonight and I am delighted to say they fit to a T and are just what I wanted. The belt is also very nice & many thanks for getting the pocket kodak films.

Thursday 8 a.m

Warren is in the infirmary and going home because he has heard that one of the babies is ill with some desease. I am so sorry & hope it is nothing serious & that he will be able to return soon.

Ever your affectionate son

FDR.

Charles Anderson was a one-eyed butler who served with the James Roosevelts for ten years, and thereafter for forty-two years with Warren Delano III and his son Lyman at Steen Valetje. *Trow's Business Directory* of 1899 carried the following small listing: "Thomas Rowland, 182 Sixth Avenue, New York. All kinds of Birds, Animals and Fish Artistically Mounted." Needless to say, F.D.R. was one of this gentleman's best customers.

∽∾

"I am having my warts burned off with nitrate of silver . . ."

[GROTON]
APRIL 8, 1898,
FRIDAY.

My dearest Mama & Papa,

I forgot to tell you before I left that I would like you to tell the post-master at Hyde Park to send all things, including newspapers, to me here while you are abroad, as anything is welcome to break the monotony of school life.

Warren left at 8 o'clock yesterday morning and the nurse told me today that it was little Kassie who had mumps. I hope she will not have a bad case of it, and that Warren may not have taken it, as I should then probably come down with it and cause a general outbreak in the school.

Yesterday after school we had a service and address from

Mr. Newbegin the clergyman of the Ayer church. Today is a whole holiday and this morning we had church at 11 o'clock and this afternoon at 3.30.

I got your letter enclosing the newspaper slip, which I thought very good, and return it to you with this letter. The Spanish situation seems to be unchanged, but I feel that every moment of delay is in the interests of peace, and that the President is doing all he can to prevent war.

After church this morning I developed two of the plates I took of Top-mast and Top-Royal and they are excellent I think. They are drying now and I will send you some pictures as soon as I print them.

I have almost finished Pendennis and I shall glance over the "Last of the Mohicans" as soon as I finish.

I am dieing to know what the Easter present is "which will be pretty for summer wear," and I am anxiously awaiting its arrival. I am having my warts burned off with nitrate of silver and it will be comfort to get rid of them, as they spread and crack continually.

I find my rubbers have disappeared, so I wish you would send me up a pair. I know you will get the right size as the shoes you buy for me always fit better than the ones I try on myself!

Ever with dearest love to you both I am your affec. son

FDR

In 1946 Mrs. George B. St. George was elected to Congress on the Republican ticket from the Twenty-ninth Election District of New York State, which embraces Newburgh, where the Delanos lived. Her candidacy had the strong support of Hamilton Fish, one of F.D.R.'s best-known political antagoists. Mrs. St. George is the former Katharine D. P. Collier, the "little Kassie" of this letter. The minister of St. Andrew's Episcopal Church in Ayer was the Reverend Edward H. Newbegin. The word "situation" in paragraph four was inserted by F.D.R.'s mother.

*"War seems to be nearer and
more probable now . . ."*

My dearest Mama & Papa,

It seems very queer to be away from home on Easter Day,
and I am thinking of you as having the Service in the Old
Church.

When we got up this morning, there was not a cloud in the
sky, but while we [were] in church it began to pour. It has
cleared however this afternoon, and everything looks greener
since the rain.

I have finished Pendennis today and am very glad I read it,
as it was not only interesting, but I am sure will greatly improve my English style.

I was much delighted last night to get your letter and lovely
Easter card, and Taddy was much touched at getting his, and
he told me he thought you were much kinder to him than his
own family! I am sorry to say that he got a D for the last
month of last term, but he says he is going to work hard all
this term.

I was much surprised to hear by your letter that it is scarlet-
fever that little Kassie has, as all the boys up here heard that
it was mumps. I have not said anything about its not being
mumps as I fancy Mr. Peabody does not want to have a panic.
I only hope none of the other children will get it, but I am
almost afraid little Sally may catch it, as it is so terribly contagious.

I am longing to hear from you, whether you are coming next
Sunday but I know how very busy and upset you will be just
before sailing and therefore fear you may possibly not be able
to come.

We have been here almost a week now and are well started
in the term. Everyone is of course looking forward to the 3
months' holidays with great delight.

193

War seems to be nearer and more probable now, and we can only hope that Spain will do the wise thing and back down completely. I very much wonder if you will be able to leave the country without difficulty in case war is declared. You must not hesitate to leave me on this side as I would be all right and I feel that Papa must not put off going to Nauheim till July, as we might then not be able to go at all.

Yesterday afternoon I went on the river with Laurie Rainsford as the weather was quite summery. We saw a number of ducks and other birds, but the season here is scarcely as far advanced as at Hyde Park a week ago.

I shall write Warren this evening and to Aunt Annie, whose basket has been a constant source of enjoyment to me and others.

Ever with dearest love to you both I am your loving son

FRANKLIN D. ROOSEVELT

P.S. We expect Goodwin to return sometime tomorrow.

The reference to the "Old Church" may be explained by the fact that St. James Episcopal Church had no heating and during the winter months services were moved into the chapel; evidently, by this Easter, the weather was suitable for the church itself.

∽

"I am to have my strength tested,
for the second time . . ."

GROTON SCHOOL
APRIL 13, 1898,
WEDNESDAY.

My dearest Mama and Papa,

I am perfectly delighted to find by your letter of Tuesday that you and *possibly* Papa are coming up here on Sunday. I shall engage a room for you & one for Calder tomorrow morning, and will go to the Powell Cottage directly after breakfast (8.30) on Sunday in case you come via Fitchburg.

On Monday the nines were made up. They are four preparatory teams, from which will be chosen in 2 weeks three regular cup nines. I am fielder on Dan Draper's team and stand a *very* little chance of making one [of] the cup nines. We play or practice every day except half-holidays.

This afternoon I went out canoeing with Laurie Rainsford, but we did not see many birds and found no signs of nests.

I got a little note from Warren saying that he hopes to come back tomorrow or next day, so you will probably find him here when you come on Sunday.

I am to have my strength tested, for the second time, tonight and hope to beat my last 336. altho' I fear I will not as I am not in very good training now.

Thursday. 12 a.m.

Warren came back just now, looking well. He had quite a nice time in Boston but he said that it was rather dull at Fair Haven

I cannot write more now as the mail is going

Ever with love

F.D.R.

Calder was Mrs. James Roosevelt's maid.

〜〜

"I am very much afraid that it
will be very expensive . . ."

GROTON SCHOOL
APRIL 17, 1898,
SUNDAY.

My dear Papa,

Many thanks for sending the letter of Mr. Tams & also for your two letters. I think you are very good to have taken so much trouble about it. I am very much afraid that it will be very expensive to build such a fine boat, and I think it would come pretty close to $1,000 in the end.

Now I never wished or expected to get that kind of a boat, and I only expected to pay $200. or $300.

Do you not think I had better write to Mr. Tams and find out if he has no fairly good *safe* second-hand boat, as I am sure there are plenty of good boats of only one or two years old on the market. If he has none, I will write to Lawley or some other firm in Boston, where I am sure some can be had. If not safe already they could have lead added and of course I should submit everything to you.

I shall however get the estimate from Richardson, and if it is over $400 or $500 I should of course think it out of the question.

It is lovely having Mama here and only wish you could have come too but of course I know how how [*sic*] terribly busy you must be just before sailing

Ever with love your affec. son

FDR.

George Lawley & Son were well-known Boston yacht builders.

∽∽

"You need not sign it as every word costs so much . . ."

GROTON SCHOOL
APRIL 18, 1898,
MONDAY.

My darling Mama and Papa,

It was too lovely to have the little visit from you, and it is horrid to think of your sailing day after tomorrow.

I hope you and Aunt Ellen had a pleasant journey home and caught the train at Troy all right.

I think Aunt Ellen enjoyed her visit here very much and I was glad she could come, although I did not have you to myself as much as if you had been alone. I shall write again tomorrow to the steamer, and after that I shall be waiting anxiously until I get your cable. You had better send it to Roosevelt—School—Groton—Mass and you need not sign it as every word costs so much.

War seems more imminent today but I do not think it will

come for at least 10 days, so you will get to the other side all right. I wonder who is the captain of the "Majestic," now?

Have you sent me any more five cent stamps? If not, could you send me some, as I have only enough stamps to last me a month.

I suppose you had a rather busy time after you got home, although with Elsie and Calder it will not be as difficult as usual.

I have played golf this afternoon and tomorrow we are to play Hopkinson. This afternoon Mr. Lehmann the great English rowing coach came up to coach our crews. He was up here last year & was at college in England with Mr. Peabody

It is time for the mail to close now so I will stop.

Ever with dearest love and lots of kisses to you both   I am Your affectionate son   FRANKLIN D. ROOSEVELT

P.S. I wish you could drop me a line to say what Papa thinks of my getting a 2nd hand boat   FDR

"Aunt Ellen" was his Uncle John Aspinwall Roosevelt's wife, the former Ellen Murray Crosby. In paragraph four Mrs. James Roosevelt added "not" to the phrase "I do think."

〰

"If there is anything I can do for him in an ornithological line . . ."

GROTON SCHOOL
APRIL 19, 1898,
TUESDAY.

My darling Mama and Papa,

It seems hard to think of you as sailing tomorrow and somehow I feel as if I would mind having the ocean between us much more than I did last year. I only trust and pray you will have a good trip and I will not be happy until I get your cablegram next Wednesday morning, I hope. I will begin keeping the letter-diary method tomorrow and will send my letter on Friday.

I wonder if you know many people on board and if you sit at the Captain's table? I wish you would send me a passenger-list and the daily runs, after you get across. This morning we did all our studying before lunch as we are to play Hopkinson in an hour. I hope we shall win but they have a very strong team.

A very curious coincident happened yesterday. The grand-mothers of 3 boys in the school died the same day. One was the Cary's grandmother, Mrs Potter I suppose & the other was Charlie Lawrance's, Mrs. Lanier I think. The third was old Mrs. Motley.

When you were up here on Sunday I forgot to tell you that Guy Cary has been made a prefect this term, and also the eldest Rainsford boy, so there are about eight prefects now.

I think you ought to have a fairly good voyage as we have had a good deal of rain lately, and ought to have fine weather now.

War seems pretty threatening now, but I shall not mind it so much when you get to the other side. You will of course get all the news from the "Paris Herald" the delightful paper I took so much pleasure in at Nauheim! I wish you would give my kind regards to Mr. & Mrs. Foleyjambey, and tell him that if there is anything I can do for him over here in an ornitho-logical line, I should be very pleased to do so.

I wonder if you will see Mrs. O'Neil and Mr & Mrs. Barclay. If you do please give them my regards.

It is almost time for the mail to go, so I will close now. Less than ten weeks now before we meet again and I feel sure it will go quickly.

With lots of love and hugs & kisses & bon voyage to you both, my dearest Mama and Papa, I am always your very affectionate son

FRANKLIN.

The *Social Register* offers some disagreement to the "very
curious coincident," recording that Mrs. Edward Motley died
April 16, Mrs. Charles Lanier on April 18, and Mrs. Howard
Potter on April 19. As regards the prefect system, there were
chosen—by the Rector, with some slight advisement from the
departing sixth form and from the faculty—a number of the
outstanding boys of the entering sixth form to act as prefects,
having a semi-authority over the rest of the school and working closely with the masters. There was a Senior and Junior
Prefect, but no set limit on the rest. Usually the first few
were selected during the summer and announced at the beginning of their sixth-form year, and others were appointed even
as late as the following spring, as noted here. Although the
boys chosen to be prefects were supposedly outstanding in
their class, at times the "selection from above," and the large
numbers of prefects named, made the distinction an empty
one. Cecil George Savile Foljambe was the fourth Baron
Hawkesbury, later Earl of Liverpool. He served for a short
time in the British Navy, retired and entered Parliament,
where he was a Liberal M.P. until appointed to the peerage
in 1893. He was a great bird-fancier, and had a fine collection at his home "Osberton-in-Worksop," in Nottingham-
shire, where F.D.R. had visited on previous trips to England.

∽∽

"War is now inevitable . . ."

GROTON SCHOOL
APRIL 20, 1898,
WEDNESDAY.

My dearest Mama and Papa,
    I am thinking of you today as going down to the steamer
and starting on your voyage. How I wish I could be there to
see you off, but it was partly made up for by your lovely visit
on Sunday. I am afraid you had a horrid day to start on as it
has drizzled up here, and I hope neither of you will catch cold
just before starting.
Thursday   April 21st

I was much delighted to get your telegram saying that you had fine weather for the start. Your two letters from N.Y. came at noon today and I was delighted to here that you got off comfortably. I hope you finally got my last letter   I sent it by the Tuesday 6 p.m mail and it ought to have got there.

It must be nice for Aunt Dora to be able to go out with you, and I am sure the change will do her a vast amount of good. It is rumored today that Spain has sent a squadron of 50 or 60 ships against N.Y. and the coast, so you may run right into them and end up in a Spanish prison! War is now inevitable and we are awaiting Spain's reply to our ultimatum. She will of course refuse to leave Cuba and on Saturday our army is to cross over and invade Cuba. I think by the time this reaches you, that Cuba will have been rid of Spaniards and Spain will be soon ready to give in.

I am so pleased to here that Aunt Kassie & Hiram did not mind Warren's coxing and I am going to write to them soon to tell them how well he gets on. I got a nice letter from Aunt Ellen today about ¾ full of old jokes (!) but don't tell her this as she was kind to write at all. It is so funny that I shall send it to you as soon as I have answered it.

We are having fine though quite cool weather here now, so I am hoping it will not be rough on the ocean. I am sure you will have a lovely time at Sir and Mrs. Foljambey's and you must write me all about it.

I am sending this to 12a Curzon St. as you said, and I hope you will get it all right. After this I shall write c/o Baring Bros. until I find where you get rooms at Nauheim. How strange it will seem to have a street & houses right thro' the lovely Huggermugger garden!

The time is passing quickly here and I don't think it will seem long until June. I have taken a room (the one Aunt Ellen had) at Mrs Powells for Sunday June 26th & Monday (Prize Day) in case you want to come up. It was the last room she had & you can give it up all right whenever you want to.

I hope you will have a nice time in London & a pleasant journey to Nauheim. Ever with best love and kisses to you both I am your affectionate son

FRANKLIN D ROOSEVELT

The rumor of the approaching Spanish squadron never actually materialized, but it did persist. A few days later, in a dispatch from Bayonne, France, dated April 27, the New York *Times* reported: "According to a letter just received here from Madrid . . . a Spanish squadron, consisting of four ironclads and three torpedo-boat destroyers, sailed for the United States yesterday. It was rumored that the squadron was to steam direct across the Atlantic and bombard northern ports of the United States."

∽∽

"War began today! . . ."

GROTON SCHOOL

APRIL 22, 1898,

FRIDAY.

My dearest Mama and Papa.

I have some news to break to you. There are two cases of scarlet-fever in the school, which broke out a day or two ago. You need not be in the least alarmed, as I have quite made up my mind *not* to get it, and as they are carefully isolated there is hardly any danger. Of course if by any chance I should get it you will have a cable, but if you hear nothing before you receive this letter you may feel assured I have escaped the plague. If I do get it you need not worry as of course I should have the very best of care, and Aunt Annie will look out for me. The two cases in the infirmary are *mild* and doing well. I cannot think how they got it as of course they did not get it through Warren, who is in the best of health.

War began today!

Spain refused to consider our ultimatum and gave Minister Woodford his passports. Our fleet has started to blockade Cuba and the first shot was fired today. The gunboat Nashville captured a Spanish merchantman off Cuba this morning, and of course everyone is wildly excited.

It is rather unnecessary for me to give you the news as you will get it all by the lovely "Paris Herald." I fancy however you will be much excited to hear of the war when you get to Queenstown Tuesday night or Wednesday morning.

I am rather afraid that the war will interfere a little with the European mails, as Spain has decided to allow privateering and that means she will search all vessels for American goods.

We are having an uneventful time up here with fine though cool weather. We play baseball every day with a game against some other school nearly every half-holiday. You must be having a lovely time in London and I hope the weather is good. I will write again Sunday and Monday.

Ever with best love to you both, I am your affec. son.

FRANKLIN.

In the New York *Times* of April 22, the text of the United States ultimatum demanding that Spain withdraw from Cuba was given. Editorially, the *Times* commented: "We go to war with Spain, not for the accomplishment of an ambition, but in obedience to the laws of nature. . . . In the patient process of historical evolution the moment has arrived when the 'opposing and enduring forces' of civilization and barbarism must meet in the Island of Cuba." General Stewart L. Woodford, a Civil War veteran and former lieutenant governor of New York, had been appointed minister in 1897, his primary object to persuade the Spanish Government to liberalize their rule over the insurgent Cubans. Woodford left Madrid on April 21 and arrived in Paris the next day, his train meeting with hostile demonstrations in Spain and being stoned at Valladolid. On April 22, as the Sampson-Schley blockade of Cuba began to take form, the *Nashville,* an American gunboat of 1371 tons, captured the Spanish merchant steamer *Buenaventura* off Key West.

∽

*"We are all kept much excited
over the war . . ."*

My dearest Mama and Papa,

You will be glad to hear that no more cases of scarlet-fever have broken out, although one boy has a sore-throat and may break out. If there are any more cases I think we shall go home for a few weeks. You need not be in the least alarmed about me, as I think there is very little danger of my getting it. I am *absolutely* well now and hope to remain so. If we are sent home for any length of time, I may come out to see you even [if] it is only for one week!

We are all kept much excited over the war. Yesterday the "New York" captured a large Spanish steamer of over 3,000 tons with a very valuable cargoe.

It was rumored yesterday that the "Paris" had been captured by Spaniards with 150 passengers and ammunition on board. It was denied in the evening and I hope will not prove true.

Warren is very well and gets on all right with his coxing. He is doing much better at his lessons and Mr. Collier will have no cause for being angry.

It has been raining both yesterday and today so there are puddles everywhere. The grass is absolutely green now and the trees look very fluffy. Our game yesterday with the Harvard Freshmen was postponed but we play some other team on Wednesday.

I can hardly wait for your cable which I hope to get Wednesday morning.

I suppose I will not get a letter for over a week and then they will come regularly. You ought to get my first letter a few days after you get to London. I envy you going to Osberton and only wish I could see the place and the birds again.

I wonder where your rooms will be at Nauheim, but I suppose you will be near the "Kurhaus" and not down by the smelly little "ooze" and the "Kaizerhof".

I have not yet heard a word about the knockabout but have written to Dr. Sturgis for Richardson's address.

Monday April 25th

I am sorry to say that today two more cases broke out. All parents were telegraphed this morning and already 20 or 25 boys have left. I have not heard from Aunt Annie, but I think she will leave me here, unless it gets worse. Warren is to stay until the school breaks up, but I very much doubt if it will, as they hope there will be no more cases.

Later.

I have not heard a thing from Aunt Annie so expect to stay here. This evening 35 boys have left in all and the place seems deserted. Edmund goes tomorrow early. I am really dieing to go home and only wish you could be there as I should then go like a shot.

I will drop you a line if I find I am to go home before Wednesdays mail closes.

Ever with best love & kisses to you both I am your affec. son.

FRANKLIN D.R.

The battleship *New York* was the flagship of Commodore William T. Sampson, commander of the North Atlantic Squadron, who was charged with blockading Cuba and containing the Spanish fleet. The *Paris* was a ten-thousand-ton steamer of the American Line built in 1889; she held the Atlantic record for four years after her launching. At this time she was bound back to the United States from Southampton. The rumor of her capture, which first appeared in the Belfast papers on the afternoon of April 23, was soon discredited, although for a time the quotations on the Madrid stock exchange soared. ～～

Following the letter of April 24, 1898, the correspondence breaks off and does not resume until the fall. It appears

that F.D.R., together with Lathrop Brown and other school-
mates, decided to be off to the wars to fight the Spaniards.
The intention was to seek out the nearest recruiting station,
and the intricate plan of escape had come nearly to fruition
when tell-tale marks appeared upon the bodies of the lead-
ers. They were quickly removed to the infirmary with scarlet
fever. F.D.R.'s father and mother cut short their trip and
returned at once, and Mrs. James Roosevelt divided her
time between her semi-invalid husband at Hyde Park and
her wholly isolated son at Groton. Since the doctors would
allow her no contact with the latter, she used to climb up
and seat herself atop a stepladder outside his infirmary
window and read aloud to him for an hour or so each day.
When the disease had run its course, F.D.R. was taken
home to Hyde Park and did not return to the school until
September.

～～

"I am all settled now in my new quarters . . ."

GROTON
SEPT. 22, 1898,
THURSDAY.

My dearest Mama & Papa,

I am all settled now in my new quarters & am getting on
well. Yesterday afternoon I took two exams: Latin and Mathematics. I passed the Math easily with a mark of 80 and am
pretty sure I passed Latin although I have not yet heard about
it. On Saturday I take History & one other.

I need not take French or English.

I got a lovely basket of fruit from Aunt Annie & am going
to write to her & Aunt Laura on Sunday.

I forgot to tell you that Taddy is in the same dormitory
with me! and his study is no better.

I have lots of work to do in various things so you must excuse this awful scrawl

I need several things & will write you more fully tomorrow

FDR.

He was now a fifth-former, and thus entitled to a study. Frank Ashburn notes: "Fifth and sixth formers had either double or single studies. A study varied from a narrow, but longish, affair just about large enough to take a desk, desk chair, and a window seat, to a considerably larger one able to take two desks, two chairs, and a window seat. No banners or pennants were encouraged and no tacks could be driven into the wall. No large, comfortable chairs were allowed."

〜〜

"I wonder if you have written to Mr. Peabody about my teeth? . . ."

GROTON
SEPT. 23, 1898,
FRIDAY.

My dear Mama & Papa—

I was much pleased to get your two letters, and to hear that you got to F.H. [Fairhaven] all right. My cold is *almost* all gone & I do not notice it at all. I passed my Latin all right and tomorrow hope to pass two more.

I wonder if you have written to Mr. Peabody about my teeth? I would like to go in next Wednesday or Saturday, as the band is all untied and doing no good. I tried to do it myself but could not get one thread in. I really have no time to let the nurse do it as we have to work very hard this year, & I can always have the band put on again next year. The valise came all right from Hyde Park and I I [*sic*] was glad to get my football things. I have not played yet, only practiced and am on the second twenty-two, playing tackle. My nose-guard did not come—if it is at Hyde Park please send it. Your letter enclosing riddles just come, I will write Catherine on Sunday. I think it is awfully nice of Ellen to send me the pillow but I would prefer a green or blue one, as the couch is green corduroy. I wish you could send me a glass inkstand and a plain blotting pad for my table. I think you must have some old one at H.P. Whatever you do *don't frame* the photos as there is a narrow rail all round the room to stand them on. I have begun to take notes for the "Grotonian" and do odd jobs for it. It is the first step towards becoming an editor although I may never become one.

Will write tomorrow

Ever with loads of love

FRANKLIN

∽∾

"You have no idea how nice it is
to have a study . . ."

GROTON

SEPT. 25, 1898,

SUNDAY.

My dearest Mama and Papa,

We have had rainy weather for the last two days and now it is cloudy though not raining. I wish you would write to the man who is marking my golf cup, to send it up here as I would like to keep it on the mantelpiece in our room.

I found the book by Mr. Soley up here when I came and I wonder if you wrote to thank her for it. You have no idea how nice it is to have a study, and do just as you like. I got my medal for the High Kick of last year and I also got a Punctuality Prize last year which Mr. Jefferson will give me soon. I stand no show of getting it again, as I am in the Old Building and it is awfully hard to get over in time for breakfast in the morning.

I took my History Examination yesterday and passed all right. On Wednesday I am to take Greek and expect to get through all right.

We have two new subjects this year, German and Roman History. We have Mr. Woods in German, and so far it is *awfully* easy. We have Mr. Higley in History, and it is rather dry. If you have not sent the other things I wish you could send me some kind of a little tray or something to keep my penholders and pencils in. It is very good for my eyes having a study as I have a hanging electric lamp with a green shade on my desk.

It is very very late & I'm wery wery cold so Goodnight.

I forgot I think to tell you I weighed exactly 130¼ with only my light grey suit on & I will weight myself tomorrow stripped. The Knickerbockers came from Hollanders and are very nice but I shall not wear them yet for some time. Ever with lots of love to you both

FDR

The golf cup was a prize won at Campobello the preceding summer. James Russell Soley had married Mary W. Howland, who was a cousin of F.D.R. through James Roosevelt's first wife, Rebecca Howland. Professor of History and Law at the Naval Academy, and Assistant Secretary of the Navy from 1890 to 1893, Soley was the author of a shelf of books about the Navy and naval history, mostly for a younger audience— *Boys of 1812, The Rescue of Greely, The Blockade and the Cruisers, Sailor Boys of 1861,* and others. The Punctuality Prize was a leatherbound copy of Bacon's *Essays;* it is now in the Hyde Park library. L. P. Hollander & Co., Costumers, was then a large Boston and New York store.

"I am in deadly fear for my teeth as I have no nose-guard . . ."

GROTON
SEPT. 27, 1898,
TUESDAY.

My dearest Mama and Papa,

I got the sofa-pillow from Ellen today and it is a perfect beauty, red with with [*sic*] black curlykews all over it. It looks very well on the blue sofa, and with two more from the other boys will make a very cozy place.

We have begun writing a horrible kind of theme, unpopularly known as "daily themes"! We have to write them every day for six weeks, and you can imagine how hard it is to get subjects if even for only one page. I have written two and am already at a loss for something to write on tomorrow.

Football began on Monday and we played a game today. In consequence I am lame and sore and bruised, and I am in deadly fear for my teeth as I have no nose-guard. It must be somewhere at home as it was taken home last Xmas and did not come up with the things Elsie sent.

Your letter from Algonac just come, & I am so sorry there there is to be a "mal de mer" in the house-hold. It would be such a pity to lose Anderson & Calder after bouncing Elsie. Do write me all details and developments!

I had to buy a pair of foot-ball shoes ($4.00) and a canvas-jacket ($.80) and I fear I must get a nose-guard unless you can find mine. Tomorrow I take Greek and Latin Composition, the last exams, as I did not have to do French or English. I think I told you on Sunday that I got through my History all right. There are 35 new boys this year, among them Lydig Hoyt and Lloyd Derby. I wonder if Coleman and Jefferson have gone to Miss Vuiton's?

Warren has got on all right in his exams, only failing one, so he will go into the 2nd form. I must close now and write to Ellen

The River must be lovely now, & I wish I could be there. Please write to Thomas Rowland to send my hawk and if the Boston birds come I wish you could put the skins in a separate box with naphaline into the bird-closet.

Ever with loads of love to you both   Affec.

                                                FDR

In this and later letters there are interested remarks about the departures and replacements of various Hyde Park domestics, of which there was a fairly large staff. "Coleman and Jefferson" were W. Coleman Rogers (*vide supra*) and Thomas Jefferson Newbold, a brother of Mary Newbold.

". . . the Rector thinks they are
too snobbish . . ."

[GROTON]
SEPT. 29, 1898,
THURSDAY.

My dearest Mama & Papa,

I got your telegram this morning, and was sorry you could not find my nose-protector. I wonder why you want me to see the dentist on Saturday. I was going on Wednesday next as there is a foot-ball game on Saturday, but when I got your telegram I wrote at once for an appointment at 3 o'clock on Saturday. I will have the band removed and my teeth cleaned.

I will get a nose-protector at once at the store. I took my strength test today and measurements for this year's chart. I got over 450 for my strength test, a good deal better than last spring, and Mr. Skarstrom says my measurements show marked improvement although my heart is still a little weak, and I must be careful in playing football not to get too tired.

Later—

The package of things came this evening and I was delighted to get them. Our room looks very nice now with pictures all round the walls and cups on the mantle-piece.

I am very glad you got me the stock and it was very good of you but the boys are not allowed to wear them up here as the Rector thinks they are too snobbish. I shall be able to wear it however at home and am very pleased to have it. The silver brush will also be nice for my hat. We are having lovely weather now, not too cold or too warm.

I must close now as it is time for my bath (the weekly one!). Many thanks for stamps and post-cards also blotter which is just what I wanted

Ever with loads of love   Your affec son

FRANKLIN

*"You would be surprised to see
how regular my teeth are . . ."*

[GROTON]
OCT. 2, 1898,
SUNDAY.

My dear Mama and Papa

Yesterday I left here at 12 o'clock and got to Boston at two. After buying a few things for the boys, I went to the dentist and got there at three o'clock. Dr. Niles saw at once that the band could do no more good, as the teeth are close together and would not move more unless the band were made longer. He therefore took the band off, but had to cut it at the end, as the cement was too hard and he was afraid my back teeth might come out with it. He then cleaned my teeth and they were not as dirty as I expected. There are several holes that need refilling but he said they would last till Xmas. I was at the dentists just 25 minutes and I told him to send the bill to you at Hyde Park.

I wandered about Boston and got a patent holder to keep pens and pencils in so you need not send me a tray. I took the 4.55 train reaching Ayer at 5.44. Mr. Cushing was there to meet his father and mother so I went up with them. It is a comfort to get the band off, and you would be surprised to see how regular my teeth are. One side is absolutely straight and the other is a. least little bit in but hardly noticeable. I really think it was worth the trouble & expense.—

I forgot to tell you last Sunday that Warren is in the choir again only this year he leads it. I shall try later on to sing tenor but at present am too busy.

It has been oppressively hot for the last three days and this afternoon we had google on the lawn at Mr. G's instead of the customary tea indoors.

By the way, I passed my Greek all right last Wednesday so am now in the V Form with everything clear.

Yesterday while I was away we played the Boston Latin

School in the first football game of the year. Although we are much weakened by the graduation of 9 out of 11 of last year's team our team did splendidly and defeated the Boston's by a score of 17 to 0. I have to get items and the lists of visitors in my work for the Grotonian and so have to work pretty hard. If there are any items by me in the next "Grot" I will send you a marked copy.

The new building is progressing rapidly, and the foundation is nearly half completed. It is very interesting to watch it going up, and there are crowds round it all the time. I was sorry I could not find the key but am pretty sure I gave it to either you or Elsie when I left. The time passes quickly but I very much want to see you again

Ever with dear love to you both your affec son

FDR.

The "new building" mentioned here was the new schoolhouse, built to replace the original building of 1884; it was completed in the autumn of 1899.

∞

"Could the naphtha have been exploded by friction? . . ."

GROTON SCHOOL
OCT. 4, 1898,
TUESDAY.

My dearest Mama and Papa

You cannot imagine how shocked and grieved I was to hear of the loss of the dear "Half-Moon" It came like a thunderbolt in a clear sky and I was completed knocked down. I cannot imagine how it could have happened. I wish you could tell me more details about it and especially how it was that *none of the men were on board?* I did not suppose she would tow unless there was someone to steer her and it was very dangerous to leave her alone, in case she might have broken adrift. Could the naphtha have been exploded by *friction?* There was naturally much friction caused by the high speed driving the water around the walls of the tank at very high speed. Other than this, I can see no immaginable cause for igniting the naptha as the tank was surrounded by water and nothing short of a great blaze all over the boat could set fire to the engine-pipes. Did she sink entirely out of sight and what part of the coast was it on? If I remember aright, I do not think she was insured, but I very much hope Papa had her insured for the voyage. Of course I realize that it is a great loss anyway, and you must of course consider the "New Moon" yours, as, if you sold her, it would help materially towards building a new "Half Moon", and I would be perfectly happy to go with you in the new boat. However, I doubt if you will build a new boat now as I hope you will think more seriously of the trip through Canada next summer!

If the Half Moon does not lie in very deep water you could have her raised for a very moderate sum in comparison with building a new boat, I think.

The weather here is perfectly stifling and today the new boys took their swimming exam, also Warren who did not take it last summer. After he passed, I took him canoeing, his first trip. In the evening it was fearfully hot and we took off everything but our neckties and sizzled. At about 11 o'clock a terrific thunder and rainstorm burst and as all the dormitory windows were open most of our things and bed-clothes were soaked. I woke up with the rain pouring on me and spent the rest of the night at the bottom of the bed.

Wednesday. a.m.

Today it is still pouring and quite chilly.

I think I forgot to tell you that I had got the punctuality prize, another little book, "Bacon's Essays". I was also given the High Kick medal I won last spring.

I have handed in my work for the Grotonian and it will appear in about two weeks. I think I may have to write a story this next month, or else take notes on the football games; either will be hard work, and will require much time, but it will help me to become an editor next year.

I have Mr. Higley this year in Greek and History (Roman) and it is not nearly as pleasant as Mr. G. but I think one learns as much.

I wish you could send me a few post-cards as they are nice to have and I cannot get them here without going to Groton.

The mail is going so I must close, Ever with best love to you both

Your affec son

FRANKLIN D. ROOSEVELT

∞

"My method of painting with iodine and then pairing it . . ."

GROTON SCHOOL
OCT. 6, 1898,
THURSDAY.

My dear Mama and Papa,

Yours of Tuesday & Wednesday and I am sorry about Papa's foot. I wonder if it is a corn, as my method of painting with iodine and then pairing it would I am sure relieve it. It has cleared today after yesterday's rain, and I think we shall have good weather now.

Saturday—

I meant to send this yesterday, but I was sent for by Mrs. Mc.Murray in the evening to play whist and so could not finish.

I have been very gay today—first I went to lunch with Howard Cary, whose mother came up just for the day. She was at Powell's and I had some very good chops for lunch. At about five o'clock I went with some other V formers to afternoon tea with Mrs Peabody and immediately after went to

214

supper with Mrs. Goodwin at Powell's. I am so full of rich food now that I can hardly walk.

This afternoon we played Hopkinson and fully expected to be beaten but by wonderful playing we managed to beat them by a score of 6–0. For the last two years we have tied them, so this year decides the rubber. Warren is captain of one of the teams on the 4th 22, and yesterday he played a little micky team from the village. He was quite badly beaten, 15–0 I think, but he is going to try again.

Your letter telling about Half-Moon has just come, and many thanks for it, and the post-cards. What wretched luck it was that neither Mr. Tams or LeMoine were in when you tried to insure the Half-Moon! I am returning Captain Delano's letter, as you may need it. I do not wonder that you feel discouraged about Campobello, but I much doubt if a certain neighbor of ours will ever be there again to trouble us.

I have written to Aunt Laura but do not know her address, so please send it. By the way has she written anything about the murder of the Empress of Austria?

Sunday.

It is a lovely day and not too warm. Today at lunch Mr. Abbott's dog got into the dining-room, and Warren had to carry him out in his arms! to the amusement of the whole room.

Have you had my lofter mended and have the birds come from Frazar's and Rowland's? Please keep the bills and I will pay you at Xmas. I do not know yet when the holidays begin, but the time is going fast, and seems hard to believe that we have been here three weeks or about $\frac{1}{4}$ of the term. There is a chance of our having a full three weeks at Xmas this year and only ten days at Easter. I would like it as there is so little to do at Easter. I hope you have begun to think of coming up, but I hope you won't come on Thanksgiving as that is only a month before we come home and I have already accepted to go for a long drive with Laurie Rainsford and Wendell Blagden.

I play foot-ball five days out of the six and have played almost every position on the team & so far have escaped serious injury.

Daily theme subjects are daily getting harder to find and we still have them for a month. I hope you will send me some thick pyjamas, as the nights are getting very cold & last night we had frost

Ever with dearest love, I am your affec. son

FDR.

"Captain Delano" was Ephraim Delano of New Bedford, a cousin. Empress Elizabeth of Austria, wife of Franz Josef and mother of the ill-starred Crown Prince Rudolf, was assassinated Sept. 10, 1898. She was stabbed on a Geneva quay by an Italian anarchist named Lucheni, who struck her in the breast with a sharp file as she was on her way to board a lake steamer. The "lofter" was a golf club corresponding to a niblick.

∽

"I wish you could bring me a new pair of yellow high shoes . . ."

GROTON SCHOOL
OCT. 11, 1898,
TUESDAY.

My dearest Mama and Papa

Yours of Sunday came last night and I am delighted you are coming up and going to bring Helen and Miss Froment. This year this St. Mark's game is on a Wednesday, November the 2nd so I do not think you had better come then as I could not see much of you. You could come, however, for Sunday the 30th October or better the 6th of November. I am crazy to see you again and am looking forward to your visit.

I am taking milk every evening at 8.15, so you need not

worry and I also take a drink of water at recess in the morning, 10.15 and whenever I can at other times between meals. We play foot-ball five days in the week, but I have not once been much out of breath or too tired.

When you decide what day you are coming write me, and I will get some rooms at either Powell's or Whitney's but I think Whitneys less crowded this year; also please mention the number of rooms you want.

I wish you could bring up when you come some old pillow that you do not want, as Hugh Minturn has been moved out of our room, and taken his pillows with him. We have in his place a boy named Andrew Robeson—the change is *not* agreeable.

I am going into parlor, nearly every time now, as I belong again to a whist set, with Edmund, DuPont and Mrs. Mac.-Murray.

I am very anxious to see the new butler Pewder, what a funny name, and also the wonderful housemaid. I wonder how Calder gets on with the new crowd? and if she will stay or follow Anderson.

I wish you could bring me when you come a new pair of yellow high shoes, heavy ones for winter as the ones I had last year are rather too tight for me now.

We are to play Worcester Academy tomorrow, and are sure to be beaten as they have a wonderful team and play Harvard and Yale

Ever with dearest love to you both   I am your affec son,

Franklin D. Roosevelt

Miss Froment was his half-niece Helen Roosevelt's governess. His whist partners included Henry F. Du Pont, Groton 1899, a member of the Delaware Du Pont family into which his son, Franklin D. Roosevelt, Jr., later married.

∽∾

*"There is supposed to be one
bottle for every year of the
school . . ."*

My dearest Mama and Papa

On Wednesday we played Worcester Academy and expected
to be disastrously defeated. We are all delighted with the result, which really means a victory for, 6–6. Their team aver-
aged 15 pounds more to the man and in spite of this we held
them well and made it a tie.

Yesterday was proclaimed a half-holiday, as the School's
Birthday falls on Saturday (tomorrow) and we were given the
holiday yesterday instead

After school in the morning I played golf with Howard
Cary. In the afternoon I took Warren out for a canoe trip up
the rapids in the Squannacook. It is only the second time he
has been in a canoe and was rather alarmed at the rapids, but
when we shot them on the way back he was much delighted.
There was not much danger in it although two other boys
upset near us.

I enclose a cutting about Jernigan which I think may interest you.

You must have had a lovely time going to Lake Mohonk
and I would have given anything to have gone with you. The
Pells must have been awfully sorry to hear about the Half
Moon. I wonder which two horses you took on the trip?

The pyjamas came last night, and I think they are very nice.
I will begin wearing them in about a week, but I think we
shall have more warm weather, although it is cold now. There
is no hurry about my winter flannels as I am still quite warm.
Tomorrow is the Birthday and in the afternoon we shall have
a game between the graduates & the eleven, and in the eve-

ning a grand fête. The fifth form are to sing the usual song in the dining room and we have practised for it:

> "Fifteen blue bottles a-hanging on the wall (twice re-
>   peated)
> Take one blue bottle from the bottles on the wall,
> And there are 14 blue bottles a-hanging on the wall
> Fourteen blue bottles a-hanging on the wall etc."

and so on down to "no blue bottles." There is supposed to be one bottle for every year of the school—Will tell you all about it on Sunday

In haste

FDR

The Reverend Prescott F. Jernegan was a promotion-minded gentleman who, in 1897, had formed a concern known as the Electrolytic Marine Salts Company, for the purpose of extracting gold and silver from the ocean. Stock was issued at $1 a share, and attracted thousands of investors—to the tune of approximately a million-dollar capitalization. A processing plant, employing over 600 men, was begun at Lubec, Maine. With the presentation at the United States Assay Office, shortly afterward, of a genuine gold brick ostensibly derived from the boundless deep, stock in the Marine Salts Company was quoted at $2. a share and higher. Then, on July 23, 1898, it became known that the Rev. Jernegan, vice-president and general manager of the company, had sailed for France with his wife and son, using the name of Louis Sinclair. He was understood to have taken along with him $200,000. in United States bonds, recently purchased. *Sic transit aurum mundi.* Since Lubec is but a few miles across the water from Campobello Island, the Roosevelt family undoubtedly had observed the operations of the company the preceding summer. It was a custom for the fifth form to sing the "Blue Bottle" song on the School Birthday, and diminutive Mr. Billings invariably led the singing, in a most vigorous and dynamic fashion.

*"Many jokes were afterwards
made on various masters . . ."*

My dearest Mama and Papa,

Yesterday morning it was raining, but cleared by 11 so we
played football in the mud and slush. After lunch I played
golf until 5 o'clock, when we dressed and had bread and butter
for tea. We then had evening school and at 8 o'clock went
to the dining-room for the banquet. First came stewed oysters,
very good, then most delicious chicken salad—I took three
helps and am still alive. Then came ice-cream, after which the
V form sang the "Blue Bottles" It went very well and their
was much applause. Many jokes were afterwards made on
various masters, and we then adjourned to the library. Mr.
Jefferson sang several good songs and also the glee club, consisting of about the whole choir, among them Warren. Mr.
Higley and Nutter performed on the p.forte. Then Mr. Gardner read his poem—the event of the evening—and everyone
was convulsed with laughter as there were jokes on almost
everyone.

After this we sang the school-hymn and toddled off to bed.
I could hardly get up this morning I was so sleepy.

This morning I saw Mr. Amory Lawrence after church and
he said he enjoyed his visit very much. There are quantities
of people up here now and nearly two dozen graduates. Coster
Wilmerding said he saw you in the Grand Central Station
about a week ago. The Grotonian is coming out next Friday
and I *may* have something in it. Next month I think I shall
write a story for it. It is lovely to think of seeing you soon
again, but I have not yet heard what day you are coming, and
so have not engaged rooms. I think there will be no difficulty,
however, as it is not a very full time.

I wish you could bring when you come the big double

Photos of Papa, that I used to have. We are going to have our lounge enlarged as it to [is] too small to lie on comfortably.

I must close now as the mail is going.

Ever with dear love to you both I am your affec. son

FRANKLIN D ROOSEVELT

~~

"The trouble is that . . . every-
thing must have some point to it . . ."

My dearest Mama and Papa

Yours of Friday and Sunday both here and I am so delighted you are coming soon and I have engaged rooms for you at the Powells. I took three for the 4th but if you need more let me know. All the rooms for the game on the 2nd have been taken at both houses so Brother Rosy & Helen could not come for it.

Warren and I are delighted that Muriel is coming too.

It was too bad Papa's visit to Pellwood was cut short, and that you could not go to Tuxedo, but it must have been lovely driving.

8c. is I think the right number for my shoes as that is the number of my present black shoes.

I am so glad Papa's foot is better, and that he got over his cold all right.

We are all much excited over the St. Marks game, now only two weeks away and I think we should do well if we play as we did against Worcester. Unfortunately several fellows have been laid up—one with water on the knee and another with a sprained arm, but I think the latter will get all right. The team I am on may play the 2nd eleven of the Groton High School next Saturday, and if we do it will be hard work as they are much heavier than we.

I wonder if you are coming on in the car? I rather fancy

you are as you are bringing Muriel and Helen and several maids.

It is too bad that Calder is leaving you and I think she is an awful fool to do so. I hope you will get a new maid who is nice, and also that Peter is nice and *clean* a great improvement over Anderson at least.

Daily themes will end just before you get here, and so far I have managed to get subjects and fair marks. The trouble is that one must write on entirely *original* subjects and everything must have some point to it.

The mail is going & so must I.

Ever with lots of love to you both

FDR.

"Pellwood" was the home of the Alfred Pells at Highland Falls, N. Y. The Groton visit of Mrs. James Roosevelt was to be by private railroad car, not by automobile.

∽

"I wish you could bring a bottle of polish and a few old rags . . ."

GROTON SCHOOL
OCT. 19, 1898,
WEDNESDAY.

My dear Mama and Papa,

Your letter from 10 West 43rd just here and I am so sorry you were knocked down by the horrid bicycle. I would have given anything to have been there, as the bicyclist would have been the jarred party instead of you, and he would have found out that I took a few boxing-lessons last winter. I am very glad you were not much hurt, and that you were close to Cousin Bammie's house. I think the man deserved penal servitude for life.

I think it very good of you to get me a new club. It came last night and I think it is a perfect beauty and I like it much better than the old one. I had no idea that you would get me a new one, as I *could* get on all right without it.

The shoes also came last night and many thanks for them. They are a perfect fit and just what I want for winter up here. The yellow shoes are always made black and spoiled by the school polish, so I wish that when you come you could bring me a bottle of good polish and a few old rags, to clean them with.

The monthly marks came out today and I am glad to say I got a B. As Krumbhaar and Rainsford also got B's & nobody got A I may have been near the top, but I think I was third or fourth. I do not think I was put back much by Scarlet fever, in fact in some things I am ahead. I think I led the form all right in German, as all my marks were 10 with the exception of one 9.

I think I forgot to thank you for the Graphic and the "Weeklies in my last letter, and they were very acceptable to me as well as many others.

It is raining hard today so we were not able to play football. So far I have managed to keep reasonably uninjured my only casualties were having my wind knocked out twice and a kick over the appendix, which may result rather fatally.

Thursday.

Yours of yesterday came this morning and many thanks for the addresses, but you did not enclose the five cent stamp. I have one, however, so you need not send any. As I wrote you on Tuesday, I have engaged three rooms at Mrs. Powells for the 4th till the 7th.

Taddy and I are much excited and amused over the new arrival at 689! It [I] am glad it is a boy and I suppose we shall hear of nothing else for many years to come! I fear Helen & James will be rather left in the cold!

I have two themes to write tonight so must close now.

Ever with dearest love to you both I am your affec son

FRANKLIN D. ROOSEVELT

Theodore Roosevelt's sister Anna ("Cousin Bammie") was always very close to the family of James Roosevelt Roosevelt. The latter's wife, Helen Astor, died while he was First Secretary at the United States Embassy in London, and Anna Roosevelt went over to act as his hostess and take care of the motherless Helen and Taddy—a warm-hearted gesture which at the time occasioned some lifting of eyebrows. It was at the Embassy that Anna met Lt.-Comdr. W. Sheffield Cowles, then naval attache, and shortly afterward married him. At the time of this letter they were living at 689 Madison Avenue in New York, and the "new arrival" referred to was their only child, W. Sheffield Cowles, Jr.

∽

"I think it will do Capt. Mitchell
good to go to sea! . . ."

GROTON SCHOOL
OCT. 23, 1898,
SUNDAY.

My dearest Mama and Papa,

Your note of Thursday came yesterday, and I am sorry neither Muriel nor Helen are coming up. However I will be able to see more of you and I am wild to have you come.

I have not got Mearns "Birds of the Hudson Highlands" but for several years have tried to get it, as it is very good. In fact I wrote to Dr. Mearns myself but he could not let me have a copy. He was I believe a great friend of Mr. Arthur Pell as he mentions Mr. P. in another pamphlet I have of his, "The Vertebrate fauna of the Highlands."

Our team did not play the High School yesterday, as we had three of our players hurt, so the other team played them and won easily. In the afternoon we played Harvard '99 the Seniors, and although the field was horribly muddy and wet we succeeded in tieing them o—o. The St. Marks game is now only a little over a week away, and we are much excited. I think it will be very close and one cannot tell at all which side will win. Two of our fellows are laid up but one *may* be able to play.

Monday. a.m.

I forgot to send this this morning & will do so now.

Papa's letter of Saturday just here and many thanks for it. It confirms what I thought from the first, that the tank did not explode, and that the men should at least have been on watch. Many thanks for sending the canvass for the "New Moon." I think it will do Capt. Mitchell good to go to sea!

We are having lovely weather now & I hope it will continue. On Wednesday we are to play Pomfret and I think we will beat them all to pieces.

Ever with lots of love   Yours

F.D.R.

Please bring up a little vaseline when you come.

Edgar Alexander Mearns was an army surgeon and a famous naturalist and collector of the time. He was a prolific author of articles on animals and birds; the pamphlet mentioned here must have indeed been a rarity, for it is not even catalogued by the Library of Congress.

∽∽

*"I was amused at the account of
Teddy's lecture . . ."*

GROTON SCHOOL
OCT. 26, 1898,
WEDNESDAY.

My dearest Mama and Papa,

Yours of Sunday here and you will be pleased to hear that the foot-ball season is almost over and we only have to play a few days more.

This afternoon we played Pomfret, and as the field was a

mass of puddles and mud neither side scored. If it had been a dry day we would have won all right, but with the rain and mud it was impossible to make long runs. Our team, however, is much laid up and we are much afraid for next Wednesday. I will telegraph you the result in the afternoon.

Many thanks for the Graphics and N.Y. Tribune I was amused at the account of Teddy's lecture and that neither B. Rosy nor Mr. N. would go.

Thursday.

Yours from town of Wednesday has come, & I was sorry to hear about Papa's foot, but trust it is much better now.

You need not worry in the least about me, as I have never been better in my life and have not had a vestige of a cold. The reason I asked for the vaseline was that most of the skin is off my arm, but it is healing rapidly.

I wish you could bring up my report for me to see. I wrote to Mr. Dumper last week, and was surprised not to have heard from him before.

I am very anxious to see the new apartment in town and especially *my* room.

This morning in French class (the V *A*) Miss Louise Cushing read to us from Athalie. You know she took the part of Athalie last year in Boston and today it was too delightful as she *almost* acted it out, hardly using the book at all.

It will be lovely seeing you next week

Ever with love & hurry (awful writing)

FDR

The "lecture" which James Roosevelt Roosevelt and Thomas Newbold refused to attend was a speech by Theodore Roosevelt, who was then nearing the end of his successful campaign for the governorship of New York State, borne along by a wave of Rough Rider popularity. The "new apartment" was still at 10 West 43rd, in the Renaissance Hotel. Louisa Cushing was a sister of Grafton Cushing.

"I have been practising on the
mandolin quite a good deal . . ."

[GROTON]
OCT. 30, 1898,
SUNDAY.

My dearest Mama and Papa,

Both yesterday [? and today] it has rained; yesterday being the eighth consecutive half-holiday on which it has rained. The result is that the regular foot-ball field is a mass of mud and slush, so we are to play the St. Marks game on another field. I spent all of yesterday afternoon in the rain digging out rocks and rolling and marking out with lime the new field. As I played foot-ball the same morning and sprained two fingers, I feel rather done up today.

I have been practising on the mandolin quite a good deal, and find that I did not do it right at Campobello at all. I did not understand the tremulo at all and it takes a good deal of practise to master it.

I saw Charlie Lovering today, he is up here staying with the Lawrences'.

Mrs. Minturn is also up here, but I have not had a chance to speak to her yet. Jack plays against St. Marks on Wednesday, but his mother, does not want to stay, as she is afraid he will be hurt!

I think Lyman will come up, as he is in the IV Form. I will show him all over the school, but it will be horrid if we dont win. You will find me very glum if we lose and just the opposite if we win. At any rate it will be a hard-fought battle and the chances are a little in St. Marks favor. Many thanks for the tube of vaseline. It is yellow, but will do alright for my arm. We are going to have our sofa enlarged as it is too small for comfort, besides being triangular. I have not yet heard what train you are coming by on Friday but hope to hear tomorrow. Will write Tuesday a line.

Ever with haste

FDR

"You need not worry about the floss-silk . . ."

[GROTON]
NOV. 1, 1898,
TUESDAY.

My dearest Mama and Papa,

You will be surprised to hear that Warren got a telegram last night saying that Aunt Kassie and Hiram Price are coming up here today, and are to stay over the St. Marks. game. By great good luck they secured one room at Powell's which was given up by someone else.

Yours of Sunday came last night and you need not worry about the floss-silk. I use it every day double but even with that I think my teeth are not quite so straight as at first. My hands get in pretty bad condition playing football, but I try do [to] clean them thoroughly at least once a week. If it is no trouble and perfectly safe I should very much like to see Mearn's pamphlets when you come up, and I will write to thank Mr. Pell

I will ask two boys for lunch on Satur'day & two for tea.

It is lovely to think of seeing you on Friday; I will be at Powell's to meet you at 6.45. You must do just as you like about coming to Parlor, but I fancy you will feel rather tired, and besides you can come on Sunday night. I am afraid you just miss seeing Aunt Kassie, but it is much nicer having you alone. I will telegraph tomorrow after the game, and am almost crazy with excitement.

My team plays almost every day and I am a little banged up, especially my hands, on which two fingers are dislocated.

Ever with lots of love and excuse a wretched pen. Affec—

FDR

The telegram after the St. Mark's game is not available, but the score is: Groton 11, St. Mark's 6—fortunately for his peace of mind, one would imagine.

"I suppose the best thing to do
is to get rid of him ..."

GROTON SCHOOL
NOV. 10, 1898,
THURSDAY.

My dear Mama and Papa,

Yours of Wednesday just came, and I was sorry to hear about
Mike, but I suppose the best thing to do is to get rid of him.
The Graphics also came, and I was delighted to get [them], but
have had no chance yet to look at them, as I have had to write
a quantity of items for the "Grotonian".

Today it is pouring so there is no foot-ball, and tomorrow
will be positively the last time I think.

Many thanks for the three ties you sent; they will do very
well until Xmas and I do not want any more.

I have written to the upholsterer at Ayer about our cushion,
but have not yet heard how much it would cost.

Yesterday I played golf in both the morning and afternoon,
first with Robeson and then with Mr. Woods. I am not playing as well as as [at] Campo, but I have improved a good deal
since I came up here.

Thanksgiving is only two weeks away & we are all looking
forward to it.

You did not tell me if you got your umbrella you left at Mrs
Lawrence's. If you did not I will get it on Sunday.

I am afraid you had a rainy day in N.Y today & I hope you
did not take cold.

Ever with dear love to you both   Your affec son
                    FRANKLIN D ROOSEVELT

"Mike" was one of the family dogs, a setter.

∽∽

*"We were all wild with delight
when we heard of Teddy's election . . ."*

My darling Mama and Papa,

We were all wild with delight when we heard of Teddy's
election, and I think he must be much pleased. On Tuesday
afternoon we heard a report that Van Wyck had won, but
when we went to bed, we heard the true result, and the whole
dormitory went mad. How splendid that even Hyde Park gave
him a majority of 81. I think Papa and Mr. Rogers must have
worked pretty hard to have such a good result.

Mrs. Rogers did not come today, I think the journey was too
long for her, and as it has begun to sprinkle a little I did not
go to the Lawrence's this afternoon!

I have smashed my bottle of tooth-powder so I wish you
could send me some more. I wish you would also send my
skates, the ones that do *not* have to be screwed on permanently, as I have no shoes for them. The pair I want will need
to have the heal part straightened, and they also need sharpen-
ing, but you can have both done at Stanton's. At the same
time I wish you could send my hockey-stick, the one with the
black tip.

I do not need the blue suit, I am quite certain, as my winter flannels, which I put on today are very heavy, and besides
I have my overcoat for going to church.

Many thanks for the "Tribune" & "Post." I was very glad to
get them, and the editorials are so good. Is it not strange about
the finding of the Maria Teresa, and that England is also trying to get her? I only hope we can have her after all this
trouble we have taken.

I am very glad you found the key of my closet and that you
are transfering the birds. I wish you could write to Rowland

again about the Sparrow-Hawk, as I very much wanted it, and it is quite rare. The monthly marks are coming out in a day or so, & I hope I shall have a B

Ever with lots of love to you both I am your affec. son

F.D.R.

Theodore Roosevelt's unsuccessful opponent was Augustus Van Wyck, a brother of the mayor of New York, Robert A. Van Wyck. Although James Roosevelt was a lifelong Democrat, blood in this case proved thicker than politics, and he and Archibald Rogers promoted T.R.'s candidacy. The latter carried the state by 25,000; his Dutchess County plurality was 2664. Stanton's was a Poughkeepsie store. As for the *Infanta Maria Theresa,* she was Cervera's flagship at the Battle of Santiago on July 3, 1898. Hit and badly damaged, she was beached; later she was repaired and refloated by American engineers, and in November of 1898 taken in tow for Hampton Roads. En route she encountered a heavy storm, and the crew, expecting her to sink, abandoned her. She was reported foundered, but actually she drifted to Cat Island, a British possession. There ensued a dispute between the British authorities at Nassau and the American consul as to possession, but finally the vessel was found to be a hopeless wreck, and abandoned.

〜〜

"There are several features that seem to me objectionable . . ."

GROTON SCHOOL
NOV. 16, 1898,
WEDNESDAY.

My dearest Mama & Papa,

Many thanks for yours of Sunday, enclosing the interesting designs of the yawl. I think them quite good, but there are several features that seem to me objectionable. 1st I think the cockpit is altogether too small, only seven feet I make it by measurement, and this must contain the helmsman too. 2nd the galley is unnecessarily large and the forecastle rather small for 3 men. The model I like very much, but you know my dislike of yawls, and how much more handsome and ship-shape she would be if rigged as a cutter!

The pictures and the lovely pillow came yesterday and I was delighted to get them. We have hung all the pictures, and put two flags, one American and one the School flag over the fire-place. The cushion I think is very pretty and it brightens the room very much.

The price for our cushion will be $5.50 or about $1.80 apiece, and it will be finished in about a week.

The cravats from Brooks have also come; they are very nice ones, but I shall save them as I do not need them yet.

I am so glad the new servants are a success and that discord has not yet broken out, but still you must miss Elsie and Calder and Anderson very much.

The watch has not yet come from Benedict, and as a result I fear I got a lateness yesterday. It does not matter however, as I must get one sooner or later this term. On Monday I received a banana all wrapped up in a box from Aunt Annie, and a note with it explaining. The banana I suppose was good, but both Warren and I make numerous faces over it! However, I shall write to Aunt A. praising it to the skies. On the golf course yesterday I met Mr & Mrs. Lawrence, and by great luck got an invite to dinner on Thanksgiving.

Thursday.

Yours of Tuesday just come, and I think you had better send Papa's No. 11 Skates, as I am sure the 14½ would be too large. Calisthenics began today and I think my running drawers and *sleeveless* jersey are at home. If so I wish you could send them as soon as possible. I am so glad you moved my birds and I will send you the key of the cabinet tomorrow. I enclose a slip from the Scientific American; it proves that you are always correct in your theories! The monthly marks came out on Wednesday, and I am glad to say I got a B. As several

fellows who generally got a B got C's, I think I must have been
quite near C. It is pouring today, and much warmer
  Ever with dear love to you both

F.D.R.

I am trying to improve my writing.

The boat under discussion here was a replacement for the
Half-Moon. Benedict, Delolme was a jewelry store on Church
Street in New York. The Nov. 13th monthly report showed
A's in Geometry, French, German, and Sacred Studies; B's in
Latin, Greek, and History; and C's in both English Literature
and English Composition. The languages he had learned with
his governesses as a child were, as usual, keeping up his grades.
The Rector's remark was: "Good."

∽∽

*"I think that at last Harvard
has waked up . . ."*

GROTON SCHOOL
NOV. 20, 1898,
SUNDAY.

My dear Mama and Papa,
  For the last three days it has rained here, but today we have
fine weather at last. Yours from N.Y came last night. I think
you are quite right to call J.R.R.Jr. Rosy, as he is known by
that name up here, and probably will be after he leaves here.
  Last night we were wildly excited over the Harvard-Yale
game & also the Freshmen game between H. & Y. I think that
at last Harvard has waked up. It makes the victory doubly
satisfactory to us as the Harvard Captain, Ben Diblee is a
Grotonian and also three other Groton boys were on the
Harvard team, and one on the Yale. We also had a number on
the Freshmen, and in all 12 out of 44 players were from
Groton, pretty good we think.
  Tomorrow we are to start a golf tournament, and the pre-

liminary round is to pick out the best 16. I may possibly get in, but I shall have to work hard for it, anyway.

We have only three weeks before the exams, and next week I shall begin studying out of school to review the work.

Monday—

I did not have time to finish this this morning so will do so now.

The watch came from N.Y this morning and also your postal. The watch looks beautifully, and is very well cleaned, but I fear you will have quite a bill to pay. I will be very careful of it, and it should not require to be repaired for many years to come.

By the way the lateness I got last week was not recorded, for some lucky reason, so I am still free from them. Last Saturday I took afternoon tea with Mr. Cushing; our form is probably going to do so every week.

I shall be very gay this week with Thanksgiving-day and a visit from (Brother) Rosy and Helen. Warren is going to drive with three other babies in the morning, and is to lunch with the Webb's (Watson Webb's people) on their private-car at the Groton Station

I wish you could please pay the enclosed bill, and I will refund you at Xmas. Also I wish you could send me last months report after you get it.

Many thanks for the box of tooth powder   It was necessary and welcome

Ever with best love to you both   Your affec son

F.D.R.

Benjamin H. Dibblee was in the class of 1895 at Groton; his Harvard team defeated Yale 17-0. The score of the Freshman game was 7-4.

〰

"I have a digestion like 10 oxen . . ."

[no salutation]

The golf-tournament has been going on for several days and I am glad to say I am now among the best sixteen. We are to continue on Friday. There is not much to say, but I will write on Friday morning all about tomorrow. We leave for our drive at 8.30 a.m., Wendell Blagden, Laurie Rainsford and myself. I don't intend to eat or drink (!) too much, but I have a digestion like 10 oxen. I got a very pretty red cushion from Muriel yesterday & will thank her soon. The skates also came from Von d. Linden, but they are very small for me now. However they will do till Xmas.

Ever yours

Too bad about Lyman   I will write to *him*.

F.D.R.

This was written on a U.S. penny-postcard. Vonderlinden's is a Poughkeepsie store.

~~

"Turkey, ham, pies (three kinds),
a whole roast pig, popped-corn . . ."

GROTON SCHOOL
NOV. 25, 1898,
FRIDAY.

My dearest Mama and Papa,

You will be pleased to know that I am still in the land of the living and just as well as on Wednesday. To begin at the beginning: Yesterday morning we woke up at 6.30 and had breakfast at 7. The day was at first fine, but soon clouded over. We started, Wendell Blagden, Laura [Laurie] Rainsford and I in a buckboard with two fast horses, at 8.45. First we drove to the village and bought crackers etc. etc. etc. then we drove to two cider-mills and at the second we got a 2 gallon jug of delicious sweet cider. Soon after that it began to sprinkle and rained for the rest of the day. We drove on however, past Pepperell to within 3 miles of the New Hampshire line, and about 12 miles from the School We returned, getting back at 1 o'clock and not at all wet. We then went in to a glorious Thanksgiving dinner, turkey, ham, cranberry-sauce, vegetables, pies (three kinds) ice-cream, pudding, fruit, etc. I just managed to stagger out of the room, and then lay on my sofa for some time to regain consciousness. I then put on rubber-boots and a sweater and in the rain played a foursome of golf with the two Rainsford & Wendell Blagden. We came home at 5, and made some hot cocoa and popped-corn, so we caught no colds. At 7.10 Mr. Billings, Mr. Ayrault and I left for the Lawrence's in a closed carriage, we were the only people from the school. We sat down 19 at table, among others the silly youth Phillip Wadsworth, who visited *Betty* Porter last summer!

We had every imaginable thing for dinner, including a whole roast pig and canvass-backs etc. I took only sweet cider, as I feared champagne might muddle me after so much grub. After dinner we talked for a while and left at 9.45. On our return we had prayers and sent the boys (about 30 of them left) to bed. As there were only four of us left at Brooks House Mr. Billings took us in to faculty-supper, quite an honor, although there were only three masters and a few graduates here—we got to bed at 5 minutes after midnight, and found the rain turned to snow. The next morning we rose at eight and found about two inches on the ground. The other boys returned at eleven & school began again. By the way, the night before, while we were in at faculty supper, the boys in Mr. Woods dormitory raided the other dormitories. Edmund and two others were caught and have been moved down to the kid table and put on bounds for the rest of the term.—

On Saturday afternoon I played my first contest after qualifying for the tournament. My opponent, Billy Burnham played very evenly with me, so that at the end of the 17th hole we were even. I luckily won the 18th by one stroke, and so one the match. The[re] are now only 8 players left, and I am next to play Jack Waterbury the Senior Prefect. However, I doubt if we can finish the match for a long time, as it began to snow hard last night and this afternoon the snow is several feet deep, and tremendous drifts. Many thanks for Papa's letter and the report. I am surprised at the marks, but you need not expect such good ones next month, as exams will take up much time. By the way it has been definitely decided that we are to return on Friday Dec. 23rd only two days before Xmas. I am very glad we are to come home so late as it makes the winter term shorter, and gives more time after Xmas. I will write to Laura for the Cotillion. Too bad about Lyman taking cold again; I will write to him but have not yet had time. It was very nice seeing Br'er. Rosy & Helen up here. I went over after breakfast and again to lunch. As the snow was so deep we had church in the School-room, but Br. Rosy & Helen & Miss F. [Froment] could not come over until it abated about 5. p.m. when they went over the school & saw our studies. The cartoon of Teddy you sent me is very amusing; is it your office at the D.&H. [Delaware & Hudson RR.] he is at in the picture? I wish you could send my toboggan cap as it is bitterly cold now. I return the report & ever with dear love to you both I am your affec. son

F.D.R.

"Faculty supper" was a frequently observed custom—several members of the sixth form, perhaps a master or two, and any visiting graduates, were invited into the Peabodys' own dining room in Hundred House, around nine o'clock in the evening. There they "found" their own snack, sat around informally, and usually departed by ten. The "Cotillion" was an annual event held at the Orange Country Club in New Jersey. Warren Delano III, Laura's father, had a house there. It was at one of these dances that F.D.R. first "met" (disallowing childhood encounters) Anna Eleanor Roosevelt, who often stayed in Orange with her cousins, the Henry Parishes.

*"He was covered with rice by
the V and VI forms . . ."*

My dear Mama and Papa,

Yours of Sunday did not get here until Tuesday evening,
so I suppose it was delayed by the snow. Everything is covered
up here, and the drifts are enormous, bigger than any we had
last winter. From all accounts you must have had a pretty big
storm at Hyde Park. Is it not awful about the loss of the
Portland, and all the coasting vessels? I only hope the New
Moon got through it all right at Campobello.

I am very glad my Sparrow-hawk came from Rowland and
many thanks for sending for it, and also for paying my A.O.U.
subscription.

I think I wrote you that we are coming home on the 23rd
instead of the 17th. Personally I am glad of it, as we shall have
more time after Xmas when everything is going on. I think I
had better go to N.Y. straight from here and do my shopping,
and then return to Hyde Park on Saturday at noon.

I think it would be very nice to have the cousins for a few
days say the week right after Xmas, if I do not have to attend
the Orange dance and other shindies then. I wish you could
let me know the dates of all the various shindies, so that we
could arrange when to have the people at Hyde Park. As you
say, we can double up with ease for a few days, and I should
think we could easily have ten people, at one time.

Yesterday morning it snowed again for about two hours, and
in the afternoon I went for a long walk on snowshoes through
the woods. By the way, last Monday Mr. Sturgis came back
after an absence of over a week and announced his engagement—! to Miss Barnes of N.Y. He was covered with rice by
the V and VI Forms and we compelled him to make a speech!
He was awfully bashful, but he soon got over it, especially

after he was again raided by the rest of the school! I suppose the dirty squaws will be pleased to hear of it! We do not know when the wedding is to take place but suppose it will be quite soon, as they have been engaged a long time.

Thursday—

It is lovely to think of coming home in three weeks, but the exams will be between now & then. I am to begin working for them pretty soon, probably next Monday.

There was a little rather poor skating this morning, but I did not go. The end of the golf-tournament has been postponed indefinitely, and as there are only 8 of us left in it, I do not suppose we can play it off till the spring. I wrote to ask Laura for the dance last Monday. It is too bad about Lyman having another cold. I am afraid he will get weak lungs or something if he does not stop having sore-throats.

The mail is going in five minutes so I must close.

Ever with best love to you both   I am your affectionate son

FRANKLIN D. ROOSEVELT

The heavy snow noted in this and the previous letter was part of a wild blizzard which affected the whole of the Eastern Coast, tieing up communications, causing many deaths and the loss of a number of ships at sea. The *Portland* was an eight-year-old sidewheel steamer of 1517 tons, owned by the Boston and Portland Steamship Co. She left Boston for Portland on Nov. 28, her captain judging that he could accomplish the trip before the expected storm broke. He was mistaken, however, and the ship sank off Cape Cod with a loss of all on board, one hundred and eighteen persons. S. Warren Sturgis' fiancee was a sister of James Barnes, who wrote innumerable books on American history, biographies of Farragut, Perry, and others.

*"I wish you would think up
some decent partner for me . . ."*

GROTON SCHOOL
DEC. 4, 1898,
SUNDAY.

My dearest Mama and Papa,

Yours from N.Y. and the note from Hyde Park have come, and also the toboggan cap.

We have had quite cold weather since the storm, and the ice on the pond is about five inches thick; it is no good, however, except in a few patches, but is very rough snow ice. Yesterday afternoon I skated for the first time and had an exciting game of hockey, on a very small clear patch of the big pond.

I have not yet had an answer from Laura about the Orange dance, but I suppose she can do it. I wish you would think up some decent partner for me for the N.Y. dance, to which I suppose I will be invited, so that I can get somebody early, and not get palmed off on some ice-cart like the [name deleted] girl!! Who do you think it would be nice to have at Hyde Park with the crowd? You had better send me a list first and I will try to add to it if necessary.

Last night Mr. Codman sang several very good songs to the school, and he has a very fine voice He sang up here about a month ago.

The Grotonian came out last week so you will probably get one soon at home. I got several items in, but my story is not yet completed (!) There is no particular hurry, however, as there is precious little chance of its being accepted. Today it has rained and snowed all afternoon, so I could not go to the Lawrence's to pay my party call, but I will go sometime this week, as they are away for a fortnight, and I would not object to missing them. You will see by the Grotonian that I have been elected into the Missionary Society. We had my first meeting tonight, and a splendid talk by a Mr. Batt, the chap-

lain of the Mass. reformatory at Concord. It was very interesting   all about the fine things they do for the prisoners.
Monday. 8. a.m.

It rained hard last night so this a.m much of the snow is
gone and bare patches are appearing here and there. The mail
is going in ten minutes so—good-bye—Ever your affectionate
son

F.D.R.

Oscar Fay Adams remarks (1903): "A feature of Groton life
concerning which a word may be said is a Missionary Society,
which, in addition to holding religious services in various
localities in the surrounding district, is largely interested in
the work of the Boys' Club in Boston, directed by the clergy
of Saint Stephen's Church. Groton men in Harvard at regular
intervals entertain the boys of the club for an evening, and the
Missionary Society assumes the responsibility for the club's
expenses." The Society also established and ran the Groton
School Camp at Squam Lake. The Chaplain of the Massachusetts Reformatory was the Reverend William J. Batt, who
founded the Union Church at West Concord, a non-denomina-
tional parish.

∽∽

"Just a line to say that I am all
mixed up . . ."

GROTON SCHOOL
DEC. 6, 1898,
TUESDAY.

Dearest Ma & Pa—

Just a line to say that I am all mixed up. I got a letter this
morning from Cousin May Soley (enclosed) inviting me to dinner the *28th* the *date of the Dodworth* dance . . . Now your
letter of Sunday says the Orange dance is the *28th also!*

Laura has accepted for the Orange shindy—What is to be
done??! please let me know if I am to accept the Soley invite.
I would not like to miss the Friday Evening class dance as it
is more fun, but I dont see what is to happen—

241

Not much going on now as we have to study hard and all the time.

We come back to school the 10th of January & if you need any to fill out I could ask Howard Cary for a few days—but not unless you think so or need him.

With lots of love   Yours in doubt

FDR

Please let me know Mrs. Soley's address in town so that I can answer *yes* or *no?*

∽∽

"I drew lots and the fateful die
fell on . . ."

Dearest Ma & Pa—

Just a line to thank you for yours of the 6th explaining about the holidays. I promptly answered Mrs. Soleys invitation accepting it, but as I was in a quandary as to whom to ask for the N.Y. dance, and not caring at all, I drew lots and and [sic] the fateful die fell on Mary Newbold, so I wrote at once. I will send the trousers tomorrow to you, and possibly some other things.

On Tuesday we had a half-holiday in honor of Mr. Sturgis' engagement and in the afternoon there was really splendid skating on the pond. I played on the second hockey squad, one higher than last year.

Yesterday as the snow is only in patches we played again on the golf tournament. By great luck I defeated Jack Waterbury the Senior-prefect in a very close and exciting match, so that I have succeeded in getting into the semi-finals or last four fellows. There are now left Archie Brown (who will win almost surely) Mr. Ayrault, Cooper Lord & myself. This morning I played 7 holes of the 18 with Lord, and we are so far even. There is no hope for me, however, as Lord is an excellent player and got the medal for the lowest score. I did not have any idea that I would get into the semi-finals, & have been very fortunate in not having to play any splendid players until now.

I am most terribly busy now with golf and the examinations only a week off. I will write at more length on Sunday when there is more time for better handwriting!

Ever your affec. son

FDR

P.S. I got this invitation (enclosed) yesterday. Is it the one you have accepted? Please answer it or tell me what to do.

FDR

Archibald M. Brown, Groton 1899, later became a prominent New York architect and partner in the firm of Peabody, Wilson and Brown (the Peabody being his classmate Julian). J. Couper Lord was another sixth-former.

∽∾

"How about Eleanor Roosevelt? . . ."

GROTON SCHOOL

DEC. 11, 1898,

SUNDAY.

Dearest Mama and Papa,

More shindies to attend to! The enclosed came last night, and what is to be done about it? If it is the date of the Orange dance (27th) of course I cannot go, but otherwise I might as well. I wish you could either decline or accept it as you think best. If you accept and there is to be a German at it, I think it would be good idea for you to ask Helen for me, for the German. It will save time and it is only two weeks off. [Name deleted] cannot dance at the Dodworth thing, (just as well); so I have written asking Muriel. I don't want to get left with the [name deleted] girl as I did two years ago to my great and

243

everlasting regret! This afternoon I am going to the Lawrence's to leave my card, as they are away from home, and it gives me a good chance.

Yesterday I finished the round of golf with Couper Lord, and although beaten by one stroke I did much better than I had dreamed of. When we began in the morning we had played 13 holes and were even; then I won two holes, but by very hard luck and losing my ball I lost the 16th and 17th hole; we were then again even with one more hole to play. I lost that by one stroke and with it the match. However I got into the semi-finals, and got third place. In the afternoon yesterday I played a hard game of hockey from 2.30 to 5, and then took tea with Mr. Cushing.

It is bitterly cold here today and a hard wind blowing, but I have worn overcoats to church, and been very comfortable in the warm study.

Have you heard anything from Campobello since the big storm, or how the New Moon came out of it? Lots of small yachts were wrecked along the Massachusetts coast, but I fancy Harbor de Lute would be pretty calm in a northeast wind.

By the way I wish you would give me a list of what you both want for Xmas, as I shall not have much time after leaving here and would like to know beforehand. Personally I can think of little but a pair of shoes, a few new shirts etc. and possibly a new golf-bag of a particular kind I have seen.

I am very anxious to see the new man Dammire and hope he will be satisfactory and trustworthy.

I am so glad Aunt Jennie's dear lambs are to be allowed to come and hope Muriel can come too. I cannot think of anyone to get up here, as most of the boys are already engaged that I would like to have, so I hope you will be able to find someone else. How about Teddy Robinson and Eleanor Roosevelt? They would go well and help to fill out chinks.

I believe Taddy has refused all invitations for the holidays and is going for a hunt to the Adirondacks, right after Xmas.

The skating at Hyde Park must be good now, and I wonder if the river is frozen?

Just think of coming home in a little over a week.

No more now & ever with best love   Your affected son

F.D.R.

One of those designated to fill out the house-party chinks was his future wife, mentioned for the first time in these letters. The other, Theodore Douglas Robinson, was the son of Theodore Roosevelt's sister Corinne. He became a member of the New York State Assembly at the same time as F.D.R. was serving as state senator, and later was appointed Assistant Secretary of the Navy under Calvin Coolidge.

*"He wants a Graphophone or a
new saddle or a dog collar . . ."*

GROTON SCHOOL
DEC. 14, 1898,
WEDNESDAY.

Dearest Mama and Papa,

I have been clearing off the pond all morning and skating this afternoon. After skating I took tea with Mr. Billings and it is now six o'clock   Last night the thermometer went to five below zero, and it is still cold, but moderating.

Thursday—

Yours from N.Y just come, and you say nothing about the Street dance, only that you have declined the Appleton one on the 27th. I also got a letter from the [name deleted] brat (!!!) accepting with thanks ! for the 28th & one from Muriel declining with thanks for the 28th. So you see I am all clear for the Dodworth dance but quite in the dark about the Streets'.

It is awfully difficult to think about Xmas presents as I want so few things and have so much already. The kind of golf-bag I wanted has an iron shaft so it can be stuck upright in the ground. However I would prefer choosing one myself in town.

I also would like to have a new pair of waterproof moccasins like the ones I had last Xmas, *unless my old ones are at home.* Any good books are acceptable, I do not get much of a chance to hear of any new ones up here, but they are all welcome. I must get two new golf-clubs this Xmas & a dozen more balls, so that would be acceptable only I should prefer choosing the sticks myself.

About Warren's wishes. I think he wants a *Graphophone* (not *Gramophone*) or a new saddle or a dog collar, chain and whip He has written his wishes to Aunt Kassie so you can find out from her. I think I would much like a holder for letters and note-paper, like the porcelain one on your desk only not of porcelain. You *must* write me both your wishes, or you won't get anything for Xmas!!!!

Ever with best love to you both & with fearful haste   Affec.

FDR

The "shindy" complicating his vacation schedule was given by Mr. and Mrs. William A. Street of New York, who had two daughters, Rosamond and Susan.

∾

"It is more fascinating each year . . ."

GROTON SCHOOL
DEC. 18, 1898,
SUNDAY.

My dearest Mama and Papa,

Just think, only a few days more! This will be my last letter unless I send a note after the result of one or two exams tomorrow. When you go to N.Y. to meet me, I wish you could bring to town an evening shirt, 2 or three of my new kind of collars and one stand-up collar. Also a pair of decent gloves. I am making out a list of the things I shall have to buy, so that it will save time. I am most awfully busy studying for the exams. I may get through all but two: Greek and Latin com-

246

position. In Greek we have Mr. Higley and it is a foregone conclusion that all (except possibly Krumbhaar) will fail.

I would much like you to get some good cider & some *brown sugar* for the holidays if possible, as I shall be both thirsty and hungry after thirteen and a half weeks up here.

I am most horribly busy so I will add more tomorrow.
Monday 8.a.m.

I forgot to say last night that Mr. Peabody's father read all yesterday the "Christmas Carol" of Dickens, as usual. It is more fascinating each year & I would not miss it for the world.

We are to have our Sacred Study exam in half an hour. I ought to pass I think, but am rather shaky on the others.

Will drop you a post card tomorrow morning.

Ever with best love to you both

F.D.R.

∾

"We had English this afternoon, very hard . . ."

[GROTON]
DEC. 20, 1898,
TUESDAY.

[no salutation]

Yours of Sunday did not come last night or today, I wonder what the matter is. I have passed Mathematics with a B, German with an A, and Sacred Studies A.

We had English this afternoon, very hard, & I do not know if I passed. Tomorrow Latin & History, both hard. Will arrive 3.30. Friday.

Ever

F.D.R.

A short penny-postcard. His final fall term average was a B. The English exam mark was a C, with B's in both Latin and History. Christmas vacation followed.

∾

247

GROTON SCHOOL
JAN. 20, 1899,
FRIDAY.

My darling Mama and Papa,

It seems as if I had been here weeks, instead of less than twenty-four hours. Everything is straightened out, my trunk unpacked, my study arranged, and lessons (unhappily) in full swing. My cubicle is four doors further up the dormitory, on the other side, the sunny one. At table I am two from Mr. Gardner, a delightful place, and with Howard Cary on one side.

I unpacked everything this morning, and have missed nothing except my heavy red sweater, but as I may need several other things you had better not send it till you get my next letter, and I can get on very well without it for a time. I have been appointed one of the two head mail-niggers for this term, with Howard Cary as my assistant. For two weeks I attend to the morning mail, then two weeks to the evening and so on. It is rather nice as the two head niggers take breakfast in the Rector's house twice during the term.

My desk now looks very nice, with the lovely red holder and the new blotter and letter opener. I shall save the blotting paper from the old blotter as it is so good.

Sunday. Jan. 22nd.

Yesterday afternoon nearly the whole school drove in barges over to a pond about two miles beyond the village. We had a hard game of hockey and then walked home, but I did not cough once. I am using the spray twice a day, and try to drink water like a fish. I hope you got the drawing-room car ticket and my hurried note all right in N.Y. and enjoyed the opera and did not find the house in flames on your return. Many thanks for your note and the toothbrush. I needed it badly as the one up here, with my sponge and tooth-powder are not to be found anywhere. I think you forgot my calendar that

Ellie gave me; I wish you could send it with the other things, if you don't mind.

We have had lovely weather so far and cold, but today it is a little warmer and looks a bit like snow. I wonder very much if the big ice-boat race has been sailed and if the great Archibald Rogers can still keep the contents of his Tiffany box?!

I enclose the blank for the Sci. Am. which I found here and said I would send. Have you written to Wil. Reed's the Boston people, about your Birthday present to me, the mocassins? Even though it is several days before my Birthday, I should very much like to get the mocassins soon, if you don't mind.

I am working every morning to make up my work but as the English books must be read in ten days I am also working on them.—You will be sorry to hear that on Friday news was received of the death of Mrs. Krumbhaar; the boys went home about a week before, as she had a tumor on the brain. It was cut out successfully but she died from the effects of it. I have written to Ned Krumbhaar.

About half a dozen boys are in the infirmary with colds and grip, the first of a long series this term   I ought to escape, as I shall try to be careful and am taking my C.L.O. regularly.

By a new system, we are to take examinations once a month, instead of only at the end of the term. They will not be so important but will mean really harder work right along. I shall have to work hard if I want to get a B this month as I am a bit behind.

When you send the other things please could you send the little picture of yourself in the little silver heart-shaped frame on my bureau, as I want it to put on my desk here.

Monday a.m.

It is still cold here and I suppose the ice-boating is still good at Hyde Park. I am longing to get your dear Sunday letter today, as I only heard from you with the tooth-brush.

Ever with best love to you both I am your devoted son

FRANKLIN.

The "mail-niggers" were boys appointed to sort the mail as it was received. Ice-boating (prior to the advent of the numerous ice-breakers of today) was a sport enthusiastically pursued by members of the Hudson River and Hyde Park Ice Yacht Clubs. Archibald Rogers' *Jack Frost* was a frequent victor in the championship race, with the result that the silver trophy usually occupied his silver-vault at Tiffany's. The year of this letter, John Aspinwall Roosevelt's *Icicle* managed to defeat the *Jack Frost*. Wm. Read & Sons was a sporting-goods store on Washington Street in Boston. The "little picture of yourself" showed Sara Delano as a girl; it is now included in the Hyde Park memorabilia.

∽∽

"You seem to think I have debts
in the school to pay up . . ."

GROTON SCHOOL
JAN. 24, 1899,
TUESDAY.

My dearest Mama and Papa,

Yours from New York and from Hyde Park on Sunday were most welcome here yesterday. I was so sorry to hear of Uncle Edward Lyman's death, but I fancy the family rather expected it, as he was so old, but he will be a great loss. I suppose you will give up all your engagements now for a little while. It was too splendid, was it not, about the "Icicle" winning the championship and proving her superiority over the "Jack Frost". I gave the description of the race to Edmund to read, and soon after he handed it back without comment to me! Uncle Johnnie must be tickled to death, *almost* as much as about that darling brat. I shall write to him soon.—

You seem to think I have debts in the school to pay up— the only one I had, if that can be called one, was the balls, and as Herman Krumbhaar is away, I will not be able to repay them.

I am glad Foster got the books all right and many thanks for sending his letter. You will be pleased to hear that I've found a Montcalm and Wolfe in the library, and have taken out Vol.2.—I won't have much time to read it for some time, but I will surely finish it as I am much interested.

By the way, I found my red sweater up here in the gymnasium, where I left it last term and forgot all about it, so you needn't worry about about [sic] it.—It is foggy and drizzling today, bad weather for you to be in N.Y. I fear, and I only hope you won't take cold. I am absolutely well altho' many are in the infirmary with colds. The time goes fast, but it is dreary thinking of ten more weeks of it. Confirmation lectures began again this week, and I persuaded Taddy to go to the first. I think he will like going better perhaps after he has been in a few times.

Warren is well, and Edmund; I take the first part of calisthenics & then stop. I am very busy reading the English books— Ever with dearest love to you both, I am your most affec son

FDR.

Edward H. R. Lyman died in Brooklyn on January 20th, at the age of eighty. He had been a partner in the shipping firm of his brothers-in-law, A. A. Low & Brother. The outside reading mentioned here in all probability was Francis Parkman's *Montcalm and Wolfe,* which had been published fifteen years before. In 1913, when F.D.R. was Assistant Secretary of the Navy, he had occasion to quote Parkman in an address entitled "Montcalm's Victory and Its Lesson," which he delivered at Oswego, New York, during the exercises opening Montcalm Park and commemorating Montcalm's victory at Oswego during the French and Indian War. The date was September 30th, the eve of the First World War; F.D.R.'s address concluded as follows: "Conflict, like everything else in modern civilization, is so complicated that preparation is essential. That is why we have our navy, our army and our militias, and that is why some of us think ahead. No one desires war today. We are all striving—army and navy alike— to prevent its occurrence. But no one can guarantee to the

American people that there will be no more war. And until that day comes, the example of Montcalm, and the lessons of the conflict between the French and the British colonies, cannot fail to inspire us to better things."

~~

"The chief news is that poor Charlie Nutter has apendicitis . . ."

My dearest Mama & Papa,

Your dear letters came yesterday and today, one from H.P. one from 10 W. 43rd and one from Orange. I only hope that neither of you caught any cold during that horrid weather, while you were in N.Y. I am all right, absolutely, although boys are succumbing daily. The chief news is that poor Charlie Nutter has apendicitis. He had a bad stomach-ache yesterday, and attributed it to bad pork, but a celebrated surgeon has been sent for and the operation takes place tonight. He is not very sick, and the operation won't be so very serious, but still he will take some time to recover. In the mean time we are to have a temporary master come up from Boston to teach us English, so that we shall lose no time before the exams next June.

The package came safely last night, and many thanks for it. You sent exactly the right things, and *not* Mama's calendar, after all. As I wrote, I found the red sweater just after I sent the letter to you, but the white one may turn out useful, and I shall keep it in my drawer until then. It is nice that the hall floor is finished, and I hope the wood matches the rest. I skated this morning and altho' the ice was quite rough we managed to get in a game of hockey.

Friday—8.a.m.

Mr. Nutter's operation took place at 8 last night, was successful, although the appendix had broken, and he passed a fairly comfortable night.

It seems hardly possible that I've been here a whole week, & the time is going. Ever with dearest love to you both   Ever your affectionate son

F.D.R.

∽

"She is an old coloured lady, living all alone . . ."

GROTON SCHOOL
JAN. 29, 1899,
SUNDAY.

My dearest Mama and Papa,

You will be pleased to hear that Mr. Nutter is getting on very well, and has not had the slightest relapse altho' when removed, the appendix was found to be broken badly. Of course he will not be up for several weeks, and I suppose he will then go away for a change of air. Meanwhile Mr. Gladwin is teaching us English, and although it is easier than with Mr. Nutter, we will not be as well prepared for the Harvard exam next June. Mr. Gladwin also plays the organ, and Mr. Ayrault teaches the choir. The music and choir are rather feeble today, but not bad considering. It is bitterly cold today with a high Westerly wind that goes right thro' one. We all sat in our coats in church this a.m but shivered in spite of it, & the service was cut short in consequence. This afternoon the service is to be in the school-room, where the thermometer has mounted up to almost 50°.

The Missionary Society has appointed Warren Motley and myself as special missionaries to look after Mrs Freeman an old woman near the school. She is an old coloured lady, living all alone, and *84* years old. We payed our first visit to her today, right after church, and talked and gave her the latest news, for nearly an hour. We are to visit her a couple of times a week, see that she has coal water, etc, feed her hens if they need it, and in case of a snow-storm we are to dig her out, & put things ship-shape. It will be very pleasant as she is a dear old thing, and it will be a good occupation for us. I shall take her all my old "Graphics," and any other papers I have.

The Moccassins came last night, but as they were a little too short I am sending them back and shall write for the next size. It is awfully good of you to have given them to me and many, many thanks for them. I can hardly realize that tomorrow I shall be seventeen, and it is perfectly *horrid* being away from you on my Birthday, but it is partly made up for by my lovely long extra holidays.

Herman Krumbhaar came back to school on Friday, but Ned will not be back for several weeks, as his father is all alone, and he does not need to study as much as his elder brother. I have forgotten in each letter to tell you that Kerr Rainsford has not come back this term as he has diphtheria; he had a very light case, and will be back very soon, and the desease did not spread at all.

Yesterday in the morning I played fives, and all afternoon I played hockey hard; the result is that I am most fearfully stiff today and can hardly raise my right arm at all.

The Scientific American came, with the back numbers, yesterday, and I am delighted to get it again. Thank you *ever* so much for subscribing for it. The Graphic came yesterday, and thanks for it also. You have doubtless seen the Campobello Golf Club Pamphlet, like the one you forwarded to me. Are they not funny and doesn't the list of members seem tiny?? I suppose Gorham Hubbard got it out, and think he deserves much credit for it.—We had one of our monthly examinations yesterday—in German—and I passed easily, with about the highest mark, I think. I forgot to tell you how pleased I was about the Canal Bill passing the Senate, and I wonder whether you think it will pass the House? I so rarely see the daily papers that I have not seen much about it, but I hope there won't be much opposition now. Don't you think I'd better have another bottle of C.L.O. The one I have it almost empty, and I know it does me good and keeps me from getting cold.

Jan. 30th

It's my birthday but I won't be 17 till this evening, so you can put off congratulations till then. I wish I could be at home now and see you both, but I must resign myself to my fate and wait a few weeks. Still your dear letter this evening will be a great comfort—

Warren has not said a word about my Xmas present to him, and I should have asked him if he ever got it, only that I forgot what *you* gave him from me. I wish you could let me know and I will ask him.—

I can hardly realize that I am now seventeen and that I shall be at Harvard next year & I don't feel a bit over 15. Please excuse this scrawl but my arm is so stiff that I have no control over it.

Ever with tons of love & kisses to you both my darling Mama & Papa   I am your affectionate son

FRANKLIN D. ROOSEVELT

Mrs. Freeman was a permanent project of the Missionary Society. Her husband had been a Union drummer in the Civil War, but had years since departed her. She was a very old lady, almost helpless, and after each snowfall, for many years, one of the first expeditions was always down to dig Mrs. Freeman out. Gorham Hubbard was a Boston gentleman who took an interest in the summer activities at Campobello and was in charge of the golf club. His daughter married T. Jefferson Newbold (*vide supra*). The United States Senate passed the Nicaragua Canal Bill on January 21st with only six dissenting votes. The bill provided for the continuation of the Maritime Canal Company, with an issue of one million shares at $100 par, the Treasury being authorized to purchase 925,000 shares.

GROTON SCHOOL
JAN. 31, 1899,
TUESDAY.

My darling Mama and Papa,

You are both of you altogether too good to do so much for such an undeserving crittur as I am, and you have given me so much in the last month that I feel as if you were quite spoiling me. I don't quite know where to begin. First, last night the delightful Thesaurus, which I shall use frequently and I hope for many years. I have written in it as coming from dear Papa; second the delightful fountain pen, with which I am scribbling this letter came tonight. It is a perfect beauty and will be a constant reminder of you and encouragement to good penmanship, and this time I shall be most careful not to lose it. At the same time came my moccassins which I had returned to Read's and the present ones fit to a T. Many many·thanks for them; I have marked them and shall keep them in readiness for the first snowstorm (which by the way looks imminent). Last night I had another delightful surprise in the large shape of a basket of goodies from Aunt Annie including apples, oranges, bananas, digs [?], figs, maple sugar, crackers & congratulations. I am writing to thank her. I celebrated my Birthday by taking two Examinations, History & English. I passed them both tho' with fairly low marks, as I had missed the actual teaching here. The results of exams are to be counted as 3 recitations on our monthly marks, so mine will thereby be pulled down considerably. I think there is very little chance of my getting a B this month (which ends Saturday) but I shall try all the harder next month. I was delighted to get your two dear letters of Sunday & one of Saturday; I am glad the Pells could get some real iceboating, & that Mr. Pell didn't get scared.

Wednesday 8 a.m

It snowed about an inch last night but we are going to clear off the pond. There is good but very dangerous coasting on the river road but I don't know which I shall indulge in. This a.m I am going to see Mrs. Freeman and take her some Graphics—

Ever with dearest love to you both   Your affec. son

F D.R.

∽

"I have only a sad and long tale
of woe for you up here . . ."

My dearest Mama and Papa,

Many thanks for your dear letter of Tuesday which arrived this morning. How angry I am to be missing all this lovely ice-boating and skating on the river! if I could only have had one good sail this year! I have only a sad and long tale of woe for you up here. First I have a slight touch of grippe which I took in the cold chapel on Sunday. It felt like bronchitis yesterday but I put a mustard plaster on my chest last night and today I am better tho' achy and sleepy and tired. As a result I failed sweetly on two examinations, which now makes sure of my getting C for the month. I had made up *almost* all my work, but to cap all on the examinations I was asked questions just from the tiny pieces I hadn't done. However I have passed Greek, by far the most important, also History, German and English, but flunked Math & Latin. But for the two pieces I missed both masters said I would have passed. The monthly exams are of course not as important as the ones at the end and I have two more chances before then, & I also do not have to study extra.

Warren has gone to the infirmary with a slight sore-throat

(together with many others) but I think he may be out to-morrow.

The bottle of CLO came tonight just in time as I had just taken the last dose of the old. This a.m I coasted with Rosy on his bob, very good fun and quite exciting & dangerous.

My head and hand are going round, and I have just taken 8 pages of English notes so I'll finish in the a.m.

Friday. 8. a.m.

I now find that I came within 4 points of passing my Math, the nearest to passing and over $\frac{1}{2}$ the form failed, so I don't mind nearly so much . . My cold is better this a.m and I think I have succeeded in stopping it entirely.

Ever with lots of love your affec. son

F.D.R.

His examination marks were below standard, with D's in Latin and Geometry, C's in Greek and History, and a B in German. Recitation marks were, however, good enough to pull his final average up to B.

∞

"He is a jolly old man and told us some good stories . . ."

GROTON SCHOOL
FEB. 5, 1899,
SUNDAY.

My darling Mama & Papa,

I was very sorry yesterday when I got your telegram as I fear you worried needlessly and I should not have alarmed you in my letter as I did.

My cold has entirely gone now and I've never felt better in my life. The mustard-plaster took all symtoms of bronchitis away and that without having to go to the Infirmary once. I hope neither of you have caught any cold in New York, and that you enjoyed the Valkyrie. I would have given anything to see it

How pleased I am that Uncle Fred has another infant, too bad it is not a boy, but the next may be. I wonder what they'll call it, most of the family names have been exhausted, but I very much hope it will be called after Aunt Annie.

Bishop Hall of Vermont is here today and preached a good sermon in the chapel this morning. He is a jolly old man and told us some good stories at Mr. G's this afternoon.

Yesterday I skated all afternoon and then took afternoon tea with Mrs. Peabody. The night before a Mr. Turner gave the three upper forms a talk on art among the primitive people; very interesting & I took notes on it for the "Grotonian."

My sponge is about worn out & my tooth-powder has disappeared, so I wish you could send me a new sponge, not too big & a little tooth-powder.

Monday—

I am in an awful hurry as I didn't finish this yesterday there is not much to be said. We have about four inches of snow but not enough to spoil the skating. Many thanks for the garters.

Ever with loads of love to you both affec.

FDR

Frederic Delano's new daughter was named Matilda. The Groton motto, *Cui servire est regnare,* had been suggested by another of Bishop A. C. A. Hall's sermons, delivered in 1893. Mr. Ross Turner was a Boston artist.

〜〜

". . . the sun thro' the clouds, a
very curious phenomenon . . ."

GROTON SCHOOL
FEB. 7, 1899,
TUESDAY.

My dearest Mama and Papa,

Yours of Sunday and Monday morning have come, and I am sorry you did not get the answer to your telegram sooner.

Yours was delivered to me at 3 p.m on Saturday and I had to hunt for nearly an hour before the janitor could send my answer. I am *absolutely* well now and expect to continue so if I am careful. I do not quite know where to send this note as you say you are going to New York on Thursday. However I shall send it H.P. in the hope that you'll get it before you leave on Thursday morning.

About three inches of snow fell yesterday and Sunday and today it has snowed *very* lightly all the time although one could distinctly see the sun thro' the clouds, a very curious phenomenon. I helped clear off the pond and got in a small game of hockey before lunch. I have begun taking all the calisthenics, including jumping and running and I find I can do it all right without becoming at all blown.

Taddy debated last night with Whitridge against Thayer and Burnham The subject was "Resolved that nations are rightly selfish". He made a pretty good speech and almost entirely extemporaneous but his opponents were too good for him and they won.

Wednesday 8 am

Thanks for the riddle about the animals in one of your letters of last week. I think it it [*sic*] is very good.

You say Uncle Jennie & Aunt Warren are going from Charleston on a cruise in the "Nerada." I suppose they are going to visit the Cuban battle-fields & Santiago etc. What fun!

Ever with lots of love & in haste—

FDR

Snowing hard again!

The yacht *Narada* was originally built for Anthony Drexel, who sold it to the King of the Belgians, from whom it in turn passed to Harry Walters, *Aunt* Jennie's brother. It was just a nice size—two hundred and twenty-five feet long, with three saloons and twelve cabins, and a crew of forty-four.

"I distinctly heard them kicking
the partitions . . ."

My dearest Mama & Papa,

Many thanks for yours of Tuesday evening and the Graphic,
Tribune and Speckled Tater; they are all very interesting—
9 p.m.

I have just got back from seeing the school stables burned
to the ground with two poor horses in it. To go back to the
beginning—about ten minutes after supper or 6.40 there was
a cry raised for the V & VI Forms to hurry to a fire in the farm-
house. We rushed & I threw on my thin overcoat and a tobog
cap and ploughed through drifts of snow to the fire which was
then burning brightly, from the front of the stable in the
harness room. A cry was raised that the horses were in it, but
we found that seven of the nine had been taken out, but the
flames and smoke were all thro' the building so we could not
save them. They were Mr. Billings horse a beauty and the
Peabody childrens pony. I distinctly heard them kicking the
partitions and we tried to cut thro' the wall to them, but the
smoke poured out in volumes so we could not reach them in
time. They probably were soon smothered and did not suffer
much. The next thing to do was to try to save a shed behind
and 20 ft. from the stables, and we managed to carry out a
quantity of meal sacks, tools and farm wagon. The sparks were
flying so thick that one had to cover one's clothes with snow
and several of us were almost knocked down by the thick
smoke. We had a rather ludicrous time in trying to get 10 or
12 big pigs from their sty; we had to carry them out bodily &
how they kicked and squealed! At about then or about ½ hour
after the fire started the hose co's from Groton arrived   2 of
them and they connected with a hydrant and kept playing on
the shed. I append a rough diagram:

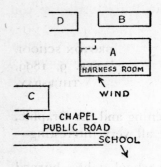

A is the stable totally destroyed.
B the shed which we saved.
C the big farm house and laundry
D the power house for the electric lights.

The dotted corner of the stable is where the two poor horses
are supposed to have been burned. The fire started in front in
harness room but as there *was no back door* we could not get
at the horses.

Friday—

I could not finish this this a.m so send a postal to N.Y. I have
just come back from the ruins, where there is a most horrible
scene. the two poor horses are lying under the débris with
their hide entirely burned off and fearfully charred. A few
bodies of hens and chickens are in the ruins and everything
is covered with a coating of thick ice which froze almost as
soon as it left the hose. You can imagine the scene last night
with the thermometer at 6° *below* zero and the awful flames!
I was wet through and one shoe froze tight   luckily my foot
escaped & is only a little sore now. There were a number of
frozen ears, fingers etc. nothing serious. The weather is bitter,
a high wind and great drifts over all. The barn and carriages
& horses were about ½ covered by insurance, the loss being
about $3,000.

—You must have loved hearing the Ring & I envy you. Many thanks for the tooth powder.

—The escape of the farm-houses is considered providential as they would have gone, together with the power-house if the wind had been different. None of us slept much last night you may imagine; my second scare in less than a month.

You will be surprised & pleased to hear that when the marks were read out I found I had a B. Saved again by Jove!

On Wednesday night we had a delightful concert, given by Mr. Gardner I enclose the program. They were two big guns from Boston; one played, the other sang, a really very good performance

I hope you'll get this by Sunday morning

Ever with fearful haste & love

FDR

"Speckled Tater" refers to the British journal, *The Spectator*. The "two big guns from Boston" were Messrs. George Proctor and Theodore Byard.

〜〜

*"We have about settled down
after the excitement of the fire . . ."*

[GROTON]
FEB. 12, 1899,
SUNDAY.

My dearest Ma and Pa,

It is snowing hard again! and is very cold, so we had church in the school-room again as the chapel can not be warmed up enough. Yours of Friday from N.Y. has come, and thanks for sending the sponge; it hasn't come yet, but should be here tomorrow.

We have about settled down after the excitement of the fire, although nothing has been done about removing the ruins or the horses bodies as the insurance man must see it and anyway everything is frozen stiff and covered with ice.

Edmund's story of the new infirmary is as yet only a project started by several gentleman, but no work or even plans have been done, and I don't think even the Rector knows very much about what is to be done.

Mr. Nutter continues to improve and he is sitting up enough to take his food and read his mail and the papers.

Yesterday afternoon I helped clear off the pond and had a good game of hockey for about an hour. I then went to tea with Mrs. Peabody, and played with the baby and Betsy until supper time.

Aunt Kassie and Hiram P. are coming up on Friday night to spend Sunday which will be nice and better than if they came three days later for the play. By the way there is no more chance of my being an usher as the number has been decreased to five, and the same ones will officiate in the village the next Saturday night.

The play promises to be fairly good and Taddy I believe has a very minor part, but better than nothing. I wonder if Rubber Boots & Helen are coming up for it?

Monday 8. a.m.

It stopped snowing yesterday afternoon but began again during the night and now there are at least 6 inches more. It is still coming down thick but is a little warmer.

Last Friday night it was so bitter in our dormitory that I slept in Aunt Ellen's sweater and was perfectly comfortable all night The mail is going so I must close.

With lots of love to you both Your affec son

F.D.R.

Excuse writing

The new infirmary, known variously as the "Pest House" or "Pain Dome," was completed after F.D.R.'s graduation, in 1902. "Betsy" was Elizabeth Rogers Peabody, the Rector's third daughter, who was then three years old. She later became an authority in the field of remedial reading, and the only woman on the Groton faculty.

"It did no good to dig her out then . . ."

GROTON]
FEB. 14, 1899,
TUESDAY.

Dearest Mama and Papa,

We have had no mail for two days, in fact none, except one from Boston, since Saturday. Everything is blocked, the drifts are mountain high, and the first snow-plough has just gone through on the railroad (2 p.m).

All yesterday it drove snow and until about 3 this a.m. In spite of the storm Warren Motley and I managed to flounder down to old Mrs. Freeman's and back to see if she was all right. It did no good to dig her out then as it was drifting fearfully. We went down again on skis this a.m with Motley and had to dig our way to her door. Her chicken-house, which must be 16 or 18 feet high was *entirely* buried except the tip of the gable on the roof. After about an hour's hard work with snow-shovels we managed to find the chicken's door and dig a narrow path to it between banks of snow which we couldn't see over. Luckily the Rector had let us off part of the last period of school, so we got back in time for lunch, but rather tuckered out with the hard work and the heavy wind We must go tomorrow and take her some provisions as the butcher or grocer havn't been near for several days.

We have all had to wear skis or snow-shoes in going from one building to another as the snow plough was burned in the barn and they have not been able to dig out the path yet.

No more now, as the mail is going   Ever   FDR.

〜〜

*"Taddy comes once on the stage
and measures a corpse . . ."*

[GROTON]
FEB. 16, 1899,
THURSDAY.

My dearest Mama & Papa,

It has at last got warmer and the huge drifts have begun slowly to grow less. Yesterday afternoon I went to Groton on skis with Lathrop Brown. It was very good fun and some of the hills were exciting. Your letters, one of Sunday and the other from the train have just come, this morning, no late last night.

Too bad you missed "Siegfried," but it must have been quite exciting bucking the snow-drifts, and what an awfully long time you were, getting to N.Y.

As you say that you are going to spend Sunday at Orange I am sending this letter there and hope you'll get it all right. Aunt Kassie and Hiram get here tomorrow night and Warren telegraphed today saying that there is plenty of room at Whitney's for Muriel & hoping that she will come.

Yesterday I went to Mrs. Powells and engaged two rooms for you, for February 22nd ~~1899~~ *1900* when I am in the play, as there is such a demand. Taddy seems to know nothing about when his people are coming, but he has a vague idea that Helen is coming *all alone* and won't be here till just in time for the play. If they come at all, they should come *earlier* than the 12 o'clock train, as that is very apt to be late.

You ask about fencing. As I came so late I found that there was no chance to take it as all the time of the fencing-master had been taken and there were already three substitutes. I am very sorry to miss it but shall take it next year if possible.

Taddy has been given a part in the play in which he comes once on the stage as an undertaker and measures a corpse. Do not tell anyone of this yet as everything is supposed to be a dead secret. The name of the play is "Turned Up," and I think will be good altho' there is not as much talent as last year.

No more now, and I hope this will reach you at Orange all right

Ever with dearest love to you both   Affec. son

F.D.R.

Of the play in which Taddy performed so gruesomely, William P. Wharton recalls that it involved the pursuit of a seafarer by a large colored lady with whom he had taken up while in the

South Seas; it ended with the Negress and the sailor doing a cakewalk.

〰〰

"I felt a sudden crack in my mouth . . ."

My dearest Mama and Papa,

I have been very gay for the last two days. Aunt Kassie and Muriel came Friday evening on time and Mr. C. (H.P.) [Hiram Price Collier] last night from Boston. Yesterday I took lunch and tea with them and in the afternoon went for a long drive of 12 or 14 miles taking Howard Cary with us in the sleigh. Today I was with them all morning and afternoon beside lunching, and we expect them to parlor later on. They leave early to morrow a.m but it has been lovely having them here, and a nice break to the monotony of the term. They all send their love to you. Thanks for yours of Thursday from N.Y & Papa's from H.P. also his postal & the Spectator. The Rector wants me to thank you very much, but he had already seen the articles as he takes it himself. I haven't had a moments time to look at them yet, but they will keep till after the excitement of the play.

It has melted hard here for the last two days and the snow is rapidly disappearing. I fancy you had quite as much at Hyde Park as we did here, but as you say you had rain it must have disappeared rapidly. I have a rather sad piece of news for you. Yesterday as I was eating some of Aunt Kassie's delicious mince-pie, I felt a sudden crack in my mouth and on looking afterwards found that a piece of my big back tooth had broken

off. The tooth is shaped like this and the corner marked broke short off to the gum and exposed the filling. I knew there was a hole there before Xmas, but Dr. Durand *assured* me there was no absolute danger and that it would last a long time longer, before needing filling. I shall go to Boston next Saturday and have something done, and I think the tooth can be saved all right.

Last Thursday afternoon we had the first of the Lenten services, & the sermon was by a Mr. Huigan of the Beverly church who spoke with a broad Irish brogue.

Monday. 8 a m

Am just going over to say good bye to Aunt Kassie, as they leave at 8.30. I positively dont want my dress suit as my function at the play is only to stand at the door and try to get the visitors names for the Grotonian. Muriel had a nice time in parlor last night & it was crowded

Ever lovingly

FDR.

The broad Irish minister was the Reverend Eugene J. V. Huiginn, of St. Peter's Church, Beverly, Mass.

〜〜

*"I don't think he is particularly
cut out for a preacher . . ."*

[GROTON]
FEB. 21, 1899,
TUESDAY.

My dearest Mama & Papa,

Just a line before the grand excitement of tomorrow. Your two letters from Orange were most welcome this morning, and it must have been nice seeing all the infants. I shall write you a full account of all that happens, and the play, on Thursday, and you will hear from Helen how it all goes off. We have skipped calisthenics yesterday and today, as the stage has been put up in the gymnasium, and there is to be a rehearsal today.

Wed. 8. a.m.

Helen & Miss Fromont and a great crowd from every State in the Union came last night, and they all came over to parlor-night.

I am to lunch with them today and I do not know what we shall do this afterday, as it is slushy and foggy and I think it will rain.

Thanks for your letter from Dumper, I hope he won't make a mess of his first sermon, but I don't think he is particularly cut out for a preacher, do you?

I shall have to sit up half-tonight as I have to complete the visitors list for the printer of the Grotonian befor 8 a.m tomorrow

No more now & excuse this abominable scrawl

Ever affec son

FDR

〜〜

"Mr. Hoyt did say a few words
to Aunt Kassie & Mr. H.P.C. . . ."

[GROTON]
FEB. 23, 1899,
THURSDAY.

My dear Mama and Papa,

To begin where I left off last Tuesday. Helen and Miss Fromont got here all right and came to parlor in the evening, and we played games. The next day, yesterday I lunched and took supper with them at Powell's. In the afternoon we went for a long sleigh-ride, altho' the ground was bare about half the way! On the way back we stopped at my old lady's, Mrs. Freeman's, and I took Helen and Miss F. in to see her. She was much delighted, and Helen will be able to tell you all about her.

Before the doors for the play were opened in the evening, about 8, I went over and stood at the door, so that I could take down all the names of visitors. It was hard work I can tell you, for a few minutes as there was a steady stream, and I had to scribble fast.

The play was really very good, *nearly* as good as last year on the whole I thought, and the acting not bad, and very

269

good in some cases; I send a programme, but won't undertake to tell about the plot, as Helen can describe it to you. There were a number of songs, quite good, although the VI form is not celebrated for singing James appeared twice at the back of the stage, and looked all right, but said nothing.

Friday.

I didn't have time to finish this this a.m. as we had to see Helen off at 8.30. Yesterday I lunched with her and went to tea with Mrs. Hoyt who is at Whitney's. They are to stay till Saturday morning so I shall see them again today sometime

Many thanks for your letter and the report which is better than I expected.

Yes Mr. Hoyt did say a few words to Aunt Kassie & Mr. H.P.C. at table, which was the only time I saw them together.

I am sorry I can't write any more as the mail goes in 5 minutes.

Ever

                                                                    FDR

Will write more on Sunday

Mr. and Mrs. Gerald L. Hoyt were the parents of Lydig and Julia, and Hudson Valley neighbors of the Roosevelts.

∽∾

*"I have almost forgotten what
school food tastes like . . ."*

[GROTON]
FEB. 26, 1899,
SUNDAY.

My dearest Ma and Pa,

On Friday evening, I went to tea gain with Mrs. Hoyt, and that afternoon went also to an afternoon tea given to the V Form by Mrs. Markoe. In all I have been out for nine meals in seven days, and have almost forgotten what school food tastes like. Still it was nice seeing everybody up here, and made it seem quite like home. Everyone has gone though, now, and we are beginning to settle down to work again. Both Friday & yesterday I tobogganed on the hill above the pond, and it was very good. Last night came the grand occurrence of the play again, this time at the Town-hall. The V and IV Forms went to it, missing evening-school (for a wonder) and the play began at 7.45. It was again very successful, and the acting on the whole very much better than last Wednesday, while the omission of jokes on boys and masters made it more real. We succeeded in having old Mrs. Freeman driven down to it and she enjoyed it immensely. I am so glad to see by your last letter that you are really coming up soon, as I am pining to see you. I hope you will let me get rooms for you this time at Mrs. Whitneys, as her house is now in thorough order and I think really nicer than the Powells and the food is improved.

You will be pleased to hear that I am to join the choir next Sunday, and if I find I can sing tenor all right I am to stay in it. We have had quite cold weather again for the last two days, and today it rained and hailed slightly. We have pussy-willows up here also and the snow is now only in patches with all sleighing over.

Monday. 8. a m.

It is horrid weather today, with rain and fog. No more now as it is time for school.

Ever with best love to you both   Your affec. son

FDR.

Mrs. Markoe was the mother of his classmate, Harry Markoe; she was a frequent visitor at the school.

❧❧

"We are against it . . ."

[GROTON]
FEB. 28, 1899,
TUESDAY.

My dearest Ma and Pa,

Yesterday, after posting my Sunday letter to you, I went to the infirmary, as I felt a cold coming on, and my throat was sore. I spent the day in bed, and as a result, I am absolutely well today, and have been to school and taken an examination so you need not worry in the least.

I am to debate next Monday evening with Polly Wharton *against* Dick Derby the president of the Society and another sixth former. The subject is: Resolved, that the U.S. & England should guarantee the integrity on [of] China. We are *Con*, against it, and if you happen to see any articles about it, one way or the other we would be pleased to have them.

You will be sorry to hear about Edmund. Last week, early, he sprained his knee playing fives and did not think much of it. When coasting with the girls on Friday he hurt it slightly again, and then on Sunday night in getting into bed he wrenched it again. On Monday he went to Boston on crutches and the doctor there put it in a plaster cast. He now hobbles round on crutches but by taking it in time I hope it will not get worse, as it is a very troublesome thing to have.

I have written for an appointment for next Saturday for my tooth, but I shall not go to Dr. Niles as I don't believe he is any good at all.

No more now and ever with best love to you both   Your affec son

F.D.R.

Less than 5 weeks more!

There was much discussion at this time about the Open Door policy in a China threatened with internal disruption following upon its defeat by Japan in 1895. A British M.P., Admiral Lord Charles Beresford, had been sent out on an investigatory visit to China; he returned in May, and published a widely publicized book *(The Break-Up of China)* in which he stated that, unless the Open Door policy were enforced, a break-up was certain to occur. Secretary of State Hay's note to the powers, asking that the policy be upheld, went forward in the autumn of 1899; the Boxer Rebellion followed in 1900. It should be noted, in connection with F.D.R.'s upholding of the negative, that the side one took in these debates was not by

choice but mainly by assignment—a rather curious custom
prevalent in most school debates, which assumes that it is more
important to develop a schoolboy's persuasiveness than his
principles.

〜〜

"I am perfectly overrun with work
—exams, debate, 'Grotonian' . . ."

[GROTON]
MARCH 2, 1899,
THURSDAY.

My dearest Mama and Papa,

How perfectly delighted I was to get yours of Wednesday
saying you are coming day after tomorrow! I can hardly wait,
and [if I get an appointment for Saturday (which I much
doubt) I shall telegraph the dentist to put it off till next week,
as there is no hurry, and I don't want] to miss a moment of
your visit. I do hope papa will be able to come too, and that
he won't have a beastly meeting.

If you want to hear my debate you must stay over till Tuesday morning.

If the weather is fine on Saturday and the roads decent, we
can go for a drive in the trap that brings you from the station
& I shall get Warren & Taddy if the weather is fine.

By the way, I wish if you have time on receipt of this you
could bring 3 or 4 of those nice gold J pens which you have.

Later—

8 p.m.

Your telegram just come. I won't cancel the appointment
the address is Dr. Wilson 85 Newbury St. and if you don't find
me there when you get there you will find a note saying where
to go.—I shall take the five o'clock train back so if your train
from N.Y is very late you can go straight to the Union Station.
I am perfectly overrun with work—exams coming all in a
bunch, debate, for next Monday and "Grotonian" work as
well.

Friday 8 a.m.

No more now—how lovely to think of seeing you tomorrow!
Ever affec son

F.D.R.

Meet you Saturday Boston

The bracketed section in the first paragraph was crossed out
following the receipt of his mother's change of plans.

∽

*"I have finished my speech and
am learning it now . . ."*

My dearest Papa,

Mama and Una are here all right, and enjoying themselves.
Too bad about Taddy isn't it? It is awfully hard luck on him,
as he wont be able to get out for at least six weeks. I suppose
Br. Rosy is half-crazy about it, but Taddy is not really ill and
it is said to be a light case. Thanks for the Spectator clipping;
it is of great use to me and I have finished my speech and am
learning it now. Mama goes to Boston tomorrow morning to
see the Sargent pictures, and comes back at 3 p.m.

Monday 8 a.m

Taddy had a comfortable night, and his temperature is down
to 101° this morning.

No more now; Mama will see you tomorrow and she has
written you

Ever with lots of love   Your affec son

FDR

Una F. Soley was the daughter of James Russell Soley, and his
cousin. Isabella Stewart Gardner, Mr. G.'s aunt, was a great
patroness of John Singer Sargent, fostering many exhibitions
of his paintings.

∽

274

"It must be inconvenient not to
be able to sit down at all! . . ."

My dearest Mama and Papa,

You can have no idea how lovely it was seeing Mama since Saturday and it already seems as if you had been away a perfect age, instead of a few hours. It was too bad Papa could not come up and most unfortunate that he had meetings in New York; however there is less than 4 weeks now before I shall be home for the lovely Easter holidays. It is too delightful to have finished my debate and I now have in its place to work up my story for the Grotonian and I also have in charge the writing up of the Fives Tournaments and the Winter Athletic Meet which begins next week. I shall probably enter the High Kick and run the risk of breaking my back, although as I am now in the I Class I shall have to compete with boys who won last year in the 1st Class. I hope you got off comfortably and got to N.Y. on time, although I fancy the snow delayed you somewhat. It has stopped snowing now (8 p.m) and I think about 6 or 8 inches fell, enough to make it horrid and slushy again as it was last Sunday. There is another boy in the infirmary today with a sore-throat and we hope and think it is not the pest. I wrote to J.R.R.Jr. today and sent him two letters from Helen. He is getting along all right and I shall write to Helen tomorrow if I get a chance to speak to him.

Don't forget to send him the oranges soon. I suppose Br. Rosy is worried half to death, and it must be inconvenient not to be able to sit down at all!

Wed. 8 a.m.

Taddy temperature this a.m is 100 4/10 and he is getting on nicely.

No more now; I hope for a letter from N.Y this a m. I send this to Hyde Park as you did not tell me when you go home.

Ever with love

F.D.R.

Taddy had scarlet fever and was in isolation, hence the letter-writing. Brother Rosy's illness can only be surmised.

∽∽

"I hope it won't recur annually
like a blossom in the spring . . ."

My dearest Mama and Papa

Your note from N.Y. telling of your safe arrival was most welcome yesterday. What a time you must have had with Br. Rosy! I hope it won't recur annually like a sort of blossom in the spring.

Friday.

I forgot to finish this yesterday so will do so and send it now.

On Wednesday afternoon the Bishop came up for Confirmation. The service was at 3.15 and 19 boys were confirmed, among them Edmund and Georgie Low. Mrs. Low & Marion were up here, but I didn't even lay eyes on them once, and only found they had been here, today. Yours of Thursday from Hyde Park have just come and I shall immediately take 3 rooms for you at Whitney's for next Washington's Birthday.

Taddy is doing nicely and his temperature is down to 99 4/10 He is very anxious to have some magazines so could you send the Graphics as soon as they come & possibly a Collier's or Harper's. Send them to me & I will glance at them & send them up to him He also would like to have a very cheap volume of one of Dicken's work; just two or three cheap but standard books.

I go to Boston tomorrow & will write Sunday

No more now, the mail goes in two seconds.

FDR

With love

The word "arrival" in the first sentence was added by his mother.

∽

"We went to Huyler's for a
drink (only soda) . . ."

[GROTON]

MARCH 12, 1899,

SUNDAY.

My dearest Mama and Papa,

Yesterday I left the school at 12 o'clock for Boston and was accompanied by no less than 11 other boys, among them Warren and Edmund, the latter to see about his knee, and Warren for a tooth. We got to Dr. Wilson's at 3 o'clock and my dental appendage was filled and put in order. The dentist said that it was a pretty close call for the tooth as the nerve was almost touched, and if I had waited till the holidays it might have broken some more. After my appointment Warren had a filling put in and we went to Huyler's for a drink (only soda) before coming out here at 5.20. I told Dr. Wilson to send the bill to you. He seemed to be an excellent dentist and said that if I wanted to have my teeth straightened I should have it done *very* soon and that it could be done perfectly well but that I should have to devote a good deal of time to it and it could not be done in a summer vacation.

I have just been to see Taddy through the window and brought him some papers, and the Graphic and Harpers Weeklies that came yesterday (many thanks for them).

He seemed cheerful and hungry as a bear[—]his temperature *normal*[—]but as yet not very tired of his confinement and anxious to hear about the goings on of the world. I am writing to Helen to tell her how he is. By the way the fruit came all right for him last night. Do you think you could send him a very cheap backgammon-checkers board, as I know it would help tremendously to while away the time and his nurse can play with him.

No other cases have developed, as I predicted from the start, and I am sure there will be no more. Last night we were given an extremely interesting talk by Mr. Barnes (Mr. Sturgis' fiancée's brother) who is an authority on American History. He told us stories of brave men in the Revolution and War of 1812 whose deeds, although practically saving their country have been almost forgotten.

The night before we also had a talk, this time from Father Osborn, the missionary. He told us of his experiences in India and South Africa where he spent seven years.

The marks came out on Friday for the past month, and again I succeeded in getting a B, and as no one got an A I may have been near the head. You will be sorry to hear that Warren was at the foot of his class with a mark of about 5.75. I feel sure that he is altogether too young for his form, and he would be just about the same age as the average of the present 1st Form. Still with such a needlessly ambitious father I suppose he will be compelled to work hard all thro' the holidays and given a terrible talking to besides. I am sure he tries as hard as anyone.

Last Wednesday was Mrs. Freeman's 86th Birthday, and we clubbed together and took her 3 pots of flowers, two hyacinths and a large begonia (excuse spelling). She was delighted. It is melting and drizzling and thundering today and the snow is once more reduced to patches. I enclose a small bill which I prefer not to pay, considering what what [sic] it is for!

Monday 8 a.m.

Just think, only three weeks before we come home! It does not seem a whole week since your lovely visit and the time passes quickly in spite of the weather. The winter meeting in the Gym begins on Wednesday and I have to take it all down for the "Grot" besides doing the Fives Tournaments which are almost over now.

No more now and ever with best love to you both   I am your affec. son

FRANKLIN D. ROOSEVELT

Huyler's Confectionary had several branches in Boston at the time. Concerning Mr. James Barnes, *vide supra.* The Reverend Edward W. Osborne was born in Calcutta, and came to the United States in 1898 from Capetown as superior of the Society of St. John the Evangelist (hence the title of "Father") and rector of the church of the same name in Boston. He later became Bishop of Springfield, Illinois. F.D.R.'s cousin Warren Robbins was eventually set back and did not graduate from Groton until 1904. As regarded his own marks, F.D.R. had improved his Geometry considerably, with A's both in recitations and the examination. He also got two A's in German, and the rest—Latin, Greek, English Literature, French, and History—were B's.

〜〜

"Crimson and black or crimson
& green? . . ."

[GROTON]
MARCH 14, 1899,
TUESDAY.

My dear Mama & Papa,

Your two letters of Sunday were most welcome, and I was sorry to hear how suffering Brother Rosy was and it was a good deal more of an operation than I thought it would be, and besides his temperament is not exactly conducive to bearing pain.

Taddy continues to improve daily and I visit every morning just before lunch. He says he feels absolutely well, but still very hungry. He is to begin on eggs next Saturday I think. He wants me to thank you for the papers which came today.

Last night we were given a concert by Mr. Jefferson. He sang alternately with a Miss Cochrane and it was very good. I enclose the program. I received a letter from Aunt Nellie today offering to make me an embroidered fancy waistcoat and offers me the choice of two colours—crimson and black with crimson sleeves—or crimson & green with green sleeves. I think I should prefer the black & crimson, don't you? I am to send her a paper pattern of the front of my largest vest, my new brown one, and she is to try it on me at Easter. Isn't it nice?

The Rector went to Boston today on a "dunning expedition." He met a big crowd at the Vendôme and already $22,000 has been promised, and a good deal more will be forthcoming. It will complete the new building, build Mr. Sturgis' house and do sundry necessary jobs in all departments. No more now & ever with dear love to you both   Your affec. son

FDR

There were two Cochrane sisters, Marjorie and Hester, but it is not recalled which one sang with Mr. Jefferson. The Hotel Vendome is on Commonwealth Avenue in Boston.

∽

"We tied on to a huge cake of ice and floated down with it . . ."

GROTON SCHOOL
MARCH 16, 1899,
THURSDAY.

My dearest Mama and Papa,

Yours of Tuesday and Wednesday was most welcome today, and I am sorry Brother Rosy is still depressed and suffering. I forgot to tell in my Tuesday's letter that we had had a choir half-holiday on Monday. I took Warren out on the river, as it was nice and warm. We did not go very far as the current was swift. On the way back we tied on to a huge cake of ice and floated down with it. An invitation came last night from Aunt Kassie to go to her on the 6th for a day or so. I should like very much to go, but am heartily sorry to discover that the little [name deleted] brat is going too!! So I am writing that I shall go to Aunt Kassie, provided you have no other plans for the sixth, and you had better write her also if you don't mind.

The Winter Athletic meet began on Wednesday and I am

kept writing every spare moment, and the Fives Tournament is not quite over, so I am busy with that too.

I can hardly make up my mind about going to Boston every Wednesday during the spring-term, it means missing so much up here. I heard of Dr. Wilson from several Boston boys up here, and I think he is extremely good. I send the waistcoat pattern, which I cut out after great difficulty to Nelly also a note thanking [her] for making it. Am I to go to N.Y. straight or to Hyde Park now that Dr. Durand is dead, or have you made an appointment at the other dentist's you told me about?

No more now and ever with dear love to you both   I am your affectionate son   FRANKLIN D. ROOSEVELT.

∽∽

"He would very much like to have 'The Meditations of Marcus Aurelius' . . ."

GROTON SCHOOL
MARCH 19, 1899,
SUNDAY.

My dearest Mama & Papa,

Only two weeks more! just think of it. Your plans for the vacation suit me to a T and I suppose I cannot arrange to have more time at Hyde Park. I am sorry to hear that Uncle Fred is not well but I trust it is nothing and that he will be all right soon.

It has poured and frozen here all day, with the result that the trees are covered an inch deep with ice, and many branches have been broken in consequence. It is lovely not to have such hard examinations to look forward to at the end of the term as formerly, and I shall not come home a mental wreck. Many thanks for the Graphic which came last night; I shall take it to Taddy when I see him tomorrow. He continues to feel perfectly well and can hardly believe anything is the matter with him. However he has begun to peal on the feet which proves absolutely that he has it. He would very much like to have a book called "The Meditations of Marcus Aurelius" in as cheap a volume as can be bought. However if it is too expensive do not send it.

Monday 8 a.m.

This effect this a.m is wonderful, every branch & twig is covered with ice, & everything glistens in the sun. Several branches have fallen, & I fear it is injuring the trees.

No more now & ever with best love

FDR.

The "Uncle Fred" in this case was Frederic D. Hitch.

❀

"I am to be a new missionary . . ."

GROTON SCHOOL
MARCH 23, 1899,
THURSDAY.

My dearest Ma and Pa,

I was most grieved to hear of Uncle Fred's illness but I am glad, that it was taken in time and that he is doing well. Still I quite realize that it is very serious in a man of his age and it makes it worse coming on top of his other operation on his neck. I only hope he will pull through all right, and I shall write to Aunt Annie. You will be surprised to hear that I am to be a new missionary. There was a lack of organ-players for the various mission houses in the neighborhood, so I volunteered and tonight I am to drive over with two other boys and Mr. Higley to hold a service at Rockey Hill in a little school-house which is about 6 miles from here. I have almost forgotten how to play the piano, but have been practising on the small organ in the school-room and can play four hymns fairly decently. We leave at 6.30 tonight and expect to return about 10, when we go into Faculty supper! The Winter Meet is

about over and You will be pleased to hear I have not kicked
as the high-kick did not take place this year, owing to the great
danger of breaking backs, arms etc. It is *snowing* again, & we
now have about 7 inches on the ground! I never knew such a
late spring as it is this year.

Ever with best love to you both

F.D.R.

How awful the Windsor Hotel fire was!

Rocky Hill was a section of East Groton, amounting to not
much more than the site of the Rocky Hill schoolhouse. The
Windsor fire occurred on March 17 while the guests were
watching the St. Patrick's Day parade from the windows of the
hotel, which was on Fifth Avenue between Forty-sixth and
Forty-seventh Streets. A smoker threw a lighted match from
one of the windows, but, since there was a breeze, one of the
curtains blew back just as the match was thrown, and caught
fire. The blaze spread instantly, causing a panic. Approximately sixty persons lost their lives, though the number of
dead was never exactly known.

∽

*"I was very busy and had noth-
ing to write about . . ."*

GROTON SCHOOL
MARCH 26, 1899,
SUNDAY.

My dear Mama and Papa,

I was much surprised yesterday at getting your telegram and
I had no idea that you would worry at not getting any letter
for half a week. I wrote on Sunday, and did not post my letter
till Thursday noon as I was very busy and had nothing to write
about. I very seldom wrote more than twice a week last year
so did not think you would worry if my Tuesday letter did not
come. I am so pleased that Uncle Fred continues to improve,
and I only hope he will not have a relapse. I think I had better

have a small coat-case to send home by Xpress but I am sure a large trunk is unnecessary. I can go to Tuxedo with my coat-case perfectly well as it is only for two days. I have a sort of idea that my own dress-suit-case is at home, and that I only brought up my hand-bag. So I think you had better take my dress-suit case to town with you and send me another to send my things home in.

I don't believe you could have got my letter telling of my visit to Dr. Wilson, for I told you in it that my teeth have 5 or six holes that *must* be filled at Easter and Dr. Wilson only said they would last till then. I shall need at least two appointments, so I fear I shall have to come to N.Y once more before coming back to school. You know I wrote you on Thursday that I had become an organ-player. Well, on Thursday night, in the midst of a blinding snow-storm four of us left in a two seated waggon. We picked up Mr. Higley who was to deliver the address, & then drove six miles out into the country to a little bit of a school-house called Rocky Hill. When we got there we found a congregation composed of the stove-lighter (who had to be there) and a little boy. It was then 8.30 and as it was sleeting and nobody was there we locked up the house & drove home again so I did not have a chance to perform. We went to Faculty supper & got to bed about 11. We are going again next Thursday and hope for a larger audience. The sports were finished on Saturday.

Monday 8 a.m.

It snowed about 6 inches yesterday but is lovely and melting today. We have about a foot of snow & ice on on [sic] the ground. Doesn't it seem absurd for the 27th of March?

Only a week more!

No more now & ever with dear love to you both   I am your affectionate son

FRANKLIN D. ROOSEVELT

〜〜

*"I have thought of moving to
the chapel and living there for
good . . ."*

My dearest Ma and Pa

Thanks for yours of Sunday and the Graphic and Harper's Weekly, which I have given to Taddy through the window.

We are having a service every day this week, so I have thought of moving all my belongings to the chapel & living there for good.

We go to Rocky Hill again on Thursday, and luckily we have the same hymns as before as we had no service last time.

The coat-case came tonight and thanks for it. I think I can manage all right now. Exams are in progress; we have had two, English and History, both of which I passed with a high B.

It has at last begun to melt hard, and it looks like rain. I am sure it is quite time for rain and spring to come.

I think I shall leave my ma[n]dolin up here during the holidays as it is so hard to carry, but if you think we could have fun with it, I think I can manage to take all right. Let me know by you[r] Sunday letter, which I will get Monday night

Ever with best love & in awful haste   Affec son

FRANKLIN D. ROOSEVELT

〜〜

*"I drummed the organ for all
I was worth . . ."*

My dearest Ma and Pa

I have been invited by Goodwin to lunch and go to the matinée on Wednesday afternoon, and as I have refused him so often, I accepted this time, and hope it will fit in with your plans. We go again to Rocky Hill tonight and hope to have a larger congregation this time.

Jack Minturn & his Mother I don't believe will come, as J. has other engagements which I fancy he prefers. I am glad to see you are to sail by the Kaiser Friedrich on the 25th and are going to get away from meetings etc. which must be tiresome.

Friday.

We got back at 10 o'clock last night and I was so sleepy this a.m that I forgot to send this letter. We had a congregation of 17, quite respectable, as it is composed only of scattered farmer's families round the school-house. We had a pleasant drive, and I drove coming back in the dark. I drummed the organ for all I was worth & drowned out the singers, but I got on fairly well for the first time and only got off the time once in the four hymns. It was hard as I had to pump, play and use the swells all at the same time. I only played the soprano & alto parts right through with an occasional bass chord. It was the last service, as they are only held there during Lent. Yours of Thursday came today, also the Easter cards, many thanks for them. I shall do as you say about the coat-case & can manage very well I am sure. I hope it will be all right about going with Goodwin to the matinée & we can go to something else in the evening. I think you ought to consult Nelly B. about that as she asked me to go & see something with her when she wrote about the vest. I shall send you a line on Sunday to 10 W. 43rd which you will get a few hours before I come. How nice our little spree of Tuesday evening will be! Edmund I believe is going with his mother, too. No more now & ever with best love

F.D.R

The *Kaiser Friedrich* was a liner built on revolutionary new principles for the North German Lloyd Company. The principles were not, however, sufficiently revolutionary to prevent the line's rejecting the ship in June of 1899, complaining that it could barely average twenty knots.

*"In it was my first real thing,
larger than an item . . ."*

My dearest Mama & Papa

Just a line to meet you in New York. It seems horrid to have Easter up here, although service is nice enough. There is a cold wind blowing and although the sun is shining it seems more like January, than April. The snow still covers everything and it freezes stiff at night.

The Grotonian for March came out last night, and in it was my first real thing, larger than an item, the prelude to the Fives Tournament. I had a good deal of work on it, as I had twelve big sheets of scores to work out first and then had to correct the first and second proof-sheets.

I have passed all my examinations that I know of so far, & only Sacred Studies is left for tomorrow. I got A in German and B or B+ in *all* the others except Greek. I took tea with Mr. Cushing on Wednesday, & with Mrs. Abbott yesterday & tomorrow I shall pay a fairwell call to Mrs. Higley. I saw Mrs. Freeman & gave her an Easter card & she was delighted & sent her kind regards to you.

Monday 8 a.m.

We have just heard that Mrs. Corning died very suddenly, is it not awful for poor Edwin. He goes home this morning.

No more now, see you tomorrow afternoon!

FDR.

The final mid-term report, dated April 4th, gave him A's in Geometry, German, and Sacred Studies, and B's in his other five subjects. Opposite Decorum, three black-marks were to be noted. The Rector's general comment was: "Good." Easter vacation followed this letter.

∽∽

"She says he is pealing very slowly . . ."

My darling Mama and Papa,

Here we are back again for ten weeks! We arrived safely at six-thirty, and had a warm pleasant drive up here, and then tea. I ate the buns and cake, also Lathrop Brown had some sandwitches which we shared. Warren appeared cheerful and played hard all the way up. Four or five boys have not come back for various reasons.

Just to think of your sailing in a week! It seems horrid to think of it, but you need not worry the least bit, as I shall be all right I am sure.

I suppose you will see Aunt Kassie off tomorrow and poor abused Hiram, no, I mean the Right Honorable Mr. Price Collier Esquire! I shall have a fearful lot of work to do for the next two or three weeks, as when I get any spare time I shall work on the "Dreyfus case" and then try for the Latin Prize. I got the mail tonight with Howard Cary and saw Mr. Peabody for a minute or two. He asked me how my cold was, (I don't know how he knew about [it]) and said nothing about Taddy or you, or anything else! I shall see Taddy tomorrow and Polly Wharton has seen him & says he is a bit depressed.

Later—

I have just seen Miss Burnett and she says he is pealing very slowly, and from present indications may be a week or *ten* days more; is it not hard on him? I shall write Helen a note about it tonight or tomorrow.

Wednesday 8. a.m.

Another lovely day & it seems so strange to be back. I have about half unpacked so there is lots of work yet. I will write you a line this evening.

Ever your affec. son

F.D.R.

The retrial of Captain Dreyfus was nearing its sensational conclusion at this time, with the French Court of Cassation hearing arguments for revision of the verdict. F.D.R. was working up an article for the *Grotonian* on the case. Miss Burnett was head nurse at the school.

∽∽

*"I have been given another duty
. . . I am delighted to get it . . ."*

GROTON
APRIL 19, 1899,
WEDNESDAY.

My darling Mama & Papa,

We have been here already a day, and it seems more like a month, as everything is running as if we had never been away at all. You see I am trying my new paper, and I think it is perfectly delightful, and nice to write on. I have been given another duty that will take up a good deal of time, but I am delighted to get it. It is Assistant Manager of the Nine. Dick Derby is the Manager, but as he is to row this year, it means that most of the work will fall on me, such as rolling or rather managing the rolling of the field, getting out the players etc. Today I had out a squad of II Formers to shove the big stone roller and I also helped lay out a diamond for the 2nd nine.

No letter came from you either tonight or this a.m. and I hope you are all right. By the way, as if I did not have enough to do without it, I have been kept as mail nigger & no changes have been made. I really think we ought to breakfast every single day with the Rector as a reward! I saw Taddy today and he looks well, and began yesterday to take walks outdoors. His heals have not pealed, and there is no prospect of their doing so; indeed it may *possibly* happen that he won't leave for two weeks, so I doubt if you see him. The seats at table have been changed, and I have a nice place, one from Mr. Gardner, on the opposite side from last term, and next to

289

Warren Motley. I will write again tomorrow and let you know if I need anything but have missed nothing as yet. My cough is better and my neck nearly all right, so you need not worry. I take the mixture four times a day, and have begun the C.L.O.

Ever with best love to you both   I am your affectionate son
FRANKLIN

The "new paper" mentioned here was a plain, porous sheet tinted a vaguely unpleasant sea-green.

〜〜

"I think I have everything I want, except a nail-brush . . ."

[GROTON]
APRIL 20, 1899,
THURSDAY.

Darling Ma and Pa,

Just a line to say that yours of Wednesday was most welcome today and many thanks. I think the sample is very pretty, I mean the dark one with the stripe, don't you. If you can get a suit of it as cheap as Brook's I think it would be very nice.

I think I have everything I want, except a nail-brush. Would you mind sending me one, a big brush without a handle, if possible, Papa knows the kind I mean.

Friday 8 a m.

Spent most of my time yesterday rolling the diamond with different squads and then I had to see that the team was well supplied with bats, balls, gloves, etc. It sprinkled a little yesterday, and today is grey but I don't think it will rain. Tomorrow we play the first game of the season; it is against Brookline High School.

This is my last letter to Hyde Park and tomorrow I shall send a note to 10 W. 43. and my Sunday letter to the Steamer It is horrid to think of your sailing so soon.

Ever with dearest love to you both. I am your most affectionate son
FRANKLIN D ROOSEVELT

". . . and indeed I don't intend
to worry in the least . . ."

My darling Mama and Papa

Yours of Thursday was most welcome this morning, and also the post-card. I shall use the delivery-stamp for my letter to the steamer. A letter came from Mr. Dumper today, and he says he shall not go to the Summer School at Harvard, as the work is too much advanced for him, and if he does not get a position as tutor for the summer he will stay in Gambier all summer and work under an instructor. He also advises me not to worry over my preliminaries, and indeed I don't intend to worry in the least.

Saturday. 6. p.m.

We have just this instant finished a successful game with Brookline High School the first of the season. I have been working on the diamond (the base-ball field) since 8 a.m., marking long lines in lime, & I am spotted with it. I hope you will get off comfortably. I am very well & the weather is lovely & warm

Will write a long letter tomorrow

In awful haste

FDR

∽∽

"Taddy is at last beginning to
peal on his heals . . ."

My darling Mama and Papa,

I wrote you a note yesterday afternoon, but unfortunately I missed the mail-bag by about 30 seconds. I shall send it to the steamer, however, just to see if it reaches you without a special delivery stamp. As I wrote in it, we had a game yesterday afternoon with Brookline High School, the first of the season. We won by the score of 14–10, a very good showing for the beginning of the season, and the diamond was in good order.

It is very warm today, and most of the boys have gone into their summer things. However I shall not change my flannels till next Sunday, nor my blue suit for two weeks. I wonder what you did about my new grey suit? If you did not order one, I shall wait till the patterns come from Brooks as we arranged.

I hope you remembered to send me "the Dreyfus "case", as I want to write an article on it as soon I get any time; I suppose my dress-suit case will come with it and the summer flannels tomorrow, or next day. I think with this weather you ought to have a good trip, and I believe the Kaiser Friedrich is a good sea-boat anyway. It will be horrid not getting any letters from you for over two weeks, but I shall expect a cable as soon as you get there, remember. Roosevelt, Groton Mass. will be sufficient, I think, & you need not sign it.

Taddy is at last beginning to peal on his heals, and hopes to leave within a week. He went out canoeing this morning with his nurse, while we were in church, and is to do it again tomorrow if it is warm. *I* shall not go on the river for some time yet, and anyway I have no time for it.

I suppose you will find it still quite cold at Nauheim when you get there, and I hope there will be somebody there you know. I will keep as usual a diary letter to you & will write at least twice a week. I got a cheque from Aunt Kassie and yesterday one from Aunt Dora. Please thank her for it and give her my love & goodbye. If you will send me her address when you get to Germany I will write her; I am also going to write to Aunt Annie every couple of weeks.

Later—

It is so warm tonight that the boys have been allowed to go

out after supper, and the Rector read aloud on the steps. I fear you will have a very early start from the apartment, and the first day will seem fearfully long, but I suppose there will be a certain novelty in going by the North German Lloyd. I am addressing my letters to Hoboken, and I hope you will get them and that it is not Jersey City.

Monday 8. a.m.

I must finish my letter now and say good-bye. By the way let me know please if you have decided to go to the Adirondacks, and if you succeeded in getting a camp.

I do hope you will have a good voyage, and I think you ought to after this lovely weather. Remember to cable as soon as you get there, & be sure you don't worry, as I shall be all right, and my cold is practically gone.

I cannot bear to think of the ocean being between us

Goodbye now, my darling parents

Ever with lots of love of hugs and kisses, I am your very loving son

FRANKLIN.

There were a number of books about the Dreyfus case being published in English at this time; the most likely to have been that requested by F.D.R. was Frederick C. Conybeare's *The Dreyfus Case*. The James Roosevelts often vacationed for a month in the St. Regis area of the Adirondacks.

$\sim\!\sim$

*"I am thinking of you as leaving
the dock in about an hour . . ."*

[GROTON]
APRIL 24, 1899,
MONDAY.

My darling Mama and Papa,

My letter to the steamer left this morning and I hope you will receive it all right. It seems very funny to be writing to you abroad, when you have not yet left this side! but I want just to send a line by the White Star boat, leaving the day after you do, so you will not be very long without news after you reach the other side. I sent a telegram to you at the Renaissance this afternoon after school, and I hope you weren't alarmed when you got it, or thought at first that I had another desease!

Thank you so much for subscribing for me to the various papers. I have received the Great Round World, also a letter from the "Osprey" people which I enclose. They sent me the piece of paper you wrapped your dollar bill up in and it was torn in ribbons but the bill inside did [not] suffer much strange to say. I destroyed the paper by mistake so can not send it to you.

I suppose that by the time this reaches you, you will be about settled, in the Villa Grunewald *not* Grünewald is it not? I really would almost like to see old Nauheim again, and I fancy it must have changed since I was there three years ago.

I got you[r] letter of Friday & Saturday this morning & am so sorry you (Mama) have a cold and you *must be careful* & not add to it (*Per order*).

Tuesday April 25th 8. a.m.

Your dear letter of Sunday from H.P. came last night, and also the sample, which I will keep. The valise also came, with the water-proof flannels and night-light, but I think you forgot my new stockings. However they may come from N.Y. and anyway they are not absolutely necessary. I am thinking of you as leaving the dock in about an hour, and I hope you have good weather for starting and will have a smooth trip. Aunt Kassie should arrive tomorrow & Warren expects news then and I shall expect it a week from today. No more now. Warren sends love, & Taddy's heals are at last pealing and he hopes to be gone in a week

Ever, dearest Mama and Papa, with loads of love and kisses to you both   I am your affec. son

F.D.R.

The Great Round World was a weekly news journal founded in 1896; it discontinued publication in 1903. Of even shorter life-span was *The Osprey; An Illustrated Monthly Magazine of Ornithology*, whose wings folded shortly after F.D.R. received his subscription.

∽∽

"You see the Old World is be-
hind the New in everything . . ."

[GROTON]
APRIL 25, 1899,
TUESDAY.

My darling Mama and Papa,

Your dear telegram from the steamer came this afternoon at about three o'clock, and I got it during afternoon school. Just to think of your being out of sight of land long before this! I can hardly believe it.

Wednesday—

Your lovely letter and the passenger list came this morning, the last letter I shall have of you for over two weeks, I am sorry to say. I am glad you have nice deck rooms, and a sitting-room all to yourself. I hope Charley Forbes won't occupy it too much, even if Aunt Dora wants him to!

The Dreyfus case & the nailbrush have come & thanks for them, but I am sorry to say that Archie Brown does not want an article on Dreyfus, as he says they had one about a year ago.

We had a very good game this afternoon with English High School and although beaten by the score of 7–6 we played a good game. I spent the morning marking out the field etc. and on the whole am kept pretty busy. By the way it is exactly a year ago today that I came down with the scarlet-fever, bad luck to it, and it seems only a few months. No pest has broken out so far, and there seems little likelyhood of it now

Thursday April 27th.

Today is a choir-half-holiday and I played golf in the afternoon. I have done this course in 46 (yesterday) three lower than ever before, so if we go to Campobello I hope to be able to break my record. Too bad we could not get the camp you thought of, but I hope we can get the other.

The doll and stockings came last night and I almost fainted when I saw the human face inside the box, & at first thought someone had sent me a dead baby as a practical joke. I carried it through the hall in my arms & soon had a crowd following, all wishing to kiss the latest addition to my family! The Peabody baby was delighted and requested me to give you her sincere thanks (she can't talk yet but said "goo-goo" & I did my best to translate it). The underclothes also came from Arnold's and I think them very nice. They were not marked so I had them done in the sewing-room.

Taddy is out all day, of course away from the other boys, and went up the river on Tuesday with his nurse and his lunch for the whole day. His heal is slowly healing and he hopes to be able to leave by next Tuesday.

I noticed you crossed with Lilli Lehmann, & who is the Miss Lee you marked on the list?

We are having perfect weather, and I think the ocean must be smooth now. Your voyage will be half over tomorrow, and I can hardly wait for your cablegram. I hope the straw hat man will come soon as it is getting rather warm to go to church in my pot-hat.

Warren is getting on all right and waiting for a letter from his mother. She did not cable him and did not intend to, when she got in, as I suppose she did, yesterday.

The roof is being put on the new building and it looks very well, and the lumber for a new stable has come & they are to begin work very soon.

No more now, I will write again Sunday.

Ever with tons of love I am your affectionate son

FRANKLIN D. ROOSEVELT

How cold it must be still at Nauheim!. You see the Old World is behind the new in everything—

Charles Stuart Forbes, a brother-in-law of Dora Delano Forbes, was an artist and lived mostly abroad. F.D.R. and Eleanor Roosevelt visited him in Venice on their honeymoon in 1905. "Arnold's" was a reference to the New York store of Arnold, Constable & Co. Madame Lilli Lehmann, the great Wagnerian soprano, was then nearing the end of her career. She had given a "farewell concert" at Carnegie Hall on the Thursday afternoon prior to her sailing. "Miss Lee" may have been some relation to Alice Hathaway Lee, Theodore Roosevelt's first wife, which would have explained why Mrs. James Roosevelt checked the name. On formal occasions in the fall and winter the Groton boys wore bowlers; these were succeeded by typically English straw hats in the spring.

〰

"My stomach is now relatively much smaller than my chest . . ."

[GROTON]
APRIL 28, 1899,
FRIDAY.

My darling Mama and Papa,

It is horrid not to be getting any of your dear letters, but I must be patient for over a week more.

I played golf today and succeeded in doing the course in 45, one better than yesterday.

Saturday April 29th.

I took my strength test & measurements this morning and succeeded in getting 565 in the test, where I was 452 last time in the autumn so you see I have gone up 113 points. Mr. Skarstrom was much pleased and said the improvement was very good especially in the shoulders & chest and stomach which is now relatively much smaller than my chest. My height sitting is relatively greater to my height standing than it was before, which is also a marked improvement. Old "cigar-stump" still swears that my heart is still weak, & I told

him that he was a liar (not quite in those words). I had intended to row this spring & try for one of the crews, but he
says I ought to give it up & I suppose it would be on the whole
safer not to, so I shall do my best at base-ball & golf. We
played Somerville High School this p.m   the best school team
around Boston. We put up a wretched game, & were beaten
15–3. However it will not hurt the nine at all to meet with
a defeat or two & will make them work all the harder. We
play St. Marks at Worcester on May 31st, & this year we are
going to fight for it.

I found the arrival of the "Teutonic" at Queenstown in the
Thursday papers, & showed it to Warren as it was the first he
heard of their arrival. I believe there is a slight chance of
Aunt Kassie going to Nauheim; how nice it would be if you
could all be there together.

Sunday April 30th

Today is the last day of April & we have been here nearly
two weeks; the time passes rapidly. Last night the photos came
from Vail, & I will send them to you tomorrow, also some to
Helen. I consider them all *excellent,* Mama's the least so, & the
group is quite worth keeping

Later—

We seem haunted up here by deseases of some kind, and
what do you suppose has capped the climax now? Yesterday
the youngest Fish boy came down with appendicitis, not serious at all; this morning two boys developed german measles,
this afternoon a third came down with it, & to beat all, it has
just been announced that Chapin has *scarlet fever*!!!!!!!!!! What
an unlucky time the poor School & the Rector are having!
The case is light, but if there is any more the four lower forms
will go home, but of course I shall stay. The weather continues
perfectly lovely, and very warm, the thermometer being over
85° all day. I have gone into my spring flannels & old light
gray suit & I am quite ready for them. I am writing Brooks to

send some samples immediately as I have absolutely *no* light knickerbockers for summer.

Monday—

Another lovely day even hotter than yesterday and I think we shall have a shower before evening. I shall anxiously expect your cable tomorrow some time & then a letter in about a week. The first swimming took place today; I went in and found the water delightful, not too warm & not as dirty as later on in the season. Before swimming I took a walk through the woods with Laury Rainsford to see if we could find any nests, but I think it is a little too early. Everything is budding, and the leaves have begun to break out on some of the trees & shrubs. The grass is absolutely green now.

You must find Nauheim lovely now, but I suppose it is still quite cool there. Please don't forget the old Graphics Paris Heralds etc!

I am not sending this till the Wednesday boat as it is only the old Saale on the U.S. Lloyd I think. No more now, I will write again for the Saturday boat

Ever with best love to you both I am your affec. son

FRANKLIN

No more deseases today!

I have sent the photos. Let me know if you have to pay extra postage on this letter. I don't think so.

The "youngest Fish boy" was Sidney, a grandson of Grant's famous Secretary of State, and first cousin of Congressman Hamilton Fish. Vail Bros. was a firm of Poughkeepsie photographers; their portrait photographs of James Roosevelt, Sara Delano Roosevelt, and of the Roosevelt family group, mentioned in this letter, have been reproduced in this volume.

∽∼

". . . the foaming cow place,
where the cow won't foam any
more? . . ."

My darling Mama and Papa,

No Cable has come today, but I suppose it takes longer to go to Southampton than to Liverpool, so I should not get it till tomorrow morning. We had a good shower last night and the leaves are now well advanced on most of the trees. I rolled the diamond with a gang of first formers and then watched the nine who were coached today by a Mr. Murphy, a Yale graduate.

Wednesday May 3rd.

Your dear cable was most welcome this morning during recess at 10 o'clock saying "Well, Good voyage." I also saw the "Kaiser Friedrichs" arrival at Southampton in the Tuesday Evening papers, which get here this evening. I shall now anxiously await a letter which I should get by next Thursday. This morning I spent marking out the diamond and in the afternoon we played a game with the Technology Freshmen of Boston. We beat them, altho' neither side played particularly well, by the score of 9–4. The weather is much cooler, quite chilly in fact, and the duck-trousers have given way to winter suits. I did not wear my ducks at all, as I thought it rather early and unseasonable.

Thursday May 4th

Still cold, and windy. You must be at old Nauheim by this time I think, unless you spent a night on the road somewhere. Please give my kind regards to Dr. Scott, no Shot; I wonder how many children he has now? Don't give silver cups to them *all* please! How is the old woman in the shooting gallery? and the foaming cow place, where the cow won't foam any more? Are there any nice people you know, and is Aunt Kassie going to take a cure there?

I have just received word that Taddy is to go home tomorrow. He is delighted and I have written Helen to have him met. Chapin the new case has moved right into Taddy's rooms, and he has a case even lighter than Taddy's with scarcely *no* fever. Still it is awfully hard on him as his parents are in Johannesburg South Africa, and old Mr. Le Bourgeois in London, but he has some other relatives over here. There are no more cases yet only Lathrop Brown, who has a bad attack of Rheumatic Fever, and is quite ill.

I am spending most of my time writing themes & reading books for Charles R. Nutter; you remember I told you he would make us work like dogs when he got back, and he certainly does. There is to be a choir festival after all & we are to go some time early in June. We practice two nights a week, so that also takes time.

Friday May 5th. 8 a.m.

I will finish this before the mail goes at nine, & you will get news quite fresh from me.

We begin the May services in the town hall next Sunday & it will be nice walking down in the evening. I wonder if the English church has ever been built at Nauheim or if the plan has fallen through? You will probably see about the Sloane divorce, & her marriage within an hour to Perry Belmont, in the Paris Herald—quite lively going isn't it?

No more now

I am your affectionate son

FRANKLIN D. ROOSEVELT.

He had missed fire; the name of the doctor under whose care James Roosevelt took the Nauheim cure was Schott. "Old Mr. Le Bourgeois" was the grandfather of Louis LeB. Chapin, two classes behind F.D.R. Jessie A. Robbins had been separated and then divorced from Henry T. Sloane under circumstances which caused some genteel censure by the society of the period. The reason for this rather adult and chatty reference would doubtless have been the fact that Jessie Robbins (daughter of Daniel Robbins of McKesson & Robbins) was a sister of Aunt Kassie's first husband, Charles Robbins.

GROTON
MAY 5, 1899,
FRIDAY.

My dearest Mama and Papa,

I sent my last letter to you this morning at 8. o'clock, and soon after I noticed the arrival of the "Kaiser Friedrich" in the Thursday Evening Post at Bremen, dated Thursday the 4th I supposed you would get in on Wednesday, and wonder if anything delayed you? or if the news was dated wrong.

I had a very funny time this afternoon—To begin with it was a choir half-holiday, the second this term, so I went and played one round of golf with Fuller Potter who is also a tenor in the choir. He had then to return to row, & just then I met Mr. Cushing, Mrs. Lawrence and "Libby" coming to play. They wanted someone to make up a foursome, so I played with Libby against the "General" and Madame. Libby was large as life, and twice as queer & we played nearly two more rounds, beating Cush and Mrs. L. all out of their boots. When we came home I had google with Mr. Cushing.

Saturday May 6th.

Another lovely day. I spent the whole morning marking the diamond, and resodding it where the grass is worn out. We played Dean Academy, and were badly beaten 19–6. They had a very strong team, and hit our pitcher hard and I am sorry to say we made a good many errors. We play the Harvard Freshmen on Wednesday next, Pomfret on the 17th and St. Marks on the 31st. We will begin drilling soon for the Decoration Day parade, which you saw last year, when John Cross was thrown off his horse.

Sunday May 7th.

We have been here three weeks almost, and the term is going fast. I forgot to tell you that Warren is coxing the first Hemenway crew, as he did last year. He was not found to be too heavy & as he hates base-ball he decided to cox. He got a letter from his mother at Queenstown last night, the first he has had; they had a rough voyage strange to say, so I fear you may have not had it smooth all the way.

I was offered the captaincy of one of the cup nines yesterday but as I may not be able to play all the time, owing to work on the first eleven, I thought I had better not accept it, and anyway I may row later on. I will finish this tomorrow.

Monday May 8th

Last night we went to Groton right after tea, having had evening school at 4 o'clock. I walked down & back with Moseley, the boy L. Brown & I are trying to reform. The preacher was the Rev. Addison of Brookline Mass, & the sermon was excellent, only he spoke too loud, while the reverse is generally the case. The big town-hall was packed & the fifth form are ushers, five every Sunday, so I shall be one the last Sunday as it is alphabetical.

I had a letter from Helen today, & she says Taddy got to N.Y. all right, & Charles packed him right off to H.P. She says "Father is out in the wilds of Canada", *I* shouldn't be surprised if he went to China! She is going up to H.P. as soon as Taddy comes back here, probably the end of this week. I ought to get your first dear letter on Thursday & I am longing for it. Just think our Jackson exams come in a month & you will be home in less than two, & the preliminaries all over.

The Grotonian came out last night, and I will send it to you be [by] the next mail, as it will probably not be forwarded from Hyde Park.

No more now & with tons of love & kisses & hugs & etc & etc, Affectionately

FRANKLIN.

I have ordered an extra of grey flannel trousers, awfully nice from the store up here & only $6.00, I thought you would not mind.

FDR

"Libby" was Elizabeth Prescott Lawrence (*vide supra*). John W. Cross later became a noted architect, associated with his brother in the New York firm of Cross & Cross which designed the City Bank Farmers Trust Building, the General Electric Building, and others. Ben P. P. Moseley, object of the reform efforts, is recalled by contemporaries as having been considerable of a non-conformist. He was in F.D.R.'s form but did not graduate. A close friend of the Rector's was the Reverend J. Thayer Addison. He was professor of the history of religions and missions at Episcopal, thereafter master of Kirkland House at Harvard and a member of the National Council of the Episcopal Church. Ernest Jackson was a former master at Groton who left to engage in private tutoring in and around Boston. He devised a schedule of examinations which was used by Groton and other preparatory schools as a measure of how well their students were prepared for college. What college preliminary examinations a boy would be allowed to take depended upon how he did in the "Jackson's."

$\diamondsuit$

*"We had some hash last night
which caused dire results . . ."*

[GROTON]
MAY 9, 1899,
TUESDAY.

My darling Mama and Papa,

The lovely spring weather continues, and the pear blossoms are out, and the apple-blossoms beginning to appear. We had some hash last night which caused dire results on the whole school, and I passed an eventful and sleepless night. As a result I can hardly move today, but we are beginning to feel better now.

Wednesday May 10th

We played a game with the Harvard Freshmen this afternoon and they had a very strong team. We did not play well I am sorry to say, and they beat us by the score of 16–6; our nine is not all good, this year, and we fully expect to be beaten by St. Marks unless they improve very much.

I got a letter from Uncle Warren today & he invites me to Steen Valetje. I shall go as we planned on Monday the third, spending Sunday at home. A letter also came from Nellie B just before she sailed, enclosing $10 for the camp and wondering if my waistcoat came all right. I shall write to her at Paris to tell her that it has been sent home & thank her for the cheque.

This evening a large box came from Brooks and in it I found two four piece suits, the *only* two they had or were going to have of the four-piece variety. One was very light and the other not quite as light grey, but as light as the one we liked and rough also. I am keeping it and like it, as I think you will also. The pieces all fit well, only the knickerbockers have no extensions, so I am sending them back with the other suit to have some put on.

Thursday—

This morning it was lovely and being Ascension-day the ground for the New Chapel was broken. Just before morning school we all went out to the site and there was a short prayer & a hymn, then Mr.G. broke the first sod, and then the Rector turned one. After that we sang the School Hymn & went back to lessons. We were given a half-holiday in honor of the occasion, and I started off with Laurie Rainsford to observe birds and play golf, but we didn't get far when it began to pour, and we got soaked to the skin, and had to come back. It rained all afternoon but cleared towards evening, and it was much needed, as it is only the second rain we have have [had] this term. I am working like a dog now, as it is better to do so than later on in June. Our Jackson exams come the first weeks in June. I *hope* to go up on 15 hours this year, more than anyone else in the form except Blagden who also takes 15, & I should be amply satisfied if I could pass 11 or 12. No letter has come today but I expect one tomorrow, as I do not suppose it caught the Teutonic which sailed the day after you got to Southampton.

Friday—8 a.m.

I must send this now as the mail goes in ten minutes. I hope you are having good weather at Nauheim & not too cold

Ever with best love   Affec. son

FDR.

Mr. Gardner gave both Groton chapels. The first, a plaster-and-timber affair, was presented to the Roman Catholic Church of Groton and moved into the village, where it still stands. Its place was taken by a stone chapel in the late Gothic style, designed by Henry Vaughan—one of the most graceful adoptions of the Gothic manner, and a landmark of the countryside.

∽∽

"Today a very important event
took place, at least I hope so . . ."

[GROTON]
MAY 12, 1899,
FRIDAY.

My dearest Mama and Papa,

Just after sending my letter this morning your dear letter and the post-cards came. I was delighted to get it, and am glad you didn't drop your lunch, even though there was a nasty swell for the last few days! You did not say whether you liked the German boat, but as you made no complaints I suppose you did, and at all events the food was good and that is half the battle. The post-cards were awfully pretty and many thanks for them; the diary no I mean dairy of the voyage was very interesting, and I will show one of them to Mrs. Freeman, although I cannot give it to her as you wrote on the other side. The old Lady has had a cough very much like mine, and has not been well lately, but she is improving and will soon be all right I think. All the apple-trees are in bloom, and the country is lovely.

Saturday May 13th

Last night I had a delightful surprise in the shape of a small round package and a letter. On opening the package I found a pair of awfully pretty golf-stockings, the long-promised pair from Frances. They have blue and grey tops, of the pattern I told you I liked so much, the only trouble being that they are awfully small in the foot and leg, so that they are pretty well stretched over my mighty muscles. Among other things she writes that the Kuhns have taken Capt. Mitchell for their boat the "Petrel," and that Hamilton is much better. The Bangs are going as usual about July 1st but the Sampsons are probably going abroad, and they themselves go to Campo the last week in June. By the way I wish you could let me know as soon as possible whether we are going to Campo or the Adirondacks, as I should like to ask some boys pretty soon.

By the way, while you are in Germany I wish you could get my new flannels as my present ones for spring and autumn are about out-grown, and are very tight besides being a little worn-out. I have not gone into my summer weight yet, and do not expect to until about the first of June.

We are to begin drilling for the Decoration Day parade this week, and although not very exciting it is always something out of the ordinary run of things. I have forgotten to tell you in my last two or three letters that about half a dozen boys in the school have had whooping-cough ever since they came back, and have been mixing with the others as usual I am quite positive that I have had a light attack of it, as I still have a paroxism or so every day, when I run hard. I am much better now, but still cough once in a great while, but it isn't in the least serious.

This afternoon we played Hopkinson and as usual were beaten, although this time not so badly, 7-2. I do not expect us to win on the 31st, as our team is really playing wretchedly.

Sunday May 14th.

It is lovely today, but quite cold. The lilacs are almost all out.

Today a very important event in the history of the School took place, at least I hope so. Four of five of us boys have with the approval of the Rector formed a natural-history society. You know a large room has been set apart in the new school-building for a museum, and there are at present no collections to put in it, so we are to do systematic work. I have forgotten in my last two letters to tell you that a Prof. Morse has come up twice and given the school lectures   the first on Japan, the second on ants. He is a most really remarkable man, a great traveller, a good artist and a wonderful naturalist. He is coming up again on Tuesday & also the following week and four of us, who are starting the society, are to be given a half-holiday and go off into the woods with Prof. Morse, and he is to give us points about collecting, etc. It will be most interesting as well as instructive, and we are all enthusiastic. Our idea is not to let everybody into the Society but only those who care for natural history & who will take an interest and really work. I will finish this tomorrow as it is time to start for Groton.

Monday, May 15th

We had a nice service last night & the sermon which was good was by Dr. Sprague of Charlestown. I walked with Harold Peabody, and it was quite chilly coming back, but I wore my winter suit and vest so was comfortable. Your letter from Nauheim the evening you got there was a delight this morning, and I'm glad you had a comfortable trip; I should have liked to see Bremen, it must be very interesting. Dan Draper also heard from his people.

Be sure you write me when you expect to leave Nauheim, and where you are going for the aftercure, which I don't suppose will be at St. Blasien, as you must be rather tired of it. I saw by the paper of the death of Mr. Ellison and doubtless Aunt Annie has written you of it. I wonder what his daughter's will do now & if they will stay at Newburgh.

By the time this reaches you your cure will be half over, and I wonder if Papa will have got to Sprudel-Stroms yet, and if you are enjoying Schwalheimer, or café-frappé and the band on the terrace.

No more now, I must close for evening mail so as to be sure of the Wednesday steamer—

Ever with lots of love & hugs & kisses & excuses for an awful scrawl   I am your affectionate son

FRANKLIN D. ROOSEVELT

Warren is well and sends love. Taddy came back this morning by the Fall River boat, looking well but a bit yellow. He is to tuitor during the summer & take exams in autumn. Helen goes to H.P.

The "Frances" of this letter was probably Frances Pell (see several later references). Old friends of the Roosevelt family were Mrs. Hartman Kuhn and Hamilton Kuhn. After Mrs. Kuhn died, she provided in her will that F.D.R.'s mother should have an option to purchase her house at Campobello (which adjoined that of the James Roosevelts) for $5000, on condition that if the house were so purchased it should be given to F.D.R. as a wedding present. Whooping-cough was so prevalent that boys were rarely hospitalized more than a day or so, in the most serious cases, and the rest of the time allowed to go freely about their business. A Groton Natural History Society had been formed originally in 1894 under Mr. Richards, then a sixth-former. It had lapsed, and was now being re-formed under the impetus of Professor Edward S. Morse's lectures. The latter was a unique little man with an engaging personality. He was ambidextrous, frequently delighting his audiences by drawing butterflies with both hands simultaneously and performing other remarkable feats at the blackboard. He settled in Salem in 1866, and was one of the founders and the curator of the Peabody Academy of Sciences there, as well as a founder and editor of the *American Naturalist*. His ambidexterity extended to the fields of learning: articles on brachiopods called him favorably to Darwin's attention, and his lectures on Oriental art inspired Mrs. Jack Gardner to begin her famous collection of Orientalia.

"He ran down the poor Chinamen
and thought too much of the Japs . . ."

My dearest Mama and Papa,

This afternoon the first trip of the natural history society took place under the leadership of Prof. Morse. We, that is the two Rainsfords, Ben Joy, Julian Hinckley and myself started soon after dinner for the woods. Prof. Morse started by turning over old logs and stones, etc. and we soon had discovered several varieties of small snails, etc. He also gave us a good idea about what to collect, how to preserve and label it, and other things about the new museum. Mr. Sturgis is to have the general charge of it and we are to try to get good collections, especially of the animals & things found in this locality. It is really very cold today and I had to wear a coat to go out, so you see Nauheim is not the only chilly place in May.

Wednesday, May 17th 1899

Last night Prof. Morse gave us his third talk, that is to the whole school; it was on China, and most interesting, although I rather thought he ran down the poor Chinamen a little too much and thought too much of the Japs. He is coming again next Tuesday for the fourth and last time, and I think we are to go off with him again.

This morning I spent in marking the diamond as usual and was a fright when through. This afternoon we played Pomfret and at last won a game with the good score of 25–11, although I must say that their team was wretchedly weak, so the score doesn't show much. You know Pomfret had a row last year with St. Marks and doesn't play them now, so this is their great game of the season, and they were promised two half-holidays if they should win, but they did not get them. It is sunny but cold today, indeed for the last week we have shivered, although the weather has been lovely. Taddy has begun work work [*sic*] again, and is rowing on the second crew, the Squannacooks, who are absolutely rotten this year, although they have a good first crew. Warren had eleven black marks last week, I am sorry to say, & the Rector has kept him off the river for two weeks, so he may not be able to cox in the race, which would be too bad, as he has worked at coxing every day this term. The ground for the new chapel is being dug up and carted away, the new building almost has the roof on, a new big barn & stables, much bigger than the old one is going up, and the contract has been made for Mr. Sturgis' house, & work will begin soon so you see we have the building craze badly; besides all this a big place in the woods near the river is being cleared and the stumps blasted out, for a new system of drainage, where the sewer will run first into one huge gravel bank, then into another, when the first is full & finally into a third, each bank for two weeks & by the time the third is full they switch it back to the first again, which is now clean, having filtered everything through to the river.

Thursday May 18th

Just a month since we came back, and the time is going like lightning. Your lovely long letter, the second from Nauheim made me happy today. I am so glad you are comfortably settled, and have such nice people as the Drapers near you. Give the old shooting woman my kind regards. I really am very anxious to see Nauheim again, after being away three years, it must have changed a good deal, especially if people begin to talk English in the shops. I am so glad you are both so well, and I hope the cure won't pull either of you down for the time being. It is cloudy & cold today & not at all like May.

Friday. May 19th 8. a.m.

Still cold & drizzling. I must send this now, as the mail goes soon. I am working hard now all my spare time in reviewing, so as not to have too much work in June. No more now & Ever with best love to you both I am   Your affec. son

FRANKLIN

Thanks for the Graphic & the excellent menu   It makes my mouth water.

[GROTON]
MAY 20, 1899,
SATURDAY.

My dearest Mama and Papa,

Your letter and the Graphics have kept me busy all the morning, and all the Nauheim news was a comfort. How nice it is for you to have the Drapers, and I wonder what villa they are in, or if they are in the old "Kaiserhof." I should think you would be tempted to play the Toupi-hollandaise all the time, and I suppose you can hear it going constantly. Are those awful people the Parrs in the Villa Grunewald again this year? and why has not the English church been built?

We played a team this afternoon composed of some men from Ayer and three or four Graduates and I am glad to say beat them until it began to rain & we had to stop. It has been a horrid day with rain at intervals & cold. We play the Harvard 2nd Varsity on Wednesday & they ought to beat us badly.

Sunday. May 21st

Another rainy horrid day, but we mustn't complain, after so much lovely weather before this.

I have some more bad news for you. Yesterday morning it transpired that there was a case of mumps in the infirmary and during the day three others came down with it. This morning four more got this and this afternoon one more, making 9 in all. It is of a light form so you needn't worry if I get it, as it does not take more than a week. We are quite resigned to an epidemic & I don't see how most of [us] can escape.

Later

It is almost time to get ready to go to Groton. It has cleared up a little so we shall walk. I am an usher so much start about half-an hour before the rest of the school.

Monday. May 22nd

It has at last cleared but is still cold. I had great fun ushering & the big hall was packed every atom of room being taken.

Just after the sermon began a crowd of ladies came in, & as the ushers had stools at the back by the door we had to get up & give them our seats, standing all through the rest of the service. Oh how my corns ached! & then we had to run home most of the way in the mud, as the ushers had to pick up the hymn-books afterwards. Your dear long letter of May 10th & 11th came today, & I am glad you are having such a nice time. This is the last letter I can send to Nauheim, that is if you do not stay longer than one month, so I shall send the next c/o Baring Bros. as I have not heard where you are going for the aftercure.

This evening after supper we had our first drill and I am the corporal of the second squad of Company B and have 7 men under me. Taddy as a sixth form is a second lieutenant & so is Dan Draper I think. We drill every evening after supper this week, and in a way I don't mind it at all, although some of the fellows hate it.

Five more cases of mumps today, but as yet only one in our form. The infirmary is *packed* & if there is a single other case they will have to turn Mr. Gladwins dormitory into a pest-house. I expect Warren to get it any moment, as most of the cases are from his form & dormitory, but it has pretty well permeated the whool school.

We only pray that one of the nine does not get it, as we should then be helpless against St. Marks.

Tuesday May 23rd 8.a.m.

The term is more than half-over and I am thinking of seeing you in six weeks. The news of the "Paris" has just come, & I am so glad the sailors & officers behaved so well, but all the same it's just as well you weren't on board. Roger Derby came down with the disease at 6 this morning & as he is on the first Hemenway crew, there may be no race this year, & it would be a great disappointment to Warren

No more now, I am still all right

Ever with best love to you both I am your affec son

F.D.R.

The liner *Paris* ran aground May 21st off Lowland's Point, near Falmouth in England. There were no casualties; her three hundred and eighty-six passengers were landed safely, and she was refloated a month later.

～～

"... *hardly appreciated, as they are 'so English you know'* ..."

[GROTON]
MAY 24, 1899,
WEDNESDAY.

My dearest Mama and Papa,

This morning I played a hard game of tennis, and this afternoon we had a base-ball game, the last before the St. Mark's game. It was with the Harvard 2nd Varsity, a very strong team as you may imagine, and we did much better than I expected, & although beaten the score was 14-8. A large basket of goodies came from Aunt Annie today, also one for Warren. In it were oranges, bananas, crackers, ginger-snaps, maple-sugar, marmalade, currant-jam, grape-jelly etc. a perfect Eden of food. So you see we are well taken care of even if you are not over here. I am sending this to Baring Bros as I am afraid it would not catch you at Nauheim if you leave after your four weeks are up. I wonder if you and the Drapers will go to the same after-cure, if you do it would be very nice.

Thursday.

A lovely hot day, just nice. I played tennis and worked a little out of school on my English. Our Jackson exams begin on June 6th less than two weeks, and I am really a bit alarmed over them, as they are harder if anything than the preliminaries.

There are now nearly twenty cases of mumps in the infirmary, only one from our form however & one from the IV Form, so I hope to escape. I fully expect to have Warren get it, as most cases are from his form and dormitory.

Friday. 8. am

I must close this fearful scrawl which I hope you will excuse. The drill continues every evening & my "four" has improved. We march Tuesday afternoon, and I hope it won't be very hot and dusty. I shall go into my summer flannels in about a week if this warmth continues.

Many thanks for the Punch and "Spectator". They were most welcome to me, to [though] hardly appreciated by others, as they are "so English you know." Just think, only a little over five weeks before you are home!

The mail goes in five minutes so good-bye—
Ever your affectionate son

FRANKLIN

〜〜

"You are truly a fairy-aunt to me . . ."

GROTON SCHOOL
MAY 25, 1899,
THURSDAY.

My dear Aunt Annie,

You are truly a fairy-aunt to me, and I cannot tell you how much I appreciated your trouble in sending all the *delicious* things to Warren and me. You have thought of every possible thing we like, and now we are well supplied for the remainder of the term, thanks to you. I am awfully sorry I forgot to acknowledge the cheque in your last letter; it came all right and many thanks for it, and apologies for forgetting to thank you before.

You probably have not heard of our latest epidemic here. Last Saturday a case of mumps developed and now nearly twenty boys have it, chiefly among the lower forms. I have never had it, neither has Warren, but we are both absolutely well and hope to escape it. It is a light form, so even if we should get it, it would only take a little over a week to get well.

I am so glad Uncle Fred is improving so fast, and is able to be out, and enjoy this lovely weather. I only wish I could be on the Hudson with you now, but the term is more than half over so I will see you both before very long.

Thanking you again and again, dear Aunt Annie, for being so good to us, and with lots of love to you and to Uncle Fred I am

Your most affectionate nephew

FRANKLIN D. ROOSEVELT

Mrs. Hitch mailed this letter on to her sister in Europe, and wrote across the top of the first page, in explanation and extenuation of the "perfect Eden of food": "Oranges, Bananas, Ginger snaps, Water thin wafers, Jams, Maple Sugar, *all harmless.*"

∽

"I am glad the English Church
is progressing so well . . ."

[GROTON]
MAY 26, 1899,
FRIDAY.

My dearest Mama and Papa,

I have been pouring over your two dear letters of May 10th & 11th and May 13th, both of which came today. I am so glad you have been having such lovely weather at Nauheim, and had such nice companions as the Drapers. Thanks for the code, it is nice to have, but I hope there wont be any necessity for using it. Thanks also for the "Paris Herald" and the "Times," both of which were interesting, and seemed like old friends. I am glad the English Church is progressing so well, but I quite understand your liking for the Lutheran service.

I have had a most busy time today; I played a hard game of tennis this morning and in the afternoon went out on the river as it was a half-holiday, given instead of the morning of May 30th. We paddled way up the river, till we got to Mr. Cush's picnic ground. There we met him and four or five other boys, and after stripping played "scrub" a sort of baseball with a tennis ball on the grassy bank, and then went in swimming. We then had "google" and cake and paddled home to a supper (?) of sure-death hash!

Saturday—May 27th.

Another roasting day—I walked to Groton to see if I could not hire a bicycle for the few days during the exams, but did not succeed there, so will have to try at Ayer, and failing that go into Boston for one the day after school closes, when there are no exams. Jackson comes on the 6th of June, a little over a week, and I hope I can do well with him, but feel rather doubtful. The marks for last month were read out yesterday and I still managed to get a B; there were only 4 others who got it so I was anyway among the first 5, if not higher. Warren was five from the tail, but doing fairly well I think.

Sunday, May 28.

Yesterday what do you think happened? Only another *dis*ease (thanks). A boy named Ladd in the second form has scarlet-fever, the second case this term & third this year. We can't imagine where it comes from, but there must be some source of infection open all the time. No more cases of mumps yesterday or today. There are now twenty & the first ones are sitting up, so we hope we have checked it. I forgot to say yesterday that we played another game with Ayer and some graduates, and I am sorry to say the team played wretchedly, and as it is just the eve of the St. Marks game we don't feel over encouraged. We leave Wednesday morning about twelve, and the team may go earlier. If they do I shall accompany them, as I shall [be] kept busy seeing that everything is all right. I suppose I shall have a glimpse of Lyman, but if we are beaten we shall not feel like doing much at Worcester.

I am revelling in the basket of goodies from Aunt Annie & so is Warren She says Uncle Fred goes out every day for strolls in the garden, so I suppose the wound must have closed. I think it is indeed a wonderful cure.

It is another showery Sunday like last one, but it only drizzles at intervals, so I fancy we will be made to walk to the last May service as usual.

Your dear letter of May 14th & 15th came last night, by what boat I cannot imagine, & it made the third letter in two days, so I feel as if I had very full news of your doings. I rather expected that you would end up by going to the Harzgebirge, and I am glad it is not so very much of a journey

Monday. May 29th

Your dear letter of May 17th to 19th got here today. I am so glad Papa's cold did not amount to anything. My whooping-cough is really almost gone, and only comes on when I run. I have forgotten to tell you some awfully sad news. We are not going to the choir festival this year, as it comes the day of the St. Marks game, day after tomorrow, & we could not reach Boston in time after the game, and anyway we should have no voices left.

I have often heard of little Paul Draper's remarkable voice, and the story is (its perfectly true) that when C. R. Nutter heard of his wonderful voice, his eye twinkled, and he said "Wait till *I* take a bit of the conceit out of him!

You speak of the death of Lady Strafford's husband. It was too bad & did it happen at Nauheim, & was she Mrs. Sam Colgate whom we all knew? She seems to have rather bad luck.

It was lovely this morning, but we had three hard showers (much needed) this p.m. but the nine managed to get in a half-hours work. Last night we had the last of the May services. A Rev. Nash preached, very good. I walked both ways with Dick Derby, and we had a talk about the arrangements for Wednesday's game. You know Roger still has the mumps. Thanks very much for the Graphic & two Spectators; they are most welcome, but I don't half like the thin edition of the Graphic, and am glad you aren't going to take it any more.

Tuesday 8. a.m.

A nice hot day. We start for the drill right after lunch.

No more now, I am well and there have been no other cases of mumps since. last Thursday, so I think we are pretty safe. Ever with best love to you both, your affec. son

FRANKLIN D ROOSEVELT.

The monthly marks included an A in German, a C in English Composition, and B's for the remaining subjects. "Excellent," noted the Rector. Evidently his mother had at last rebelled against further "deseases." The "boy named Ladd" was William F. Ladd, Jr., later a prominent broker on the New York Stock Exchange. Paul Draper, Groton 1906, was a member of the William H. Draper family and father of the noted dancer of the same name. A famous Groton story concerned the rumor of his death by drowning. While at the school, he fell into the river and got well soaked, but neither caught and died of pneumonia nor drowned. Both these versions of his fate, however, passed through the school like wildfire, and before anything could be done about it had reached a number of parents. In its most lurid form, the tale credited Mr. Peabody with remarking, when asked if the body had been recovered: "It will come up in the spring." A dispatch from London dated May 16th reported that the Earl of Strafford, special equerry to Queen Victoria, had been decapitated after falling in front of the Cambridge express which was passing through Potter's Bar station in Hertfordshire. His wife was the former Cora Smith, whose first husband had been the wealthy American manufacturer, Samuel J. Colgate. She later married George H. Gould. She was a colorful figure of the period, and a doubtless apocryphal story concerning her third marriage relates that she once was refused admittance at a hotel because she insisted upon registering as "Cora, Countess of Strafford, and Mr. Gould."

∽

"We are all tired and cross . . ."   [GROTON]

MAY 30, 1899,

TUESDAY.

My dearest Mama and Papa,

This a.m. we had lunch at 12.30, and right after left in barges for the village; we lined up just on the outskirts and marching to the town-hall joined the veterans and from there marched to the cemetery. We then had lemonade and oranges in a hut near the cemetery and then marched back to the town-hall, & disbanded. I had a soda and walked right back as the nine had their last practice. I fear the outlook for tomorrow is not very promising; the nine has fairly good capabilities but utterly lacks team play & snap. I am afraid Edmund will not play tomorrow as he is a substitute. It is hot today, but not unpleasant, and luckily the roads were not dusty. Dr. Rainsford gave a talk to the school after supper on his hunting-adventures in the West, and they were really very good and funny, to make up as he said for a long sermon he preached here at the beginning of the term.

Wednesday May 31st 9.p.m.

Well, we were beaten as we expected, 25–6. We left here at 12 o'clock, I in the nine's barge. We had [a] special train and got to Worcester at 1.30. Special trolley cars were waiting for us, and we reached the grounds about two, before the St. Marker's arrived. In the first two innings we led, but our pitchers went all to pieces and we only made one run after that. The cheering was incessant & I am hoarse. We got back here at 8. and we are all tired & cross. As I sat with the nine and had to be with them all the time, I did not get a chance to speak to Lyman or even to see him but Warren saw him, and he said he was well etc.

Thursday June 1st '99.

Warren got a letter from his mother today saying that they are going to return with you on the 28th. How lovely for you all! You must be delighted.

I am thinking of you as just about leaving Nauheim now for the Harz. I only wish I were with you. It is a piping hot day, with the thermometer over °90. I have just come back from a canoeing on the river. It was lovely except for the 'squitoes and a good swim afterwards refreshed us.

I saw Lathrop Brown yesterday at Worcester. He just came

320

up for the game, and is still pretty weak so he will not come back again this term. He goes abroad for a cure I think the end of this month, so he will not take his preliminaries until the autumn.

Friday 8.a.m.

I must finish this with apologies for such a poor & scrawly letter, but it is hot, & I have had every moment occupied.

Ever with lots of love I am your affec son,

FDR

My pen is too pointed & catches at every stroke.

◇◇

"It is a place of considerable responsability . . ."

My dearest Mama & Papa

The crew races took place this afternoon, and I am delighted to say both the first and second Hemenway won, and Warren coxed them both. It was a hot day & I started for the finish in my canoe at 4.30. Warren coxed the second Hemenway also, because its regular cox has the mumps. You know Taddy was the captain of the second Squannacook, he being the only sixth former on it, and they had absolutely raw material. Still they pulled a very plucky race, and did well considering, being beaten three lengths.

After that Warren was rowed back to the start, & got into the the [sic] first crew boat. When the boats came round the curve at the finish we saw the Hemenways well ahead, & they won easily. Warren was delighted & get[s] a nice blue jersey with an "H" on it & also a cup.

Sunday—June 4th.

Another sweltering day, & it was fearful singing in the choir. No May service, so we could not have a nice walk home in the evening. I wrote to Muriel & Aunt Dora so have not had much time to add to this. Just think, prize-day is only 3 weeks from tomorrow, & then come the dreaded exams.

The Jackson's begin day after tomorrow & I have reviewed today on various subjects.

Monday June 5th

You know we have been having the "June system" since Thursday, and although rather a strain to work right up to lunch on these hot mornings, it gives us the whole afternoon free. This p.m I studied till four then went out on the running track for a run, and practised the broad jump a little. You know we are to have an out-door Athletic Meet on the 20th & I shall enter several events.

You will be pleased to hear that today I was appointed Manager of the nine, in place of Dick Derby, for next year. I am much pleased, as it is a place of considerable responsability. Two teams are coming up this week to play the second nine, so I shall have to take care of them.

Tuesday. June 6th 8. am.

I am sorry I have not written a longer & better letter but it is 92° in the shade now & I am soaking wet.

The mumps has broken out again with fearful fury, 3 more from *our* form, also *Edmund* & 3 or 4 others. My turn next

We have Latin & Greek today with Jackson. I *hope* to pass.

Ever lots of love

FDR

Please excuse

∽∽

"In the same tyrannical way the Rector . . ."

[GROTON]
JUNE 7, 1899,
WEDNESDAY.

My dearest Mama and Papa

If you can imagine what it is like to be studying and taking exams from morning till night, with the thermometer at 90° in the shade, why you can know how I feel. Yesterday morning we had two hours solid of Latin awfully hard but I hope I may

322

have scraped through, then two more hours of Greek, which I am sure I failed on, together with ¾ of the form. This morning we had two more hours in an English exam, which took over twelve large sheets of quick close writing, but I hope I may possibly have passed then, a Latin Comp exam, which I also think I passed, and to wind up the day the worst Greek Composition exam I have ever seen in all my born days. Only 9 of the whole form as much as handed in their papers, and I am sure I failed. The trouble is that these exams are harder than the Harvard exams, and unless we pass them we cannot take the preliminaries in the things we fail in. Otherwise I am *perfectly capable* of taking 15 hours for Harvard, and I think I could pass at least 12 or 13 out of the 15. But if I am not allowed to take more than 9 or 10, I may not pass many hours, so you see if we had our own way, we could probably pass many more hours. In the same tyrannical way the Rector may not allow Wendell Blagden & me to take German this year. Why? He *acknowledged* that *we both* could *easily* pass it, and probably take an honour, but he says we would have to take advanced German next year in a course by ourselves, while the rest are still doing Elementary work. Personally I dont see how this bears on the subject at all, as it would be *worse than useless* to take another easy course such as this years and I should much prefer to take a course in Higher Mathematics or something like that.

This afternoon the second nine played the Ayer High School, at four o'clock and I had to receive them & see about the arrangements.

Thursday June 8th

Today we had two more exams, Geometry & Algebra. I fully expected to pass Algebra, but was doubtful about Geometry. However I just had hard luck in the Algebra, & I think I passed the Geometry all right   I am going to kick if I don't go up on Algebra, as I have been very near the head of the form in it this year

I have been running and jumping every afternoon for the

last week, training for the sports. There are new cases of mumps every day now, & I think nearly 20 more have it. I see everyone falling round me, but so far I am all right

Friday June 9th 8. am.

We take History this morning & I hope I may pass. I am sorry to write these horrid short letters, but we don't feel like writing when so much else goes on. I am so glad you return with Aunt Kassie; Warren & I will meet you on the dock. Sorry you cant go to the Harz. Thank Ruth Draper for the problem. It is very good. No more now, lots of love

F.D.R.

This letter was misdated "1898," presumably under the strain of the series of examinations. At this time preparation for college was under the "anticipation plan," which stemmed from the very great influence upon American education of President Eliot of Harvard and his elective system. At Harvard there were certain prescribed courses which Freshmen had to take; once these were out of the way, students were free to "elect" nearly any course they chose. Fifth-formers in the preparatory schools, if they passed their college preliminaries, were allowed to "anticipate" these prescribed Harvard courses by taking them in their sixth-form year at school. F.D.R. did this, and like a large percentage of the Harvard men of that time, was thus able to complete Harvard College in three years, and spend his fourth year doing graduate work. After Eliot retired, this "speeding-up" trend was reversed. The "Ruth Draper" mentioned in this letter is the famous monologist, another member of the large William Draper family.

～～

*"I really do not understand what
has saved me from the mumps . . ."*

[GROTON]
JUNE 10, 1899,
SATURDAY.

My dearest Mama and Papa,

Yesterday morning the dreaded Jacksons were finished with a History (Greek & Roman) exam. I think I passed it all right

324

Old man Jackson will come up this evening with the first few papers corrected I hope, & will finish the others up here.

The second nine had a game just now with a team from Ayer. They put up a very good game and beat the Ayers 19-11. Harry Markoe has been elected captain for next year, and I manager, as I wrote you last time.

Yours of May 27 to 30th came yesterday and was most welcome. I am glad you are having such nice weather, and you must enjoy the Drapers. You will be leaving [for] St. Blasien in a few days, and I am sure you will like it as usual, and hope you will be able to dine with the Clanwilliams. Give Mr. C., I mean Lord, my kind regards, also Mrs. and Lord Foljambe, if you see them again.

Sunday June 11th

A lovely day—Mr. Jackson has corrected three papers, I have passed Latin and English but failed Greek, together with 17 more in the form; only 4 passed so we shall have another exam. I really do not understand what has saved me from the mumps. There are now 33 cases of it, making over fifty boys who have had it this term, many of them for the second time. The boys I sit between at table both have it, and I expect to come down *any* moment. The average case lasts *less* than a week, and only one or two have had it badly. Edmund is coming down tomorrow. Mr. Gladwin's dormitory has been turned into a pest-house, and their are trained-nurses everywhere. Warren & I are about the only boys who have not had it before & escaped it so far.

Just think we shall be sixth formers in two weeks, I can hardly realize it. I shall of course have to go to Cambridge this year to see about my rooms, I thought we talked it over at Easter, but I will find out about Dan's [Draper] rooms. Most of the boys go either to Randolph or Claverley.

Monday June 12.

Only two weeks before prize-day and a trifle over three before you will be on the dock at New York. There is some talk of giving up all the Prize-day ceremonies if the Mumps outbreak does not stop, but I hope they won't.

Mr. Jackson finished correcting all the papers, and to my utter surprise I passed *all* except Greek as I wrote, & I append the marks on another sheet. In the two hour subjects & the two compositions a mark over 70 is an honor, but I shall be pleased if I can get even 1 honor at Harvard, as they dont fly very thick for everybody. We took another Greek exam this p.m. & I hope I passed. I am to take an *Advanced* German paper this evening, just to see how I come out on it, & I am almost sure I shall be recommended on Elementary German. If so, & if I pass my Greek, I shall go up on 15 hours, & Wendell Blagden, more, I believe, than anyone before in the school.

I shall write again by the Saturday steamer, and my last letter will go Monday. I can hardly realize that you will be back so soon as the time has flown by, much more quickly indeed than this time last year in the ———— Infirmary. The present cases are doing well, Chapin will be out soon, and Ladd the other boy who has scarlet-fever also has the mumps, but he is not at all ill.

Tuesday June 13th 8. am.

The weather is perfect, not a cloud in the sky, & yet the temperature is pleasant. Next year you must be at home for June.

No more now, I hope you wont either of you get cold in London, & that the weather will be fine

Ever with best love to you both, your affec. son

FRANKLIN

I go up on the following subjects and to get into college without conditions I must pass 16 "hours." This year I take *15* & *if* I pass them all it will only leave 1 hour for next year.

	Mark with Jackson	Harvard Hours
Latin	74	2
Latin Composition	72	1

	Mark with Jackson	Harvard Hours
Greek	44	2
Greek Composition	77	1
English	73	2
Algebra	60	1
Geometry	59	1
German	no exam	1
French	" "	1
Advanced French	" "	2
History	75	1
		15

I took my Greek again and passed it.

Richard James Meade, the fourth Earl of Clanwilliam (Ireland), made his career in the British Navy, where he eventually attained the ultimate stripes of an Admiral of the Fleet. Upon his death (in 1907 at the age of seventy-five), the *Times* of London commented: "He affected the tight, very short jacket, which—forty years ago—was thought the sign of the true British sailor; and a certain roughness of manner, which was at times rather puzzling to his subordinates. Throughout his life, he was before everything a sailor. . . ." Randolph and Claverly were dormitories next door to each other on Bow Street, at the corner of Mt. Auburn Street, in Cambridge. They were part of the group of "Gold Coast" dormitories built by private enterprise in the eighteen-nineties, and offered luxurious (by comparison with the "Yard") quarters to Harvard students who could afford them. They were later purchased and incorporated into the rest of the college. Randolph, built in 1897, was a large five-story building which looked like a city apartment house, while Claverly was distinctly a miscarriage of architecture, exhibiting martello towers for corners.

[GROTON]
JUNE 13, 1899,
TUESDAY.

My dearest Mama and Papa,

I forgot to thank you in my last letter for the two Graphics you sent, they were most welcome. This will be the last letter you will be sure of getting, as you may miss the Queenstown letter, so I will tell you about the plans, which I have told you of before, I think.

I leave here July 1st at 5 o'clock in the afternoon, and as it is too late to catch the Fall River boat I think I shall take the midnight train to N.Y, getting there Sunday morning at 7, & taking the 8 o'clock train to Hyde Park. Then on Monday morning I shall go up to Steen Valetje & stay till *early* Wednesday morning & will meet you at the dock, as I dont believe you will leave it before 11 o'clock.

It has been practically decided to give up the social functions of prize-day because of the mumps, but there will be the regular affair for the school, & the laying of the corner-stone of the chapel.

Wednesday June 14th

It has been decided that Blagden and I are to go up on 15 hours, the school record I think. Last night the form went into the Rector's study and we were told what we should go up on. I passed my Greek easily so I go up on all I can. For once in my life at least I have got ahead of Krumbhaar, as he, with about 5 others take 14 hours & the rest less that that. The thing is now to pass them all, but it is extremely unlikely & I should be amply satisfied with 12 hours.

The rest of the school go home on Tuesday the 27th and that day and I [*sic*] the next I shall have no exams to take so I shall make a couple of bicycle trips, and I am thinking of riding to Concord & seeing the sights on Wenesday with Mr. Gladwin and several other boys; it is only 17 miles there. It looks a little like rain, and we need it very much. Everything is dried up and the farmers say the hay crop is almost ruined, but I hope it is not quite as bad as that and that they have had more rain at Hyde Park.

Thursday June 15.

It threatened to rain all day, and this afternoon when I was about half way round the golf course it began to come down in buckets, & is still pouring. I was thoroughly soaked but changed & took the chance to send off my winter clothes to Mr. McFarland with a note asking him to return the coat-case. I have just bought at the store a grey neck-less sweater. They are thin and just the thing for golf at Campobello.

Your last letter from Nauheim was most welcome tonight, also the Graphic, Times & Spectator, many thanks for them. I am sorry you worried about the mumps but I still survive although one or two new cases go up every day, also one or two cured boys come down. The average case is only a week, and most of the boys who are getting it now have had it before. Warren & I continue well, however.

Just think you be be [sic] home in a little over three weeks! The term seems to have gone very fast. Give my love to Aunt Kassie & Muriel. Warren has not yet been invited to spend the 4th at Steen Valetje but I hope he will be, as it would be very stupid for him all alone at Tuxedo. We will both meet you on the dock and are looking forward to it and counting the days.

You can send your last letter to me to Steen Valetje.

Friday 8 a.m.

The weather is lovely again and I am crazy to get to Hyde Park & see the place.

Ever with dearest love to you both & apologies for the wretched letter   I am your affec. son

FRANKLIN D. ROOSEVELT

∽

[GROTON]
JUNE 18, 1899,
SUNDAY.

My dearest Mama & Papa,

The weather continues lovely, and yesterday I spent the afternoon playing scrub base-ball. Yours from Freiburg came last night, and I am glad you had a pleasant journey down from Frankfort. I am sure you liked seeing St. Blasien after an absence of two years, and I fancy the place must have changed somewhat since then.

This morning a curious catastrophe occurred; Mr. Billings got the german measles! He has been run down for the last week with something the matter with a vein in his leg, so I suppose he caught it easily, as there are three cases of germans in the infirmary. It came probably from Ayer where they have it. We are all so sorry for him, as I don't believe he will be down before school closes.

Today after church I met Mr. Amory Lawrence and lunched with him, also another boy Fuller Potter went. Mr. L was alone with Mr. Osgood Sheppard whom you know—we met him at Albany on the D & H car last summer; he asked after you, also Mr. L. Delicious lunch *etc.*

School closes in a week and it seems glorious to think of. We have a complete holiday on Monday, (prize-day) Tuesday, the day the rest of the fellows go home and Wednesday. On Thursday we take Latin Greek, and Latin Comp exams, practically occupying the whole day, then Friday we have Geometry, Algebra, and English and on Saturday Advanced French, History, Greek Comp, Elementary French and Elementary German, finishing at 5 p.m. I can hardly wait for that moment to arrive.

The time seems horribly short before we shall be in the midst of them, but I hope to pass *most* of them.

Monday—June 19th.

Your dear letter, the first from St. Blasien, came this a.m. I am so glad you have nice rooms and enjoy it there. Thanks for the suggestion about the blazer and ducks; I will write at once to Brooks about sending them to Hyde Park.

I think the birds you saw must have been magpies, as they are just like the ones you described. I forgot [to] speak about the curious Nauheim bird, which I do not know, as I am not very well up on the European species and would have to see it first with my own eyes & a book in my hand. I think it is so nice for you all to return together, and you may count on our meeting you unless even now we fall victims to the mumps or german-measles, or if I flunk *all* my exams which I *guess* isn't likely!

I hope you'll have a smooth voyage and I'm sure you ought to at this season.

Just think only *two weeks* till we meet again on the old dock. Give my love to the P.C.'s.

I wrote Uncle Warren today about going there, and I mildly hinted that Warren would be all alone for the 4th so I hope the little fellow may get an invite up there with me, as he wants to very much.

Good bye, my dearest Mama and Papa, & I hope you'll have smooth seas, & that this will catch you at Queenstown.

Ever with tons of love and kisses and hugs I am your affectionate son

FRANKLIN

What followed upon this letter was—the mumps.

∾∾

*"I am reduced to my normal size
once more . . ."*

GROTON SCHOOL
JULY 2, 1899,
SUNDAY.

My dear Aunt Annie,

I am reduced to my normal size once more and feel very well. I shall leave here tomorrow afternoon and take the night

train from Boston getting to New York on Tuesday at 7 a.m
and shall take the first train up the river to Algonac, just to
spend the day and night before meeting Mama and Papa. I
will let you know what train I take by telegram as I do not
know the Hudson River trains this year.

I was well enough to take the examinations on Thursday
Friday and Saturday, although my face was a sight to behold,
and I had to take them all alone in a little room up here in
the infirmary. The boys all went last night and it seems horribly lonely up here now, but it won't be for long.

I think this note ought to reach you early Tuesday morning,
so you will get it just before I arrive.

No more now and with much love to you and Uncle Fred
I am your affectionate nephew

FRANKLIN D. ROOSEVELT

This letter was incorrectly dated "June." His slightly delayed
summer vacation was spent at Hyde Park and Campobello,
and the following fall his last year at Groton commenced.

∽

"All is confusion and Babel . . ."

GROTON SCHOOL
SEPT. 19, 1899,
TUESDAY.

My darling Mama & Papa

All is confusion and Babel; the new infants are like the sands
of the sea, the new building is not finished, and E.V.R.T. is
Senior Prefect, of which we are all very glad. The five prefects
are Krumbhaar, the *two* Rainsfords (!), Gerry Chadwick and
Jimmy Jackson. Yes I am a full-fledged dormitory-prefect in
charge of Mr. Woods' dormitory, which is this year the dwell-
ing-place of the kids. Both Jefferson [Newbold] and Coleman
[Rogers] are under my wings & Mrs. Tom [Newbold] begged
me to take special care of Jefferson. My cubicle is at the end
on the West side (the best) & I get sunshine most of the winter.
My new study where I am now writing is on the north side

of the VIth form hall and is one of the five best single studies. Mr. P. has congratulated me but nothing further has resulted. Wendell only passed 14 hours failing on Greek Composition so I am the record holder. I think about six boys got 14 hours, & poor Euey only 4 & Andy Robeson 6. The form however got *28* honors altogether, the record, & one to be proud of. I think I must have contributed a number as Mr. P. said I *more than* passed

The new building wont be ready for a week, & then only partly open. Howard [Cary] & Lathrop B. have not yet returned, but do so in a few days. *Push* [Mr. Griswold] is alive & kicking & sends kind regards. No more now. Will write more tomorrow

Ever your affec. son

F.D.R.

I sit next Mr. Cushing at table.

"E.V.R.T." was Eugene Van Rensselaer Thayer, also known as "Euey." He later became president of the Chase National Bank. James Jackson, Jr., another classmate, was afterward treasurer of the Commonwealth of Massachusetts. Mr. Woods's dormitory was located in Hundred House directly over the Library. This letter, by comparison with those preceding, shows quite a change in tone—brief and almost exuberant (considering it followed upon a pleasant vacation), with unusual familiarity in the references to other boys and masters: a sixth-former at last, and really enjoying Groton, one would gather.

<center>~~~</center>

"I must go up to see that the kids in my dormitory are behaving . . ."

GROTON SCHOOL
SEPT. 20, 1899,
WEDNESDAY.

My dearest Mama & Papa,

Just a line to say that every [thing] is going on smoothly and as if nothing had ever happened in the way of holidays. The summer vacation now seems like a delightful far-away dream, and I can safely say I have never enjoyed holidays as much as the ones just past.

This afternoon we played football, I am trying for the second eleven, and it was so hot that I lost 5 pounds actual weight in the course of the practice.

The kids are innumerable, 37 new ones, and they seem to be a nice crowd.

My study is delightful, also the dormitory and you see things were not quite as bad as I feared. I must go up to see that the kids in my dormitory are behaving themselves.

Jeff. & Coleman are happy & well.

No more now will write to H.P. tomorrow
Ever

F.D.R.

My portfolio is here

∽

"I stay up every night until 10:15 now . . ."

GROTON SCHOOL
SEPT. 21, 1899,
THURSDAY.

My dearest Mama and Papa,

Today is Mama's birthday and I wish you many happy returns of the day, and I am sure you are having a birthday party at Fair Haven. The stamps and stamped envelopes came today and many thanks for them, they will easily last through this term.

Friday.

I forgot to finish this last night so will do so now. I stay up every night until 10.15 now, as the dormitory prefects have that privelege, so Kerr Rainsford & I sit in Mr. Woods room while he is down at Faculty supper, and read. The kids have behaved very well so far, and Coleman and Jefferson get on well and are in the best of spirits. Thank you for thinking of sending $5 but I really do not think I shall need it as I have

334

plenty without it. Yours from the Fall River Boat has just come. My study is so nice and I have plenty of things for it and everything I want. I should not be allowed a big chair or lamp and I have a rug, but anyway I have tied my electric light back of my chair so that it shines over my shoulder and will not hurt my eyes.

The football practice continues daily of the 1st & 2nd elevens. I am playing end on the latter and feels rather stiff & bruised.

It rained most of yesterday but is lovely weather now. I hope you found all well at H.P. & are all right yourselves. Howard Cary returned today looking thin but much grown. No more now

Ever with love

F.D.R.

∽∽

"By the way, I still sing tenor . . ."

GROTON SCHOOL
SEPT. 24, 1899,
SUNDAY.

My darling Mama and Papa,

Your letter from 10 W. 43rd was most welcome yesterday, and thank you very much for sending the suits. They have not yet come, but I expect them tomorrow and shall return the one I do not want. My hat and shoes have come from Boston and are very nice.

I wish you would send me my clothes-bag which Mrs. McMurray says must be at home as it is not here, and also please send my new heavy pyjamas as the nights are very cold, and we have already had frost. The boys are behaving well in the dormitory, & you can tell Mrs. Newbold that Jefferson get[s] on well and has as yet had no blackmarks or latenesses. There are 16 boys, all new in the dormitory and I have not yet been able to master all their names, but know most of them by now. Little Paul Draper is also there, and he is very much liked and seems to be one of the nicest of the new boys, as well as being

335

the greatest addition to the choir. By the way, I still sing tenor, and I fancy I shall stay in the rest of the year. The new chapel is getting on well and the walls are already nearly 1/3 up, but they say we will not be able to get into it until *next* autumn, so I shall not be in while I am here. The new building is an unknown, the Rector hopes to get into it in about a week, but personally I think it will be almost a month, as the plastering even is unfinished and the carpenters are not nearly done. It has a huge gilded dome on top of the tower which I think is rather inappropriate, but otherwise the exterior looks very well.

Yesterday for the first time we lined up against the first eleven and contrary to my expectations I did not find myself in such bad condition and managed to stop several plays of the first. Euey Thayer, the Captain of the first was hit in the head and was out of his head for several hours, although otherwise he was perfectly well, and he kept talking the most utter nonsense for some time, although today he says he feels alright and remembers nothing of what took place. Morin Hare, who played against me, and Leaycraft were both hurt though not badly. I survived & am only a bit stiff & sore, & I am in very strict training no sweets or rich desserts or nuts.

By the way my clothes-brush also is at home and I wish you could send it with the other things.

I went to see Mrs. Freeman today and she is well. There are the greatest quantity of graduates and I have had one or two in my study most of the day.

Monday 8. am.

There is a dense fog over everything and it is raw and chilly.

Some of the graduates saw Taddy in Cambridge a few days ago. They say he looked like a tramp with flowing hair, and he refused to look at any of them, but scurried away!

No more now, will write again tomorrow

Ever your affec son

FRANKLIN.

336

"Nothing matches anything else . . ."

My dearest Mama and Papa,

Your letter of Sunday was most welcome last night. My sofa pillows are all different and I only have three on the seat, so I think I should very much like another one. The walls of my study are dull pink but my window-seat is green so nothing matches anything else.

We played against the 1st for the second time yesterday and about half-a-dozen were hurt. My left leg was squashed by Mr. Marvin, the new master and my knee nearly went out but I kept it in hot water for half an hour last night, and it is nearly all right now so I shall keep on playing today. It is foggy again this a.m, as bad as it ever is at Campo. I am so glad Mike is nearly well and Nardo improving.

No more now
Ever with best love

F.D.R.

George D. Marvin was a master at Groton in 1899, and again from 1903 to 1909. "Nardo" was another family dog.

∽∾

"I think it is simply too pretty . . ."

My dearest Mama & Papa,

Yours of Tuesday came last night and I was glad to hear about everything and that Taddy was having a nice visit at home. Yesterday I golfed in the morning with Mr. Abbott and played football most of the afternoon and managed to bang my knee again, but it is only a bad bruise I think and not serious, and I keep on playing just the same.

My cup came last Monday from Boston, I forgot to mention

'it in my last letter. I think it is simply too pretty and makes a great addition to my other cups & my study. By the way did the servants bring your photos from Campo and did they have a terribly rough trip?

The suits came from Brooks Monday night and I am taking the lightest colour of the three as the other two suits (one with red & other blue thread) are two small in the coats. I am sending back the others today and I am very glad to have it as the weather is beginning to get really cold and we have had several frosts. Many thanks for the "Graphic" and "Tribune." I should much like to see the "Herald" & "Trib" accounts of the parades. I hope you wont be in N.Y. during them as the crush must be terrible. What a joke that "Jewey" got here two days ahead of time! Last night the Rector read to ½ the form from "the Coming of Arthur," at 9 o'clock & we went in to Faculty Supper after that. Have you heard of Mr. Collier's splendid present to the school of an autograph letter and portrait of every President of the U.S.? We saw one or two samples last night & they are magnificent

No more now   Ever affec.

F.D.R.

This was the time of the triumphal New York reception for Admiral Dewey. Mr. Price Collier's collection is still to be seen in the Schoolhouse, and has been kept up to date.

∽

"We were glad to have one day free
from buffets and bruises . . ."

[GROTON]
OCT. 1, 1899,
SUNDAY.

My dearest Mama & Papa,

Yours of Friday came yesterday & I am so glad you will get a chance to see the procession which from all accounts must have been splendid. I wonder where you saw it from & whether you were not detained on the train going or returning. I was so sorry to hear of the Parker boy's death and it will be a terrible shock to his family. The valise came on Friday with everything all right and in good condition. The Doré looks lovely on my wall and has been much admired. The cushion is a perfect beauty, the prettiest I have, and many thanks for it. I have begun wearing the night-clothes which I remember you got last winter, and today I put on autumn flannels, as the days are chilly and it goes to about °30 every night. Many thanks for the "Graphic" and cuttings about the "Shamrock" which are most interesting. I suppose you only go to N.Y on Tuesday just for the race so I will send this to H.P. as you have written nothing to the contrary. I got a post-card from Aunt Dora with a view of "Fort Chabrol" being beseiged. When does she return? Let me know if there is time to write and the address.

Yesterday we played the first game of the season, against Boston Latin and I am glad to say won easily, 17–0 and the team did well. Naturally the 2nd got a rest and we were glad to have one day free from buffets and bruises given by the 1st. If I can stay on the 2nd and don't get injured I shall go to the Harvard-Yale game in November. Now we get crackers & milk every evening free of charge. Lathrop Brown Jack Minturn & Jackson, having finished their prelims, have returned. Brown got 14 hours & Jack passed about 1/3 for his Yale entrance. Paul Draper sang a solo today at P.M. chapel It was remarkable & everyone was pleased. Mrs. D. is up here for the day with Dan. I hear Taddy is seen little of & never intends to visit Groton again. No more now.

Ever with best love   Affec son,

F.D.R.

This year saw the appearance of the first of the five *Shamrocks* with which Sir Thomas Lipton unsuccessfully contested the America's Cup over a period of thirty years. In 1899 the races were sailed against the Iselin-Morgan yacht *Columbia*.

"Pen bad, ink bad, writing bad
& a glorious time . . ."

GROTON SCHOOL
OCT. 4, 1899,
WEDNESDAY.

My dearest Mama & Papa,

How I envied you yesterday! We heard several reports about the race and *this morning* at 10.30 I got your telegram for which many thanks. I am so glad the Columbia did so well, but it was too bad they could not finish. Your letter describing the parade and all the newspapers were most welcome. I will return the valise very soon, but I am still wearing my summer suit as I find it warm enough with these heavy flannels.

What do you think is the latest news?

Mr. G r i s w o l d is e n g a g e d
! ! ! ! ! ! ! ! ! ! ! ! ! ! !

It came out this morning and there was a celebration!!!!!! He was carried round by the VI form and cheered, etc. Tell Helen & tell her to break the news gently to Taddy & Miss Fromont. I feel that this is quite enough excitement for one letter so will write you the name of "she" tomorrow.

Faculty supper again last night & reading in the "Idylls of the King."

Foot-ball, bruises, afternoon teas, lack of sleep, gossip & engagements come thick & fast so no more now

Every yr. devoted son

F.D.R.

Pen bad, ink bad, writing bad & a glorious time

The first of the Cup races was sailed over a thirty-mile course between Asbury Park, N.J., and the Sandy Hook lightship, on Oct. 3rd. Because of light winds the race could not be finished within the stipulated five and one-half hours. The *Shamrock,* though trailing, appeared to have sailed the better race, and there was some criticism of the *Columbia's* skipper. S. Nicholson Kane (*q.v.*) was chairman of the N. Y. Yacht Club committee in charge of the races. Mr. Griswold's fiancee was Miss Norah Brewer, daughter of Professor Brewer of the Yale Scientific School.

∽∾

". . . by holding up her photo and
saying laconically 'She's mine!' . . ."

GROTON SCHOOL
OCT. 6, 1899,
FRIDAY.

Dearest Mama & Papa,

Just a line to say that I expect to go to Boston next Wednesday to be operated on by the dentist. Your letter about the race & also the Graphic & Herald were most welcome. I am thinking of you as going to it again tomorrow & hope there will be a good race this time.

The future Mrs. Griswolds name is Miss Brewer, of New Haven, & her father is a Yale prof. He (Push) met her abroad & with a large party travelled thro' Palestine together. Push broke the news to Mr. Billings first by holding up her photo and saying laconically "She's mine"!!!!!!!!!

We had a half-holiday yesterday in consequence & I golfed in the a.m & went for a long canoe trip in p.m. Tomorrow we play English High School.

Today we practiced in a pouring rain & I have a slight cold as a result not anything at all

Ever affec. son

F.D.R.

Xcuse scrawl—

∽∾

"Xcuse writing which I do with
2 fingers . . ."

GROTON SCHOOL
OCT. 8, 1899,
SUNDAY.

My dearest Mama & Papa,

Yesterday afternoon we were again victorious and beat English High School 12–0, I am glad to say. The team played well and no one was hurt for a wonder. I am still unhurt, comparatively, and my cold is slight. Today I went over to lunch at Whitneys with Mrs. Goodwin who is up here to see her two boys. Mrs. Blagden is also here.

I went to see Mrs. Freeman after afternoon church, & she is well but afraid that her house, whose owner has died will be sold; however I think she will have it all winter anyway.

Last night Mr. Nutter was telegraphed for as his father is very ill, so Mr. Gladwin ran the choir today.

My two medals have come from Mr. Hubbard and they look very nice on my photo moulding. By the way I wish you could send me my red frame holding the six pictures as I suppose it was left out of my trunk by some mistake.

Monday.

I forgot to finish this this a.m so will do so now.

So sorry the race on Saturday was a fizzle & that you went all for nothing, but I think there ought surely to be wind on Tuesday & there should be a good race.

It is raining but we play foot-ball just the same

Xcuse writing which I do with 2 fingers as I smashed one in a door yesterday

Ever affec.

F.D.R.

On Oct. 5th and 7th the Cup yachts again failed to finish. Good sailing weather finally came along a week later, and the *Columbia* proceeded to win three races from the *Shamrock I,* successfully defending the Cup.

*"Shall send the note just as soon
as the tusks come out . . ."*

My dearest Mama and Papa,

I entirely forgot in my Sunday letter to tell you that I am not to go to Boston tomorrow after all. I got a note from Dr. Wilson giving me an appointment for *Saturday* at 2 o'clk. I cannot get to Boston till *2.30* so have written asking if 2.30 will do just as well. Your Sunday letter enclosing letter-sheet came *today* and I shall send the note just as soon as the tusks come out. Dr. Wilson says he will accompany me so you need have no anxiety.

I wrote to Abbott Frazar last week to have the birds sent home, but he sent them up here by mistake. I shall send them on to you by Xpress soon and they have been much admired here.

What a fake the old races are! I am still hoping I may get a chance to see one or two in the Xmas holidays!

Football continues; tomorrow we play Worcester Academy, a much bigger and heavier team & they ought to beat us.

Ever with lots of love   Your affec. son

F.D.R.

Cold almost gone. Sore hand

⌒⌒

*"Why don't they get some com-
pressed air for the old boats? . . ."*

My dearest Mama and Papa,

Yours of yesterday was most welcome today, and I was sorry Loulie did not do better in the Tournament but I suppose she got badly rattled, as she often does at Campobello. Yesterday we moved into the school-room of the New "School-House as it is to be officially called. The room is 15 feet longer than the big dining room, so with 150 desks in it you can imagine that it is an enormous room. Only about five or six other rooms are ready so we still recite in various nooks, and the calsominers and carpenters will not be entirely through before Christmas.

In the afternoon we had the game with Worcester Academy and contrary to all expectations we beat them 11–0. They fully expected to win and their team was much heavier and older, but we were too quick for them. Your letter telling about the St. Markers broken arm caused great excitement here and we think it must be Mackay their Captain, as he did not play in their game last Saturday with English High School, which they beat 12–0, just what we did. They have about the best team they have ever had at St. Marks this year and they ought to beat us, as nearly all are old players, while ours are mostly new ones. The game is at Southboro on November 2nd so I shall see Lyman then.

Friday. a.m.

The weather is lovely and warm & I hope it will continue so tomorrow. I shall follow your directly [directions] about not eating & the dose of Harmless, & will send the note from Boston. Sunday is the School's Birthday, but they celebrate it in the evening tomorrow, after I get back from Boston. They have the usual poem from the Billywag (alas, I hear I am in it!) & songs, etc. On Wednesday afternoon Mrs. Peabody had a fair in the children's play-house to support the district nurse. We all went and I spent a dollar, & got a tiny pine-pillow & much trash from the grab-bag. They had ice-cream, cake, candy, etc but I took none of it as the first & second elevens are in strict training.

Many thanks for Harper's & the Trib; they are most welcome. Why don't they get some compresseed air for the old boats? I begin to think the "New Moon could beat them.

Ever with lots of love   Affec. son

F.D.R.

You must have enjoyed the visit from Mr. Pell & Miss Bangs, also, the Hubbards.

〜〜

"I was told I got a bit sky-blue scarlet . . ."

My dearest Mama & Papa,

Today the School is fifteen years old. Over twenty graduates came up last night after the Dewey parade in Boston and got here in time for the grand feast at 8 o'clock. We were allowed to break training for the occasion and had a glorious feast. After supper we adjourned as usual to the library and songs followed from Mr. Jefferson, Paul Draper and the quartette. Paul sang very well and was much applauded. Besides we had violin solos from Mr. Griswold who played with a lighter touch than ever before (!) & from Alvah Crocker, a banjo solo from Randolph & piano recitals from Joy & Heaton. Finally as a climax came the poem from Uncle William Billywag, a howling success. Jokes on everyone, including one on the goings on of your son during the summer, which they got on to and utterly perverted in some way, so I won't repeat it, but I was told I got a bit sky-blue scarlet which I don't believe.

I played golf yesterday afternoon and broke my record on the links, doing 41, which is within 2 strokes of the record of the course, held by Joe Swan.

Oh, yes, by the way, I forgot to mention it before, my teeth are still in my head! Yesterday morning I got a telegram from Wilson saying, "Do not come today, see letter." The letter has not yet come, but I suppose I suppose [*sic*] he wanted to see Dewey. I hope I can go next Wednesday instead.

I have decided to keep the two bird skins here and they are hung up on my study wall, and look well.

Today I took supper with Mr. Gardner. One or two of the sixth form go to him every Sunday night, and it is delightful to get good beef-steak & cream for once.

For a wonder we did not play foot-ball on Saturday, and I was glad as I felt pretty well banged up as on Friday I was hit in the head.

This a.m before church I helped Mr. Griswold with his Sunday school in the old building. We had 10 children & I played two hymns

Monday—

Time for school.

Goodbye with love

F.D.R.

Of the Boston reception for Dewey, Bishop Lawrence wrote (in his biography *Roger Wolcott*): "It was a brilliant day. The population from all parts of the State had poured into Boston, for it was the day on which the Commonwealth and the city gave their welcome to Admiral Dewey, the hero of Manila. The morning was given up to the procession. The whole state militia was in line. Later the officers and sailors of the flagship Olympia led the column through the gates of the Common to the parade ground. The Governor took his position on the slope of the hill just below the soldiers' and sailors' monument. Two hundred trumpeters gave the call to colors, and seventeen sergeants with their colors stood before the Governor. The commanding officers took their positions in front; and one by one the officers turned the colors [flags borne in the Spanish-American War by Massachusetts servicemen] over to the Governor." A. Bertram Randolph, the boy who played the banjo, was a form behind F.D.R. He was a stepson of William C. Whitney, the noted financier and Secretary of the Navy under Cleveland. Randolph, fighting with an English regiment, was the first Yale graduate to die in World War I. As for the Birthday Poem reference to "the goings on of your son," the following passage is excerpted from Mr. Gardner's poem: "His maple-sugar kisses were / The sweetest thing on earth. / Like Roosevelt at the candy pull / When maidens in their mirth / Threw the molasses at his face. . . ."

∞

"Singing really should come before speaking . . ."

GROTON
OCT. 18, 1899,
WEDNESDAY.

My dearest Mama and Papa,

I found the remains of a block of this paper in the Confiscation closet yesterday. I think they must have belonged to Rosy, but as there are only a few sheets I will use them up. Yours of Tuesday came today, also a Tribune from Papa, and I shall write "Nelly" soon, only I am somewhat behind in my correspondence as I have such a lot of work with foot-ball, etc.

Thursday—

Today I got somewhat banged to pieces against the "1st" receiving a crack on head, a wrench of the knee and my thumbnail was bent back, and I fear I may lose it. We play Pomfret on Saturday, but alas, I shall miss it as my teeth come out then, and I do not return till six.

What do you think! I am going to take singing lessons! A Miss Reid comes up here once a week, and gives lessons in either singing or declaming. However singing really should come before speaking so I have decided to take one lesson a week, as they are not very expensive. By the way, I suppose you are going to pay for old Wilson so I shall keep a strict account of my dentistry expenses. We have had one row in the dormitory, a grand one, and Jeff got 6, also Paul Draper but Coleman escaped. They made a row after lights were out and Mr.

Woods gave in all 36 black-marks. By the way I wonder if you have had any prints of your kodak-pictures done, as I think there is one of the "New Moon," & I should like to see them all. Have you written yet to Randolph Hall? There is not much time left & most rooms are already taken.

How splendid that the Columbia is doing so well! Many thanks for the two Tribunes & two Graphics which are most welcome.

No more now

Ever with loads of love

F.D.R.

This letter was written on Hyde Park notepaper. The "Confiscation Closet" was a depository of (a) all illegal objects found in the possession of Groton students, and (b) all objects left lying around by same. Miss Reid proved such a great success that even the Faculty began to take singing lessons from her. She eventually settled in Groton.

∽∽

*"I had delightful day-dreams
during the process . . ."*

[GROTON]
OCT. 22, 1899,
SUNDAY.

My dearest Mama and Papa,

I sent a note to you last night by the evening mail which I wrote on the train and in Boston, and I hope you will get it tomorrow afternoon. I am feeling all right after the gas and I did not mind the operation at all, and had delightful day-dreams during the process. Mr. Gardner went down with me as he had a very painful tooth and we went with Dr. Wilson, who is also his dentist, to the extracting parlors. I went in first and was "under" about 15 minutes I think. Then he went in and took about the same time. Mr. G. had to go back with Dr. Wilson to have some work done, so I went to the "Touraine" and had a hair-cut which I needed very badly. I then went to Wright and Ditson's and bought some head-protectors for the eleven and started for the station in a trolley. However we got into a block and I had to get out and run about half a mile to catch the train, so I did not have time to post your letter as I just got there in time. I came up with Anson Stokes who came up for Sunday to see his kid-brother Harold.

I forgot to tell you in my last letter that we have had a very serious case of illness among us. One of the new boys, Harold Hadden, Billy Hadden's brother, who is in my dormitory and next to me, came down with typhoid after he had been here a little over a week. On Thursday last he became very much worse and had a temperature of over 106°. Mr. Peabody who was away came back, also a lot of doctors. On Friday he was still in a critical condition but yesterday he became better and now is getting on well.

It is a lovely day with not a cloud in the sky and quite cold; Mrs. Cary and Mrs. Brown are up here besides several graduates. They say Rosy does not associate with anybody at Cambridge, but sees Polly most. I hope he will come up here as it is rumored he & Poll have made a contract not to come back and the other boys are all down on them.

We, Mr. Griswold and I, held our second Sunday-School today with good success, although I got somewhat twisted in playing one of the hymns.

Later. 9 p.m.

I took afternoon tea with Mr. Billings after chapel, and at 6.30, right after supper he and I started to drive to Ayer. We got there at seven and went to the Church which is a sort of offspring of our church, but has a separate minister Mr. Newbegin. Mr. Billings preached to quite a congregation, and I sang in the local choir, which consisted of two sopranos, an alto, two men bases & myself as tenor. We have just got back and the drive was most enjoyable.

I am now going in to Faculty Supper, and will finish in the morning.
Monday.
It is cloudy and damp and I think we shall have rain. I forgot to say that on Saturday while I was away we beat Pomfret 30–0 It was a splendid game and a great victory which we did not expect.
No more now Ever your affec. son

F.D.R.

The Hotel Touraine (then the Waldorf-Astoria of Boston, today quite changed in character) was on Boylston Street at the corner of Tremont; the firm of Wright & Ditson Sporting Goods on Washington Street. Anson Phelps Stokes, at this time studying for the ministry at Episcopal Theological School, was to become a noted author and educator, serving as trustee for numerous foundations and on the boards of many welfare committees. He performed important social service work in the city of Washington during F.D.R.'s presidency, and became especially prominent in the field of Negro education. Harold Phelps Stokes, his brother, turned to newspaper work, and was successively European and Washington correspondent for the *New York Evening Post*, secretary to Herbert Hoover from 1924 to 1926, and later an editor of the *New York Times*.

〰️

"Groton ingenuity may win . . ."

GROTON
OCT. 25, 1899,
WEDNESDAY.

My dearest Mama and Papa,
Yours of Tuesday and Papa's postal with the London News and Punches were all very welcome today. I was glad to see the photos and I think you deserve great credit for taking such good ones. Helen's and Papa's I think excellent, but Frances' and yours are not quite so good. I want to keep them

all except the two of me and two blurry ones which I am returning. Isn't the one of Mike good? Too bad the one you took of the "New Moon" did not come out well.

How does the Pomeroy boy happen to be in the Harvard Scientific School? When we crossed the ocean with him about five years ago he was younger than I and a horrid little baby with fat cheeks.

You must have enjoyed your visit to the Staatsburgh links. I can just imagine Rubber Rosy in green. Is he too delicate to play himself?

The little Hadden boy is better but has lost his power of speech; still the doctors hope he will recover it as he gets stronger. You have doubtless heard of the death of Mr. Russell Sturgis. I forgot to mention it, but suppose you knew. Mr. S.W.S. [S. Warren Sturgis] went down a week ago last Saturday but got there too late.

Thursday.

I forgot to finish this yesterday. We play football daily, and the "first" are getting their finishing touches. St. Marks have easily the best material this year but Groton ingenuity may win. Wait till a week from today. *If* we win I shall send a "telegram" but you may *not* get it. I expect to go surely to the Harvard-Yale game now, as I am regularly on the second, usually as end, but when Mr. Sturgis does not play I take his place at half-back. My knee is still somewhat tender, the joint is all right, but a few more knock might bring water.

I go to Wilson on Nov. 5th. I wish you could write a note to the Rector, just saying that it is absolutely necessary to have the straightening this year. I have not said anything about it, but a word from you will be a help.

Ever affec.

F.D.R.

Please send me a new spool of floss silk!

∽∾

"I got both knees banged again
and my head cracked . . ."

My dearest Mama and Papa,

I forgot to enclose the photos I do not want in my last let-ter, so am sending them back now. What a nice time you must be having at home now, I wish I could be there, & I am sorry to miss Nelly. I am glad you are still having warm weather and can enjoy rowing and driving. Up here we have one day cold and the next warm. Yesterday a *thick* fog hung over every-thing, worse than any we have at Campo. Still we played Foot-ball all afternoon and were watched by the whole school, as it is the last line-up before the game and there will only be signal-practice between now and then. I got both knees banged again and my head cracked, but very hot water and massage took down the swelling and I am nearly all right. The joint is all right but it gets badly bruised every now and then. On Tuesday the 2nd is to play the 3rd eleven, of course we shall beat the 3rd (of which Howard Cary is capt.) but it will not be as hard work as against the "first". Mr. Sturgis has been made a "1st" substitute so I now fill his place at half-back, hav-ing been moved there from end, and the substitute end has taken my place, so you see I am sure of going to the Harvard-Yale game on Nov. 18. It is overcast today but quite warm.

Monday. 8 a.m

Cold and clear. Nothing much to write about. I will send a line on Wednesday & write about the game after we get back on Thursday, & will send a telegram if we win. No more now

Ever with loads of love

F.D.R.

Xeniphon Examination.

I, Translate: ὑμᾶς δ' αὖ ἡμῖν δεήσει ὀμόσαι ἦ μὴν πορεύσεσθαι ὡς διὰ φιλίας ἀσινῶς, σῖτα καὶ ποτὰ λαμβάνοντας ὁπόταν μὴ ἀγορὰν παρέχωμεν. ἢν δὲ παρέχωμεν ἀγοράν, ὠνουμένους ἕξειν τὰ δ' ἐπιτήδεια. Ταῦτα ἔδοξε, καὶ ὤμοσαν καὶ δεξιὰς ἔδοσαν Τισσαφέρνης καὶ ὁ τῆς βασιλέως γυναικὸς ἀδελφὸς τοῖς τῶν Ἑλλήνων στρατηγοῖς καὶ λοχαγοῖς καὶ ἔλαβον παρὰ τῶν Ἑλλήνων. Μετὰ δὲ τὸ δεῖπνον ἔτυχον ἐν περιπάτῳ ὄντες

10. πρὸ τῶν ὅπλων Πρόξενος καὶ Ξενοφῶν.

II Write in Greek in the form of indirect discourse after ἔφη the first sentence (through the 1ˢᵗ παρέχωμεν.)

Give prin. parts of ὤμοσαν, ἔδοσαν, ἔδοξε and ἔλαβον. Construction of ἕξειν (l.4), ὠνουμένους (l.4) ὄντες (l.9). Account for the mood of παρέχωμεν (twice.)

Decline γυναικός. (l.7)

III Write in Greek: Clearchus made the following reply to those who said that Tissaphernes was plotting against the Greek army. "I bear all this in mind also. But we must not abandon Ariaeus who, while Cyrus was a-live, was our ally. If, however, Tissaphernes breaks his oath and attempts to do us any harm, we will de-fend ourselves as valliantly as possible."

πειρῶται

ἴδοιμι

δεδοκι

σωδ.

σω

F.D.R. learned from his parents, to whom the report was mailed, that he had scored a gentlemanly 76% in this exam.

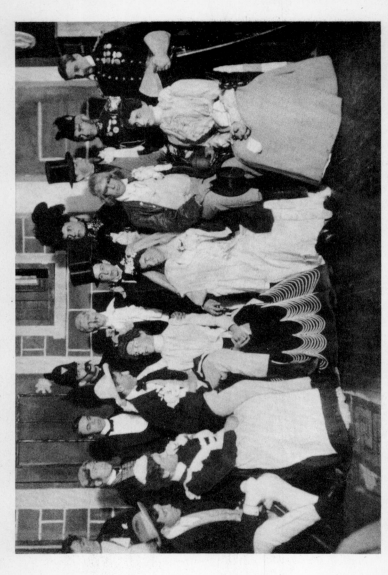

He wrote home for "a tail coat . . for an old county bumpkin in his best London clothes." The Groton sixth-form play, showing F.D.R. third from right, standing.

*On a winter's day at Groton, Franklin and classmate
Warren Motley coasting on a hill near by the school.*

*Bowler-hatted half-brother James Roosevelt Roosevelt; half-
nephew J.R.R.jr.; F.D.R.; and half-niece Helen R. Roosevelt.*

Eighteen years old, he gave this picture of himself to members of his Groton class at graduation.

Portrait of Anna Eleanor Roosevelt at the age of eighteen.

Sunday.
Oct. 26.
1902.

Dearest Mama –
I am packing
the valise today with
the books and my old
gray suit, and will
ship it tomorrow.
Yesterday I went out
to Dedham just before
lunch rode for two
hours in the afternoon

on a horse which is
the counterpart of
Bobby and returned
here at 10 p.m. after
dinner. I intended to
go to Groton today, but
have so much work that
I couldn't get off.
It has been very chilly
for the past week and
the buildings have been
cold through lack of
fuel, but now that

the strike is settled
the coal has begun to
come in small quantities.
In spite of his success in
settling the trouble, I
think that the President
made a serious mistake
in interfering – politically
at least. His tendency
to make the executive
power stronger than the
Houses of Congress is
bound to be a bad thing,

especially when a man
of weaker personality
succeeds him in office.
Howard Cary stood his
running very well, and
feels perfectly well. He
has gone home for Sunday.
I have to run the Crimson
every Sunday in November
so fear I can't get
home or see you until
Thanksgiving.
Ever with love
F.D.R.

A Harvard undergraduate sees danger in the tendency
of Theodore Roosevelt to strengthen the executive
power of the President at the expense of Congress.

Two views of the original Hyde Park house.

At Campobello, with one of the "cottages" in the background.

GROTON
OCT. 31, 1899,
TUESDAY.

My dearest Mama and Papa,

I was delighted to get yours of **Sunday** and what fun you must have had at Hyde Park! Also I was pleased to see my marks, as there were only five in the form who got B and the rest had C. You are surprised at the small number of studies we have, but our form did so well in the preliminaries that there are very few things left to take. I do take German, Blagden & I are reading "Wilhelm Tell" of Schiller for our advanced course, but we never recite so don't get marked. Also we spend a great deal of time on physics which is hard but most interesting.

I forgot to mention that I got at least 3, and and [*sic*] possibly 4 or 5 honors in my preliminaries, in French, Advanced French, German, and maybe two others which I do not yet know of.

Wednesday.

Tomorrow comes the final struggle. The team had its last practice today amid cheers and a drizzle. It is a toss-up which team wins but we hope for the best. We leave at 12 tomorrow and you *may get* a telegram.

On Saturday Mr. Cushing sold some awfully pretty sporting prints he got at an auction in Boston. I got the pick of the lot, a perfect little beauty for 1.50 this shape [image of a horizontal print frame] & a steeple-chase. I have hung it in my study which is now better fitted up than any other *I think*. Many thanks for the Graphic & St. Stephen's paper. Good for Campo! Are they really waking up? Is Harold Weekes Arthur's boy?

No more now, may write on black edge next time but hope not.

Ever Affec.

F.D.R.

Could you send a few stamped envelopes?

353

On his Oct. 21st report, F.D.R. got B's in Latin, Greek, and Physics, a C in English, and a "Good" in Sacred Studies. The Rector's initial comment for 1899-1900 was "Very good. He is developing most satisfactorily." The St. Stephen mentioned here is the New Brunswick town near the head of Passamaquoddy Bay and not far from Campobello. Harold Weekes was the son of Mr. and Mrs. Arthur D. Weekes of New York City. There was a family connection here, as his aunt, Mrs. John A. Weekes, was the former Alice Delano, a cousin of F.D.R.

"Awful hard luck . . ."

⟨≈⟩

[GROTON]
NOV. 3, 1899,
FRIDAY.

[no salutation]
  Awful hard luck.

Groton 5
St. Marks 6

Each side made one touch-down, both on tricks.
St. Marks kicked their goal and Euey Thayer in attempting to kick our goal slipped so we missed. Still, it does not in the least show their superiority as we played fully as well if not better & gained more ground in the end.

[no signature]

Heavy, doleful ink lines framed this communication.

⟨≈⟩

354

*"By which people with some taste
are somewhat shocked . . ."*

My dearest Mama and Papa

I sent you a note on Friday telling of our hard luck at Southboro. We left here Thursday at 12.30 and reached Southboro
at 2.30, where Lyman took Warren and me up to his room
which bristled with autograph photos of Dewey, yellow soap
posters about five feet square, "EAT H.O." signs, etc. by which
people with some taste are somewhat shocked. The game began
at 3 and after ten minutes play St. Marks made a touchdown
by a trick. In five minutes more we made one by another trick
but as the ball was way over to one side we tried to make a
"kick-out" to enable us to kick the goal from the middle of
the field. Euey tried to catch it but the sun was right in his
eyes and he slipped and missed it thus making the score 6–5
through a piece of individual hard luck but not at all poor
play. For the rest of the time neither side scored and the
teams were very even. We tried to kick a goal from the field
and the ball rose beautifully but *hit the crossbar*. If it had been
½ *inch* higher we would have beaten them 10–6! Anyway they
can't crow as the game shows of course absolutely no superiority of their team. After the game I saw Lyman for a while and
we left at 6, getting home at 8. We do not feel at all badly
as the result is not a defeat. We play the Freshmen next
Wednesday.

Nothing much has happened besides my visit to Boston yesterday. Old Wilson took two or three more casts of my mug in
plaster and I go again next Saturday to have two jack-screws
put on, one in each jaw. The screw I work with a tiny screw-
driver & it is to fill up the holes where the teeth were taken
out.

355

Thus 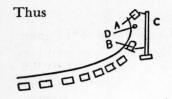 The screw C I turn a little every day & it pulls the teeth A & B together. D is the cavity where the tooth was taken out. He says it will take practically all winter! but I feel it is amply worth it.

A good many graduates are up for Sunday & they say Taddy is never seen in Cambridge & very few boys know of his existence. Remind me when I see you to tell you of some very funny hazing Taddy went through on "Bloody Monday" night. It was told me confidentially & I must say I think it was rather too much.

No more now. I bought a twelve-trip ticket to Boston yesterday, & it will save Papa about $4.00 in the end.

Ever with love & haste

F.D.R.

"Bloody Monday" was an engagement between incoming Freshmen and upperclassmen at Harvard, following upon the official Freshman Reception at Sanders Theatre. For a fuller description, *vide infra.*

∽∽

"I am sure it must be bad for
him as it is for everyone . . ."

GROTON SCHOOL
NOV. 6, 1899,
MONDAY.

My dearest Mama and Papa

I was too distressed to get yours of Saturday this morning, and to hear about dear Papa's upset. I am so glad you were able to get Dr. Ely and that he is better now Your Sunday note is just here and I am glad you are back at Hyde Park and Papa is steadily improving.

I do not think Papa ought to go to New York for business at all as I am sure it must be bad for him as it is for everyone, and I do hope he will give it up this winter.

356

Do let me know again soon how he is.

I forgot to tell Mr. Rogers was up here the day of the game and I sat beside him at table. You will doubtless have seen him since then.

Tuesday 8 a.m.

I must send this as it is time for morning school.

Hoping to hear that dear Papa is all right again I am ever your affec son

FRANKLIN D. ROOSEVELT

Many thanks for the stamped envelopes

Dr. Albert H. Ely was a family doctor not only for the James Roosevelts, but also for the family of Anna Eleanor Roosevelt. Besides being a general practitioner, he was the attending gynecologist at City Hospital.

∽

"If anyone else had been laid up
I should have had to go in . . ."

GROTON
NOV. 8, 1899,
WEDNESDAY.

My dearest Mama and Papa,

No letter has come today to tell me how Papa is getting on but I trust he is all right again now. However I was most agreably surprised and delighted this evening to get a box with the picture of you which I consider just like you and a striking likeness. Many many thanks for it; you say the frame is mine, but I don't quite remember where I got it and who gave it to me. I shall keep the frame on my desk where I can see it all the time.

We played the Freshmen today and had awfully hard luck. Very soon after starting we had four of our best men laid up. Euey Thayer was again hit in the head and made silly, Leaycraft broke his nose badly, Markoe wrenched his leg, Hare sprained his back, and there were many minor injuries. They

beat us 17–0 but our team played a splendid up hill game.
If anyone else had been laid up I should have had to go in as
all the substitutes were called in and they should have had to
draw from the second eleven.

No more now, I hope to get a letter tomorrow morning.

Ever with lots of love to you both your affec son

F.D.R.

∞

"Hurrah for the Boers! . . ."

My dearest Mama and Papa,

Yours of Wednesday and Thursday were most welcome and
I am delighted that Papa is nearly all right again, and I am
sure you are right about the diet, as even I feel the difference
after a long autumn of training and abstaining from sweets.
I go to Boston again tomorrow and am to have the screw put
on, and several teeth filled. It will really be the first of the
straightening process, and I shall try to go on Wednesdays
hereafter as you suggest. Next Saturday the 18th we go to the
Harvard-Yale game so I cannot have an appointment that day.
How do you admire the ink I am using? I got seven ounces
of it, 5 different colors in little pills for 10 cents! You dissolve
it in water and it is indelible and delightful to write with.

Many thanks for the most interesting Graphic. Hurrah for
the Boers! I entirely sympathise with them. I have a slight cold
so omitted my singing-lesson today. I have had two and can
sing one song which I will bring at Xmas!

I will go to see Mrs. Lawrence soon, but it is terribly hard
to find time. There is to be a hare & hounds chase tomorrow
and I am sorry to miss it.

There is little to write about, football is over and I suppose we shall have snow soon. I have taken up golf again but played vilely as a result of no recent practice.

Ever with lots of love to you both your affec son

F.D.ROOSEVELT

Green was the color of the ink used here. The South African War had commenced the previous month, with the attacking Boers everywhere successful. At the time of this letter they had driven the main British forces under General Sir George White back into the Natal colony of Ladysmith, and were besieging that town.

∽∽

"Lathrop Brown and I have decided
definitely to room together . . ."

GROTON SCHOOL
NOV. 12, 1899,
SUNDAY.

My dearest Mama and Papa,

I had a most dismal day yesterday to go to Boston. When I left here it was snowing hard, with about half an inch on the ground, but when I got to Boston it had turned to rain and mud. Dr. Wilson filled two teeth, but had to do some wedging before putting on the screws, and I am to go in again on Wednesday to have the screws put on.

It is a lovely day, but very cold and windy and muddy with a little snow on the ground which makes one think of winter. Just think, the term is two-thirds over and we go home in five weeks! I do not know the exact date but I think it is the Friday before Xmas.

The Hare and Hounds chase was not run yesterday on account of the weather but they are to have it next Wednesday. The boys who were hurt in the Freshman game are getting on well but Harry Markoe's leg now has water on it and Jack Minturn's foot is badly swollen and they think he has a mild case of blood poisoning. I have a pretty sore finger which I put out of joint the last time I played, Tuesday, and it has festered a little back of the nail but I don't think it will come to anythink.

Monday.

I forgot entirely to finish this this morning It is awfully cold here today, but clear.

What do you think? Lathrop Brown and I have decided definitely to room together next year! We are going to Cambridge together sometime during the holidays, probably the last day, to see about rooms, so if you hear anything from Randolph Hall you can tell them I don't want a single room there. We are much inclined to go to the new place, Russell, but we can decide later

No more now Ever with loads of love to you both your affec. son

F.D.R.

Russell Hall, another of the Gold Coast dormitories, was completed in 1900; in appearance it was much like Claverly. Later it was incorporated, under the "house plan," into Adams House.

∽∽

"I also told her about the chickens . . ."

GROTON SCHOOL
NOV. 15, 1899,
WEDNESDAY.

My dearest Mama and Papa,

About ten minutes before leaving for Boston yesterday, I got your two letters, and I am sure you can imagine how delighted I was that you are coming on Saturday. I did not get back till 7, & will go over the first thing in the morning to get rooms for you at Powell's as I agree with you that the food there is infinitely better.

I had a successful visit to Wilson although it was another horrid drizzly day. He put on the screw arrangement on the lower jaw, and it is in full operation now.

Thursday.

I have been to Mrs. Powell, and she thinks you will be the only people there, and can have the whole house to yourselves. I also told her about the chickens.

I have not the faintest idea how soon we shall get home after the game. If we are lucky in getting out after the game from the field we *may* catch the 5.15 and get to the school at 6.30, but I think we cannot probably get back till after 8. so I am afraid you will not see me till Sunday at 8.30. Still, I shall make every effort to get a glimpse of you Saturday night & will tell Warren, & I think he may meet you. I do hope you will have good weather, and I think you should after the last storm. They must have had a terrible storm as several boats were wrecked near there and one schooner was wrecked at *Schooner Cove,* the Henry F. Eaton, which brought up my knockabout. The crew were nearly drowned & the Capt. may die. I have cut out the account from the Boston Globe and will show it to you.

No more now. How lovely to think of seeing you again in 3 days.

Ever in awful haste & love

FDR

⌒⌒

*"It was born Monday morning,
a she, worse luck . . ."*

GROTON SCHOOL
NOV. 22, 1899,
WEDNESDAY.

My dearest Mama and Papa,

I intended to write you last night, but was so tired that I lay on the sofa all evening. The reason of it was a paper-chase, the first ever held here and a howling success. The cause of the paper chase was a half holiday, and the cause of the half-holiday was——a baby. It was born Monday afternoon, a she, worse luck, and weighs nine & ½ lbs. They are going to call it Dorothy.

361

Betsy was most amusing over it, and was wild to have her called Kenneth for some unknown reason, or failing that Hamilton.

The half-holiday was most welcome and the paper-chase bagan at 3.30. The school was divided into four squads to find the trail near the buildings, and I was in charge of one squad, the master of hounds, carrying a tin horn to assemble my hounds. When the start was found we dashed on the dead run past the village, the Lawrences and Sears places to the river and thence to the boat-house, & there the trail ended and we raced for home. The course was a good *six miles* !!!!!!!! Your son finished fourth out of a field of nearly a hundred, and I was almost exhausted as I tottered in. Indeed two boys lost their lunch, the pace was so quick, and the winner who was just ahead of me fell after crossing the line & nearly fainted. I am so stiff today I can hardly move.

Later—

Just back from Boston, where I had a rather unsuccessful visit to old Wilson. He only did two fillings & could not put on the other band for some reason.

Yours from N.Y. was most welcome and I am glad you had a comfortable journey.

No more now,

Ever your affec son,

F.D.R.

Your visit seems like a delightful dream now, & about a week ago, but we only have four weeks from tomorrow!

He was getting the most out of his investment in colored inks: the pages of this letter alternated between blue, green, and red. Dorothy Peabody was the youngest of the Rector's five daughters. She married a Groton boy, F. Trubee Davison, who was Assistant Secretary of War for Air under Coolidge and Hoover, administrative assistant chief of air staff during World War II, and (since 1933) president of the American Museum of Natural History in New York. The word "dream" in the postscript to this letter was added by F.D.R.'s mother.

*"What a horrible barbarity at
Lawrenceville! . . ."*

My dearest Mama & Papa,

My overcoat came Friday night, most opportunely, as yesterday was very cold and I was glad to wear it to Boston. Dr. Wilson put *two more* whirly-gigs into my mouth, one directly in front in the lower jaw and the other above corresponding to the one you saw when you were here. I made an appointment for Wednesday, but I find Aunt Kassie is coming here on Wednesday so I am writing today to cancel it and make one for Saturday instead.

I hope you have written to Randolph to apply for a double room for us; we are also applying at Claverley and Russell in case we get nothing at Randolph.

Taddy came up with me last night, also several other graduates. He appeared cheerful and has been in my study part of the day. He seems to get on well in studies, though I don't believe he is doing much else. He may go home next Sunday, and I think could perfectly get permission to leave Friday night as several others are.

Later—5 30 p.m.

Rosy has just gone back with the others, having first lost his hat which has just been found, & then he discovered that he had no money! It has been a most perfect day but we are reminded of winter by the board walks and shields to keep off the snow-drifts. Our Sunday School was a howling success, 12 children, from 6 to 20 years old. It seems like a month since you were here, and I keep thinking of your lovely visit; only a little more than three weeks now and we shall be home!

No more now,

Ever with best love to you both your affec. son

FRANKLIN

What a horrible barbarity at Lawrenceville!! Glad I'm at *Groton*.

Inquiry among contemporary Lawrenceville students, and at the school itself, has failed to reveal the nature of the "barbarity" here mentioned, nor do newspapers provide any clues. At this time morale at Lawrenceville was not of the best; there had been a change of headmasters two months before, and it is possible that the event which aroused F.D.R.'s excitement followed from this shakeup—the expulsion of a large number of students, or something on that order, which would have loomed barbarous to a rival schoolboy. It was a Groton master, after all, who twenty years later went to Lawrenceville and built it into the outstanding boarding school which it is today.

$\sim$

". . . not being able to think of anyone else . . ."

GROTON SCHOOL
NOV. 29, 1899,
WEDNESDAY.

My dearest Mama & Papa,

Aunt Kassie and Muriel got here today at 12, and we were very glad to see them. I lunched & teaed with them and during the afternoon we took a drive for about an hour. Tomorrow we leave at 11, as it is more comfortable, altho' most of the boys leave at eight. In the afternoon we are probably going to the Harvard Museum to see the flowers (glass) and in the evening are to see Robespierre I am delighted to say.

The marks for the last month were read out today and I am glad to say I got B, altho' I rather expected a C. Warren was 7 from the tail, which is better, but our two Hyde Parks boys did not distinguish themselves. Poor Coleman was foot of the class, alas! with an average of 3., out of a possible 10. Jefferson was next to him, with 3.25/100!!! I quite blushed for them when it was read out as they are both about the lowest marks on record! The invitation from Mrs. Soley came yesterday and I have accepted it; also I have written to ask [name deleted] for the Dodworth dance, not being able to think of anyone else. I am also writing Laura for Orange. Howard Cary is to dance with Muriel at the Dodworth, I am glad to say, & he was over there at tea tonight.

It is 9.30 & I must go to bed as we have to be up at 6.30

No more now

Ever with dear love to you both your affec son

F.D.R.

Sir Henry Irving, then sixty-two years old, was touring America with his notable Lyceum Theatre production of Victorien Sardou's *Robespierre*. F.D.R.'s November marks included an A in Latin Composition, a C in English Composition, and B's in the remaining subjects. Rector's comment: "Excellent."

∽∾

"I don't think I ever saw a better play in my life . . ."

GROTON SCHOOL
DEC. 3, 1899,
SUNDAY.

My dearest Mama & Papa,

Your lovely long letter of Friday came yesterday just before I left for Boston. I am sorry I can't go to the Metropolitan dance on the 23rd as I should like to go to Hyde Park that night, but I suppose I must go to the dinner now, as I have already accepted it. I am asking Lathrop Brown up for some time after New Year's and I will let you know definitely soon, but he may not be able to come. I am also thinking of asking some others up, possibly. You must have had a nice Thanksgiving dinner, too bad the toast fell flat, still it is somewhat what one would expect. We left here at 11.30 Thanksgiving Day, and reached the Touraine at 1. After lunch, accompanied by the great P.C. we went to Cambridge and saw the glass flowers and other Harvard sights. We got back at 5.30, I took a bath (!), we had dinner at 6.30, turkey etc. and then went to "Robespierre". I don't think I ever saw a better play in my life and Irving was splendid. We came back at 10 on Friday and yesterday I went again to Wilson and must go more next Wednesday. Today the Toms [Newbolds] are here and Mrs. Hoyt & the Elephantine [name deleted]. I lunched with Mrs. N. and took supper with Mr. G. & am now going in the Faculty Supper, so I will surely have a bad pain in the night! No more now, I have tons of things to do.

Ever with love

F.D.R.

2½ weeks more!!!!!
What shall I do about the enclosed? Must it be answered? *What a bore!*

F.D.R.

The Metropolitan dances, given during Christmas and Easter vacations, remain today one of the leading social institutions for the New York "sub-debutante set."

〜〜

"... dont quite understand why
I should not go too??! ..."

G.S.A.A., GROTON SCHOOL
DEC. 8, 1899,
FRIDAY.

My dearest Mama and Papa,

Yours of Tuesday is most welcome, also the Graphic. I am sorry not to have written sooner but I have not had a moment to sit down. I went to Wilson again on Wednesday, but he merely looked at the teeth and told me to come again next week. I have already asked him about the enamel but he says

366

it cannot be used on me. I shall ask him again, however. I am sending you my dress-suit and will try to answer the questions. 1. The trousers need letting down and the coat out, especially under the arms. Also the waistcoat needs letting out *and down* to meet the trousers. I can't think of any wishes, O, yes, you know I thought I would like a tin box, like your missionary society cash-box, with a combination lock. Any good book would be acceptable indeed anything, for you know I am not especially hard to please. Anything for my room at college next autumn I should like, such as pillows, etc.

Skating really began today, although only a few boys went to a small pond, as our big one has not yet filled up, and I doubt if it does so now, but we can have no good skating unless it does. I have had several challenges for next year's team and shall be kept busy from now on. I am writing on some [Groton School] Athletic Assoc. paper as mine has run out.

I will write at more length Sunday although I am behind hand in work, I have so much to do. Mary Newbold & Laura have accepted. I hear that Jack & Hugh Minturn are going to the Metropolitan club dance on the 23rd so dont quite understand why I should not go too??!

Ever with loads of love, your affec son

FRANKLIN.

〜〜

"Only Bookstores & Candy-stores
and cheap hardware-stores! . . ."

GROTON SCHOOL
DEC. 10, 1899,
SUNDAY.

My dear Mama, & Papa,

I can hardly believe that I shall be really home in a little over a week. Goodwin is coming up on Jan. 2nd. Brown *probably* also and I may ask one other, possibly Kerr Rainsford. I am to dine with Brown the night of the 8th, (the day before we return) go to the theatre & take the midnight on to Boston.

Mr. Griswold and I are going to Boston early on Wednesday to buy Xmas presents for our Sunday-School; and in the afternoon I have an appointment with Wilson. My lower teeth are very nearly straight, but I bust the instrument today and it cannot be put on again till Wednesday. I have had really no time at all in Boston to buy presents and it is on the whole a most unsatisfactory place for that. Only Bookstores & Candystores with one or two cheap hardware-stores! The rest of the city is taken up by Commonwealth Ave. and Dentists as far as I can make out! And the Subway! Dont you think we had better ask up one or two girls for the 2nd? A Draper girl or anyone, I don't know any so will trust to you entirely. Only not the [name deleted] brat! please!!

Monday—8 a.m.

The weather continues clear, but much warmer today Please excuse the awful scrawl, but I have only had about ten minutes to write it in.

Ever with loads of love, affec son

FDR

∾

". . . then I found a smelly old,
tough mutton stew waiting . . ."

GROTON SCHOOL
DEC. 14, 1899,
THURSDAY.

My dearest Mama and Papa,

I am sorry not to have written sooner but yesterday I went to Boston with Mr. Griswold at 11 o'clock, skipping part of morning school, to buy Xmas presents for our Sunday School. The day was *hot* and fine & I bicycled to Ayer with "Push" at a furious ~~gate~~ gait, having on a covert-coat. When we got to Boston we had a substantial lunch of beans of the Boston Baked variety. We then walked or rather ran to Jordan and Marsh, the Boston Siegel Cooper, and we were there walking the floor for *two mortal hours!!!* We bought everything, toys, games, cards, books, etc. till I could hardly stand up. Then at 3.30 we left & I went to Dr. Wilson, who kept me waiting an hour, & then just looked at my teeth, but they are moving nicely. I caught the 5.15 train back, & bicycled *up* (!) from Ayer in the dark, at 80 miles an hour. I nearly expired, & then I found a smelly old, tough mutton stew waiting for supper, & did not eat any.!!!

I return the report for which many thanks. It is better than I expected Yours of Tuesday is most welcome. Glad the infants are coming. I would just as soon go out to Orange Thursday night, if nothing in N.Y. turns up but you can decide. Very nice that [we] dine with Coz. Corinne the 27th.

Lathrop Brown has asked me to dine with him & he is to have a little party & go to the theatre afterwards.

By the way, one of the Xmas presents I should like is a "Life's Gibson Calendar". You can get it anywhere.

Awful rush. Love

F.D.R.

The New York department store of Siegel, Cooper Company, on Sixth Avenue, was known as "The Big Store," and had for its slogan: "Meet Me At The Fountain." It was sold in 1901. Restrained counterpart of today's "Esquire Calendar" was that drawn by Charles Dana Gibson for the old humorous magazine *Life;* it was an equally popular wall adornment.

∞

"Most were in skins & I never
saw anything finer . . ."

[GROTON]
DEC. 17, 1899,
SUNDAY.

My dearest Mama and Papa,

Next Friday! Just think! We are coming home by a special train of three cars & a dining-car, & we ought to get to N.Y. by 2.45, but I will write definitely to 10 W. 43rd. Please take down for me my blue winter suit, dress-suit and a dress-shirt & tie & all my collars. Also a new pair of gloves which I think you have at home. I had a most delightful experience yesterday. Mr. Jefferson is the nephew of Wm. Brewster the President of the A.O.U. We left, Mr. J., Roger Derby & six other bird-boys at 11 o'clock for Cambridge & on arriving there went straight to Prof. (in the College) Brewster's house where we had lunch and then went to a delightful little house in his yard, "The Museum" where he has the *finest private collection of American birds in the world!* Most were in skins & I never saw anything finer. I will tell you more about it on Friday We got home in time for supper & after supper Mr. Peabody's father began reading the Xmas Carol as usual, which he continued all day today.

Today I have tead with Mrs. Sturgis & had a most successful Sunday-School where we gave presents.

Monday.

The mail is off, I will write once more

Ever with love

FDR

Professor William Brewster was assistant in the Department of Ornithology and Mammalogy at the Harvard Museum of Comparative Zoology. In his final fall-term report, F.D.R. got a B average. Christmas vacation followed; the promised Friday letter is not to be found.

∽

"The air break made a horrible noise all night . . ."

THE TOURAINE [BOSTON]
JAN. 9, 1900,
TUESDAY, 2:30 P.M.

Dearest Mama & Papa,

Here I am after a most successful trip, just going to Dr. Wilson. Last night I reached town [New York] safely & on time, *saw* my trunk taken around, left my valise & went to the Renaissance for a wash, etc. I found there a letter from Nelly B which I will enclose from Groton. I took a handsome (!) to the Brown's (247 Lex.) & got there on time. Mrs. & Mr. B, Lathrop, "the Kid" & I, that was all. Mrs. B. *very* nice & we got on swimmingly. Mr. B. also most kind, but I should not say he amounted to as much as Mrs. (first impression) We (Mrs., Charley, L, & I) went to Sherlock H. & had a most delightful evening, splendid play. Did not get through till 11.30 when we went back to the Browns for a bite of scrambled eggs toast & milk. Then we caught the midnight by the skin of our teeth. Found Mr. Ayrault on board & did not get to bed till 1 a.m. It was so cold I slept little & was uncomfortable for the first time in my life as the air break made a horrible noise all night. We got to Boston at 7 with *fearful* cold & ran here for hot coffee & a good breakfast. Then to Cambridge & we caught Archie Brown just getting up but Taddy had gone. Then we went [to] the different agents & went over all the buildings, Randolph, Claverley, Russell & Westmorely. We saw many rooms, but the pick was at Westmoreley, *1st floor corner, looking on the South-West,* and guess the price? *$400* without extras. The plan is roughly like this:

We both thought it a chance and are sure of getting it as we will be given 1st choice on Mar. 1st. On the W. side of Westmoreley is Russell, then Randolph, then Claverley so all four buildings are together. The sitting room is large enough for two desks, & the bed-rooms & bath room light & airy. The ceilings are very high.

Lathrop went back at 12 o'clock & I found J. [Taddy] and lunched with him & Kellogg who appears quite nice. I saw all the Groton contingent & now am off to Wilson. I will write a line when I get to school. Am well, still somewhat sleepy! Ever with tons and tons of love, I am your affec. son

F.D.R.

"The Kid" was Charles S. Brown, Jr., younger brother of Archibald and Lathrop, who succeeded his father in the New York realty firm of Brown, Wheelock & Harris. The previous November, William Gillette had opened "in his new play called 'Sherlock Holmes' "—a performance which he was destined to repeat many times during the next thirty years. Westmorly Court was a pleasant, spacious, vaguely Tudor building built in 1898. F.D.R. roomed there, in Number 27, all his four years at Harvard.

～～

*"I wish the vacation might have
been just two days more . . ."*

GROTON
JAN. 9, 1900,
TUESDAY, 8 P.M.

My darling Mama & Papa.

I wrote you at 3 o'clock from the Touraine this afternoon about my doings in the little town of Cambridge, and I hope you have received my letter. I went to Wilson and he took off my upper screw as it was bent but nothing more could be done until a new one is made and I am to go again either Saturday or next Wednesday. I did my best to impress on him how hard it was for me to go every week and he says he will do his best. I shall keep telling him to hurry and I think it will have effect. At the station I met all the Boston boys and we got to the school at 6.30. Everything is too familiar, alas, and the prospect of eleven weeks of it is not sweet. I am still at the New Building, luckily, no one changed yet, and am all alone in the dormitory as Kerr is to be operated on and will not return till next

372

month. I think we have really secured good rooms, and I am sure you will be pleased with them, and besides, the price is so much less than we expected. I have not yet unpacked, in fact I dont even know if my trunk is here, they are only just beginning to arrive. I fancy you have had very cold weather since I left, as it is bitter here. I wish the vacation might have been just two days more, I don't feel as if I had seen half enough of either of you. But we must be resigned and wait till Feb. 22nd. Mr. Cushing says he has a good play in mind—Don't tell anyone, though. No more now, I still feel tired & sleepy, tho' the cold in my head is *really better,* and I have not coughed so much.

Ever lovingly your son

FRANKLIN.

∾∾

*"I fear I cannot get the Boer
question . . ."*

GROTON SCHOOL
JAN. 11, 1900,
THURSDAY.

My dearest Mama and Papa,

Yours of yesterday was most welcome this morning. The memorandum book, paper-holder, umbrellas and "Wild Animals I have known" have all arrived, and many thanks for them, also for the floss-silk. Yesterday afternoon I worked over my correspondence, took a walk and had tea with Mr. G.

Today was lovely and as there is splendid skating on the river the choir decided to take a half-holiday. We played hockey steadily until 4:30, then skated about two miles down the river and back, and I am tired out now, but my cold is better, and I hardly notice it. It has begun to snow now, and the ground is already white. I fear it will be deep in the morning. The play has been decided on but not the parts yet, I can't breethe a word to anyone. I enclose Nellie's letter. I shall write to thank her for the basket & cushion. Please ask her to send them to Hyde Park, as I shall not use them till the autumn.

I am to debate in two weeks, but I fear I cannot get the Boer question as we debate second, and the first batch will take it.

Friday. 8. a m.

It has stopped snowing, there are only 6 inches, but it is enough to spoil the river skating.

No more   Ever with loads of love,

F.D.R.

Ernest Thompson Seton's *Wild Animals I Have Known* had just been published.

~~

"My chief work is kissing the heroine . . ."

My dearest Mama and Papa,

I was too distressed to get yours of Thursday telling of Papa's bad turn again. It seems such a strange thing, and I hope Dr. Weber will understand it. However I am only too glad it was not as serious as the one in N. Y. and that Papa is nearly all right again. I hope your next letter will say he is perfectly well.

Last Friday we spent the whole time clearing off the pond, having been let off calisthenics to do it. However the snow was so heavy on the ice that the pond overflowed on top, making a nasty slush, so that we cannot do much skating now. A hard crust has formed and there is good coasting on Joy's Hill. Yesterday I visited several of our Sunday School children's families, with Mr. Griswold after lunch, going to four or five houses in the neighborhood. Then at 4.30 we went to Mr. Cushing's for the first rehearsal of the play, merely to see what characters we were to take. There are only four or five girls in the play and as only two have at all good parts, I decided to try for a man part, in which I appear constantly, have little to say, but *lots* of acting and Mr. C. says it is a hard part. As yet nothing is decided definitely, but I don't want you to say a word of this to anyone, even Helen, as it *must* be kept secret. My chief work is kissing the heroine (I am her cousin) and thus I enrage the hero, her fiancé. The name of the play is "Wedding March," a translation of the French "Un Chapeau de Paille d' Italie", you may have heard of it. Remember, *Mum's* the word. Impress the importance of it on Papa, as it would spoil *everything to have it known*

I cannot help thinking of poor Debby, and that I shall never see her again, but I fully realize that it is for the best as she is in such a condition. You ask what foods I bought in Boston. I got absolutely nothing as I had no chance. However chocolate is my favorite diet, but if you send anything up let me know just before as I will bribe the express niggers not to open the box. Laurie Rainsford has Lathrop's study this term as he & Kerr were in a double one and they were separated at their own request.

I think I shall have to go to Boston on Wednesday, but I have not yet heard from Wilson and shall not go until I do. Many thanks for the umbrellas and note-book which I had hunted for everywhere.

Monday. 8. a.m.

A thick fog is over everything although I think the sun will burn through. I took my first fencing lesson Saturday, & found it most interesting but as they come on Wednesdays and Saturdays I fear I shall miss a good many by going to Boston.

Ever with best love to you both your affec. son

FRANKLIN.

The Washington's Birthday play being a sixth-form production, F.D.R. was at last having a chance to satisfy what seems to have been a considerable histrionic ambition. The drama chosen for this year was *The Wedding March—An Eccentricity in Three Acts,* an English adaption by W. S. Gilbert of *Le Chapeau de Paille d'Italie* by Michel and Labiche.

∽∽

"I think it rather hard as there
are so few girls . . ."

My dearest Mama & Papa,

I was delighted to get yours of Sat. and Sunday, saying that Papa is nearly all right again. I do hope he will be most careful and never go to N.Y. for the day and not go as much as he has been doing.

Paul Draper has not returned yet, I dont understand it as apparently he is perfectly well & has been seen at the theatre and opera. We had the most extraordinary weather, this morning it drizzled and there was slush everywhere, but tonight it will freeze up everything as it is much colder and there should be a good crust for coasting tomorrow.

I have tried another part in the play, a woman's, but shall not have it, as it is being saved for Kerr Rainsford, who will be back from the operation the first week in February! I think it rather hard as there are so few girls and I am sure I could do as well as Kerr. As it is now I doubt if I get a good part at all, and Mr. Cushing is being bullied by his Boston friends (!) to give *them* all the best parts!

I shall not go to Boston tomorrow as I have heard nothing from Wilson and he promised to write. As it is I have no appliance on my teeth now and a whole week has been utterly wasted. I am writing him a very angry letter.

Wed. 8. a.m.

It is a glorious day and there is a fine crust, so I shall go coasting as I have a fencing lesson this morning. Mrs. Sturgis has a "house warming" this afternoon for the VI form, tea at 4.30, and Mr. G. & Mr Cush are away, so there will be no rehearsal.

No more now.

Ever with dearest love & haste   Affec son

F.D.R.

376

Two editorial assists from his mother: the addition of the word "well" in the second sentence of the second paragraph, and in the third paragraph, the alteration of "women's" to "woman's."

∽∽

". . . but he finally backed down . . ."

[GROTON]
JAN. 19, 1900,
FRIDAY.

Dearest Mama & Papa,

Just a few lines to tell you how the world moves here. Last Wednesday there was a heavy crust over everything, so Mr. Griswold and I put on our skates and *skated* on the crust, 'cross' country over barbed-wire fences to Groton, and from there more than a mile beyond, to visit the family of a member of our Sunday-School. I never had such a long skate but it was glorious fun and we went awfully fast.

Yesterday, Thursday, was a half holiday, for the honors of last years form at Harvard. They got so few that the Rector w'd not let us have one last term, but he finally backed down.

I went coasting on the Joy's hill with Laurie Rainsford and Markoe and as the crust was splendid we went very fast, but only had one or [two] spills.

It is foggy and melting hard today so everything will be spoiled unless it freezes.

I am going to Boston tomorrow and hope Wilson will do something as he telegraphed for me to come

I must close as it is time for me to go in to faculty-supper, it is my night.

Ever with loads of love, Affec. son

F.D.R.

∽∽

*"I cannot help feeling that the
Boers have the side of right . . ."*

My darling Mama & Papa,

In my last letter of Friday I was in such an awful hurry that I entirely forgot to thank Papa for his lovely birthday present to me and his letter. I have sent the cheque and I am delighted to have the Scientific American for another year. Many thanks also for the two Graphics, which were most interesting. I think you misunderstand my position in regard to the Boers. I cannot help feeling convinced that the Boers have the side of right and that for the past ten years they have been *forced* into this war. I am sure you will feel this if you only read up the Boer case. *However,* undoubtedly, now that the war is actually on, it will be best from the humanitarian standpoint for the British to win speedily and civilization will be hurried on, but I feel that the same result would have been surely obtained without war.

Mr. Jacob Riis was here today and this evening he spoke before the misionary society, and told stories of his experiences with "Teddy" on the police-force in N. Y. I am going into faculty supper in a few minutes and I hope he will be there. Yesterday it poured and I did not have a nice time in Boston. Wilson found that my teeth had changed during the week so could not put on the appliance he had made, so he has decided to have me down on Wednesday & he will put in a rubber plate. I have cursed him out but he says he is doing his best. Today everything is frozen, but there is very little snow left on the ground. I have written five letters to teams today so cannot write more

I debate a week from tomorrow, (Monday) on the Phillipine question, & am working hard.

Ever with tons of love, Your affec son

FRANKLIN.

A common interest in bettering social and political conditions in New York City provided foundation for the close friendship between the Danish immigrant, Jacob Riis, and Theodore Roosevelt, which began when the latter became president of the New York Police Board in 1895. Riis, a journalist, was not actually on the Police Board as suggested in this letter. His famous autobiography, *The Making of an American,* appeared the following year.

∽∽

"We are pros, that is in favor of independance . . ."

[GROTON]
JAN. 23, 1900,
TUESDAY.

My dearest Mama & Papa.

Yesterday it melted hard so there was no outdoor exercise to be had, and I worked somewhat on my debate which is on the Phillipine question: Resolved, that the U. S. should promise the Philipinos independence when they are in a fit condition to receive it. We, that is Sam Hinckley, Morin Hare & myself are pros, that is in favor of independance, against Warren Motley, Roger Derby and Duane Humphreys. Our opponents are pretty strong but I hope we can win. Tonight there is a debate on the Transvaal, & I intend to make a two minute speech. Mr. Riis stayed over yesterday and last night gave a most interesting lecture on the poor in New York, with stereopticon views, and there was great enthusiasm over him & the whole school cheered when "Teddys" picture was thrown on the screen. Today it is still melting hard and there is no snow left, except in the woods. I walked down to the river this a. m. It is still frozen but I fear will break up tomorrow if it does not freeze. I see by the paper that the Hudson is open at Albany so I suppose must be at Hyde Park. Many thanks for the newspapers which are most interesting. I go to Boston tomorrow and shall miss my fencing for the second time! It makes me tired, but I suppose it is inevitable.

Wed. 8. a.m.

During the night it has grown bitterly cold. I am off at 12 o'clock & shall wear my ulster. Edmunds side won the debate last night in favor of the Boers & I made a two minute speech. It is so cold I can hardly hold the pen

Ever with love

F.D.R.

The Filipino independence movement had not been sidetracked by the substitution of American for Spanish rule in 1898. Early in 1899 fighting broke out, and although the results were disastrous for the Filipinos under Aguinaldo, they retired to the hills and continued a deadly guerrilla warfare not actually ended until 1901. At the time of F.D.R.'s debate, the United States Army's military government of the Islands was under Lieutenant General Arthur MacArthur, father of Douglas MacArthur; and Judge William Howard Taft, of the Sixth Judicial Circuit Court of Appeals, had just been appointed president of the Philippine Civil Commission, to proceed to the Islands in March preparatory to restoring civilian control. As for the Transvaal debate, that was again the Boer question; British encroachment into this last stronghold of Oom Paul Kruger and his Boers, notably the unsuccessful Jameson Raid of 1895, had been one of the basic causes of the South African War.

∾

"I have to wash the plate every day and cannot talk well . . ."

GROTON SCHOOL
JAN. 25, 1900,
THURSDAY.

My dearest Mama and Papa,

Yesterday I went to Boston in a fine drizzle and for the first time in *over a month* I have an appliance on my teeth which is really working! And such a machine! It consists of a complete roof to my mouth made of hard rubber fastened on to several teeth, but to cap the climax there are four angry hooks on the bands around the teeth and between these are stretched rubber bands as tight as possible which are pulling hard all the time. I have to wash the plate every day and cannot talk well now and the plate & hooks are in the way of my tongue. However it is well worth the inconvenience if it will straighten the tooth in 2 weeks as Wilson says it will. It is sleeting today and the ground is slippery & wet. I missed a rehearsal yesterday but am still hoping for the part I wanted, of the foolish cousin I wrote you about. Still nothing is decided definitely yet and Cush is in Boston today & won't be back till Saturday. The best part of my appliance on my teeth is that I don't have to go to Boston again for two mortal weeks and I will have a good chance at the rehearsals for a while.

Friday 8. a.m.

It is clear again but not very cold. I am working all the time on my debate and hope to be able to say it off well. It comes next Monday night and if I win it will mean four years debating without a single defeat.

There are a lot of graduates up here now, who are having a holiday between exams. Rosy may come up but it is doubtful.

No more now, Ever affec son,

FDR

∽∽

*"I cannot in the least realize
that I am eighteen . . ."*

GROTON SCHOOL
JAN. 30, 1900,
TUESDAY.

My darling Mama & Papa

I cannot in the least realize that I am eighteen today, and only wish I could be at home with you now, as a Birthday at School seems too much like any other day. Indeed today I I [*sic*] have done nothing but work, either on lessons or on my debate which comes tonight. I don't believe that we will win as we have by far the poorest side of the question. The box of goodies came last night and they are the most delicious things I ever tasted. I have sent to Groton for a tin of condensed cream, and we shall have a feast in the dormitory I am so terribly busy I will send this scrap off & write again tomorrow

Ever with loads of love and kisses & thanks to you both your affectionate son

FRANKLIN.

∽

". . . made the American eagle
crow as loudly as he could . . ."

My darling Mama and Papa

Your three dear letters from New York have all come and I am glad Papa has not been upset by all his gaiety. What a dinner that must have been at the Reid's! I will gladly *try* to get a room for Nelly but just at present I am suffering from a slight cold in the head and have not been out today, but have sat and read in my study all morning. The infirmary is *packed* with colds, Jeff among them but it is not serious, although he thinks he is very ill. But to go back and give you the news. On Monday night we had a talk on South Africa from Father Osborne, a missionary, and it was most interesting. Tuesday, my birthday I celebrated by working hard, and in the evening losing my debate, through no fault of my own. The first speaker on my side, Hare, made rather a failure, as he didn't know his debate at all. Sam Hinckley my other colleague had an excellent speech but he rattled it off so fast that no one could understand him! On the other hand our opponents were all fair, and had the entire sympathy of the audience & made the American eagle crow as loud as he could, and Blubber Derby was so ludicrous that the whole room was convulsed at the funny way he spoke. However when the votes were counted they stood 21 to 19 against us, so you [see] we were not so very bad. Last night there was a reception in Ayer to the new clergyman, and as Mr. Billings wanted to go he took me with him. We left at 7.30 in a sleigh and when we got there found the reception in full swing, every member of the church, mostly old women and deaf men. I talked to everyone, said the same thing to everyone for two mortal hours, and a young woman with a voice that sounded like tearing oil-cloth sang two songs, and another recited two stories. I nearly died. Then supper was handed round, that is tea (?) a juiceless olive on a toothpick one mouldy sandwich, one-half of a cracker and one green and yellow doyley. Still it was interesting and novel and when we got back at 10.30 we had faculty supper. Today I have stayed in the house on account of my cold.

Friday.

My cold is a great deal better and I go out this afternoon to a rehearsal. Last night a Mr. Wilson came here and told us about the Nova Scotia Coal mines & asked for money for his hospital. I think it is a really worthy charity & gave $2.00 (!)

No more now. Will go to Powell's tomorrow.

Ever affec. son

F.D.R.

The dinner party mentioned here was given by Whitelaw Reid, successor to Horace Greeley as editor of the New York *Tribune,* and father and grandfather of owner-editors of the merged *Herald Tribune.*

∾∾

"Sunday school was small today
on account of the bad walking . . ."

GROTON SCHOOL
FEB. 4, 1900,
SUNDAY.

My dearest Mama and Papa,

It is damp and chilly today, and I fear there will be snow. My cold is practically gone, and yesterday I had a fencing lesson in the morning and stayed in during the p.m. till five when we went to Cush's for a rehearsal. My part will be decided positively in the next few days, and I have hopes of getting it, but they are doubtful. Our Sunday school was small today on account of the bad walking. By the way there is one boy in the infirmary with pneumonia, who is very sick, the Haight boy.

Monday.

I forgot to write more on this yesterday but there is nothing to say. Will write more tomorrow.

Ever

F.D.R.

∾

"I suppose it is criminal to rejoice
but I cant help it! . . ."

GROTON SCHOOL
FEB. 11, 1900,
SUNDAY.

My darling Mama and Papa,

Joyful news! I have a part in the play at last and entirely by accident. Jimmy Jackson had the part of the old hayseed countrified uncle of the bride. He is sick in Boston with rheumatic fever & water on the knee so wont be back again this term. I suppose it is criminal to rejoice but I cant help it! I've got his part, and it's one of the best in the play!!!! I have begun to learn it hard and shall have to work hard as the play is only ten days off. We have had 3 rehearsals last week & I did well I think, tho' I dont know my part yet. Remember, dont breathe a word to anyone yet, till the play-bills are out, & I will try to send you one this week.

All your letters of the past week have been most welcome. I dread going home to find no more Debby in her stall but I suppose it is for the best. I am so sorry Papa had that expedition after the yacht for nothing and do hope he will be able to get something he likes. By the way I wish you could send me my old (Papa's) flannel trousers, and the shortest and baggiest pair of duck trousers I own, as I must try several costumes for the play. Mrs. Rogers is here. I went to lunch with her yesterday. Coleman has a cold. She goes back tomorrow & will see you I suppose.

Ever in haste & with dear love. Excuse awful pen.

F.D.R.

Will write Tuesday.

∽

". . . better yet Papa's straw beaver
that he got in London . . ."

GROTON SCHOOL
FEB. 12, 1900,
MONDAY.

My dearest Mama and Papa

Yours of Saturday almost knocked me down with surprise this morning, and I am glad on the whole that you are going to the Lawrence's and simply delighted that you will stay over Sunday, as you will see the play on Saturday again, the [in] the town-hall at Groton! As I wrote you yesterday I really have a good part in the play, although I shall have to work like anything to learn it as I got it so late in the day. I want very much a tail coat and if I remember right Papa has an old dress suit coat that he never wears. Do let me know as soon as possible, and *send it on* if I can have it just for the occasion. Also if you have a farmer's hat, or better yet Papa's straw beaver that he got in London last year. Anything that you can suggest for an old country bumpkin in his best London clothes! I am delighted that Nelly is coming & I shall say nothing to Mrs. Powell, so that we can have the big double room. Let me know what day you get here & what time. Wednesday p.m we have the dress rehearsal & Thursday is a half-holiday so come early if you come Thursday.

It is *pouring* today and there is no snow left, only puddles.

I can hardly wait till next week to see you but this term has gone like lightning and is already half over.

No more now.

Ever with love

FDR.

〜〜〜

*"At last my ambition of tieing
with Krumbhaar is satisfied . . ."*

My dearest Mama & Papa,

Yours of Wednesday night has just come. Please bring the high hat besides sending the other things as it may be most useful. I don't believe I shall see you Wednesday night but shall go to the Lawrences at 12 on Thursday. Please bring also my low yellow shoes, the heavy ones with hob-nails in them. I went to Boston Wednesday, but Wilson only kept me ten minutes so I went out to Cambridge & had nearly an hour with Rosy. He is well and will come up for Sunday when you are here and will go to the play in the village.

The marks for last month were read out today and you can imagine that I was somewhat surprised when my name was read out for an A. the first (and last) in my school career!

Krumbhaar also had one, so that between us we led the form. I was delighted as at last my ambition of tieing with Krumbhaar is satisfied. It came as a complete surprise as I have not worked harder than generally, this term, and I think it is due chiefly to good-luck in recitations. Warren also did well and was just in the upper half of his form with 6.74 for his average. You know A means an average of 8.50 or over & the Rector told me he was much pleased. I sent you a poster yesterday, and I don't mind you showing it around as they are now posted all over town. I have four good seats for you, & four for Aunt Kassie but the gym. will be terribly crowded and there are no more seats left. Warren is to play the cymbals in the orchestra between the acts, & he is delighted and will go to the rehearsal on Wednesday. I just have heard from Cush that he has lots of old top-hats, so don't bring Papa's but send the straw, also please bring my red cotton socks.

[no signature]

The ultimate A was a product of C in English Composition, B's in English and Greek, A's in Latin and Physics, and a "Good" in Sacred Studies.

∞

"I am learning how to manipulate the tails . . ."

GROTON SCHOOL
FEB. 18, 1900,
SUNDAY.

My dearest Mama and Papa,

For the first time this winter we have had a good snowstorm and this morning there must be over a foot on the average, although it is drifting terribly. We are to have chapel in the School-House, as it would be too hard to get to the Chapel. On Friday night I was delighted to get the first batch of clothes and last night the second box came. The checked flannel trousers are *perfect*, with the seat coming about my knees, and the legs reaching only to the *tops* of my shoes. I have not decided yet on a waistcoat, but will probably wear the buff one, and the dress coat is simply perfect, and I am learning how to manipulate the tails when I sit down. Dont tell anyone, however what I am to wear.

The stage is being rapidly put up, and the stage-rehearsal comes Tuesday, and the grand dress-rehearsal, on Wednesday. I hope you have sent Papa's *straw* top-hat as I cannot decide whether to wear it or an ordinary beaver till I see the straw-one. You ask if you can continue to Groton in the Fitchburg train. You know Groton is on the Boston & Maine R.R. *not* the Fitchburg, but the two roads cross at Ayer. I have looked in the time-table, but can find no train from Albany reaching Ayer at 6.32 However there is one which leaves Albany at 1.10 getting to Ayer at 6.08. If you take that, you can get into a B.&M. train at Ayer and get to Groton at 6.30 about. However the connection is fairly close & you could not make it if you do not reach Ayer till 6.32. I shall not see you Wednesday but will try to get down to the Lawrences at 12.30 on Thursday & I can stay to lunch & be with you all afternoon. I have got four tickets for you, & 4 for Aunt Kassie, but you are lucky to have any as if I had not been in the 6th form you [would] have had horrid seats. The gym. will be the worst kind of a jam and even the running track upstairs will be utilized. Standing-room is at a premium, and it will be the biggest affair we have had at Groton. A special train is coming from Boston & will take the Boston people back the same night.

Later.

We have had both morning & afternoon chapel in the new school-room. It has stopped drifting but the snow is pretty deep. None of my Sunday-School children came today as the roads are all blocked.

Monday. 8.a.m.

It is a glorious morning & cold. I wish you could bring me a bandana or some bright handkerchief for the old Uncle Bopaddy to wear.

Ever with loads of love your affec. son   FDR.

∽

"I went to the Bank on Monday
& had my book balanced O.K. . . ."

GROTON SCHOOL
MARCH 14, 1900,
WEDNESDAY.

My darling Mama & Papa,

Your three letters have made me so happy that dear Papa continues to improve and I only hope he will not overdo.— I thought that the bird was not only too far gone, but its plumage was in bad condition, and one eye was too far gone, in fact had been all eaten away, so I did not telegraph, and hope you will throw it away. A very funny thing has happened. The letter you enclosed was from Thurston the agent of Westmoreley asking me to sign the lease which he sent me on Feb. 28th. Now no lease has come and I can find no trace of it! I have written him to send another and I hope it will be all right. I have just returned from Boston & Wilson had me for two hours, but he spent most of it in trying to make a new band which took so much time that he could not finish it in time, so I have nothing on now, & am to go again on Saturday.

I have tons of work, base-ball letters, my 15 page essay & all the back work to make up. Tomorrow I am to go in to breakfast with the Rector. Warren debates this evening & I shall go to hear it. The weather is lovely though quite cold. I went to the Bank on Monday & had my book balanced O.K.

Ever with loads of love & I hope the improvement will continue steadily.

Your devoted son

FRANKLIN.

9.30 p.m.

Warren has won. Very good debate Just got the enclosed from Mr. Hubbard, I don't quite know what to do. I should like to take the job, but don't know whether people would object. I wish you could telegraph me upon receipt of this whether you think I'd better take it, so that I can write Mr. Hubbard at once, & return the letter when you write. It will not entail my going up to Campo any earlier I don't think, as Eliot can put the course into shape.

Ever

F.D.R.

The dating of this letter, and of the one which follows it, is not clear. In each case, F.D.R. wrote the day of the week, and his mother jotted down "March 1900," but omitted to add the day of the month. There is also a gap between this letter and Mrs. Roosevelt's departure from Groton on Feb. 26th after the sixth-form-play weekend. He may have had a short illness or been taken away for a short period by his parents.

∽

"I don't mind the slanders of our neighbors . . ."

My darling Papa & Mama,

I meant to have written Friday but I have never before had so much to do. Yesterday I went to Boston by the 11 o'clock train & met Mr. Hubbard at the Puritan Club. He said that two members of the Exec. Committee could appoint a new Sec. & Treas, so I am now S. & Treas. but I only took it after he said there was no one else. Gannett would be good, but Louly would run everything in his absence so Hubbard don't want him & there is no one else who will be there all summer. He will send all the books etc. to H.P. soon, so be on the lookout, & dont open them as there is money inside. I don't mind the work, & don't mind the slanders of our neighbors, & I intend to hand the position back with the Club in as good condition as when I take it.

Wilson put on a plate *just like the one Dr. Richmond put on!* only a bar instead of a band, & he hopes to finish my teeth in 3 weeks! They are really much better & if you look at the model before he began you will see a great change. The snow is frozen tight, about four inches, it don't look like spring. I am so delighted Papa is doing so well, & was overjoyed to get the Speckledtater addressed in his own hand. I have worked day & night on my 15 page essay on Pope & I read it tomorrow. One week more! I breakfasted at Mr. G's this a.m at 9.30!!!! so had a good sleep out. I am going in to Faculty Supper now so goodbye. Tell Papa not to take too many baths!

Ever with loads of love affec. son

FRANKLIN.

At the request of Mr. Gorham Hubbard, he had accepted the position of Secretary & Treasurer of the Campobello Golf Club, a job which involved everything from seeing that the greens were in shape to dunning members for dues and contributions.

∽

". . . splendid to hear of Papa's
continued improvement . . ."

GROTON SCHOOL
MARCH 19, 1900,
MONDAY.

Darling Mama & Papa,

I enclose my lease which came today and is all right. I have signed it and after Papa has done so & had his signature witnessed please send it to Mr. Charles S. Brown 247 Lexington Ave. New York.

I am writing him to sign it & send it to Lathrop. Also please sign a cheque for $112 50/100 for my semi-annual share of the rent & you had better send it right on with the two bills & the lease, so that Lathrop can send the whole thing back to Thurston together.

Your letter was most welcome, but I hope you understand that the only reason I accepted Sec. & Treas. was because there is no one else. It is splendid to hear of Papa's continued improvement. It has begun to rain, & the snow is going fast

The mail is going

F.D.R.

The dating of this letter is not certain. Mrs. James Roosevelt wrote what appears to be "Jan. 22/00" on the first page, but the handwriting is not very clear and internal evidence would indicate that this letter must follow the references to the Westmorly lease and to Gorham Hubbard in the preceding correspondence.

∽

391

"The honor is now no longer an honor . . ."

My dearest Mama & Papa,

I have decided to leave here on Tuesday at 6 a.m. for Boston, see Wilson & catch the 10 o'clock Limited for N.Y. reaching there at 3. & will take the 3.30 for H.P. I will send my trunk with the boys, & get it in N.Y. I want to see Aunt Doe off but think I can take the early train down on Wednesday, as I dont believe she sails till noon. Your telegram has just come & I will bring home my pictures of the eleven but you have the ones of the buildings & I can get them at Hyde Park. The ones of the play are excellent & I will bring them home. I went to Wilson yesterday & my teeth are nearly straight, just think! I went to the Lawrences today but they were out, saw Dick & Jim. Three more prefects made today, but I'm glad not to be one after the choice! [name deleted] (what a swipe), [name deleted]!!! & [name deleted] who is all right. Everyone is wild at the Rector for his favoritism [three words deleted], but the honor is now no longer an honor & makes no difference to one's standing. I have just had supper at Mr. Gardner's & I had afternoon tea at the John Lawrence's as several of us went to call on Marion Peabody who is staying there.

No more now see you Tuesday at five-thirty. Ever

F.D.R.

Here again the correct day of the month can only be guessed at from the contents of the letter itself. "Dick and Jim" were sons of Mr. and Mrs. James Lawrence, and brothers of Elizabeth Lawrence. Marion Peabody was a sister of Harold Peabody and a niece both of the James Lawrences and the Rector.

⌁

"I ordered a pince-nez . . ."

Dearest Mama & Papa

Here we are again, after a most successful day in Boston. I had a *very* comfortable journey in the sleeper, & we (Harry Markoe, Krumbhaar, L. Brown) & I had breakfast at the Touraine, then a hair cut & then to Cambridge. We saw our rooms, they are only one flight up, & the walls are light brown. We saw a few pieces of second-hand furniture which Lathrop may get for his room.. We lunched at the Groton table, and I left at 1.30 & saw Dr. Morgan who examined my eyes & says I must wear glasses to study to prevent my getting more near sighted. I ordered a pince-nez, & spectacles, & they will be here tomorrow. I went to Wilson at 3, & saw him. I must go for a retaining plate again   Bought two pair of shoes & got here at 6.30. Where is Warren? My trunk came all right. Mr. Woods is shooing us to bed. Will write tomorrow

Ever

F.D.R.

〜〜

"Next time you see me you won't know me . . ."

My darling Mama & Papa,

I'm writing in "specks"! It seems so strange, & I got them this morning, a pair of spectacles & a pair of "pince-nez". Next time you see me you won't know me. The package of delicacies from N.Y. came last night, also my two new pair of shoes, which are very nice, & the tennis-raquet & balls from Slazenger. They sent a *lady's* white hat, so I shall send it back & get a real one. Hugh Minturn is now in the dormitory as Kerr has gone to the other house, & I find the change rather nice. Yesterday I spent the morning laying out the diamond, & in the p.m. I rolled it & dug out & put in some new pegs. The nine had its first practice & we play Technology 1902 on Saturday. At five yesterday we had service in the chapel & I saw Mrs. John Lawrence who asked all about Papa. Also Mr. & Mrs. Peabody have inquired.

Today it is raining, & I am sure it is needed. Tomorrow we have no lessons & it is just like Sunday. No more now, your letter from N.Y was most acceptable. I do hope the trip did not tire dear Papa, & I expect a letter from H.P. tonight. The mail is off.

Ever your aff son

FRANKLIN.

〰️

"The first is impossible & I dont intend to do the second . . ."

GROTON
APRIL 22, 1900,
SUNDAY.

My darling Mama and Papa,

At last I am able to write you a little more than a line. My eyes are all right so you need not worry in the least. Dr. Morgan the first day was unable to examine them thoroughly, so on Wednesday he completed the examination with the aid of belladonna. I did not get over the effect of it for two days but am all right again now. Dr. Wilson intended on Wednesday when I saw him to send up an appliance which the Groton dentist could fix, but I got a letter yesterday saying that he must see me again! and can't put it on. Now I dont want you to think that I am not just as anxious as you are to get the teeth straight, but you do not realize what it means my being away on days of games. I should have either to give my work to the Ass. Manager, a V former or else *resign*. The first is impossible & I dont intend to do the second, as it would lose me not only the ribbon but the respect of the entire school. Wilson does not realize this & you can't make him, so I shall write him definitely to put a retaining plate on, & I will try

394

to go down some day in the next two weeks, although we have a game *every* half-holiday & I can't possibly go any other day, so I shall have to miss one game I fear.

But to go back to the history of the School for the past week. On Saturday the 14th we were beaten by Technology 1902, but we made up for it on yesterday by defeating Somerville High School, an even stronger team than the first by the close score of 10–9. The team did very well, and although I fear we won't beat St. Marks still we will do better than last year anyway. On Friday we had the first choir-half-holiday, & I went canoeing on the river with Burnham. Mrs. Freeman is quite ill, heart-trouble arrising out of grip. Added to this her house has changed hands, & she must [the rest of this letter has been lost.]

～～

"I declare, I have less time every day . . ."

GROTON

APRIL 26, 1900.

THURSDAY.

My dearest Mama and Papa,

Yesterday we played Boston Latin School, and in a very close and exciting game they beat us by 1 run, 3–2. I worked from morning till night, and am looking forward to another 5 weeks of the thankless task. It is blowing hard tho' bright sunshine and it is cold for April, and I think the spring is *very* late, just think we are nearly in May, and the birds can hardly be seen.

Friday. 8 a.m.

I declare, I have less time every day. I was called off in the middle of writing this, & now the mail is going in five minutes. It is still bright & chilly; We play Dean Academy tomorrow & it promises to be a hard game. Hope Papa wont get worried about the "Brynlys" Let Barbey do everything & have her sent to Hyde Park if you want to see her. She can be towed up. No more now

FDR.

The yacht which eventually replaced the original *Half-Moon* was a sixty-foot, eighteen-ton auxiliary schooner, the *Brynlys,* launched three years earlier. James Roosevelt purchased it from Nathan and Henry Clifford through the ship-broking firm of A. Cary Smith and Barbey, and renamed it the *Half-Moon II.*

∽∽

"I wonder where the engine will go . . ."

GROTON SCHOOL
MAY 4, 1900,
FRIDAY.

My dearest Mama & Papa,

Here I am down again, writing in my own study, perfectly cured, if indeed I was sick at all. I forgot to thank you for the clothes and doll, I didn't have time to deliver it before I came down with disease, but shall do so soon. The paint is cracked off the nose, but I don't think it matters, as it would be licked off soon anyway! Also many thanks for the Graphic & letters from the Capt. I hope [he] is a good man & not too delicate! I *don't like* the idea of a flush deck as they are not comfortable in any kind of a breeze and you would feel always unsecure, unless you have a rail. You must have all rigging renewed as by all accounts it is unsafe. Yours of yesterday has just got here with the cheques, for which many thanks and Capt. Newells letter. I think he has indeed been quick and I hope to hear of her safe arrival in N.Y. in a very few days. By the way, where did you get Newell? I wonder where the engine will go, and why have you changed from Daimler to Globe? Yesterday we had a splendid rain, but it cleared in the afternoon & has brought out the shrubs & trees wonderfully; still the leaves are not out of the buds yet, & I suppose you are much further advanced at H.P.

No more now, what a farce German Measles is any way! The poor Lawrence kids haven't got it yet, so I have hopes.

Ever,

F.D.R.

396

F.D.R. headed this letter "Friday"; his mother added "April 1900." However, on the internal evidence of preceding and following letters, May 4th would seem to be the logical date. The doll was another present for a Peabody baby, probably for Margery, *aetat.* three.

∽∾

"Jack Minturn as May Queen, in
short skirts & a sun bonnet . . ."

GROTON SCHOOL
MAY 7, 1900,
MONDAY.

My dearest Mama & Papa,

I did not have a single moment yesterday to myself, so could not write. On Saturday we had a glorious victory over the Harvard Freshmen, the first time we have beaten them at baseball for five years. The game was exciting & close throughout & in the end we [won] with the score 8–7.

Yesterday immediately after lunch I went to call on Mrs. John Lawrence, & I am glad to say none of the children got the disease from me. At four o'clock we had school & directly after supper we went to Groton to the first May Service, & had a good sermon from Dean Briggs of Harvard.

Today the VI form celebrated the time-honored custom of May-day, though a week late. At 6 o'clock this evening we got the Jefferson's donkey & with Jack Minturn as May Queen, in short skirts & a sun bonnet, on the donkey's back we paraded round the School, & then wound up the May pole. After a game of tag, we all went to tea at Mrs. Peabody's & had a real feast, then games in the parlor ended the evening.

I am terribly busy making up the work I lost, & the base-ball, & I am beginning to write the golf letters & have written 50 Camp letters. Yours & Papa's of Sunday most welcome & I am so glad the "Half Moon" is such a good boat, & has been re-rigged. Also it is comfort to feel that Newell is such a good & experienced man. I go to Wilson on Wednesday

No more now. Ever your devoted son

FDR.

397

Le Baron Russell Briggs was one of the great Harvard figures of the period, respected as a teacher and beloved as a man. He was then Dean of Harvard College. In 1902 he moved up to become Dean of the Faculty, and in 1903 began a twenty-year tenure as President of Radcliffe College. The "50 Camp letters" might refer either to Campobello Golf Club correspondence, or to work in connection with the Groton School Camp, which (being a member of the Missionary Society and a sixth-former) he attended as one of the "Faculty" in the summer of 1900.

～～

"After all there are plenty of good
butlers in the world . . ."

[GROTON]
MAY 13, 1900,
SUNDAY.

My dearest Mama and Papa,

Yours of Friday was most welcome yesterday, though I was awfully sorry to hear about Todd's leaving. I quite realize what a great loss he will be to you and I only hope you can get another man who is equally clean and good at valeting & who is a little spryer & better at the table. Don't let Papa worry about it, as after all there are plenty of good butlers in the world.

I am so glad [you] had a successful trip to see the Half-Moon, & I was sure you would like her. I am glad you are to have an enlarged cockpit, instead of a flush deck. You do not say where the engine is to go, but I presume it is forward of the cabin, as the cockpit is to be enlarged. By the way when you order the new flags have the "Half-Moon" flag *red* with a white half-moon instead of *blue*.

You ask if I don't want to go to camp the first week. I should like to very much, but it is absolutely necessary for me to go to Campo as soon as I get out, so as to get the Golf Course in shape, so if I go there on June 30th I will have nearly two weeks before going to camp on the 10th of July. It is very good of you to want to write some of the letters for me, but I think the letters should be personal notes, & as I wont send them out till I get to Campo, there is no particular hurry, & it will be easy to write 30 or so before leaving school. Mrs. Minturn is up for Sunday, and has asked me to visit them at Islesboro next summer. We have the second May service tonight, & it is time to start.

Today is *broiling*, & *five* boys fainted in church this a.m. I'm very well & going to walk with Jake to the service. Must close now.

Ever your affectionate son.

F.D.R.

The color preference with regard to the new *Half-Moon* may fairly be taken as Harvard patriotism. "Jake" was a nickname for Lathrop Brown. When the May 12th marks came out, F.D.R. got a B general average, and a "Good" from Mr. Peabody.

〜〜

"I have spent most of the week at the telephone . . ."

GROTON
MAY 20, 1900,
SUNDAY.

My darling Mama and Papa,

I am so sorry I did not write you during the week, but I was so flooded with work until yesterday that it quite slipped my mind. I have spent most of the week at the telephone, having received an average every day of two telegrams and three calls over the 'phone, and all about the blessed base-ball. On Wednesday we played Pomfret, and defeated them 22–7, an easy victory, as they had a wretched team. We, that is the rest of the school was not allowed to see them as they have scarlatina at Pomfret, so *I* received them alone at Mrs. Powell's, which we rented for the occasion, and they did not go near the rest of the school. Yesterday we were to have played Thayer

Academy, but it poured all day, and they did not come. Next Wednesday we play Cushing Academy and on Saturday the grand culmination of the season, St. Marks. As the game is here this year all the responsibility for arrangements will fall on me, so I shall be busy every moment of the week. I shall hope to see Lyman but it is doubtful as I shall have so much to do about the team.

It is cool today and Dr. Parks (of Boston) is to preach this evening at the Third May Service in the Town Hall. We have begun drilling for the Decoration Day parade and I am a sergeant. Three of the "nine" have the German measles, but they will be out tomorrow. Edmund is one of them and I only trust no more will come down.

It it [is] time for supper so I will stop, & try to send a line on Wednesday, but don't worry if I don't.

Ever with love

F.D.R.

∽

". . . and Mr. Sturgis stepped up
to the bat . . ."

[GROTON]
MAY 27, 1900,
SUNDAY.

My dearest Mama & Papa,

Well, it's all over, and a more glorious victory there never has been. Imagine a 12-inning—not the usual 9—game and a win by the score of 7–6 in the end! I've never seen such a game in my life. At the very beginning St. Marks made four runs, & we felt a bit discouraged. Then in the third inning we made three, then St. Marks two, making the score 6–3. St. Marks was wild with joy, & I saw Lyman waving a huge flag across the field. Then for three innings the score did not change but in the eighth by some good hits we got three more runs, tieing the score! For four more innings, we stayed the same, turn & turn about, both sides unable to score, tho' we came very near it once. Then in the 12th inning when we thought it would never end, we got one man on bases, and Mr. Sturgis stepped up to the bat. The very first ball that came, he banged away out over the right fielder's head, easily bringing in the winning run! My, but there was a din! The team was carried off the field, and I rescued the winning ball from a St. Marker's hands. Lyman disappeared!!!!!!!

In the evening I went to Ayer during supper-time & got some fireworks & at 8 we had the greatest bonfire on record, & the nine, coach & manager were all cheered again & again. There are crowds up here & today is lovely. All my work is over, & over successfully, & there has not been a single complaint. I am going to row for the rest of the year, as I want some good exercise, & I know it won't hurt me.

I'm so sorry you had to part with Mike, but I know it was necessary. Too bad Emfred & Clara are going. I hope the new people will be successful. By the way do send the cheque for my Chapel seat to Mr. G. for $100. *not* $200. as $100 is the price of one complete stall. About my teeth, I have a gold band around each front tooth, covering the entire tooth, & a piece of wire behind the two side teeth, so it does not look so badly. I'm so glad the Half-Moon is getting on so well, have you given any orders about my boat?

Monday 8 a.m.

We had the last of the May services last night, Mr. Sprague of Charlestown preached, & it was delightful walking home in the evening. We are still hoarse from Saturday's shouting & I don't think St. Marks will get our cheering out of their ears for some time!

No more now, Ever your affec. son

FRANKLIN

Do send some *stamps!* About 25.

The cheque sent Mr. Gardner was toward a fund for placing stalls in the new chapel; contributors were to have their names on the seats.

*"It is lovely and warm, & the
swimming is just right . . ."*

GROTON SCHOOL
MAY 31, 1900,
THURSDAY.

My dearest Mama & Papa,

I can hardly realize that the great game is over and so successfully at that. Last Tuesday we were given a half-holiday to
make up for the time lost in marching on Wednesday, & I
took my first lesson in rowing & got on all right   I don't believe I shall race at all this year, tho' there may be a short one
just before we leave. Yesterday we drove to the village &
marched to the cemetery, I at the head of a company, & after
the usual exercises, marched back again. I rowed before lunch
& spent the afternoon canoeing with Laurie Rainsford. Today
has been a choir half-holiday & I took Warren out canoeing, &
in for a swim, as the VIth form are allowed to go in whenever
they like. I lunched with Lathrop's Mother at Powell's. They
are up here, Mrs. & the little girl [Lucy], for a week or more.
The June system begins tomorrow, when we have all lessons in
the morning. It is lovely and warm, & the swimming is just
right as it hasn't got too warm yet. I hope I can have the room
I had last year at Campo or the room next it as the big guest
room is not nearly so cosy. If this lovely weather continues I
don't suppose you will go till July 1st but I think I must go
straight from here as the course must be put in order by the
1st. No more now   let me know how the Half Moon is getting
on & if you are to have her on the river

Ever

FDR.

Many thanks for stamps & report

402

*"You have never told me where
the engine is to go . . ."*

My dearest Mama & Papa,

Yours of Thursday, telling of your visit to the "Half-Moon" & to Tuxedo is most welcome. I am so glad the boat is getting on so well, but you have never told where the engine is to go, tho' I have asked several times. Also are you going to have the flag changed to red, and will you have charts, china, linen, international code signals, etc.? It is pouring today, and we are glad not to have to go to the village again. I am having my golf-club notices printed down at Ayer, and it will save an amount of work.

The rowing is great fun, and there will be a regatta about the 20th in which I think I shall row, tho' the race will be at all events a very short one, not over ⅓ mile

Monday. 8 a.m.

The weather is bright & lovely tho' quite chilly. I am still pretty busy making up the "nines" accounts, and am trying for one or two prizes. Will write again Wednesday

Ever with love

F.D.R.

Please thank Papa a thousand times for his Whitsunday present. Mr. G. is very much pleased, & has over half the stalls already promised.

〰

*"I hope to get on sliding seats
within a few days . . ."*

My dearest Mama & Papa,

We are having the most heavenly weather I have ever seen, not too hot, but simply perfect. I row everyday for an hour and a half in a four-oar, but you must not think it is like ordinary rowing, as the stroke is most complicated to learn, and we are coached regularly by Mr. Abbott or Mr. Richards. I am rowing stroke the best place in the boat, and although we are still on fixed seats I hope to get on sliding seats within a few days. At the end of the term there is to be a grand water-carnival with tub-races, greased-poles, & races etc. Tonight the nine went to tea with Mrs. Jefferson, & I went with them. We had a delicious feed, & enjoyed it immensely. Next Wednesday the wedding takes place in the chapel, & the choir are going. Then the reception comes at Mrs. Whitney's cottage, which the Rice's have taken for a week. After the wedding guests go the whole school has been asked to a spread at Whitney's about 6 o'clock.

Thursday 8 a.m.

Another lovely day. I am glad the flag is red, but it is a shame not to have the cups done in red, as I have often seen them with red flags very well done. I shall have the bowsprit put on my boat the week I am at camp.

No more now

Ever your affec. son

F.D.R.

∽

"Tonight I go to serenade Miss Rice . . ."

[GROTON]
JUNE 10, 1900,
SUNDAY.

My dearest Mama and Papa,

I hope you are safely at home again after your Burlington trip, and I think you must have had good weather, and not too hot. I am so glad Aunt Annie and Uncle Fred may come here next Sunday, I am writing them the trains.

Monday—.

404

I was so terribly busy yesterday finishing the prizes I am trying for that I forgot to finish your letter. I am trying for all three prizes, Greek, Latin, and English Essay, but I do not expect to get *any* of them as it is a forgone conclusion that Kerr Rainsford with [will] get the Latin, Greenough or Krumbhaar the Greek, & Motley the English. You will be surprised to hear that there is chicken-pox, and real measles in the School. The chicken-pox has been going for over two weeks, & there have now developed about five cases of *real* measles, in addition to a number of German measles patients!! Thank Heaven I have had them all! so I am not in the least alarmed.

Today the "nine" went for a picnic with Mr. & Mrs. Peabody about five miles off to a high hill where there was a most glorious view. We all enjoyed it immensely, & had a roaring good time. Last Saturday our dormitory had a grand picnic up the river, & we all crammed ourselves chuck-full of delicacies. After our return this afternoon the "nine" was photographed & I with them. Tomorrow the VI form will be taken, & tomorrow p.m comes Miss Rice's wedding to Mr. Lawrence. The choir will be there and the school is to have a spread at 6. Tonight I go to serenade Miss Rice with the quartet, in which I now sing.

On some day towards the end of the week the VI Form has a picnic. Will write Wednesday.

F.D.R.

P.S. I will add a line to let you know about my plans. My last examination here come from 4 to 6. on Friday afternoon the 29th of June. I can get to Boston in time to take the 7.45 train for Campobello. However Mr. Griswold's wedding is the next day, Saturday, at New Haven & I *may* go to it, & take the train for Campo Saturday night. But I shall only do this if the wedding is early in the day. Also there may be a VI Form farewell dinner here at Powell's on Friday night, so I can't yet tell when I shall leave, but I'll let you know inside of a week. My list of exams is as follows:

Tuesday	June	26th	9-11.	Advanced German.
Wednesday	"	27th	3-6	English A.
Thursday	"	28	4-6	Advanced Latin
Friday	"	29th	8-9.	Physics,
			4-6	Advanced Greek.

Also Tuesday afternoon I shall go to Cambridge for the Physics Laboratory Exam. You see I have very few to take & shall have a lovely two or three days here. Blagden & I are the only boys who leave Friday, all the others have to stay over till Sat. morning.

Ever

F.D.R.

P.P.S. Your Sunday letter is just here. So glad you had such a nice trip. I must say I think it would be better to have the flag blue as the china is blue, & it will be nice to have the old flag. I will let you know on Wednesday whether I can go on Friday night or must stay up for the dinner, but I *think* I can go.—

Mr. Amory Lawrence married Miss Gertrude Rice; she was his second wife. His daughter Edith was a bridesmaid, and his son Amos was best man.

〰

"Youthfulness handicaps one in so many ways . . ."

GROTON SCHOOL
JUNE 13, 1900,
WEDNESDAY.

My dearest Mama and Papa,

What a lot I have to tell you! The school has gone home, in the first place! Yesterday morning there were two new cases of measles & one of chicken-pox, so it was decided to send the four lower forms home, if their parents wanted them. This a.m about 70 went, and Warren among them. It was all so strange & hurried, & we that are left can hardly realize it yet. About 30 boys are in the infirmary, and besides the V & VI forms about twenty unfortunates are still here whose parents are either abroad or don't want them home. But the worst piece of news is that Warren will re-enter the 3rd Form next autumn. He was discussed in Faculty meeting last night, & owing to age, character & lessons it was thought best for him to drop a form. The poor little fellow felt dreadfully about it when told, but I am quite sure it will be by far the best thing for him, as youthfulness handicaps one in so many ways. He will be thankful in years to come that he had another year at Groton, & in many ways I envy him. He will now be the leader of his form among the boys & have a good start in lessons. We of course go on as usual up here, only it seems very strange. Jefferson & Coleman (who has one of the diseases I've forgotten which) reënter the first form again, as I predicted. Yesterday at 4.30 we had the grand Lawrence-Rice Wedding, & it was "more sport than a goat." Only the choir went, & we sang "Lohengrin" etc. All Boston turned out and they looked quite nice, for Boston. Edith L. was a bridesmaid & Amos gave his Father away. There was a profusion of flowers & the bride & maids wore pure white & they looked rather ghostly & poor Edith nearly colapsed. There was a grand reception at Whitney's afterward, & the guests went at 6, & the School went over for their spread & we had a glorious time. How we ate! Today the boys left at 7.15 & this afternoon I played tennis & rode to Ayer on a bicycle to have the Golf Club things printed. Alas, we shall have no prize-day, no regatta, no out-door sports events, now that everything is bust up. Your letter came this a.m. & I am so glad Muriel is at H.P. tho' I am awfully sorry to miss her. The stalls on the chapel are not to have name-plates according the the [sic] latest plan, but if they do I will have my name put in full.

Now about Taddy——. I was not very much surprised to hear that he had been put on probation, as I had heard from *all* our graduates that he was not doing well, & I am very sorry this should have happened. He will *not be* kept over for probation, as the studies end the 1st of June & from then on, the time is taken up with exams. However the probation may be carried over the next autumn. I do not know what the direct cause has been, whether lessons or bad conduct, but I think I should tell you now that I *know* that Taddy has been on to N.Y several times without letting anyone know of it. If his last exam came June 7th he may be off on a bat now for ought I know. I think the very strictest measures sh'd be taken, but of course Papa must not worry in the least, as after all it is no affair of ours. Some measures should be taken to prevent his having his full allowance next year, as even this year he has had just *twice too* much.

The weather is too lovely, & I have never felt better, tho' very sleepy.

Ever with loads of love your affec. son

FRANKLIN

P.S. I have definitely decided to leave here Friday the 29th. I arrive Boston at 7.30 p.m. & can catch the 7.45 & private-car for Campo.

～～

*"I think it is hardly worth while
for about twelve hours . . ."*

GROTON SCHOOL
JUNE 17, 1900,
SUNDAY.

My dearest Mama & Papa,

Today, I am glad to say has been ideal for Aunt Annie's & Uncle Fred's visit. They drove straight from the station to the Chapel, & were just in time for morning service. Of course there was no choir, but I think they enjoyed it. Then after Church we went over the new Chapel, Brooks House & the School-House, then back to lunch at Powells. After lunch I showed them all over the Hundred House, and took them to my dormitory & study, then for a short call on the Rector.

They left again at 4 o'clock, but it was lovely seeing them here and makes up in a slight degree for not seeing you since April. I am very much wondering whether the "Half-Moon" is on the river yet, and when you intend to send her around to Campo. I find now that Push's wedding does not come until 4 o'clock on Saturday, so I could not get home from New Haven the same night, so c'd not arrive till Sunday noon. Therefore I think it is hardly worth while for about twelve hours. However if you do not come till Monday I can get on very well at Campo alone for a day or two, & I shall be working from a.m to p.m. anyway on the golf-course, as I have decided to enlarge several greens & teeing-grounds, & have various improvements made which can't be done until I get there. I get to Boston Friday Evening at 7.30 & as the train leaves at 7.45 for Campo, I shall have a pretty close shave, but can do it all right, as I shall Express my trunk the day before. Isn't this weather too perfect? There is to be an informal prize-day after all, but I dont think many people will come. I will send a list of things I want taken to Campo in a few days. No more now, my Sunday-School picnic comes on Wednesday.

Ever your devoted son

F.D.R.

I played in the Tennis Tournament yesterday and was beaten by a very close margin.

∽∽

"I shall need a good wheel in Cambridge next year . . ."

GROTON SCHOOL
JUNE 20, 1900,
WEDNESDAY.

My dearest Mama & Papa,

Your two letters, from the train & 10 W. 43rd were most welcome. You do not seem to understand that if I go to Mr Griswold's wedding I should have to spend *two* nights travelling and could not reach H.P. till 1 o'clock Sunday. Then I would have have [*sic*] to leave again at 6 the next morning, so I can't say that I think it worth while. As it will be chilly in the house the first few days, perhaps it would be better for you not to go till Monday, and I can get everything in order before you come. However if you come on Friday I will meet you at Ayer at 3.02 and have my trunk put on the car. Then I will go back to take a two-hour exam, & meet you in Boston at 7.30.

I am going to buy a new bicycle! A Columbia chainless for $60. As I shall do a good deal of riding this summer, going to the Hotel etc, and shall need a good wheel in Cambridge next year, I thought this a chance, as the wheel costs ordinarily $75.

I hear Taddy has left college entirely. He was summoned to appear before the dean, & did not go, but simply left college, and he will now be unable to return if he ever changes his mind. [Sentence deleted.]

We had our Sunday-school picnic this p.m, and went in a boat, 10 of us, for about a mile up the river & joined there with the Woodville Sunday School under Mr. Sturgis & landed. We had a delightful time & got back at seven.

No more now, the weather is too lovely. It is a shame about the "Half-Moon," but I hope she will leave the 28th at the latest.

Ever

F.D.R.

The hotel at Campobello was the Tenafly; it no longer exists.

〰

*"We the departing form, are
feeling very blue . . ."*

[GROTON]
JUNE 24, 1900,
SUNDAY.

My dearest Mama and Papa,

Yours of Friday came last night and I am sorry you read my letter aloud to Papa if he worried, but I meant it only as a

410

suggestion that I should go on first to Campo, in case you *both* preferred to stay on over Monday, as the golf-club is the only reason I could not go back, and personally I feel that I would have given anything for only a few hours at home. As it is the arrangement is splendid, I think, and on Friday I will meet you at Ayer at 3.02 and put my trunk, valise and new bicycle on car 500. I have a Greek exam at 4 so will drive right back to the School and to the train again at 6.32 reaching Boston at 7.30, and from the train will walk straight around to the car.

I have had a lot of score-cards, invitation-cards and bill-heads for the club printed, and enclose a sample. Don't you think they are rather nice?

As they [the] end of School approaches we the departing form, are feeling very blue, and I would give anything to have been dropped as Warren has. We had the last services that will ever be held in the chapel today, as they expect to be in the new cathedral the first Sunday next autumn. Mrs. Goodwin was here today and I lunched with her, then took supper with Mr. G. this evening. On Friday last Mr. & Mrs. Peabody gave the annual VI form picnic. We went to the same hill as on the "Nine" picnic & had a glorious time. Yesterday I played tennis part of the afternoon, and drank google the rest at Mr. Cush's. Tomorrow is Prize-Day and my fate will be soon decided but I don't really expect to get one, so shall not be disappointed. About fifty people are expected, and a spread will be held in the dining-room at 1, when the prizes will be awarded. In the afternoon everyone will amuse the numerous girls, and I dont think I know one that is coming, but will probably be shelved with a "pill." On Tuesday at 9 I have Advanced German, and at 11 shall go to Boston to shop, and have Wilson fill a tooth.

I will give you a rough list of the things I want at Campo, so dont forget to pack them, but there are probably lots of things I have forgotten, so please look through my things and bring anything I may possibly need.

Acetyline Bicycle Lamp & extra charges.

The *two* big American flags, (we'll be there the 4th)

My rifle. Send by express.

Clabrough gun " " " but wrap the case carefully in
                                    paper

Collecting   "   Will go in trunk.

All golf sticks at home, including my new sticks and Mama's. Also all balls.

All shirts, ties etc. socks stocks.

Patent-leather shoes,

Gun-cleaning case.

New score-book which someone gave me last Xmas.

Prize-Day. Monday. 8 a. m.

It is a perfectly heavenly day, and the crowds will begin to arrive in a few hours. I will drop you a post-card tonight if I get a prize, but 16 to 1 you won't get it!

No more now

Ever your affec. son

FRANKLIN.

∽

*"Scarce a boy but wishes he were
a 1st former again . . ."*

GROTON SCHOOL
JUNE 25, 1900,
MONDAY.

My darling Mama and Papa,

"The strife is o'er, the battle won!" What a joyful yet sad day this has been. Never again will we hold recitations in the old School, and scarce a boy but wishes he were a 1st former again. This morning after one Sacred Study exam, which developed into a talk from the Rector the VI Form went out and gathered wild-flowers for over an hour, to decorate the dining-room. Then at 12 o'clock the guests began to arrive, till there were about fifty. I only knew a few, and before lunch showed Elizabeth Tuckerman over the place.

At one we all went to the dining room for a spread, and

after all were full, the Rector made an excellent speech, then one from Mr. Atwood. Then the Rector's Father gave out the prizes from the head table, the Form Prize to Krumbhaar, the English Essay to Warren Motley, the Greek to Greenough, then I was somewhat taken aback when my name was called for the Latin Prize. I was presented with 40 volumes, the Temple Shakespere just like yours & you may imagine I feel rather tickled. After that Lathrop & I took the two little Peabodys, Helen & Rose, also Hester Lawrence on the river, as they had never been before. The guests left at 5, and I went down to say goodbye to Mrs. Lawrence who goes to Islesboro tomorrow but she was out. After supper we sang songs on the steps till nine o'clock & the V Form serenaded the VI. It is time for bed now. I go to Boston to shop tomorrow afternoon. This will be the last letter I can write as you leave so early Friday morning. I will meet you Ayer 3.02. I am sending my pictures to Westmorly 27, where they will be taken care of till I arrive.

No more now, I can hardly wait to see you but feel awfully to be leaving here for good.

Ever with loads of love to you both your affec. son

FRANKLIN.

Elizabeth Tuckerman was a daughter of Mrs. Bayard Tuckerman (*vide supra*). A fellow student at Episcopal, one of the Rector's closest friends, with whom he carried on an extended correspondence over the years seeking opinion and advice in the conduct of Groton affairs, was Bishop Julius Walter Atwood of Arizona. Helen and Rose Peabody were the Rector's first two daughters, then ten and nine, respectively; Hester Lawrence was the John Lawrences' daughter, a niece of the Rector. F.D.R.'s last Groton report showed B's in Latin, Greek, English, and English Composition, a C in Physics, and a "Good" in Sacred Studies, for a general average of B. The final comment from Mr. Peabody was: "He has been a thoroughly faithful scholar & a most satisfactory member of this school throughout his course. I part with Franklin with reluctance."

HARVARD

HARVARD

THE HARVARD to which Franklin Roosevelt came in the autumn of 1900 was entering upon the fourth and final decade of Charles W. Eliot's presidency. Eliot (like James Bryant Conant sixty years later) was both a scientist and a young man when, in the face of considerable opposition, he was appointed president. In the course of his career he engineered the transformation of Harvard from a small, provincial college to one of the great modern universities, exerting as he did so a liberalizing influence upon higher education throughout the whole United States. The first two decades of his presidency had seen tremendous expansion in plant, endowment, and teaching staff. Notably it had seen the introduction (again over strong opposition) of the "elective system" and its corollary, voluntary attendance at classes. Students became free, within the barest essential limits, to study what they would; as the eminent historian of the University, Samuel Eliot Morison, wrote: ". . . _fin de siècle_ marked the zenith of undergraduate liberty at Harvard." This observation remains true even in comparison with the Harvard of today. The elective system caused students to use the library to a degree before unknown, and the number of volumes grew from less than one hundred thousand in 1869, when Eliot was appointed, to half a million in 1900. The size of the undergraduate body more than tripled in this same period, reaching an enrollment of 1750 when F.D.R. entered.

As students were liberated, so were great teachers attracted. Only recently Harvard had buried three of her Pericleans, James Russell Lowell, Francis Parkman, and Dr. Holmes, but this meant no default of glory: in the *Catalog* for 1900-01, listed among those who held chairs in the department of Philosophy, were William James, Josiah Royce, and George Herbert Palmer. An assistant professor of Aesthetics then beginning to make his mark was George Santayana. Teaching English were cultivated, witty Barrett Wendell of daily-theme fame, and that famed Shakespearean scholar and Harvard immortal, George Lyman Kittredge. The famous drama laboratory, "47 Workshop," training school of Eugene O'Neill, Philip Barry, Thomas Wolfe, and many others, had not yet come into existence, but its founder, George Pierce Baker, was an assistant professor; and the English department was further glorified by William Allan Neilson, later president of Smith College, and Charles Townsend Copeland, the matchless "Copey," who were then instructors. Edwin Arlington Robinson had just completed a short period as secretary to President Eliot. In History there was that great debunker of historical legend, Albert Bushnell Hart, and scholar-librarian Archibald Cary Coolidge; Hugo Münsterberg held his revolutionary lectures in Psychology; Langdell was dean of the Law School, Shaler at the head of the Lawrence Scientific School; professor of the Science of Government and future president of the University was Abbott Lawrence Lowell (brother of Amy); Taussig was lecturing in Economics . . . the list of great names is long.

In the courses it offered and in the men who taught them, the Harvard of 1900 was brilliant and liberal. In its social life it was brilliant. Endicott Peabody often decried (and, being an official preacher to the University, spoke out against) the "gap between Mt. Auburn Street and the Yard." In and around Mt. Auburn Street were such expensive dormitories as Westmorly

Court (where F.D.R. lived), and such exclusive clubs as the Fly (which F.D.R. made) and the Porcellian (which he did not); on the other side of Massachusetts Avenue lay the Yard, within which stood the recitation halls, and the old, unprepossessing buildings, badly in need of repair, where lived those who could not afford better—and they were the majority. Financial security and family background very definitely made a difference in all non-scholastic undergraduate activities. Except for friendships which grew up out of common interests at class, and the premier sports of football and crew, there were few opportunities for students of different social spheres to come into normal contact. Graduates of such preparatory schools as Groton usually ate (as Freshmen) at their own special tables in Cambridge eating houses, not in the large common dining halls. Sophomore and Junior societies and the exclusive Senior "final" clubs drew from these ranks. In F.D.R.'s day, the Harvard Union made tentative steps toward bridging the gap, but in essence no foundation for democracy in the social sphere was laid until the coming of the "house plan" twenty-five years later.

The atmospheres of the city of Boston and the University across the river have always influenced one another profoundly, and something should be said here of the relationship between the two at the turn of the century. Harvard's first professor of the History of Art, Charles Eliot Norton, he who lamented the sight of the smoke of industry in New England skies, had recently retired, but his influence was still enormous and the memory of him at Harvard was bright. Santayana (son of a Boston mother and a Spanish father) recalls in *The Genteel Tradition at Bay* the "sweet sadness of Professor Norton," who "would tell his classes, shaking his head with a slight sigh, that the Greeks did not play football." It was Norton who inspired Isabella Stewart Gardner to form the famous art collection later housed in her palace, Fenway Court, under construction at this time. Skeptical at first, Boston finally accepted "Mrs.

Jack" as symbol of her golden afternoon, and could be amused to see that lady conducting a young lion on a leash through Back Bay streets, and unawed when she got down on hands and knees to scrub the steps of the Anglican Church of the Advent on Good Friday each year.

One whose salon rivaled Mrs. Gardner's in its display of Boston notability was Sarah Wyman Whitman. Though not given so dramatically to extra-social eccentricities, she was nevertheless an outstanding figure in the intellectual and artistic life of the city. At her home James, Royce, Holmes, and many another Harvard great were often seen. From the evidence in the letters, one may presume Franklin Roosevelt had opportunity to drink at these Pierian springs.

In Mrs. Gardner's Italian palace, as in the "Richardson Romanesque" of Trinity Episcopal Church, Boston's break with her Puritan past could readily be seen. As Van Wyck Brooks pointed out in *New England: Indian Summer,* "those who called the moment Alexandrian knew their history well."

Lace-bonneted Julia Ward Howe might still be found at any meeting which involved a cause, and as always her recitation of the *Battle Hymn* would take place before adjournment, but she was becoming a tradition, and so were causes. In Cambridge septuagenarian Miss Sarah Palfrey, daughter of a renowned New England historian, could be seen pedaling her tricycle around Fresh Pond before breakfast each day. New religions had sprung up in the previous quarter-century. Mary Baker Eddy, who regarded sickness and death as errors, had many followers and her Christian Science flourished. In the drawing rooms of Beacon Street swamis from the East were often to be found. And the large Irish population of the city inherited the Puritanism which the Yankee stock disavowed.

Boston, having passed from her Athenian to her Alexandrian period, was perhaps a more tranquil place than ever before. And Harvard Square was relatively quiet, too. The era of hazing and explosions in the Yard was almost over. Only rarely were inscriptions in paint or lampblack to be found on Harvard's walls. Thirty years had passed since the last serious mischief—the blowing up of the top floor of Hollis Hall—had occurred, and for more than a decade the College drain had performed its humble duties undisturbed by gunpowder. Such pranks and disorders were legacies of a time when the average Senior was little older than a Freshman in F.D.R.'s class. President Eliot's efforts to raise the scholastic standards made it necessary for prospective students to spend an additional year or two in preparation for entrance; the undergraduate body was soberer for being a little older.

Such were the Boston and Cambridge to which Franklin Roosevelt was exposed. His letters continue to concern themselves primarily with the classmates whom he saw regularly, with the friends in whose Boston homes he dined—people his mother knew. As to his career at college, he lived on the Gold Coast, belonged to a number of the better organizations, took regular exercise but, with the exception of crew in his first two years, never participated in team sport. He devoted enough time to his studies to pass with satisfactory grades, but took no honors. He was active in the Political Club, of which he became president. He served on committees for the Harvard Union, the Memorial Society, and the Hasty Pudding Club. He did not waste time. Living within the confines of the "Mt. Auburn Street system" for the most part, he ate at a Groton table and later on at one of his clubs, attended Beacon Hill and Back Bay parties, and did the usual things—with one exception. His work on the Harvard *Crimson,* which consumed a great deal of his time, provided opportunity for an extension of viewpoint beyond that of most undergraduates in his circle. As one reads the letters which follow, one comes to the conclusion that the *Crimson* was the most important element in his Harvard career. Not only did it broaden his interests, but it became the means of attaining a reassuring prominence in his class—something he was never able to achieve at Groton.

*"In twelve hours I shall be a
member of the Class of 1904 . . ."*

My dearest Mama and Papa,

Here I am, in Cambridge and in twelve hours I shall be a
full registered member of the Class of 1904. The journey from
New York was uneventful, and I got off at the Back Bay Station
to save the long distance from the Terminal, and arrived at
our rooms at 9.15, finding Lathrop in an agony of correspondence, but delighted at his appointment as Manager. I have
already seen a number of fellows I know & came out in the
trolleys with Jimmy Jackson. The rooms look as if struck by
sheet Lightning, the sitting-room having the chairs and tables
but no curtains or carpets. The bed is in place in my room &
it looks inhabitable but one trunk is the sole piece of furniture
of Lathrop's room, his belongings not having arrived. He is
sleeping on his cousin Harold Brown's couch, so I shall be
alone for the next few nights. Tomorrow afternoon I shall go
in to Boston to get my trunks & do general errands. I am
hoping to hear of the "Half-Moon's" arrival & do hope Papa
will not get too tired in N.Y. I will try to drop another line
some time tomorrow.

It is late & I must make my bed. With a great deal of love
to you both

I am ever your affectionate son

FRANKLIN.

Lathrop Brown had come up to college early, and had won
the pre-season competition for manager of the Freshman foot-
ball team (in his final Harvard year he was manager of the
varsity).

∾

422

*"Bought some evening shoes, derby
hat, went to the bank etc. . . ."*

WESTMORLY COURT
SEPT. 28, 1900,
FRIDAY.

My dearest Mama & Papa,

I did not get a chance to write yesterday as I was very busy.
But to go back—. On Wednesday Morning I signed on and
shopped, and spent most of the afternoon consulting with
Mr. Coolidge about courses, with the result that my schedule
is much altered. I am now taking History, Government,
French, English, Latin and Geology, 5 ½ courses in all. Yesterday I went to Boston in the morning and did some shopping.—
bought some evening shoes, derby hat, went to the bank etc.
In the p.m I went to the first lecture, in English, & then saw the
foot-ball practice. At 8.30 I went in to the Sturgises where there
was a grand reunion & welsh rabbit & didn't get back till 11.30.

Your letter & pincushion are most welcome this morning and
I am so glad you got "Tip", I am dieing to see him. Too bad
about the "Half-Moon". I have three courses today, and of
course the real work does not begin until Monday.

There is a Freshmen Foot-ball talk tonight and play begins
on Monday. I shall go to Groton tomorrow afternoon & stay
until Sunday night.

Our Groton table is great fun & most informal. Breakfast
7.30-10. Lunch 1-2   Supper 6-7.30.

I will try to send a post-card from Groton on Sunday. I am
very well & Lathrop awfully busy.

No more now

Loads of love to you both, Ever your affectionate son

F.D.R.

The adviser who helped plan F.D.R.'s first-year courses was
Archibald Cary Coolidge, then assistant professor of History.
Coolidge (brother of Julian Coolidge) had as a young man been

private secretary to his uncle, Thomas Jefferson Coolidge, when the latter was minister to France in 1892, and also secretary in the American legations at Vienna and St. Petersburg. He forsook a diplomatic career for Harvard, where his "History One" course became famous. In 1910 he became director of the Harvard library, which in no small measure owes its preeminent position to his efforts. The Widener library building, with its great collections, was a particular project of Coolidge's, and has been called as much a memorial to him as to Harry Widener. F.D.R. (as noted) anticipated most of the prescribed Freshman courses while still at Groton, with the result that he already had considerable leeway in what he could elect. The schedule he followed in 1900-01 consisted of:

(1) *French 2-C.* A course in French Prose and Poetry, studying the works of Corneille, Racine, Moliere, Hugo, de Musset, and Balzac, under the general direction of Assistant Professor P. B. Marcou and Dr. J. D. M. Ford. This was a full-year course; classes met Mondays, Wednesdays, and Fridays at 10 A.M.

(2) *Latin B.* A full-year course in Latin Literature; texts were Livy (Book I), Horace (odes and epodes), and Terence. Professor Morris Hickey Morgan supervised the course, with five other teachers assisting. The classes were large, and held Mondays, Wednesdays, and Fridays at 11, or Tuesdays, Thursdays, and Saturdays at 12, depending upon the individual's schedule.

(3) *English 28.* An outline course in the History and Development of English Literature, whose instructors included Dean Briggs, Barrett Wendell, Kittredge, and George Pierce Baker. This was a full-year course, meeting Tuesdays and Thursdays at 10, with Saturday conferences "at the pleasure of the instructor."

(4) *History 1.* Medieval and Modern European History, under the general direction of Professor Coolidge, meeting Mondays, Wednesdays, and Fridays at 9. A full-year course.

(5) *Government 1.* A full-year course in Constitutional Government, under the supervision of Professor Silas Mac-

Vane, with the assistance of Abbott Lawrence Lowell. It met Tuesdays, Thursdays, and Saturdays at 9.

(6) *Geology 4.* A half-year course in Elementary Geology under Dean Shaler, meeting Wednesdays, Fridays, "and occasionally Monday" at 12.

(7) *Geology 5.* The second half-year: Elementary Field and Laboratory Geology, with afternoon classes.

"Tip" was a Pomeranian Spitz, destined to be killed by a train. It was a custom for Groton graduates to return to the school on the first Sunday of their first college year, and attend chapel. This "Freshman Sunday" was particularly fostered and made attractive by the hospitality of Mrs. Peabody.

∽

"I am pretty well unpacked tho'
no pictures are hung yet . . ."

CAMBRIDGE
OCT. 5, 1900,
FRIDAY.

My dearest Mama & Papa,

I have such a lot to write about that I dont quite know where to begin. But to go back to Monday— In the afternoon the first foot-ball practice with a long run made us stiff, but after supper the fun began. Most of the Groton, St. M., & St. Pauls & Pomfret fellows were in at Sanborn's, and last night I visited the Lords. The curtains haven't come but I am writing J.&M. Paine will send the rug for my room in a few days. I am pretty well unpacked tho' no pictures are hung yet. There are still over 100 candidates for the 04 team & I shan't make it but possibly a scrub team. I am crazy for a picture of Tip.

No more now. Will write Sunday. I lunch at Sturgises then. Ever with lots of love your affec son

F.D.R.

This was not "Westmorly Court" stationery, but bore his own monogram—the florid, entwined initials "F.D.R." Sanborn's was a billiard parlor and smokers' supply store on Massachusetts Avenue in Cambridge. There are frequent references in subsequent letters to the Lords, who were old family friends. Their son, Sidney Archer Lord, married Beatrice Sturgis' sister Anne, referred to in F.D.R.'s correspondence as "Nancy." "J.&.M." is Jordan & Marsh, the large Boston department store; "Paine" is the Paine Furniture Company.

$$\sim\!\sim$$

*"When you come, please bring
my new pipe . . ."*

CAMBRIDGE
OCT. 14, 1900,
SUNDAY.

My dearest Mama & Papa,

How perfectly delighted I was to get your letter saying that you intended to come on to Boston next Saturday! I can hardly wait until the day, and I shall be at the Union Station at 3 to meet you. I will get five seats at the Theatre & ask 3 boys to dinner. I don't know whether you intend to go to the Touraine or the Somerset, but I fancy it will be the Touraine.

I have just got back from Groton, but I must go back to the beginning. I went up on Friday at 3 p.m, and that evening about 20 graduates only came. On Saturday morning about 200 people arrived and the Consecration Service began at 11.30. The graduates marched by forms to the Chapel, the original form consisting of 1 grad. The service was most impressive, there were 50 clergy in their robes, & the Chapel had 400 persons in it, on chairs, camp-stools, etc, it was an event which none of us will ever forget. After the service there was a big stand up lunch in the dining-room, and in the afternoon a foot-ball game with Hopkinson which Groton won, 6-o.

Last Wednesday I had received an invitation from Mr.

Higley to spend Sunday with him so I moved over to his house (also Warren Motley) on Saturday & had a most delightful visit there, away from the awful crowd at the school. There was a grand dinner at the School in the evening & speeches & songs afterwards. Today there was Communion & the regular services, & I came back tonight at 7 o'clock. When you come, please bring my new pipe (Uncle Ned's) as it was forgotten when I packed. I am not smoking as I am in training for foot-ball.

No more now. Will write on Tuesday.

Ever with lots of love your affec son

FRANKLIN.

The Somerset Hotel in Boston is on Commonwealth Avenue. At the opening of the fall term at Groton, the new chapel was formally consecrated. The single original graduate mentioned here was George Rublee, Groton 1886. The original owner of F.D.R.'s appropriately collegiate accessory had been his Great-uncle Edward Delano.

∽

"I am also trying for the 'Crimson' . . ."

WESTMORLY COURT
OCT. 19, 1900,
FRIDAY.

My dearest Mama and Papa,

What a funny mistake we made about your coming on! Your letter said Saturday the 17th, nothing about November, as without looking up the date I took it for granted that next Saturday was the 17th. However I shall look forward to seeing you in a short time. I have been very busy this week, or would have written before. On Monday I went to a "Beer-Night" in a Senior's room. It is a regular institution by which a senior has a few of his classmen and about 20 Freshmen in to his room in order to get them acquainted with eachother. I left the Freshmen team on Saturday & the squad is now very small. As I wished to continue playing I put my name down for one

427

of the 8 scrub teams which are to play till Nov. 5 for a Cup. We had our first practice yesterday & I was elected Captain of the Team. It is the only one composed wholly of Freshman & I am the only Freshman Captain. Billy Burnham is also on the team. I am also trying for the "Crimson" & if I work hard for two years I may be made an editor. I have to make out notices & go to interviews so I am very busy.

I dined at the Lord's on Tuesday evening & Mrs. Lord wanted to be remembered to you. I shall call on the Porters tonight, they live next door to the Lords & I have not seen them yet. Many thanks for the Graphics & photo on board the "½ Moon". By the way, Nancy wants to see the others taken that day, so if you have any extra prints you might send them to me.

Tomorrow I am going with Moseley to spend Sunday at Newburyport where his place is & we are to shoot ducks. It is not the pleasure of going with him that induces me to go, but the chance to get some good duck shooting, which I have never had, & to see a new place. Gerry Chadwick may go with us. I was asked to go to Naushon for Sunday by Alex. Forbes who is in our class, but I should have had to take 3 cuts so thought it better not, as I dont take any going to Newburyport. I expect to get back Sunday night. So glad you're going to keep "Tip." Very sorry to hear about Mr. Olyphant I hope Papa won't get tired. I want very much to see the new horses, do send a photo of them, also of "Tip," & the other photos at Campo. Will write Sunday night or Monday.

Ever with love

F.D.R.

The Harvard *Crimson* first offered its news services to the University on January 24, 1873, for a name drawing upon the then undefined college colors. When, two years later, it was officially given out that the Harvard flag was crimson, the *Magenta* gladly followed suit. Today the *Crimson* is a large (13½" x 20") daily; in 1875 it was a biweekly half the size, competing in many of its features with the literary *Advocate*. It had a number of mushrooming competitors: the *Daily News,* the *Echo,* and the *Herald,* which produced a disadvantageous financial position, so in 1883 the *Crimson* and *Herald* merged, became the *Herald-Crimson* for a while, and after 1891 reverted to the original title. In 1900 the *Crimson* had offices on Massachusetts Avenue, and the following year moved into the new Harvard Union building. It was in the process of shedding the leisurely traditions of its past, and emerging more and more as a true newspaper, with wide sports coverage, occasional extras, straw votes preceding national elections, and speedy "breakfast-table" delivery. The A. S. Porters were the parents of Betty Porter *(vide supra)* who was F.D.R.'s age. Naushon Island is in Buzzards Bay not far off Fairhaven; Alexander Forbes, who invited him there, was a Milton boy who later became professor of Physiology at the Harvard Medical School, and president of the board of the George Junior Republic.

〜〜

"Moseley got 2 ducks, I none but
had a splendid time . . ."

CAMBRIDGE
OCT. 23, 1900,
TUESDAY.

My darling Mama and Papa,

I cannot tell you how distressed I was to get your Saturday letter saying that Papa had had another attack in the night. I came very near going on, but was so glad to get your Sunday letter saying he is better. Remember that it is *very* easy to go home, & I can get permission almost any time. I do not think it would be at all good for Papa to come to Boston, so I shall hope to go home for Sunday the 11th of November, and I need only take one cut to do so.

[Three sentences deleted.]

I forgot to mention in my Friday letter that last Wednesday I went to Southboro' & saw Lyman who is in the infirmary with a strained stomach, which was serious for a few days. He got

it in football but hoped to be up in about a week. I got back
yesterday morning from Newburyport. We shot Saturday &
Sunday at 4 a.m. Moseley got 2 ducks, I none but had a splendid time. We took a long drive Sunday afternoon & got back
in time for the first recitation on Monday. I have had most of
the skin on my left hand kicked off in foot-ball, but it is not
bad. Uncle Fred was here in Boston yesterday & he came out
at 6. I supped with him & showed him the room. He has a
meeting tomorrow & goes back in the evening. It was delightful
seeing him. No more now. I hope to hear of Papa's complete
recovery.

Ever your devoted son

FRANKLIN.

The deleted portion of this letter is a reference to his half-
nephew, who had just contracted an alliance judged unfortunate by the society of the time. A certain furor ensued, understandably in view of the fact that Taddy was a grandson of
the nonpareil Mrs. Astor. F.D.R. implanted, in his saturnine
appraisal of the event, the advice: "It will be well for him . . .
to go to parts unknown . . . and begin life anew."

∽

*"Last night there was a grand
torch-light Republican Parade . . ."*

WESTMORLY COURT
OCT. 31, 1900,
WEDNESDAY.

My dearest Mama & Papa,

I feel ashamed not to have written you for a week. To go
back to last week.—I played foot-ball every afternoon & on
Thursday evening paid the Porters a call. Our team being by
far the lightest of the eight, we have of course no show for the
cups but we have made a very good showing & won two games
& lost two. We are called the "Missing-Links" & I am the only
Freshman Captain. We finish the series next Saturday & I shall
then play golf or row. On Saturday the game with the Carlisle

430

Indians took place & I took Miss Lord to see it & went there to dinner afterwards. It was a most exciting game & Harvard finally won, 17-5. The next morning we slept until 10.30 (!), then cooked some griddle-cakes over a chafing-dish (which Harold Brown provided) & had some chops brought up from down-stairs. We dressed in time for lunch & lazied round until 4.30 p.m. when we went for afternoon tea to the Sturgises & then dined in style at the Touraine, the first time this term.

Last night there was a grand torch-light Republican Parade of Harvard & the Mass. Instit. of Technology. We wore red caps & gowns & marched by classes into Boston & thro' all the principal streets, about 8 miles in all. The crowds to see it were huge all along the route & we were dead tired at the end. The weather of the last few days has been *horrid* cold & damp & drizzly; I do hope Papa won't catch cold.

The big game with Pennsylvania comes on Saturday & the outcome is doubtful. I can leave here *on Friday the 9th* getting to N.Y. at 9 p.m. if you are to be there. But if you are to be at H.P. I will take the 1 o'clock train & catch the 6.30 up river. So you must let me know which to do. The Dean won't count the two cuts necessary to go home. Many thanks for the papers. I'm pretty well banged up with foot-ball, but it will be over in a couple of days.

The monthly exams are beginning next week so I'm working hard. No more now.

Ever your affec. son,

FRANKLIN.

The presidential campaign of 1900 was nearing its climax, McKinley's running-mate being Theodore Roosevelt. The campaign, in addition to providing F.D.R. with an opportunity to march if not vote Republican, gave him a very important *Crimson* scoop. The Harvard *Democrat,* an evanescent publication appearing only in election years, had on October 20th reprinted large portions of an article written for *The Outlook* by President Eliot, in which the latter discussed the issues at stake, criticized faults in both parties, and

431

did not declare himself for either Bryan or McKinley. The *Democrat* made great capital of Eliot's criticisms of the Republican candidate, and a letter to the *Crimson,* signed "Lovers of the Truth," pointed out that the *Democrat* had deleted unfavorable references to the Democratic Party in its reprinting of the *Outlook* article. To ferret out whom President Eliot would vote for thus became a great prize for the competing *Crimson* candidates. At the time there was a rule against candidates' interviewing the president of Harvard, but F.D.R., newly come and unaware, paid a call at Eliot's home. He was doubtless severely rebuked, but in any event he got his story; the *Crimson* of October 29th headlined: "President Eliot Declares for McKinley," and continued: "President Eliot gave the Crimson the following statement last night concerning his article in the Outlook about which there has been so much discussion: I intend to vote for President McKinley, Governor Roosevelt, and Representative McCall, and I have never had any other intention." The story was picked up by newspapers all over the country, and very probably assured F.D.R.'s election to the *Crimson*. There is surprisingly no mention of the event in this letter; however, it seems probable that there are some letters missing in the period following, which may have contained a detailed account.

~~

"Nine-tenths of Cambridge was tight . . ."

[CAMBRIDGE]
NOV. 6, 1900,
TUESDAY.

My dearest Mama & Papa,

I was too delighted to get yours of Sunday & to hear about the cottage at Aiken, and I know you will both enjoy it there. Of course Papa will take "Bobby" with him. Last Friday we finished foot-ball, and our team came out about the middle of [the] series. On Saturday, the Pennsylvania game was magnificent and altho' Harvard was not the favorite we won easily, 17-5. In the evening we all, that is about half the college went to the theatre, "The Monks of Malabar" and regularly "rough-

432

housed" the play. They had to lower the curtain half a dozen times and missiles flew all over the place. After it was over, everyone went to the Hotels, I to the Touraine with 3 others, & 9/10 of Cambridge was "tight"! Lathrop & I remained sober as judges, but couldn't get a car back till 2 a.m.!!!!!! We slept till 12 on Sunday, then went to lunch with some cousins of Jake's, the Thachers. I studied most of the afternoon for exams, and in the evening called on the Porters & Lords.

Yesterday I played squash most of the afternoon, & called at Bishop Lawrence's house in the evening.

I leave on the 1 o'clock Friday & will see you in the station at 6. It is too lovely to think of seeing you so soon. I won't bring my Tuxedo home unless you wire me to do so, & will bring just my coat-case, also the big trunk with some summer flannels. You wouldn't know that this is election day here, all is so quiet, we haven't heard any returns yet, but I think there can only be one outcome.

I am sending a cheque to Frazar today. I tried to pay him before but the store was closed, & I didn't want to send a cheque for 75 cents, but have done it now.

Ever with loads of love

F.D.R.

His father's health was worsening, and his mother had rented a cottage at the famous South Carolina resort. "Bobby" was James Roosevelt's favorite riding horse.

〰️

"What's the matter with 1904? . . ."

CAMBRIDGE
NOV. 19, 1900,
MONDAY.

My dearest Mama & Papa,

On my return from Groton last night I was too distressed to get your note of Saturday, saying that dear Papa has had another attack. I am sure the Doctor ought to absolutely forbid his going to N.Y. I hope that you will get off by *Dec. 15th* for Aiken, as that will be the only way Papa can have absolute rest and forget about the everlasting D.&H. I only wish I were at home & c'd take the responsibility off his hands.

Later.

Yours of Sunday is most welcome & I do hope Papa won't try to overdo.

I went last Friday afternoon to Mrs. Kuhn's & saw her for an hour. She is well; Hamilton not any *too* well, & they leave for Washington on Monday next. I am to dine with them next Wednesday.

On Saturday I went to Groton & had a nice visit, coming down Sunday p.m with the Rector. Saw Mrs. John Lawrence after Church & she sent kind regards, but c'd not find time to walk all the way to the James L.s. I got back here at 6, found Jake & we dined at the Sturgises & had a pleasant evening. Today is horrid, drizzling & muggy. I am going this evening to teach at the boy's Club in Boston. I have been asked by the Lords to take my Thanksgiving dinner with them & shall do so.

Make Papa rest. I shall write again in a day or so. What's the matter with 1904? Harvard 1904-17, Yale 1904-0. A great victory & Jake is wild.

Ever affec. son

F.D.R.

I shall wear my dress-suit to the Kuhn's on Wednesday.

Continuing to play a part in the Groton Missionary Society (*vide supra*), F.D.R. spent a good deal of time at the St. Andrew's Boys Club in Boston . . . teaching, helping out with entertainments, participating in sports.

∽∽

"My dress-suit looked like a dream and was much admired . . ."

WESTMORLY COURT
NOV. 23, 1900,
FRIDAY.

My darling Mama and Papa,

I am so glad Papa is really better, and I only hope he will be absolutely well again in a few days and not go to New York again, for it is not *necessary* I am quite sure, and is bound to be bad for him, no matter how quietly he takes it. I feel that it is most important that Papa should realize this, even if he has to be forbidden by the Doctor. Also I am sure it will be best for you to start for Aiken by the middle of December, and I should feel much more happy if you take Miss Galloway with you.

On Monday last I went in to the boys' Club and helped amuse them for two hours in the evening. It is in one of the poorest quarters in Boston and it is the head church mission of that part. On Wednesday I dined at the Kuhns and Nancy was the only other guest. My dress-suit looked like a dream and was much admired. After leaving the Kuhns I paid a short call at the Sturgises & saw Rebecca Newhall who is staying there for a few days.

Last night I went to see Alice Roosevelt at the Lee's, she came on Tuesday. She is going to the Saturday Evening, not the Friday as you thought.

I leave tomorrow morning at 8 o'clock in a car of 50 other Freshmen, and we arrive at New Haven at 12 p.m We leave again at 6 & arrive in Boston about 10 p.m. I only hope Harvard will win, the chances are about even. I doubt if I see Helen as she sits on the Yale side & the crowd will be awful, but I will try to find her.

I shall anxiously await the clothes on Monday, I hope you didn't forget the double-breasted coat. Our piano is coming tomorrow, $40. for the year which is $10 off the regular price. It is a very nice one and of good tone.

With loads of love to you both I am ever your loving son

FRANKLIN.

Miss Galloway was one of Sara Delano Roosevelt's Baltimore friends. "Princess Alice" was staying with her grandparents, the Lees, and attending a Boston social institution known as the Saturday Evening Dancing Class. There is no further mention of the Harvard-Yale game; score: 28-0, unfavorably.

"She wore white and looked very well . . ."

My dearest Mama & Papa,

Your telegram came this afternoon and I think you will have found good weather in New York, although very cold I fear, for it is freezing now and promises to be cold tomorrow. I am just back from Nancy's tea and it was most successful in every way; she wore white and looked very well and there were crowds there, three or four hundred, I should judge. Susan [? Lee] was there to help besides many buds, to many of whom I was introduced, also Lathrop. I was there about an hour, and met every old fogy from Campobello I have ever seen

Wednesday.

I forgot to finish this last night so will do so now. On Monday night I went in to the St. Andrews Club & spent two hours. I have arranged to umpire a foot-ball game tomorrow, Thanksgiving Day morning, between a team from my Club and that of some other boys' club. That will take up all morning, and I am to have one grand dinner at the Sturgises' in the middle of the day, 1.30, and then at 7 I go for another to the Lords, so that my digestion must be strong to stand it. I got any [an] invitation yesterday from Cousin Frank Forbes to take my Thanksgiving with them in Boston, but of course I can't go. It is very good of them to ask me, as I don't even know them, but I shall go to see them on Friday. I got the cheque safely and many thanks for it, also the wrapper etc came & the butterflies are most ornamental. One of the Brooks suits is just right, double-breasted waist-coat, not coat, the $31 one, & I wore it to the tea yesterday. No more now, I shall go to bed early tonight, 9. o'clock.

Ever your affec son,

F.D.R.

I hope Papa will be all right in this very cold snap, let me know what Dr. Ely says.

"I dont like the awful *** pill
& don't know the *** pill . . ."

WESTMORLY COURT
DEC. 3, 1900,
MONDAY.

My dearest Mama & Papa,

I am too distressed about Papa and cannot understand why he does not improve more quickly. I cannot help feeling that a change of air will do him good, so I only hope his strength will improve sufficiently for him to think of Aiken.

It is very good of you to bother so about my dances, I am writing Ellen & Laura, and as I dont like the awful [name deleted] pill & don't know the [name deleted] pill I shall ask either Alice Draper or Jean Reid for the Metropolitan. Please answer the enclosed or keep it, I dont know what it means.

But to go back. On Thursday morning I went out to Franklin Park & umpired a football game, went to lunch at the Sturgises, and to dine at the Lords, so I was pretty well filled, (with food I mean) and had a most pleasant day. On Friday I recuperated and on Saturday went to lunch with Mrs. Brown at the Touraine and went to the theatre in the evening. On Sunday (yesterday) I met Sidney Lord in Harvard Square at 9.30, & we went to Oakley and had a very good game of golf, & met various members of the family.

I hustled back at 12.30 & went in to a stag lunch with Willy Burnham. After lunch, at 3.30 I went to Dr. Parks Church for afternoon service. After service I paid several calls, one to the Forbes but they were out. I hustled back here & in again to dinner at Gerry Chadwick's where I stayed all evening. Tonight I go in to the boys Club again.

If you decide to remain in New York over next Sunday, which I think is doubtful please telegraph me and I will spend Sunday there with you, without taking any cuts, as I will take the 3 o'clock Saturday afternoon. I do hope Papa will improve, as it must be discouraging to you both but I feel confident

437

that your next letter will bring better news. No more now; I go to Wilson this week, have written for an appointment. Lovingly,

F.D.R.

Alice Draper was a sister of George, Ruth, and Paul (*vide supra*); she married Edward C. Carter, secretary-general of the Institute of Pacific Relations. Jean Reid, daughter of Whitelaw Reid, became the wife of The Hon. John Hubert Ward, equerry to Edward VII. She and Eleanor Roosevelt, when they were debutantes, taught classes for children at the Rivington Street Settlement House in New York. Five days after this letter was written, on December 8th, James Roosevelt died at the Renaissance Hotel, with his wife, both his sons, and Mrs. Franklin Hughes Delano in attendance. He was seventy-two years old. F.D.R. did not return to Harvard until after the New Year. From all available evidence, it appears that the loss of her elderly husband proved a deep shock to Sara Delano Roosevelt, and that in the immediate and ensuing years she turned more than ever toward her son for a replacing companionship.

∽

"You must tell me what is the thing to do . . ."

CAMBRIDGE
JAN. 4, 1901,
FRIDAY.

My darling Mummy,

Yesterday I worked all morning and most of the afternoon and evening, and I saw all the fellows. Our table you will be glad to hear began at lunch yesterday & the crowd is a very nice one & next to the table of some of the other Grotonians.

Today my trunks arrived and I have been unpacking most of the time. My bronze is much admired. I am too worried about dear Uncle Warren, I hope you will telegraph if he is really worse, I am beginning to fear that it may be typhoid.

I received the enclosed from Sidney. As I don't know

whether a wedding is considered a "society" event like a dance I don't know what to say to it but you must tell me what is the thing to do.

It is cold today & tonight I shall work while most of the fellows go to the Friday Evening.

Do write me about Uncle Warren.

Ever lovingly

F.D.R.

I am wondering if you are going to N.Y. tonight or tomorrow but don't know so will send this to Hyde Park

This letter, and most of those which followed it during the course of the next year, was written on heavy black-bordered stationery.

～～

"The prints came last night and are much admired . . ."

CAMBRIDGE
JAN. 6, 1901,
SUNDAY.

My dearest Mummy,

Two letters from you, one from H.P & the other from N.Y. came yesterday, and I am surprised that you had not received at least the letter which I posted Thursday morning soon after my arrival here. I telegraphed & your Saturday letter from N.Y. speaks of receiving it. Yesterday afternoon I went out to Hammond's Pond & skated and played hockey

Today I slept till 10 o'clock and then Lathrop Harold & I cooked a most sumptuous breakfast on two chafing-dishes, scrambled-eggs, sausages, toast, etc. As it was so late we ate no lunch, & this evening we are to cook our supper in the same way, & are to make griddle-cakes. I am glad that Uncle Warren's illness is still called grippe, and only hope it will not develop into typhoid

I am writing Aunt Laura today and will post it tomorrow morning.

The prints came last night and are much admired by everyone, as is the bronze. My hat came also, thanks for it, and the Lessing has come too; I am writing Aunt Annie.

Just think I shall be home two weeks from next Friday.

Lovingly,

F.D.R.

You gave me *plenty* of money & I haven't used it up yet. I am going for the Book-Case this week.

~~

"I feel as you do that dear Papa
would have liked me to usher . . ."

CAMBRIDGE
JAN. 8, 1901,
TUESDAY.

My dearest Mummy,

No letter from you today but yours of Sunday made me happy yesterday. I am too sorry Uncle Warren's case has been pronounced typhoid, but I hope that the worst of the suffering is over and that tho' slow his recovery may be without any setbacks.

I feel as you do that dear Papa would have liked me to usher at the Lord's in June. I have not told them I w'd yet as Nancy is in Phila. and Dr. Lord in the South, on a shooting trip.

The delightful rug & quilt came today & are too pretty, the rug is already down & looks so well. I am using my old quilt to cover my trunk & my rooms is perfect now.

It has been warm yesterday & today & the ice too soft to skate on, so I have worked & hung my new pictures.

I *may* spend next Sunday quietly with Tom Beal in Boston as he says he should have no one else & we s'd go to church with his family Sunday morning, but I shan't do it if he has a single other person in the house. In case I do I shall go to Groton the Sunday after. No more now, I have a vile pen & viler ink & I am going to bed as it is 10:30. Good hours you see.

Ever lovingly

F.D.R.

One of F.D.R.'s Harvard classmates, a good friend and an usher at his wedding, was Thomas Prince Beal, later president of the Second National Bank of Boston.

～～

*"I wish I could be home to help
mark the trees . . ."*

My dearest Mummy,

Yours of Wednesday and Friday are most welcome. I am so glad the ice is in, we have had a good fall of snow, that is about 6 inches, and there is sleighing. I hope the men will get the wood in while the snow lasts. I wish I could be at home to help mark the trees. It rained Thursday, snowed part of yesterday and today.

I have been working for the exams, and this evening am going to Tom Beal's for Sunday, and will not come out here till early Monday morning & will write you again then.

I am glad Uncle is not any worse, and I trust his recovery will be steady. On my letter to Aunt Laura I put a two-cent postage-stamp, but realized it too late, after it was posted. I was in Boston yesterday & left my card-dye [die] there as it is easier to have it done there; I ordered 50 cards.

No more now, I shall be home a week from next Friday & can hardly wait for the day.

Ever lovingly,

F.D.R.

I will buy Julian Coolidge's present tomorrow

His former Groton master, Julian Coolidge, was now an instructor in Mathematics at Harvard; on January 17th he was married to Miss Theresa Reynolds.

～～

"Tom & I went to see a bicycle
race on an indoor track . . ."

CAMBRIDGE
JAN. 16, 1901,
WEDNESDAY.

My dearest Mummy

I am sorry not to have written since Saturday and there is
much to tell; On Saturday evening I went in to the Beal's
about 6 pm. and after dinner Tom & I went to see a bicycle
race on an indoor track.

On Sunday we all went to Trinity Church in the morning
and in the afternoon Tom and I took a very long sleighride
way out into the country. We passed a quiet evening and returned to Cambridge just in time for a 9 o'clock lecture Monday a.m. Yesterday was a horrid day, melting, and today is the
same   everything swimming

My exams come on the days I told you but on very bad
hours, on Friday the 25th I have Geology at 2.30 p.m, lasting
till 5.30, so I shall take the midnight and go to Hyde Park by
the earliest train Saturday. I hope Aunt Doe got in safely, I
hope to see that the "Majestic" is in by the morning papers.
I am writing her to Algonac.

I am glad all the ice is in before this thaw. Sorry about Top-
Sail. Have you heard anything about the "Yacht". If you write
me I will go to Stearns in Boston & tell him about her and also
advertize in the "Rudder". No more now, will write on Friday.

Lovingly

F.D.R.

I go to Groton for *Sunday.*

One of Sara Delano Roosevelt's reactions to her husband's
death was a desire to sell the *Half-Moon II,* which had been
very much a part of their life together; the boat was consequently being advertised in the two yachting magazines mentioned, and also offered through Stearns Marine, a Boston
ship-broking firm.

"I have found some additions to our family tree . . ."

CAMBRIDGE

JAN. 21, 1901,

MONDAY.

My dearest Mummy,

I wrote you [a] note on Saturday, just before I went to Groton but I found it in my overcoat pocket this morning, having forgotten to mail it. I went to the School after lunch on Saturday and came back here last night I had a nice stay at the Rector's and yesterday lunched alone with the John Lawrences.

I saw Mrs. James L. and she sent her love to you and thought it very good of you to let her have the apartment. I began work today for the Freshman Crew, it consists for the next month of work in the gymnasium on machines. I am not sure if we can get off during the mid-years more than once, but I will come home Friday unless I telegraph you. I will leave here by the 5 o'clock train, reaching N.Y. at 11 o'clock & will go straight to the Renaissance.

On Saturday it was *terribly* cold, & I had a very cold drive up to the School, but today it is very warm again with puddles everywhere. I have found some additions to our family tree, the genealogy of the Pomeroy ancestors who married Experience Woodward in 1661. I will bring it home on Friday, & it will give us several additional dates. Give my love to Aunt Doe. I am working hard for the mid-years.

Lovingly

F.D.R.

Experience Woodward married Medad Pomeroy the son of Eltweed; from this Puritan joining-together arose Thankful, who married Benjamin Lyman who begat Joseph Lyman, who was the great-grandfather of Catherine.

∞

*"It seems to me I like the Angel
of the Resurrection best . . ."*

[CAMBRIDGE]
FEB. 3, 1901,
SUNDAY.

My dearest Mama,

I have been so busy that I haven't had time to write a line
for days. Yesterday I took the English 28 exam and think I
passed. I worked all evening while Lathrop went to the theatre,
and today I slept late & we cooked our own breakfast-lunch
combination. The package of goodies came from [S.S.] Pierce
yesterday, just in time to aid us in our feast today. They are all
delicious and a most delightful birthday present, which will
give pleasure to a large number of boys.

Yours of Friday arrived this a.m. and it seems to me that I
like the idea of the Angel of the Resurrection perhaps best
with the "Good Shepherd" as second choice. You must decide
about it, and let me know the details more fully. Wasn't Nelly
thoughtful? She sent me also a blotter & paper holder for my
birthday & I am writing her straight to California. I sent a note
to F.A.D. [Frederic A. Delano] to the Adam's House, in Boston
where he stayed last time, but have heard nothing from him
today. Are you sure it was *this* Sunday & not *last* that he was in
Boston. The rowing continues, & is pretty hard work. French
exam tomorrow & Latin on Tuesday. I fear I can't get off the
rowing possibly on Saturday so may go to Groton for Sunday.
No more now

Love to Aunt Doe
Ever affec

F.D.R.

The discussion of Biblical figures here pertains to a memorial
to her husband which Sara Delano Roosevelt was considering
having placed in St. James's Church. It was to be a window;
not until more than twenty years later was it actually installed.
The old Adams House, on Washington Street in Boston, was
especially famous for its dining room.

444

"I found it in his pocket today . . ."

My dearest Mummy

I wrote you a note Friday & gave it to Gerry Chadwick to post & I found it in his pocket today so I will go back to the events of last week. I took the Government exam on Thursday and rowed Friday afternoon Friday morning I went down to Beverley with T. Beal & we sleighed for two hours, a beautiful day & I came back & lunched with him & came out here in time to row at 3.30. On Saturday Lathrop & I left at 10.37 & got to Fairhaven in time for lunch. After lunch L. & I drove all over N. Bedford & Fairhaven in a buggy & saw a fire in N.B. & had a glorious time. On Sunday morning we all went to Church in N.B. & visited the Swifts afterwards. After Lunch Uncle W. [Warren Delano] L & I went to the Fort & I paid a visit to the Church cousins. After a luscious tea we left at 5.30 & got back here about eight.

Nancy is to be married in April, they changed their plans suddenly a few weeks ago. Of course I shall not be usher & have told Sidney how sorry I am. The cake came safely & was most delicious, we all enjoyed it, & the last of it went today.

Tuesday.

The weather continues cold & fine. The rowing squad has been cut down & half the fellows are dropped. I am still kept strange to say & there are only 50 left. I am taking a new half course, Geology 5 which is laboratory & field work. I have heard from two of my exams, History, B, Latin D+ so I got thro' the latter better than I expected, & got an honor in History. There is a very slight chance of my coming home for Feb. 22, 23, 24 but *very slight.*

No more now, love to Aunt Doe
Affec.

F.D.R.

The Swifts were the parents of his Harvard classmate, John Baker Swift, Jr. A feature of the Revolutionary scene at Fairhaven was Fort Phoenix. The "Church cousins" relationship came through Deborah Church who married the original Warren Delano.

〜〜

*"I have rowed every day & had three
Glee Club rehearsals . . ."*

[CAMBRIDGE]
FEB. 16, 1901,
SATURDAY.

Dearest Mummy,

I am just off to Groton for Sunday (3 p.m) & shall come back Monday a.m.

Aunt Jennie & Uncle Warren came here on Thursday afternoon with Cousin Archie Howe & saw the room. I have rowed every day & had three Glee Club rehearsals this week. The concerts begin in two weeks.

Last night I went out to Oakley with the Lords to toboggan. The slide was perfect & there were no other people there

My train goes in 20 minutes. I will write when I get back. I dont believe I can get off next week to go home. I shan't go to the play at Groton the 22nd as there would be a crowd there.

I got a C+ in Geology 4 & a B— in French so have had two honors & still have two subjects to hear from.

With love & haste

F.D.R.

F.D.R. was a member of the Freshman Glee Club, but did not make the University. "Cousin Archie Howe" was related through Catherine Lyman.

〜〜

"I shall stay here quietly . . ."

CAMBRIDGE
FEB. 18, 1901,
MONDAY.

My dearest Mummy,

I got back from Groton this a.m at 9 o'clock, just in time for History, and found yours of Saturday. I am glad you have not decided anything about the window until you see English designs. I think the idea of the consecration service is very good.

I got to Groton Saturday at four o'clock and had a nice visit there. Nothing much happened, but I saw the remains of the Jefferson's house which burned down last Wednesday. They managed to save most of the furniture (it was at 4 p.m) but the house being of wood burned to the ground. It belonged to Mr. Gardner, & Jeff's furniture was insured. The J's are now living in the Griswold's house & the G's have moved to Brooks House. There were four or five other graduates there & we had a nice time together.

I can't come home on Saturday as we get off *only* for the 22nd. I shall stay here quietly. I do not know whether I ought to go to Groton for the 2nd play on Saturday. Aunt Kassie will be there & I should like to see them but dont want to see a crowd, so I am undecided. The book-case turned out to be just ½ inch too wide for the space, & it was the narrowest I could get. I have got a beautiful table & it looks very well between the two front windows.

Love to you & to Aunt Doe

Affec. son

FRANKLIN.

∾

"I sang 'Maggie Dooley' . . ."

CAMBRIDGE
FEB. 22, 1901,
FRIDAY.

My dearest Mummy,

I am delighted that you are going to Fairhaven next week, and if you go on Friday, I can get there on *Friday* at 6.20 in the evening. I hope you will be able to do this as I c'd then be with you for two whole days in Fairhaven. It will be lovely seeing you both so soon & I am looking forward to it. Lathrop may come down Saturday, he is up at the play at Groton. I am going up tomorrow afternoon, but shall keep in the background as I dont want to see many people. They will be chiefly villagers, anyway, but I shall see Mrs. Rogers. I believe Aunt Kassie & Muriel are coming to Boston on Monday, at least Pierre Lorrilard tells me so, & I hope they will come out to see my room.

The weather is fine but melting. The annual dinner of the Groton Club of Harvard was held on Tuesday night at the Somerset & was a glorious success. All the old play songs for several years back were resung & I sang "Maggie Dooley". Last night I tried for the "Varsity" Glee Club & sang "Matinata". Of course I have no show of making it but it w'd be a great thing if I c'd ever get on it. The Freshman Glee Club has just had a rehearsal here in our room, & we have 3 a week so you see it all takes time.

No more now. Love to you & Aunt Doe

Affec.

F.D.R.

Pierre Lorillard, Jr., scion of the tobacco family, was in F.D.R.'s Harvard class. The senior Mr. Lorillard had, years before, purchased a large section of land surrounding a small lake about twenty-five miles southeast of Newburgh, where he and a few friends built homes and had a shooting club. This eventually grew into the privately owned community of Tuxedo Park, where Aunt Kassie lived.

◇◇◇

"At ten o'clock the fire bell rang . . ."

[CAMBRIDGE]
MARCH 7, 1901,
THURSDAY.

My dearest Mummy,

Yours written on the train came this morning & I hope you got home safely & comfortably. I am to lunch with Aunt Doe today at Mrs. Russell's & dine with her somewhere this evening.

Last night there was a great excitement here. At ten o'clock the fire bell rang & Trinity Hall an old wooden building had the two upper stories entirely gutted & everything else soaked. I was in the building helping save some stuff & got soaked by

448

water & was nearly frozen afterwards! About 15 fellows lost nearly all they had, & the fire was not out till after midnight.

I cannot tell you how I enjoyed seeing you at Fair Haven & here & will come home if I possibly can get off my rowing.

This is just a line as I am awfully busy

Affec

F.D.R.

His cousin Mary Russell was Frank Forbes' sister.

∽

"We have all been to Church here . . ."

THE HOMESTEAD [FAIRHAVEN]
MARCH 10, 1901,
SUNDAY.

My dearest Mummy,

Aunt Doe, Harold Brown and I came down here last night arriving at 6 o'clock. As Lathrop could not come nor Alexander Forbes, I brought Lathrop's cousin Harold instead. But to go back, on Thursday I lunched at Mrs. Russell's with Aunt Doe and dined at the "Touraine" with her and Mrs. Low. On Friday afternoon I went with her and saw Mrs. Frank Forbes, also left a card at the Murray Forbes. I had to go back early to row & had a Glee Club rehearsal in the evening.

We have all been to Church here and been to the fort. After lunch Harold and I are going for a short drive & we leave by the 5.35 train.

It drizzled yesterday and is cloudy & damp today, but quite mild. I found your letter here and know how busy you must be. I was surprised to see the enclosed slip in yesterday's Herald (N.Y) I am delighted that Mr. Bacon has taken the house if it is true.

Poor Mary is really ill, & the Doctor says she will be in bed for several weeks.

No more now, I will write from Cambridge in a day or two.

With lots of love

F.D.R.

449

The James Murray Forbes' were some more of his multifarious
Forbes cousins, all related through Aunt Dora's two marriages.
John Murray Forbes, who died in 1898, had been one of the
first and most successful of the Russell and Company partners.
The "enclosed slip" referred to a small "Society" note which
appeared on page 10 of the *New York Herald* for March 9th,
and read: "Aiken, S.C., Friday—Mr. Robert Bacon, the well
known polo player, who has sub-rented the Henderson cottage from the estate of James Roosevelt, will arrive on Monday." Mr. Bacon, remarked in this item for his polo, became
rather better known for his distinguished ambassadorship to
France from 1909 to 1912. "Poor Mary" was Mrs. Mary Olsen,
housekeeper at Fairhaven for over three decades.

∞

*"I am glad not to have my Stamp
Album as I really have not time ..."*

[CAMBRIDGE]
MARCH 19, 1901,
TUESDAY.

My dearest Mummy,
    I forgot to write last night as I went in to the Boy's Club.
I got here safely yesterday morning, the train being 1½ hours
late, so that I did not reach Cambridge until 8.45. Still I had
time for a very good breakfast before my nine o'clock recitation. I rowed both yesterday & today, & I assure you it was hard
work & bitterly cold.
    I cannot tell you how much I enjoyed my two days with you,
& the Sunday walk. I am glad not to have my Stamp Album
here as I really have not time. My Scientific American has begun coming & I am very glad to have it again.
    No more now
    Ever devotedly

F.D.R.

∞

*"There is no hurry and we must
have a good one . . ."*

My dearest Mummy,

I feel as if much had happened since I last wrote you, and I was much shocked at Mr. Pell's death. I know what a comfort you must have been to Frances and her Mother. I fully intended to come on for the funeral, but seeing in the papers that it was to be private, I telegraphed you. If I had come I sh'd have had to cut rowing and three recitations.

I was much amused over MacCarty's letter but he is indeed a great loss and is a fool not to keep his good position as he is sure to come to grief some day. I hope Frederick's infant will help to keep him steady; also that you will be able to get somebody good for a butler. I hope you wont decide too soon as there is no hurry and we must have a good one.

On Sunday evening I dined at the Frank Forbes Mr. & Mrs went out elsewhere but the young people were in & I had a nice evening. Tonight I am to dine with Mrs. Low at the Albemarle & then go to the Boy's Club & after the Boy's Club to the Lord's.

I am off for rowing.

Lovingly

F.D.R.

Mr. Alfred Pell was the old family friend mentioned often in previous letters.

〜〜〜

*"It is much colder & the river is
not pleasant . . ."*

My dearest Mummy,

The most important news is that last night was held the election of officers of the Freshman Glee Club.

President—Geo. Lawton,
Secretary—F. D. Roosevelt
Gen. Manager, L. Brown.

Lathrop will have to make all arrangements for the concerts of the 1904 Musical Clubs, & he will have hard work, I don't have so much but have to sign the membership certificates for the whole Club.

On Wednesday the Newell crews were temporarily graded. I was put on the fourth as Stroke and was elected Captain but there is talk of regrading us & I may be taken up to the 3rd crew.

I think I shall go to Groton for Easter Sunday, but as the '04 races are not until the 25th April or thereabouts I wont get off for more than two days during the holidays.

Sunday.

I forgot to finish this Friday. Our crews were regraded yesterday and I am now on the 3rd Crew and was elected Captain of it last night. It is much colder the last few days & the river is not pleasant. I went this a.m to hear Mr. Peabody preach at Emmanuel Church & lunched at the Beals afterwards. I am going to the Lords now & shall stay to dinner. My Crimson work begins tomorrow so I shall be terribly busy, as I intend to work very hard for it. Yours of Friday telling of the silver came this a.m. I am most touched & am very anxious to see it. It is a thing we must always cherish.

Goodbye now as it is time for me to dress. I will write again in a day or so

Affec

F.D.R.

At Harvard there were two boating clubs, the Weld and the Newell. In the spring, following the class championship races, the club crews were graded—senior, junior, and intermediate —and in May raced for the various club championships, and in the local Boston regatta. The best of the club crews often rowed outside races with other colleges. The Weld Boat Club was formed in 1890, following the gift of a boathouse by

George Walker Weld of the Class of 1860. Nine years later, while Lehmann was coaching the varsity, the Newell was organized to compete with the Weld; it was named after Marshall Newell of the Class of 1894, a fine athlete who had rowed on three varsity crews and who was killed in an accident in 1897. The mention here of "the silver" refers to a legacy from F.D.R.'s father.

〜〜

"I have promised Frances to give
a talk to her boys . . ."

My dearest Mummy,

Well, I am here in Cambridge instead of being at Groton. Last night I intended to go up but was given so much work to do for the "Crimson" that I could not get away & was much disappointed. I find that I have to work three or four hours every day on the "Crimson" assignments. Today I went for morning service & Communion with Lathrop to Emmanuel Church & after that to lunch at the Thorndike's. I have worked again for the Crimson from 4 p.m. to 11 p.m & I am now off for bed. I will be home on Saturday night or Sunday morning & will be able to stay for three days, then I must come back for the rowing. I have promised Frances to give a talk to her boys on Monday afternoon so will have to be in town that day. I must stop now as it is late, I am going to bed every night at 11. I wish I c'd have been at home for Easter but have been working as a reporter instead.

Lovingly

F.D.R.

The Thorndikes were the parents of his classmate John R. Thorndike. Frances Pell was at this time listed as a "Non-resident Volunteer Worker" for Hartley House, a settlement house in New York which had been opened four years previously by the N. Y. Association for Improving the Condition of the Poor. The buildings were the gift of Marcellus Hartley. In the first annual report, it was stated that: "The idea of the Association in establishing Hartley House was, primarily, to create a small 'homekeeping' school, where poor girls could be taught how to make and keep a home neat and tidy and attractive." By 1901, at the time when F.D.R. spoke there, a "Young Men's Club" had been added to the program of the settlement.

$\sim\!\!\sim$

*"I am hoping & praying that he
wont get well . . ."*

[CAMBRIDGE]
APRIL 20, 1901,
SATURDAY.

My dearest Mummy,

I arrived safely at three on Thursday, and we rowed immediately, & the exercise was hard after a comparative loaf at home for five days. As my trunk could not be brought out the same day & as my dress shoes were *in* the trunk I c'dn't go anywhere to pay calls, except to the Lords where I went last night. Yesterday we rowed both morning and afternoon, & I am nearly half through Adam Bede. The stroke of the second crew became ill & today I stroked the second crew. I am hoping & praying that he wont get well before the race as it would be glorious if I c'd stay on the 2nd & at stroke too. I have been in bed at 10.30 every night. I did some work for the Crimson today & will have to work all tomorrow afternoon & evening so wont be able to go to Groton. Sorry Uncle Warren is ill again

Affectionately

F.D.R.

The demands upon a *Crimson* candidate's time were very great, considering that he was also expected to attend and pass his regular courses, and usually keep some sort of sports or social career going as well. W. Russell Bowie, who was a

454

classmate of F.D.R.'s and managing editor of the paper when the latter was president, wrote in an article for the *Harvard Year Book, Class of 1904:* "After the talk to the candidates by the managing editor on the night when they first reported, [the system existing in 1900-01] allowed them during their time of candidacy for the paper to go to practically any man they chose and to cover all departments of news ... the candidate obliged himself to keep track as far as he could of everything of consequence going on all over the College. The task was heavy, the drain on the candidate's thought and time exhausting. The candidate was everywhere; he was 'the arrow that flieth by day, and the pestilence that walketh in darkness.' "

∽∽

*"I am still on the Crimson, two
more have been dropped ..."*

[CAMBRIDGE]
APRIL 27, 1901,
SATURDAY.

Dearest Mummy,

The race on Thursday was glorious. I stroked the 2nd crew and we beat the 2nd Weld by 3 lengths. It was awfully rough & the other Weld crew by steering way in shore in calm water got ahead of us & although we spurted beat us by *4 feet* in 2 miles. I have not been kept for the Freshman crew as only the first 2 crews & one or two extras will go to the training table. I shall try on Monday for one of the Club crews which rows in the Metropolitan regatta on June 17th. I am still on the Crimson, two more have been dropped but two others are trying again so there are still eight left.

I will write about Europe on Sunday. I almost think I favor *Europe* this summer. I go with Aunt Annie to St. Marks for tomorrow afternoon. I haven't had ¼ second to myself since I came back.

Love

F.D.R.

455

The University records list F.D.R. as stroke of the Second Newell Crew which finished fourth in the interclub eight-oar races. The Metropolitan Regatta was rowed in the Charles River Basin, under the direction of the Boston Park Commission, with a number of Boston boat clubs participating.

∽

"Last night I got a 'scoop' about Cousin Theodore's talk . . ."

[CAMBRIDGE]
APRIL 30, 1901,
TUESDAY.

My dearest Mummy,

To go back—On Sunday I went out to Southboro with Aunts A. & T. [Annie & Tilly] & we had a most successful visit and got back at 7.30. I dined with them but had to get right back to the "Crimson." I am working about 6 hours a day on it alone and it is quite a strain.

Last night I got a "scoop" into it about Cousin Theodore's talk, about which I enclose a most amusing, highly colored and inaccurate piece from this evening's paper.

Now about abroad. 1 You ought to go. 2 The Pells want us. 3 We will be of benefit to them, & shouldn't get a chance next year. 4 I want to go.

I like the plan of staying at Hyde Park most of the summer except in its most important particulars. That is I dont want to go to Campo, neither do you; I dont want to stay on the river in August, I dont want you to; I dont like to go visiting this summer any more than you do.

On the other hand, If we sail say on the 8 of July we sh'd have a good long time at Hyde Park & you will see Uncle Warren for a long time, and we could get back to the river for 2 or 3 weeks before I return to College. Also we can have a trip abroad which will do us a world of good, and also we can give a great deal of help and pleasure to Mrs. Pell and Frances who w'd otherwise be quite alone. Besides this I know that we both will enjoy seeing new places & new things and it will quite take us out of ourselves. I sh'd not enjoy visiting by myself, and I sh'd not want to leave you and we w'd be mutually unhappy if we stayed at home. I have accepted Aunt Kassie's invitation to go to the Harvard-Yale race on June 27th as I want to go anyway & it is a good chance & will take but a short time. Read my reasons thro' two or three times & I know you will agree with me. I am so sorry for the Drapers.

Affectionately

F.D.R.

As the story goes, F.D.R. heard that Theodore Roosevelt was staying with Abbott Lawrence Lowell, and telephoned him to get a *Crimson* interview. The Vice-President suggested that they meet the next morning following a lecture he was to give before Professor Lowell's class in Government. At any rate, the *Crimson* for April 30th displayed this banner headline: "Vice-President Roosevelt to lecture in Government 1 this morning at 9 in Sanders," with a brief story below: "Vice-President Theodore Roosevelt '80 will lecture this morning at 9 o'clock in Sanders Theatre before the class in Government 1. Mr. Roosevelt will speak about his experiences as Governor of New York." The Draper mention referred to Dr. Draper's death.

～～

*"We can make some delightful tours
in the vicinity of Hamburg . . ."*

CAMBRIDGE
MAY 24, 1901,
FRIDAY.

My dearest Mummy,

Yours saying that you have booked the passages on the "Deutschland" is most welcome. She is a splendid boat and [will] give us one day more than the "Cymric", besides obviating the long and tiresome and costly journey from Liverpool to Hamburg. As you say we can make some delightful tours in the vicinity of Hamburg. You say nothing about our state-rooms on the "Prinzessin Louise". I conclude you have taken them. Do let me know more definitely & the numbers of ours and the Pells and I can look them up on Teddy's diagram. We race on Saturday, tomorrow, instead of Tuesday and we will be beaten I fear as the Weld Junior is very fast. The Crimson work continues arduous as ever but there is only three weeks more of it. If we win tomorrow I will telegraph.

We go tonight to Lexington for our third & last Musical Clubs concert

It is hot but lovely & I am crazy to get back to the place.

Ever with love

F.D.R.

Feature of the European trip was to be the North Cape cruise. With Teddy Robinson and the Pells, F.D.R. and his mother sailed to Plymouth, then at Hamburg picked up the "cruising yacht" *Prinzessin Victoria Luise*. In one of the Norwegian fjords they came upon Wilhelm II aboard the imperial yacht, and a number of the vacationists—F.D.R. included—were invited to inspect the boat during one of the Kaiser's absences ashore. The tale holds that F.D.R. came away with a prize souvenir from the royal writing desk, but if so, that particular trophy has not yet turned up amongst the Hyde Park memorabilia. The Harvard Glee Club, the Mandolin Club, and the Banjo Club, with their Freshman affiliates, formed what was known as the "Harvard Musical Clubs," and gave occasional entertainments around Boston and even farther afield. As for his 1901 rowing career, in the race mentioned here F.D.R. stroked the Newell Junior to a victory over the Weld Junior. Three weeks later, in the Metropolitan Regatta, he rowed number two on the Newell Junior and won one race. Summer vacation followed.

∽

*"The Union was opened last night,
a most impressive ceremony . . ."*

[CAMBRIDGE]
OCT. 16, 1901,
WEDNESDAY.

Dearest Mama—

You will be surprised to hear that I shall probably be home for Sunday next. There are several reasons for this. I can get off rowing & there is no football game here to watch as Harvard plays West Point, & I want to be here the following Saturday, also I want to see Muriel and get home again before all the trees are bare and also I am crazy to see the photographs. As I row Friday I will take the midnight to Albany and arrive Hyde Park at 9.28 a.m Saturday—which is quicker than via N.Y. Before I leave Friday night I am to dine at Mrs. Alfred Roosevelt's quietly. *But* I will telegraph you whether to expect me or not.

I had a very nice time at Groton, with a good football game on Saturday. I tead with the Sturgises on Sat. & on Sunday lunched with the Joys & had afternoon tea with the John Lawrences. Mrss. Joy, Lawrence & Peabody sent their love to you. I got back on Monday a.m. and have been rowing every day, still stroking the second Newell, but I doubt if I stay there. The Union was opened last night, a most impressive ceremony.

Warren was well & doing very well at football. He sent his love to you & M.D.R. [Muriel Delano Robbins.]

Will telegraph. With love

F.D.R.

LATER

What do you think of my taking M.D.R. Helen [Roosevelt] & Mary Newbold to see the Harvard-West Point game at West Point Saturday afternoon. The game begins between 3 & 4 p.m & will be most interesting.

459

If you approve make arrangements as to trains.
I shall come *ten to one*

F.D.R.

Hope the new butler is a success & wears the blue ribbon.
Please get my guns from Po'keepsie.

The dating of the correspondence from this point on is often
uncertain; unfortunately Sara Delano Roosevelt did not jot
down dates as invariably as she did for the Groton letters, and
in some cases the dates she did furnish are inaccurate. For
example, she wrote "Nov. 6th" on this letter, but since the
Harvard-West Point football game came on Saturday, October
19th, her dating must be revised. Mrs. Alfred Roosevelt, the
former Katharine Lowell, had married a first cousin of
Teddy Roosevelt's. The Harvard Union was the gift of Henry
Lee Higginson of Boston. It was a club for one and all,
housed in a big building just off the Yard. Debates, rallies,
and entertainments of various sorts were held there. There
were billiard and game rooms, reading rooms, a library; in
an annex were the team training tables; the *Crimson* moved
in and occupied the basement. The Union was a frank en-
deavor to democratize Harvard social life. At first it was enthusiastically pushed by everyone, but eventually the undergraduate clubs took back their own. In his Sophomore year,
F.D.R. had the following courses:

(1) *English 22.* A half-year course in English Composition,
considered to be rather dull, meeting Tuesdays and
Thursdays at 1:30, with occasional conferences.

(2) *English 10.* Second half-year. A course in Public Speaking, "intended for students somewhat advanced in platform speaking." It met in five groups at various hours,
under Messrs. Winter and Hills.

(3) *Economics 1.* A full-year course: Outlines of Economics.
It met Mondays, Wednesdays, and Fridays at 9, under
the direction of Assistant Professor Abram Piatt Andrew
(*vide infra*). Numbered among the instructors in this
course was Gilbert Holland Montague, later a prominent lawyer and chairman of the N. Y. Bar Association's Committee on the National Industrial Recovery

Act, in which capacity he termed the N.R.A. "a gold-fish bowl" that was opaque and from a constitutional viewpoint would not hold water. Speaking at the American Academy of Political and Social Sciences in Philadelphia on April 6, 1935, Montague had this to say of the handiwork of his former pupil: ". . . hastily, absent-mindedly, without any intention or realization that it was acting fascistically, the N.R.A. snatched at a form of executive law-making that was unconsciously but nevertheless essentially fascistic . . ."

(4) *Geology 14.* General Paleontology, a half-year course under Dean Shaler, meeting Wednesdays, Fridays, "and usually Monday" at 10.

(5) *History 10.* First half-year: American History to 1783. Meeting Mondays, Wednesdays, and Fridays at 11. One of the instructors in this course was Mr. Hiram Bingham, Jr., later to become a famous author and explorer, governor of Connecticut and twice senator from that state.

(6) *History 24.* Second half-year: Constitutional & Political History of the U. S., 1783-1865, meeting Mondays, Wednesdays, and Fridays at 10, under Mr. William Garrott Brown.

(7) *History 12.* First half-year: English History from 1688 to the Reform of Parliament, meeting Tuesdays and Thursdays at 2:30; and:

(8) *History 12.* Second half-year: English History Since the Reform of Parliament, meeting at the same hours. Both the last-mentioned courses were given under Silas Marcus MacVane, then McLean Professor of Ancient and Modern History. He was an extremely nearsighted gentleman, and once he had settled down to his lectures, it was no trick at all for a student to remove himself from the classroom for parts elsewhere and more entertaining. On one occasion practically an entire class performed this feat, proceeding one by one out a window in the rear of the lecture hall and down a fire escape, leaving the Professor's historical periods assailing empty air. Among the departing group was observed the author of these letters.

"I shall get Lathrop to rub it . . ."

Dearest Mama

I got here all right & on time, and found that Cousin B's telegram had been repeated to Poughkeepsie but I got a copy at the telegraph office & have just sent the following.

"Unable to go to Farmington today. Can meet you New Haven tomorrow if convenient." And I hope to hear from her this afternoon. In case she can arrange I shall go by the first train tomorrow. I have *at last* got the Savings Bank nuisance within my grasp & I enclose it, but have a feeling that the letter will go astray. My back is still sore this morning so that I doubt if I row today, and I shall get Lathrop to rub it.

I have received my invitation to the Saturday Evening Dancing Class and shall accept at once. No more now

Love to Muriel

F.D.R.

The Cowles family home was in Farmington, Conn.; Cousin Bammie had done it over in 1900, and lived there part of the year. The rest of the time was spent in their house at 1733 N Street in Washington, where Captain Cowles' duties required him to be. It may be noted that, after McKinley's assassination, Theodore Roosevelt stayed at the Washington home while waiting to move into the White House, and it was for a time called the "Little White House." On October 20th to 23rd of this year Yale University held its Bicentennial Celebration, which F.D.R. attended for the *Crimson*.

∽

"Quite primitive but nice . . ."

Dearest Mama,

I have been so busy with make-up work since I have been back from New Haven that I haven't had time for a line.

I will not go into the details about the New Haven trip, only it was well worth it & most impressive. I am going to the Penn game at Phila. on Nov. 9th with Teddy, and return to H.P. that night late with T.D.R. & Eugene Thayer & spend Sunday. This is *probable* Teddy may not come.

I am asking Mary Newbold to go to the Yale game if she is in Boston then, Nov. 23rd, and I think Lathrop & I may have a tea after it.

I may go to Groton next Sunday. Last Saturday I dined with Nancy & Sidney Lord in their little flat. Quite primitive but nice. On Sunday I worked & payed a call on Mrs. Beal & Elfrida Roosevelt.

I am rowing every day & am now sure of stroking the second Newell in the race on Nov. 13. It is very cold work & hardly pays in the autumn.

I am so anxious for you to get the Kuhn's house. You must arrange it.

Affec

FDR

Elfrida was the daughter of Mrs. Alfred Roosevelt.

∽⌒∽

"The Crimson election is in two weeks . . ."

[CAMBRIDGE]
NOV. 12, 1901,
TUESDAY.

Dearest Mummy,

We had the most exciting kind of a race yesterday and won by four feet. On Saturday it was so rough that we couldn't row and yesterday it poured and was so rough that we got half full of water. Just before we started one of our crew broke his oar and had to borrow an old one. The Weld crew got ahead at the start, but I quickened the stroke near Harvard bridge ½ way and we caught them. From there it was terribly rough and once I jumped my slide off the track and lost several strokes. Just before the finish we spurted and got several feet ahead but

Kerr Rainsford's oar suddenly snapped. We crossed the line just four feet ahead of the other boat.

I am too sorry to hear about Cousin John Weekes, it must have been very sudden. I suppose you will see the Pells off today, it is horrid weather for the ocean, cold & wet. Can Alice Draper come to us on the 19th? I won't ask Alexander Forbes till I hear from you as we must have an even number. I have not decided whether to continue rowing until the 17th or not. Recitations end today & my first exam is on Friday. The Crimson election is in two weeks & I am still working hard.

Affec.

F.D.R.

∽

"Please copy for me all the extracts
in our old Dutch Bible . . ."

[CAMBRIDGE]
NOV. 18, 1901,
MONDAY.

Dearest Mama,

We rowed last Friday & lost in an exciting race by a length, it was very cold & I am thankful to have it over with. On Saturday I dined at the Touraine with Aunt J. & Uncle Warren and we went to the theatre afterwards. They went to Southboro yesterday. I did not go to Groton as it w'd not have paid for so short a time. Instead I lunched with Jack Swift & in the p.m went out to Chestnut Hill to see Rebecca Newhall who was staying with the Wilsons. I am very busy with a thesis for History 10 on the "Roosevelts in New Amsterdam." I have been in the library constantly looking up old records, but nothing much is to be found. Do please copy for me all the extracts in our old Dutch Bible & send them to me. Also the old brown genealogy which you have, a pamphlet, & any other records you have. I will be very careful of them & bring them back on Dec. 6th. I must have them as soon as possible as my notes must be in in a week. I have ordered a beautiful frock coat, vest, & trousers for $70. Horrible   I am broke.

Ever

F.D.R.

The last crew race in which Harvard records list F.D.R. as participating was the Weld-Newell Fall Regatta on November 15th. He stroked the Second Newell, which finished fourth. The thesis mentioned in this letter can be seen today in the Hyde Park library.

~~~

"Lathrop made the last ten & is
running now, a physical wreck . . ."

<div align="right">CAMBRIDGE
NOV. 29, 1901,
FRIDAY.</div>

Dearest Mama—

I got back from Groton this a.m. having gone there Wednesday & had a very nice Thanksgiving. The Newbolds were there & have doubtless seen you since. On my return I found a note from Frances who is spending Sunday at the Vendome with Mrs. Hoe. I called there this p.m. but she was not in. Tomorrow I have promised to return to Groton for Sunday & to play hockey as the ice there is very good.

There is some doubt about my getting to Muriels tea   10 to 1 I *do* but I have a ghost of a show for the D.K.E. which begins Thursday. I will telegraph Thursday if there is anything doing, but you can expect me to arrive N.Y. 11 p.m Thursday.

Lathrop made the last ten & is running now, a physical wreck. Do not say a word of this to a soul.

My new clothes I have tried on & they are a dream! Will be ready by Wednesday. I have accepted the Met. dance on the 21st & not to Orange so I will try to get some fellows for Dec. 27th. Many thanks for the genealogy. It is hard work but I am still at it, & will be for several weeks

No more now

Ever affec son

<div align="right">F.D.R.</div>

D.K.E. fraternity, always referred to as the "Dickey," had
then a shadowy, complicated relationship with a larger group,
the Institute of 1770. The latter, Harvard's oldest club, com-
prised about one hundred members of the Sophomore class;
the first third of these members, in order of election, formed
the umbrageous Dickey, which controlled the affairs of the
whole Institute. Undergraduates were elected to the Dickey
in groups of ten, to the accompaniment of a variety of self-
abnegating initiation ordeals known as "running for Dickey."
A contemporary account states that this was the business of
"doing all manner of fantastic things about Harvard Square,
and even in Boston." Indeed, legend reveals that the imagina-
tion of the initiators must have been unlimited. No doubt it
all had medieval origins, or was even related to pagan rites,
for in many cases a worship of the earth featured the activity.
The more painful elements of the torture had by this time
been removed, following a deal of fuss raised by William
Lloyd Garrison in 1891, who complained in the public press
that his son had been made badly ill as the result of being
branded on the arm by a lighted cigarette. He threatened to
sue—but of course, no one knew who the Dickey really was.

~~~

"... but it was paid for by we
five new editors ..."

[? FAIRHAVEN]
DEC. 8, 1901,
SUNDAY.

Dearest Mama—

I have accepted Cousin Corinne's invitation to dinner & the
Dodworth dance afterwards on Dec. 26th. I thought it would
be a good chance to work in Algonac for a short visit also.
Thayer Lindsley is to come to me on the 28th or possibly the
evening of the 27th & stay until New Years day. I hope you
have asked Jack Minturn & that A. [Bertram] Randolph &
M.D.R. can come too. If Jack can't come how w'd it do to ask
Lyman, that is if it won't be too many. I am here for Sunday,

it's beastly weather & I haven't left the house. Very busy with thesis, stamps, photos, & odd jobs at the last minute. Thayer Lindsley is the son [of] a missionary or something or other in Japan. He is very popular & rowed on our Freshman crew last spring. I have refused Mrs. Dan. F. Appleton's dance on the 23rd as I know nothing about it. We had a Crimson dinner & theatre-party on Friday, great fun, speeches, songs etc. but it was paid for by we five new editors, about $30 apiece. No more now

    Love,

                                  F.D.R.

Mrs. Daniel F. Appleton was the former Susan Cowles of New York, and her husband the son of the publisher.

⌒⌒

"I went to the White House for tea . . ."

CAMBRIDGE
JAN. 6, 1902,
MONDAY.

Dearest Mama—

I got here all right this a.m. at 8, & have been unpacking most of the day. To go back—On Thursday evening the Groton dinner was a great success, good speeches by the Rector & some of the older graduates. On Friday Aunt Kassie, P.C. & M.D.R. & I took the train at 10.50 & had a very comfortable journey to Washington. I went straight to the Kean's, & from there, in obedience to Cousin Bammie's note to Mrs. Townsend's tea, which was interesting & filled with New Yorkers whom I knew. I dined at the Keans, (old Mrs.) & there were 40 there. Then to the dance, which was most glorious fun. The Washington people weren't in it with the New Yorkers & from start to finish it was glorious. I am sure M.D.R. had a good time. We left at 2 a.m. & I slept till 12 on Saturday. After lunch Mr. Kean took me over the new Congressional Library, & at 4 I went to the White House for tea & stayed till 6. All most interesting. We dined quietly, & at 10 went to

467

the Austrian ambassador's reception, where I saw many diplomats. On Sunday I went to Church with the old Keans, & afterwards went again to the White House. Lunched at Cousin Bammie's & left on the 4.50 train for here. On the whole it was one of the most interesting & enjoyable three days I have ever had. Found every thing all right here. Your 2 notes have come. It is time to go to bed.

Ever

F.D.R.

Please bring when you come the "dog" tobacco jar on my bureau. This is the first of many afterthoughts. Trunk is here all right.

The events recounted in this letter revolved around what was unquestionably the social occasion of the year, if not of the age: Alice Roosevelt's debut in the White House. An account in the *New York Times,* dated January 3rd, commences: "Miss Alice Roosevelt, the President's daughter, made her social début to-night at a ball given in her honor by her mother. The White House was filled with young people, and they enjoyed themselves after the manner of young people. The state apartments had been turned over to them, with no other injunction put upon them than that they would incur the great displeasure of the President if they did not make a jolly night of it. They appeared to heed this injunction, for no jollier company was ever assembled in Washington. . . ." Farther down the column, under the heading "Invited guests included," one finds the name of Franklin D. Roosevelt, sandwiched between Miss Pansy Roosevelt and Ogden M. Reid. Helen Roosevelt, together with Helen Cutting and Jean Reid (*q.v.*), as well as Lucy Kean, daughter of the John Keans with whom F.D.R. stayed, were among the feted debutantes in this Capital whirl. On January 4th: "Mrs. Roosevelt was at home this afternoon from 5 to 6, when a large number of visitors were received by invitation. The ladies of the Cabinet, Miss Roosevelt, and Mrs. Cowles assisted in receiving. . . ." Then back to Harvard.

~~

"I am about to be slaughtered,
but quite happy . . ."

CAMBRIDGE
JAN. 9, 1902,
THURSDAY.

Dearest Mama—

I am about to be slaughtered, but quite happy, nevertheless. I heard this a.m that I am the first man on the next ten of the Institute of 1770 & the Δ.K.E. I am to be taken out for the former in about ½ hour, & will finish this later.

8:30 p.m.

My back is a bit raw, but I am through the first ordeal O.K. Feeling fine. Tomorrow night I begin running. L.B. is running me & I hope he will take me to Groton for Sunday.

The Agony will last till Wednesday night next, but don't worry about me at all. I will telephone you Thursday morning if I can, or get word to you. I hope I can see you Thursday p.m. about 5 o'clock, as I have recitations before that.

I did not find Tom Beal's pipe when I unpacked. It was in an envelop, & I left it with the other things. Please bring it with you as it is important. Also please bring my DOG tobacco-jar. Also my riding-pants. Also some more of my cards.

I am sorry I can't see to anything about the house, but I shall be otherwise engaged—Will drop a line tomorrow if I have time.

Ever

FDR

Please pay enclosed, it is not worth a cheque.

Sara Delano Roosevelt, for the winter months of 1902, and again in 1903, took a house in Boston, where she had many friends. Hyde Park was probably a lonely, empty place, and she could be near her son. Hence there are no letters extant from these periods.

〜

"I am just back from the Class Dinner . . ."

Dearest Mama.

I got back after a comfortable journey at 8 a.m. and have been rowing this afternoon. I am just back from the Class Dinner, where I was on the Reception Committee. The information bureau at Albany was closed, but I will ask about my train here some day this week. I race next Monday, or Tuesday, so can leave positively on Friday.

No more now—Lots of love

F.D.R.

Let me here about Laura.

2 Holyoke Place was the address of the Alpha Delta Phi Club, to which he had been elected the previous winter. Alpha Delta Phi, founded in 1836, was usually called the "Fly Club," which name was officially given it in 1910.

∽

"On Saturday I interviewed about six Captains . . ."

Dearest Mama,

I have been meaning to write you every day for the last week but somehow every instant has been taken.

First, about the skipper. On Saturday I spent the morning at Lawley's Ship-Yard in South Boston, & interviewed about six Captains, all of them excellent, but all of them terribly high-priced, about $150 a month, and all have been accustomed to big yachts etc. I then telephoned to Crowninshield & Boardman, but they had nothing at the time, may later, also to Mr. H. S. Bigelow who referred me to his Captain. This morning I have heard of a promising man named Nicholson, who is to come out here tomorrow morning, and I hope he may do. If he does not suit & I hear of nothing else before tomorrow night I shall telegraph you to let Mr. Tams secure one, although I should prefer to get one myself.

To go back. A week ago I spent at Coz. Malcolm Forbes', at Milton & had a most delightful quiet Sunday. On Wednesday I dined with Coz. Mary Russell & went with them afterwards to a little play given by the "Sir Galahad Club" of poor boys.

On Thursday I went to the Hasty Pudding Play with some fellows and again on Friday with the Quincys' & dined there also. Saturday afternoon after rowing I went in to the Touraine & saw Muriel for ½ hour, she was on with the Poors, and I then took the 8 p.m train for Groton & am just back from there after a nice quiet Sunday. By the way, the 3 youngest John Lawrence children have scarlet fever, light cases, & are getting on well. Mrs. L. is quarantined with them and Hester has been shipped off to relations.

I shall send of[f] my big valise in a few days, but so far it has been so cold that I have been wearing heavy things.

Many thanks for the cheque, it is awfully good of you. I have given $25 of it to the library & we have got a complete set of St. Amand's works and also a Rousseau, both of which we needed. I am now on the library committee & it is very interesting.

I have written to Brooks to send my suit straight here.

Next Sunday I am to be with the Malcolm Forbes' again & go to a Glee Club dance in Milton the night before. The Sunday after I *may* come home.

We race probably the 15th & I shall do no more rowing this year. A lot of old oars have come out to try for the Annapolis crew, so I am relegated to the Junior crew, the same I was on last year, but this year it is much better than last.

No more now. Let me know how the place is etc. When does Helen sail etc.

Ever

F.D.R.

Written on Club stationery; the letterhead reveals a green leopard rampant, regardant, and throwing off a chain. The fate of the *Half-Moon II* was still in doubt; F.D.R. was trying at this time to get a captain for her, although his mother was still inclined to dispose of the boat. The Hasty Pudding Club (which today includes both the Institute of 1770 and the Dickey) was founded in 1795, coming by its name from the members' custom of eating hasty pudding at meetings, as relief from the usual bread-and-milk supper of students in those days. In the beginning it had a literary tone; the minutes were kept in verse (James Russell Lowell was one of the Pudding secretaries). By F.D.R.'s time the Pudding was a Junior organization; fried mush and maple syrup had replaced the hasty puddings; and the society's main effort was the production of an annual musical show. F.D.R. was on the library committee of the Harvard Union. On May 24th the First Weld beat the Naval Academy crew; the records do not show whether F.D.R. raced on the Junior crew in this regatta.

∞

"I like his face . . ."

CAMBRIDGE
MAY 12, 1902,
MONDAY.

Dearest Mama

I am just back from Milton where I went Saturday evening & was at the Musical Clubs dance that evening. Yesterday I played tennis most of the day.

I have actually taken a Captain as I wrote you, Chris *Michelson* is his name, pronounced like Nicholson. He is a Dane, has been on yachts & knows the coast. He has not been Captain of large vessels heretofore as he has only just taken out his master's license as a navigator. I like his face & his recommendations are good. Mr. Robert Saltonstall & Mr. Rantoul both recommend him; I telephoned to them.

Michelson will meet you between 12 and 1 on Wednesday at the Renaissance & he is to take orders from you.

I am sure that the Bacon offer is N.G. I have not heard from him, but know exactly what a cruising boat built in 1889 would be like: Slow, uncomfortable and not easy to handle. Besides this she would be even more difficult to dispose of than the Half-Moon, as otherwise she would not be offered in exchange. At any rate she is not worth $2,000

Later—

Yours of yesterday has just come. By *all means dispose of the Half-Moon to Mr. Tucker* if you can. Don't go below $5,500. I can easily charter a knockabout for the summer, & our hands will then be free. I don't believe in any exchange proceedings.

Employ Michelson's time somehow. He can begin work at once. Had he not better be under the immediate orders of Tams & Lemoine? It will save you trouble and I cannot boss him from here very much. I prefer T.&L. to Cary Smith & Barbey. It is a young firm all through, whereas C. Smith himself is a back number and Harry Barbey a well meaning but stupid aristocrat. One thing must be made clear to T&L: The outfitting must include only absolutely necessary things —nothing like frills to be allowed.

I may get home for Sunday. I race on Wednesday but have a sore back from having fallen down stairs, & may not row. Will telegraph.

If Tucker is Allanson Tucker of Phila. he will pay our price, but insist on *immediate action*.

Love to Helen & bon voyage.

Ever lovingly

F.D.R.

Vile pen.

Robert Saltonstall and his brother-in-law, Neal Rantoul, were both boating enthusiasts; the former was a cousin of the Rector, and a first cousin once removed of Senator Leverett Saltonstall. The Emperor of Germany apparently did not share F.D.R.'s opinions regarding the firm of Cary Smith & Barbey, having given them the commission to design and

473

superintend the building of his yacht *Meteor III*, launched the previous February and christened by Alice Roosevelt. Alanson Tucker *was* from Philadelphia; he did *not* purchase the *Half-Moon II*.

◇◇

"I talk with a lithp and look like a thight . . ."

ALPHA DELTA PHI CLUB
MAY 19, 1902,
MONDAY.

Dearest Mama

I got back safely after a most comfortable night, and went to recitations. After lunch I went to the dentist, and am now minus my front tooth. He cut it off very neatly and painlessly, took impressions of the root and space, and is having the porcelain tip baked. I hope to have it put on next Friday, and in the meantime I shall avoid all society, as I talk with a lithp and look like a thight.

Please don't forget about the stanchions etc for Michelsen. No more now

Affec.

F.D.R.

◇◇

"I may *become a confirmed batchelor . . ."*

WESTMORLY COURT, SOUTH
MAY 27, 1902,
TUESDAY.

Dearest Mama,

My tooth is no longer a dream, it is an accomplished fact. It was put in on Friday and is perfect in form, color, lustre, texture, etc. I feel like a new person and have already been proposed to by three girls. My best friends don't recognize me and say "Who *is* that handsome fellow?"

I rode Saturday a.m. with Mr. Andrew, saw Harvard defeat Yale in the afternoon in the track games and went to Groton in the evening.

Sunday was hot and I spent the afternoon wheeling Marjorie & Dorothy Peabody down to the John Lawrences in a baby carriage, accompanied by Mrs. P., Betsey, Rose, Helen and Hester. It gave me excellent practice, but I *may* become a confirmed batchelor.

I got back here Monday early and am working like a pup for the make-up exam in Economics on Thursday. However I shall go to Groton for the St. Marks game tomorrow afternoon

Aunt Tilly is here and I dine with her Friday. Sunday I go to Beverly.

Ever affectionately

F.D.R.

Abram Piatt Andrew was an assistant professor in the Economics Department with whom F.D.R. took courses his Sophomore and Senior years. Andrew taught what was then a fairly unusual subject. He was a handsome, brilliant man, later left Harvard to go into politics, and was for a number of years congressman from Essex County in Massachusetts, and also Assistant Secretary of the Treasury under Taft.

〰

"Do not tell Michelsen I may visit him . . ."

BEVERLY [MASS.]
JUNE 1, 1902,
SUNDAY.

Dearest Mama.

On Wednesday I went to Groton & saw us win a wonderful game over St. Marks by the score of 5 to 3. I spent the night there and took part in the celebration which was marred only by the accident to poor Fulton Cutting who had the ends of two fingers blown off by a dynamite cracker.

I had my make-up Economics exam on Thursday afternoon, & think I passed it. On Friday I worked all day at Groton & had a History 24 Exam yesterday, coming down here right after

it. I have been to Church today & leave Tuesday a.m. I may
go to N. Y. by the Tuesday midnight, see the Half Moon
Wednesday a.m, & come to Hyde Park Wed. at 1 o'clock, if
not an earlier train. I should leave for Cambridge again
Thursday night as I have an exam on Saturday. I will telegraph if I do this. The weather is perfect. Do not tell Michelsen I may visit him. You can catch me by a line to the Renaissance where I shall go on my arrival Wednesday morning.

Lots of love

F.D.R.

The summer following his Sophomore year was spent at Hyde
Park and Campobello.

∽

*"There have been more newspapers
articles about me . . ."*

Dearest Mama,

I have not written you for over a week, but it is not because
I have not thought of you constantly. To go back—On Tuesday, a week ago, I went to see the Half-Moon and made the
best arrangement possible with the man at the dock, of which
I suppose the Capt. has written you. If you want the sails
etc insured, write the Capt. & he will attend to it. I advise
$500 insurance, & this will cover about everything stored in
the locker, which is not in a fire proof building. It sh'd cost
not more than $10.

On the next few days I worked like a dog on the Crimson,
& was elected Ass't Managing editor on Monday, along with
W. R. Bowie. I am delighted to get it, and now run the paper
every Monday & Thursday nights. On Saturday I went to
Beverly to the Beals, played golf that day, & on Sunday went
to the Sohier's camp on a neighboring lake for the day, re-

476

turning here Monday a.m. A ten of the D.K.E. was taken out last Thursday, so I have been amused.

Today Alice Sohier left for Europe & I saw her off on the "Commonwealth."

Now (11 p.m) I am just back from a Dinner of the Mass. Republican Club, of 1,000 people, at which Sec. Shaw of the Treasury and Senator Lodge made most interesting addresses. Mr. Beal gave me the ticket & it was a chance of a lifetime.

Lyman seems to be doing well, and he is rowing & trying for the Crimson. I have just decided to return to Aunt Annie's anniversary, & Lyman returns also probably. I leave here Wednesday night the 15th & get to Algonac Thursday a.m. & stay at H.P. till Sunday, & L. with me if he can get off. I have given your note to Howard [Cary], & he will let you know. Teddy may come too. I am not yet unpacked & don't know when I will be. I have bought a few books which I will bring home. The weather has been bad until yesterday.—

Leslie Ames is also trying for the Crimson—

I haven't had an instant to think of driving lessons, singing lessons, or teeth filling, but I *may* have more time next week. The Club library has kept me two whole days, and I am on the Committee on Receptions to Freshmen, & must give an entertainment for 10 in my room next week. My new job on the Crimson will get me into a great many things & there have been more newspapers articles about me which make me excessively 'tired.'

Next Sunday I must be here for a Club function.

I will write again in a few days to let you know definitely about coming back.

No more news. Lots of love. How about our whole party going to the Harvard versus West Point football game on Sat. the 18th?

Do the girls come Friday?

Lovingly

F.D.R.

Ascension unto power on the *Crimson* went something like this: Candidates began to heel the paper as soon as they entered college; starting after the Freshman mid-year, and continuing into Sophomore year, candidates were elected by the Board of Editors; at the beginning of Junior year two of the successful competitors were elected Assistant Managing Editors, and at Junior mid-year one of these was named Managing Editor for the rest of that year, becoming the head man on the *Crimson* from his class; at the beginning of Senior year the Managing Editor became President of the paper, and the remaining Assistant Managing Editor replaced him; then, for the second half of Senior year, a similar shifting of positions took place, with the President retiring into a supervisory position. F.D.R. and Russell Bowie held these last-described positions from the class of 1904 (the latter afterward went into the ministry, was for sixteen years pastor of Grace Church in New York, and since 1939 professor of Practical Theology at the Union Theological Seminary). Alice Sohier was considerable of a Boston belle at that period. Lest there be confusion as to how she traveled to Europe, it should be noted that the *Commonwealth* was a ship of the now-defunct Fall River Line running between Boston and New York— hence only the first stage of her transatlantic crossing. Those from whom F.D.R. (who seems to have been quite attentive to Republican doings at this epoch) heard talks included Leslie Mortimer Shaw, a former governor of Iowa whom Theodore Roosevelt had appointed to the Treasury in 1902; and Woodrow Wilson's notable opponent, Henry Cabot Lodge, then in his second term as senator from Massachusetts. As for the "newspapers articles," these were in Boston papers, which took at intervals a chitty-chatty interest in the doings of any Harvard undergraduates who had newsworthy relations. F.D.R.'s *Crimson* election was picked up locally because of the connection with Theodore Roosevelt, most of the papers being under the impression it was closer than it was. One of the articles began: "Franklin D. Roosevelt, President's cousin, elected secretary of *Crimson*"; another, later in his Junior year, headlined: "Franklin D. Roosevelt, nephew of President

Roosevelt, heads movement 'Harvard Fund for Boer Relief.'"
What must have been particularly annoying was the tone of
the articles, which were full of rather snobbish references to
his prominence, wealth, and democratic-ness—none of which
must have helped his relations with his classmates.

∾

*"The house-party was great & we
all had a glorious time . . ."*

CAMBRIDGE
OCT. 21, 1902,
TUESDAY.

Dearest Mama,
We got back all right yesterday a.m. though ½ hour late.
Howard had a fairly hard day, but so far he is all right. I am
packing the valise etc. and send it tomorrow. It is a vile windy
day, and this p.m. I go on a booking excursion in town.

Next Saturday I go to Dedham to ride with the Quincy's so
wont come home, and Sunday I may have to run the paper.
There is no news—The house-party was great & we all had
a glorious time.

Ever

F.D.R.

Although one might not guess so from this letter, F.D.R. had
a good full class schedule his third Harvard year, one which
pointed up clearly where his main interests now lay:

(1) *English 18.* The Forms of Public Address, under the
direction of George Pierce Baker. Met Mondays,
Wednesdays, and Fridays at noon.

(2) *English 34.* A half-year course on the English Letter
Writers, with Charles Townsend Copeland. Mondays
at 11.

(3) *History 13.* The Constitutional and Political History of
the United States, 1783-1865. Meeting Tuesdays, Thursdays, and Saturdays at 12, under the direction of Professor Edward Channing (a noted teacher, author of

the monumental, unfinished *History of the United States*). This was a half-year course, and preparatory to:

(4) *Government 4.* Second half-year course on the Elements of International Law, with Mr. Albin L. Richards; Mondays, Wednesdays, and Fridays at 1:30.

(5) *Government 16-A.* First half-year, on the Administration of the Government of the United States; classes on Tuesdays, Thursdays, and Saturdays at 9. This course was given under the direction of Charles Sumner Hamlin, who had been Assistant Secretary of the Treasury during Cleveland's second administration, and later served in the same capacity under Woodrow Wilson. Hamlin was an exemplary public servant, a member of many government boards and commissions. At the end of F.D.R.'s first presidential term he was appointed special counsel to the Board of Governors of the Federal Reserve System.

(6) *Government 16-B.* The second half-year, a course in Tendencies of American Legislation, again meeting Tuesdays, Thursdays, and Saturdays at 9. Director of the program was Frederic Jesup Stimson, a distinguished lawyer, later first American ambassador to the Argentine, and the author not only of authoritative law-books but, under the pseudonym "J.S. of Dale," of a number of adventure tales including *The Crime of Henry Vane.*

(7) *Philosophy 1-A.* General Introduction to Philosophy, meeting Mondays, Wednesdays, and Fridays at 2:30. F.D.R. took the first half-year of this course, Logic, under Josiah Royce, but missed the second half-year, which was Münsterberg's famous class in Psychology.

(8) *Fine Arts 4.* The Fine Arts of the Middle Ages and the Renaissance, with Professor Charles H. Moore; Mondays, Wednesdays, and Fridays at 9.

～～

480

F.D.R. and Helen Roosevelt on the Hyde Park lawn.

Friday
Dec. 4th
'03.

Dearest Mama —
I have been absolutely rushed to death since I came back, with a thousand things to attend to & meetings of the nomination committee (for Senior Class elections) lasting up to 2 in the morning. I am to be nominated anyway for an

office & am naturally delighted — You will be as surprised as I was when you hear what office — But I don't stand a ghost of a show of being elected to it though I am pleased at the honor of nomination. Dearest Mama — I know what pain I must have caused you and you know I wouldn't do it if I really could have helped it — Mais tu sais, me

"You will be as surprised as I was when you hear what office — But I don't stand a ghost of a show of being elected . . ."

voilà! That's all that could be said — I know my mind, have known it for a long time and know that I could never think otherwise: Result: I am the happiest man just now in the world: Likewise the luckiest — And for you, dear Mummy, you know that nothing can ever change what we have always been & always will be to eachother — only now you have two children

to love & to love you — And Eleanor as you know will always be a daughter to you in every true way

I shall be here over Sunday working all the time but will write you a longer letter then —

Excuse this hurried scrawl, it doesn't express anything but you know what I mean

Your ever loving

F.D.R.

know my mind, have
own it for a long time.
Result: I am the hap-
est man in the world;
ewise the luckiest—"

THE HARVARD CRIMSON, SENIOR BOARD

W. DRINKWATER   H. OTIS   W. E. SACHS   A. V. DE ROODE   A. A. BALLANTINE   R. T. HOLT   E. B. KRUMBHAAR
C. W. BLOSSOM   W. R. BOWIE   F. D. ROOSEVELT   P. DANA   H. DE H. HUGHES

His work on the Crimson may well have been the most important element of his college career.

THE HARVARD CRIMSON

W. C. CLARK '03, PRESIDENT
A. F. NAZRO '03, MANAGING EDITOR

C. H. DERBY '03, BUSINESS MANAGER
W. FIELD '03, SECRETARY

CAMBRIDGE,   Sunday,   Nov. 2

Dearest Mama_

          I am trying my hand at this machine
as the copy is all in , and the proof sheets re
not done yet. I am just back this evening from Salem,
where I went last night after the game to stay with
Harold Peabody.We studied all morning, and took a
long drive after lunch.
          LastWednesday I came down with a kind of grippe
and was quiet for three days; I wasachy in my bones,
but had very little cold and it passed off very
qickly. Yesterday the Carlisle Indian game was most
exciting and we won with great ease , 23 to o.
The CROWN/PRINCE of SIAM was at the game , and came
to the FLY after it for some"   " afternoon-tea,"

i. e., a little champagne!
                         We are in the midst of the
hour-examinations now , and they will last off and on
for a couple of weeks. I may get home for SUnday
the I6 th,possibly,if I can get off from this job
that day. Next saturday I have to run the extra
edition on the occasion of the Pennsylvania game,and sh
shall consequently see only the second halfof it.
     The valise is'nt off yet! but I intend to send
it tomorrow surely, with the Stevenson and the coat
and waistcoat of the old gray suit. As I wrote you,
the trousers must be at home , asthey are not here
and nobody would have stolen them.
               No more now, I hear the printers
callings- it is an early paper, for it is only just
midnight and I should get away by I o'clock.
               Loads of love-

                    Ever affectionately,

                         F. D. R.

To his mother from Cambridge, "I am trying this new machine. . . ."

CLASS DAY OFFICERS

L. Grilk   R. Sanger   H. G. Dillingham   A. D. Ficke   C. H. Robinson   F. D. Roosevelt   R. S. Wallace   A. Goodhue
R. Foster   W. K. Bowie   C. B. Marshall   J. A. Burgess   E. C. Rust   E. B. Krumbhaar   J. Daniels   S. A. Welldon
A. A. Ballantine   P. Dana   J. H. Densmore

F.D.R. was elected chairman of the Class Committee in the winter of his senior year.

Twenty-two years old, Franklin D. Roosevelt, Harvard '04.

F.D.R.'s bride wore "a white satin princess robe . . . with a court train. Her point-lace veil was caught with orange blossoms and a diamond crescent. Her pearl collar was the gift of the bridegroom's mother."

"The President's tendency to make the executive power stronger than the Houses of Congress is bound to be a bad thing . . ."

[CAMBRIDGE]
OCT. 26, 1902,
SUNDAY.

Dearest Mama—

I am packing the valise today with the books and my old gray suit, and will ship it tomorrow.

Yesterday I went out to Dedham just before lunch, rode for two hours in the afternoon on a horse which is the counterpart of Bobby and returned here at 10 p.m. after dinner. I intended to go to Groton today, but have so much work that I couldn't get off. It has been very chilly for the past week and the buildings have been cold through lack of fuel, but now that the strike is settled the coal has begun to come in small quantities. In spite of his success in settling the trouble, I think that the President make a serious mistake in interfering—politically, at least. His tendency to make the executive power stronger than the Houses of Congress is bound to be a bad thing, especially when a man of weaker personality succeeds him in office. Howard Cary stood his running very well, and feels perfectly well. He has gone home for Sunday. I have to run the Crimson every Sunday in November, so fear I can't get home or see you until Thanksgiving.

Ever with love

F.D.R.

In May of 1902 the anthracite miners, after eighteen months of discussion, finally agreed at a convention in Hazleton, Pennsylvania, to go out on strike. They were led by union president John Mitchell, who tried—unsuccessfully—to get the bituminous miners to join his group. Union demands were a twenty-per-cent wage increase, an eight-hour day for men paid by the day, and that 2240 lbs. (not 2750) should constitute a ton. The strike dragged on through the summer, with neither side giving an inch, and seemed destined to continue deadlocked. In October Theodore Roosevelt asked the mine operators to join with Mitchell and come to Washington for discussions; they rejected this offer forthwith. On the eleventh of the month, Secretary of War Elihu Root paid a visit to J. Pierpont Morgan aboard the latter's yacht in the North River; two days later Morgan forwarded the President a statement by the operators agreeing to arbitrate, whereupon T. R. appointed a commission and on October 17th, when the miners accepted this, the strike ended. The importance of Theodore Roosevelt's action was that it marked the first active intervention of Government in Labor-Management disputes in any way resembling the modern sense; in this respect, and in the light of later history, F.D.R.'s remonstrance becomes provocative.

〜

"No more now, I hear the print-ers calling . . ."

THE HARVARD CRIMSON

W.C.Clark '03, President C.H.Derby '03, Business Manager
A.F.Nazro '03, Managing Editor W. Field '05, Secretary

CAMBRIDGE
NOV. 2, 1902,
SUNDAY.

Dearest Mama—

 I am trying my hand at this machine as the copy is all in, and the proof sheets are not done yet. I am just back this evening from Salem, where I went last night after the game to stay with Harold Peabody. We studied all morning, and took a long drive after lunch.

 Last Wednesday I came down with a kind of grippe and was quiet for three days; I wasachy in my bones, but had very little cold and it passed off very qickly. Yesterday the Carlisle

482

Indian game was most exciting and we won with great ease, 23 to o. The CROWN/PRINCE of SIAM was at the game, and came to the FLY after it for some "afternoon-tea," i.e., a little champagne!

We are in the midst of the hour-examinations now, and they will last off and on for a couple of weeks. I *may* get home for SUnday the *16*th, possibly, if I can get off from this job that day. Next saturday I have to run the extra edition on the occasion of the Pennsylvania game, and shall consequently see only the second halfof it.

The valise is'nt off yet! but I intend to send it tomorrow surely, with the Stevenson and the coat and waistcoat of the old gray suit. As I wrote you, the trousers must be at home, asthey are not here and nobody would have stolen them.

No more now, I hear the printers callings—it is an early paper, for it is only just midnight and I should get away by I o'clock.

Loads of love—
Ever affectionately,

F.D.R.

This letter was written on *Crimson* office stationery with a typewriter, and is filled with the usual errors of an untried hand. The *New York Times* for November 2nd carried a story on the visit of Crown Prince Chakrabongse and suite to Harvard; they were entertained by President Eliot at the Union, saw the football game, following which "tea was served at the Alpha Delta Phi Club." F.D.R., when he wrote this letter, was "putting the paper to bed." Russell Bowie recalls, in this connection, that the *Crimson* was printed by two Scotsmen named Mac and Ed, journeymen printers who had a small plant in the Union building to the rear of the paper's offices. They called themselves the Crimson Printing Company; and as they had other work besides the newspaper, they were very insistent upon getting it on the presses at a set time. F.D.R. however, Bowie remembers, could always jolly the old Scots into opening up the forms whenever a last-minute news break occurred.

*". . . in consequence am feeling
very sleepy . . ."*

[no salutation]

Got back safely, although the train was over an hour late. I cannot tell you how much I enjoyed the three days, and I am anxiously awaiting the Fairhaven trip. Owen W. did not return with us and probably will not until after the game. I am running the paper tonight and in consequence am feeling very sleepy. Teddy Kendall, a clubmate is to be married tomorrow in Boston, so there will be a jamboree. How are the horses!!! Also the wheel—!

Ever

F.D.R.

A penny-postal sent to his mother at Hyde Park. "Owen W." was Owen Winston, a classmate, and one of F.D.R.'s ushers; he later became vice-president of the New York store which guides undergraduate presentability through life: Brooks Brothers.

∽

*"Today I have browsed in whale
books . . ."*

Dearest Ma—

I came down here yesterday at 10 with Howard and found everything fine except the weather. It snowed and blew all yesterday, last night and this morning, and we have been in the house the whole time except for a short walk this p.m.

when I went to see the Church cousins. We go back at 6 a.m. tomorrow and tomorrow night I shall be taken into the Signet. Today I have "browsed" in whale books etc, and done a little studying. The food has been wonderful, and we have been too full to move.

On Friday night I went to the Warren's dance in the new ballroom at the Somerset. It was an enormous affair, great fun, and I didn't get back to Cambridge till 6 a.m. As I had a 9 o'clock and had to pack to come down here I did not go to bed at all or close my eyes, but slept 10 hours last night.

I have heard the provisional dates of my midyears, and get 12 days off in the middle, from Jan. 24 to Feb. 5th!

With lots of love

F.D.R.

The Signet had been founded in 1870 as a protest against the abandonment of literary traditions by the Hasty Pudding. At this time it occupied the former A.D. clubhouse on Mt. Auburn Street, engaging the attendance of such faculty luminaries as Kittredge, Neilson, and others. A certain proportion of the members were drawn from the undergraduate publications; every effort was made to maintain an atmosphere of "literature at ease"; and the initiations were a particular feature of its activity, being framed with elaborate literary humor, pseudo-punditry, and participated in by faculty members. The club's motto was from Plato, suggested by George Herbert Palmer: "Work and ply the Muses." From the large gaps in the correspondence here and hereafter, it can be presumed that Mrs. James Roosevelt did not keep (or later mislaid) a good many of the Harvard letters. She again spent the winter in Boston, which accounts for part of the gap; F.D.R., of course, was much freer than ever before to go home for weekends, and during examination periods, which accounts for other lacunae.

◇◇◇

*". . . breakfasted at the Touraine
with Ogden Mills . . ."*

THE HARVARD CRIMSON

A.F.Nazro '03, President   C.H.Derby '03, Business
                                                              Manager
F.D.Roosevelt '04, Managing Editor   A.C.Travis '05, Secretary

CAMBRIDGE
APRIL 27, 1903,
MONDAY.

[no salutation]

I got here this morning after a very comfortable journey on,
and breakfasted at the Touraine with Ogden Mills. After my
recitation at 9 I found immense quantities of work to do in the
office which took till 3.30. I then took my coat to the tailor's
and went to Bartlett's to see about some Club books, with the
sad result that I invested in a few volumes myself. They are to
be sent home and you can open them. The Smollett is a very
nice old edition, as are the Junius letters and the Dryden's
Virgil.

I have been thinking over the month's trip abroad, and as I
can't come to any decision myself, I really want you to tell
what you would want me to do. I have told you what I feel
about it: that it would in all probability be good for me, and
a delightful experience; but that I don't want to be away from
you for four weeks in the summer; also that I don't want to go
unless you could make up your mind not to care at all. I feel
that really it would be a very thoroughly selfish proceeding
on my part.

Next Sunday I may go to Gloucester to stay with Mr. Andrew,
one of the professors. If I don't go there it will be Groton. The
Thesis will keep me at work all day tomorrow, except the
hour's agony with Hopkins. I tried to get Sally some book, but
saw nothing suitable. Hope to have better luck tomorrow. Will

be through with the paper by 1 a.m. Hope to unpack within a week or so

    Ever affectionate son

                                                F.D.R.

Ogden Mills (actually in the class of 1905, although he took his B.A. in three years and graduated in 1904, entering the Harvard Law School) became Secretary of the Treasury in the last year of the Hoover administration; he was one of the most emphatic opponents of the New Deal. Bartlett's began as a drugstore, afterward becoming a sort of general students' supply store. Hopkins was another dentist; Sally, presumably, Sara Delano (Redmond), his first cousin, then nine years old.

∽

"We had a wonderful rest by the sad sea waves . . ."

<h2 style="text-align:center">THE HARVARD CRIMSON</h2>

A.F.Nazro '03, President	C.H.Derby '03, Business Manager
F.D.Roosevelt '04, Managing Editor	A.C.Travis '05, Secretary

CAMBRIDGE
MAY 6, 1903,
WEDNESDAY.

Dearest Mama—

    Just a scrap to say that I am alive & well. I had a most delightful all night dance last Friday, a subscription affair & went to Gloucester Saturday to Monday to stay with Dr Andrew, Professor of Political Economy. T. Beal & Leverett Bradley also there & we had a wonderful rest by the sad sea waves. I was elected to the Memorial Society last Monday on the first ten—it is a good thing to make. C. E. Norton is head of it. Last night I became head librarian of the Fly for ensuing year. This between ourselves. I have been working like several canines. I sent home my best purchase yet—the best possible set of Morte

487

d'Arthur & very hard to get. I have had an order for it for over a year. Be careful of it & open it nicely! Rode with Eleo Sears Monday & have been getting out six-page papers & standing on my head generally.

It was *horrible* about Uncle W. & Aunt J. Also about the Steen Valetje stable! Also about Aunt Doe. Also about my going abroad (I have applied for room). Also about its being 2 a.m. Will write by Friday sure

Ever lovingly

F.D.R.

Leverett Bradley was both a Groton and Harvard classmate of F.D.R.; he later taught at Francis Riggs's Indian Mountain School. In 1895 the Memorial Society was founded "to perpetuate a knowledge of the history of the University, and to commemorate the great men who have been students or teachers here." The Society raised money, which went toward the purchase of historical books, the giving of lecture courses about Harvard, preservation of the University grounds, and the like. The then head of the Memorial Society was Professor Emeritus (History of Art) Charles Eliot Norton, translator of Dante, co-founder of *The Nation,* intimate of literary great and host to Kipling—(Norton's daughter, Sara, is credited with having rescued from Kipling's scrap-basket, and caused to have published, the poet's *Recessional*). Eleanora ("Eleo") Sears was a cousin of Julian and Archibald Cary Coolidge, and of Mary Newbold, (*q.v.*). She was also a half-niece of Richard Sears, national tennis singles champion from 1881 to 1887, and a most formidable sportswoman in her own right. It may even be said that she was the emancipator of "the weaker sex" in the field of sports, relegating that invidious phrase to limbo. Her well-fortified position as a Boston Brahmin gave her license to defy the conventions—she was the first woman to ride astride, the first to play squash racquets . . . she drove a car, she flew an airplane, she was four times U. S. doubles champion in tennis, and she once walked forty-seven miles from Providence to Beacon Street in nine hours and fifty-three minutes to win a bet. On walks of this order she frequently used Harvard undergraduates as pacemakers, but they very rarely were with her at the end. For a full generation she was the spectacular epitome of the American sportswoman. The "horrible" events were mainly a fire at Uncle Warren Delano's Steen Valetje stables, in which a number of fine horses were lost.

⌇⌇

"Dont worry about me—I always
land on my feet . . ."

S.S. "CELTIC"
JULY 24, 1903,
FRIDAY.

Dearest Mummy

The boat is just out in the stream & I am only just beginning to realize that I am actually off for t'other side o' the Duck Pond.

5.45.

I have just stood on the after deck & saw the Priscilla move out just behind us with you on board I trust. I saw a figure in front of the pilot house that I fancied was you as it waved. I am so glad Moo is with you & will be a week at Campo. You will all have a nice visit at Fairhaven.

I have opened one basket of fruit, the only one which has appeared yet—Aunt Kassie's & it is delicious. Tell Aunt Annie her's will be even more enjoyed when we get several days out. And *your* basket I am going to eat *all alone* & give none of it to C.B.B!

The purser says he must have all letters at 6 p.m. so I must hurry. He expects an absolutely smooth voyage as the Oceanic which is just in had a rough one & it is never rough two weeks running at this time of year.

I shall unpack after we leave Sandy Hook, but I want to see the last of land. I will write a long steamer letter & send a cable from Queenstown—but you may not get it till Monday as the office might be shut.

Goodbye dear Mummy I am longing for Aug. 25. Dont

489

worry about me—I always land on my feet—but wish so much
you were with me.

Ever your devoted

F.D.R.

He was off aboard the twenty-one-thousand-ton White Star
Liner *Celtic* on the previously debated European vacation.
The *Priscilla* was another Fall River Line boat, bearing his
mother and Muriel Delano Robbins ("Moo") in the direction
of Campobello. His traveling companion on the trip was a
classmate, Charles B. Bradley, an usher at F.D.R.'s wedding
and in later life general counsel for the Prudential Life Insurance Company.

∽

"There will be some oil in the
vinegar anyway! . . ."

WHITE STAR LINE
JULY 24, 1903,
FRIDAY.

[no salutation]

The boat is nearing Sandy Hook & this is a last line. Delightful breeze, cool, & smooth sea. A Groton boy, John Symonds
[Simons], is on board & I am told also Mr. [Arthur] Woods
(I haven't yet seen him) so there will be *some* oil in the vinegar
anyway!

Loads of love   Hope Half Moon has come.

F.D.R.

A picture-postcard to his mother at Campobello.

∽

"Saturday—up at 9:15—delightful
bath—enormous breakfast . . ."

S.S. "CELTIC"
JULY 24, 1903,
FRIDAY.

Dearest Mummy

It was so nice seeing the "Priscilla" go out just astern of us,
but I *almost* wished I was on the familiar old Sound route

490

instead of passing out through the Narrows. We dropped the pilot all right about 7 o'clock and I am just through dinner—at the second table on the port side & I am just able to hold the pen now owing to great internal pressure. It is very smooth and a most perfect evening, with Fire Island light in the distance. Will add to this occasionally

Saturday—

Up at 9.15—delightful bath—enormous breakfast—then straightened out a few belongings and before I knew it lunchtime and another gorge took place. Now about sundry others on board—The Pitnays—C.B.B.'s uncle and aunt are very nice; also they have a small son aged about 10. But the best acquisition to the human menagerie is Mr. Woods and John Symonds—who is in Warren's form at School and a very good lad. Also at our table is Arthur Gordon, of Savannah, the brother of Mrs. Wayne Parker, and he appears very nice.

We ran today 249 and are taking a very Southerly course. I long for a possible pen—these in the library curl up and die if you press on them at all.

Sunday—

Up in time for the last of breakfast and went to the service with the Pitnays, Mr. Woods & Mr. Gordon, contributing 50 cents to the plate thus securing a safe passage across. There is a very slight sea but this leviathon "passes no remarks"—merely plugs along at 17 knots day in & day out, and you wouldn't suspect the existence within a hundred miles of machinery worth ten or fifteen thousand horse-power. Run 401 miles—very fair—Usual routine of gormandising. C.B.B. doesn't feel quite up to the mark.

Monday—

Exciting games of shuffleboard, quoits & push-golf today with Messrs. Woods, Gordon & Symonds. Run 391. Same slight sea and S.W. wind. I find Gordon most interesting—he was at Yale in '93 and knows many of my friends.

491

Tuesday—

C.B.B. feels quite ill & thinks it indigestion. He hasn't moved from his chair & will see the Dr. if not better tonight. Same weather & water conditions & the boat absolutely steady. Run 395. It is a bit hazy now & looks like fog. We are far south —just beginning to turn northward—and only 400 odd miles from the Azores.

Wednesday.

Last night C.B.B. felt so badly that he got the Dr. & found temperature of 103. We were rather alarmed but Dr. says it is a mild attack of malaria and will wear off in a few days. Funny place to get such a disease. He is in bed of course and feels wretchedly.

It became foggy early this morning but has lifted occasionally during the day, so we have not been bothered much by the whistle. Run 402.

Thursday—

Today I have spent most of the time in interesting talks with Arthur Gordon—on negro, political, educational & other topics.

Charley feels a good deal better and brighter and he has almost no fever but stays in bed. It is too bad as he is missing a good trip. The sea looks fairly rough, but it takes close watching to see our bow or stern lift and dip what looks to be about six inches on the horizon. It is still very foggy though not especially wet and it has not prevented exciting games on deck. Run 392.

Friday—

Charley did not feel so well this a.m. but I think it is merely because he is tired of being all the time in a narrow berth as he feels fitter this p.m. and the Doctor says he ought to be up tomorrow. He may go straight to London with me as he couldn't go to Scotland on Sunday owing to lack of trains and doesn't want to run the risk of not being well there. We expect to get to Queenstown tomorrow morning about 8 o'clock—too

492

late to get to Liverpool that night—so we ought to land early Sunday morning and get to London in time for lunch. It has cleared up today and the run was 400. The "Celtic" has made a remarkable record for evenness of speed—all the runs have been between 391 and 402—and we have—or had—301 miles from noon today to Queenstown.

By the way, the Carnegies on board are the A.C. 2nd's, he being a *nephew* of the real article and cheap enough, I gather.

I have accomplished a good deal on the trip—have done a lot of work on my editorials—reading over last years with the comments on them—, have read 2/3 of "John Percyfield," when it was stolen out of my deck chair in broad daylight, much to my disgust as I liked it and thought it clever. The fruit—yours, Aunt Kassie's & Aunt Annie's—has been a constant source of delight, and has been the means of saving the inner man. Our plans are still quite at sea—no joke intended —and we shan't decide between Normandy, the Italian Lakes, Interlaken and the Tyrol until we get to London.

I am thinking of you as just getting settled at Campo & am so anxious to hear about the house—also about the "Half Moon". I have a horrid feeling that something has gone wrong with her just because I am not there to save you the worry of it all. Give my love to the Pells—et écrivez les nouvelles— I am so glad Moo is with you, she is so dear, I am only too sorry to miss her visit. Hope Uncle Fred has gone up on the yacht. Also that Aunt Tilly will go to you. You wont hear from me again till via the *Wednesday* steamer which is the Teutonic or Majestic I think.

With lots & lots of love your devoted Globe Trotter—
Have you finished the Lightning Conductor?
Also I have read 150 pages of Notre Dame de Paris.
This must go to the mail bag tonight. 11 p.m

F.D.R.

Seaboard reading, which he thought clever, was the just-published *John Percyfield, the Anatomy of Cheerfulness,* by

493

Charles Hanford Henderson. Also receiving some reflection were his *Crimson* editorial duties, which would begin the forthcoming Harvard year when he took over as president.

∞

*"Those infernal Bank Holidays—
the invention of the devil . . ."*

BURLINGTON HOTEL, W.
AUG. 3, 1903,
MONDAY.

Dearest Maama,

I cannot tell you how happy it made me to get your letter from the Fall River Boat. It seemed so strange to get news from home at Queenstown! We got to that place at 9 Saturday morning, and just as we were leaving we saw the King come into the harbor on the "Victoria and Albert," accompanied by four battleships. It was great luck but unfortunately we were at least a mile away. We got to Liverpool at 10 p.m. Saturday, too late to land so we had a quiet night in the harbor. We landed at at [*sic*] 9 o'clock yesterday, Sunday, & I came straight up to London with Arthur Gordon arriving at 2. Charley, who felt of course much weakened after the malaria went to Scotland by the Doctor's advice, spending last night in Liverpool or Chester, I don't know which. He will not come to London until next Saturday a.m. so until then I am on my own hook.

As it is no fun to put on "lugs" when one is alone I decided not to go to Claridge's, so came here on the recommendation of S. Hooper Hooper, the locally celebrated Ward McAllister of Ye Little Town of Boston, who was on the "Celtic" with us, but who got off at Queenstown to see the King or kiss the Blarney stone, I don't know which. The *Burlington street side* of the house is fearfully costly, but the side I am on, on *Cork Street* is more liked by my purse—made up chiefly of bachelors' rooms and patronized by many army officers. I have a nice room up two flights, at 5 shillings.

Eh bien, when I got here at 2 I promptly lay down and slept till 6 when I had a bath and dined at Claridge's. Most excellent meal—with a pint of Burgundy and a good "seegar"—then I went for a 'bus ride and went to bed at 11. The change of air made me sleepy and I slept until 11.30 this morning. To my chagrin I discovered that today was one of those infernal Bank Holidays—the invention of the devil—so of course not a thing was open & I can't get mail or anything till tomorrow. This p.m. I called on the Edwardes, they are all in Godalming & I left cards—shan't have time to go down to see them. Then I paid a call of an hour on Alice Parker who is staying with her Aunt Mrs. Low, Arthur Gordon's sister. Tomorrow night I dine with the Lows at Claridge's & Cousins Douglas & Corinne [Robinson] & little Corinne will probably be there too

Tomorrow I shall go to the City early—see Lord Revelstoke if he is in and then order clothes. Also I shall probably hear from Lady Cholmely and if she wants me I shall go to Easton on Wednesday & return Friday. I have wired E. Bell to come here Friday. Nothing more decided about plans. I will post this tonight to catch the North Germ. Lloyd & will write by the White Star boat again.

Ever affec.

F.D.R.

Edward VII, with Queen Alexandra, after a state visit to Ireland was just departing for Cowes, to observe the British naval maneuvers which commenced August 5th. A Boston combination including various parts of Ward MacAllister, Harry Lehr, Charles & Co., and Bellows, was the justly re-nowned Mr. S. Hooper Hooper, who came of a well-estab-lished Back Bay family. Since he was also a wine merchant of renown, with a store near the Racquet Club, he conveyed both social and spiritous grace upon the beau monde of his day. Henry George Edwardes, a younger son of the third Baron Kensington, had been a friend of F.D.R.'s father and mother; he was in the British Legation in Washington in 1887 during the winter the Roosevelt family lived there. He had two children F.D.R.'s age, and who are probably those referred to in the letter: Cecil, who died in 1905, and Sylvia Gay Edwardes, Maid of Honour to Queen Victoria from 1897 to 1901. The branch of the Baring family with which the Roosevelts were most closely acquainted had received the barony Revelstoke of Membland. The "Lord Revelstoke" mentioned here was John Baring, a partner in Baring Brothers and, as a usual concomitant to this latter, a director of the Bank of England. "Lady Cholmely" was the former Edith Sophia, a daughter of Lord Rowley, who had married Sir Hugh Arthur Henry Cholmeley (a family not to be confused with the Marquesses and Earls of Cholmondeley, hereditary Joint Great Chamberlains of England). She and her husband, the third baronet, lived at Easton Hall, Grantham, in Lincolnshire. They had three daughters (*vide infra*) roughly F.D.R.'s age: Mary Selina, Winifred, and Aline Janetta. Before inheriting his title Sir Hugh had been for twelve years a Member of Parliament from Grantham. The family were old friends of James Roosevelt and his wife. "E. Bell" was Edward Bell, a Harvard classmate, later counsellor of the American Legation in Peking. "Little Corinne" was the daughter of Corinne Roosevelt and her husband, Douglas Robinson, a well-known New York real estate operator. She married Joseph Wright Alsop; the newspaper columnists Joseph and Stewart Alsop are her sons.

〜〜〜

"It was delightful & Miss Truax
whistled for us afterwards . . ."

EASTON, GRANTHAM
AUG. 5, 1903,
WEDNESDAY.

Dearest Mum—

Just got here today at 5 o'clock—but I will go back to where I left off my last. Tuesday a.m I went to Barings, saw old Mr. B. & he was very nice, got letter of credit & notes from Aunt Doe & Winnie Cholmeley—the latter asking me to come Aug. 4 or 5, so I wired acceptance. Then I went to Johnstone & or-

496

dered 1 dress-suit, 1 dinner-coat suit, 1 winter suit, two summer suits & 1 frock coat & trousers! Prices not as high as Poole—but they weren't low! Then I went to Thresher & Glenny & ordered riding breeches & had the good luck to meet Gerald Boardman & Allen Sumner, so we went together & saw St. Paul's, lunched at Ye Olde Cheshire Cheese—Sam Johnson's "joint" & then went to several book-stores & Westminster Abbey. This took up all p.m. so I had no more time to shop. At 8 I dined at Mrs. Low's & she had also Alice Parker & her Father, Arthur Gordon, Lord & Lady Munson (she was recently Mrs. Turnure) a Miss Richardson of New Orleans & Munro [Monroe Robinson] & Corinnie! It was delightful & Miss Truax whistled for us afterwards. At 10.30 Corinne, Munro & I drove home in a hansom & I saw Cousins Corinne & Douglas for about 15 minutes. It was so nice & made me feel quite at home.

This a.m. I packed most exquisitely & then ordered riding boots & patent leather button shoes & had my first fitting at Johnston. At 2 I caught a very fast train & got to Grantham at 4.05 & here in ¾ of an hour, finding the three girls. Lady C. is unfortunately seeing no one but her husband—it is a kind of rest cure for nervousness I fancy—so I shan't see her. I remembered nearly everything perfectly—even the girls—May is rather *better* looking but it is not saying a great deal, though she is very nice. Winnie is I think the nicest & quite stately & Aline is really quite pretty & less large than the others.

I walked to the stables & farm on arrival & then played a game of tennis which nearly melted me as I had on travelling clothes. Delicious dinner & Sir Hugh evidently desired me to sample his wine cellar but I only took one kind—for which I have been alternately patting myself on the back & kicking myself ever since!

This house is a Dream of Nirvana & as the situation much resembles ours I am taking notes & measurements of everything. The whole place is almost too good to be true, & if C.B.B. isn't well by Saturday I shall return on the 12th & shoot,

another dream.—Friday I return to London & Saturday a.m
Charley comes.—The Newbolds went to Scotland *two days*
before I arrived! Ned's dinner is on Sunday so we don't go to
Continent till Monday. Loads of love. I expect letters on return to L.

F.D.R.

Allen Sumner was in F.D.R.'s class as Harvard, Gerald Boardman a year ahead. Sumner fought with the United States
Marines in the First World War, and was killed in 1918. An
amusing religious note in the *New York Tribune* for July 14,
1902, records the first blossoming of "Miss Truax" before the
public eye: "At the service in the Lexington Avenue Baptist
Church yesterday morning Schumann's 'Traumerei' was whistled by Miss Louise Truax. Miss Truax whistled her solo
while the collection was being taken. So pleased were the
worshippers that after the service they induced her to whistle
'The Mocking Bird.' Miss Truax is nineteen years old. . . .
Six years ago, while living in Detroit, she discovered her natural gift, and she immediately started to cultivate it. She practised daily for several hours, until she acquired a register of
three octaves. Two years ago she made her first appearance in
public as a whistler. . . . Mme. Cappiani and Miss Emma
Thursby became interested in her. They aided her in the
cultivation of her whistling power." And to this it should be
added that Miss Truax sibilated from one international tri-
umph to another, eventually performing at royal command
before Edward VII.

⤬

"I walked up to the best looking
dame in the bunch & said 'howdy?' . . ."

GRAND HÔTEL VICTORIA, INTERLAKEN
AUG 12, 1903,
WEDNESDAY.

Dearest Mama—
I have been trying to find a moment to drop you a line ever
since the first day at Grantham, but didn't succeed.—

498

The day after I got to the Cholmeleys was perfect and in the morning I fished with Aline & caught four trout—one of them over a pound—& the others we threw back. It seemed quite too wonderful to be getting excellent sport within a couple of hundred feet of the house—and what a house! The family must have thought me crazy to rubber so at the pictures & library, for it was *almost* my model library—with three distinct parts and yet all thoroughly liveable and satisfactory.—After luncheon Winnie, Aline & I drove over to Belvoir—a chance I at once jumped at as I have heard Papa speak of it so much that I was wild to see it. The family were all out but the old housekeeper showed over the entire "see-able" part of the house—only not the actual living rooms of the Duke. I thought it magnificent and the paintings are very fine—but it is of course distinctly a show place and the Castle is not entirely home-like. Then we walked about the gardens—the situation of the Castle is indeed perfect—and met the old Duke on horseback in a high hat, accompanied by his Chaplain. The Duke is 87 or so & very old in looks—but it is wonderful that he can ride—just as my Great Grandfather R. did.

On our return to Easton at 6 we four had a set of tennis & after dinner played bridge again. On Friday I was to returned to London—but somehow did not as the programme was too alluring. In the a.m. I fished again—downstream—but it was too sunny & I only got two small ones. After luncheon we played fives on the billiard table, & at three Sir Hugh, Aline & I drove over to the place of the Lord-Lieutenant of the County —beyond Grantham. The place is called Belton I think & *his* name was as near as I could gather *Brownel* or something like it. It is a most perfect place & house & there was a large house party there besides lots of neighbors—all having tea on a heavenly terrace. As a large detachment of volunteers were encamped in the park there were officers there too—among them Gen. Gatacre of South African war fame. As I knew the uncivilized English custom of never introducing people I had about three fits when we arrived & got at once separated from Aline & her Father—but I walked up to the best looking dame in the bunch & said "howdy?" Things at once went like oil & I was soon having flirtations with three of the nobility at the same time. I had a walk with the hostesses' niece over the entire house which was really perfect in every way—I mean the house —although the walk wasn't bad—I will have to wait to tell you about it in person—again I mean the house. Then I inspected the gardens with another 'chawmer' & ended up by jollying the hostess herself all by her lonesome for ten minutes while a uniformed Lord stood by & never got in anything except an occasional "aw" or an "I sy." We stayed about an hour and I made about 15 bosom friends & got on so well with about 10 of these that I found out their names! After our return I fished for a half-hour—had dinner (*and some port* of about A.D. 1800 that made me almost weep for joy) & then played bridge again. On Saturday I had a nice walk about the place before leaving at 11.30. Winnie went to London with me—to visit somewhere in Kent. I tried on at tailors & met Ned Bell & C.B.B. at 4 p.m. The latter was quite recovered I am glad to say. We dined at the Trocadero & went to "The Schoolgirl" which wasn't bad. On Sunday we all lunched at Princes & had a drive in p.m. and found George Williamson. We had a most heavenly 21st Birthday dinner of Ned's at the Cafe Royal—just the four of us—we [with] goldfish on the table—music etc—all in a perfect little private dining room.

On Monday I had to hustle to get through—make arrangements to have Johnstone send me a trunk to the Steamer at Southampton—& packed my other things. C.B.B. & I left at 9 for here via Dover & Basle—had a *vile* channel crossing— which came so near to upsetting my digestion that my stock of English French and German profanity absolutely ran dry. There was no Wagon Lit on the train—so on arrival at Calais we wrapped up in rugs & lay out on the seats. Got to Basle at noon & here at 5 p.m. yesterday.

500

Today we slept till 9, saw the town & spent the rest of the day on a delightful trip through Grindelwald, Scheidegg, Wengernalp & Lauterbrunn, about 6 hours nearly all the time in an observation car. We really saw all that is possible outside of long tramps & the views of the Jungfrau, Wetterhorn Monch, Eiger etc were *magnificent,* you almost felt you could touch them.

Tomorrow we go to Giesbach & Meiringen & Friday drive over the Grimsel pass to Brieg, 54 miles. Brieg as you know is close to Zermatt at the mouth of the new Simplon—& on Saturday we go to Geneva or Montreux—then to Paris Sunday night & sail Wednesday a.m.

There you have it all & I will be home a few days after this letter—It has been perfect so far & great fun but I wont be sorry to get home—though I could have a good time right here for a month—

Ever dear mum   Lovingly

F.D.R.

Belvoir Castle, in Leicestershire, had been given to the ancient and noble Rutland family by Henry VIII. The "old Duke" whom F.D.R. encountered was John Manners, 7th Duke of Rutland, who had succeeded to the dukedom in 1888. Prior to that time he was for a while actively associated, as a member of the House of Commons, with the "Young England" party under the leadership of Disraeli, wherein he worked to restore the political prestige of the aristocracy through a more enlightened attitude toward the working classes. Adelbert Wellington Brownlow, third Earl Brownlow and Lord Lieutenant of Lincoln County, lived at Belton House. General Sir William Forbes Gatacre commanded a British division in the South African War, and was rather ill used by the Boers. Three months prior to the date of this letter, *The School Girl,* produced by George Edwardes and Charles Frohman, had opened at the Prince of Wales Theatre. A contemporary newspaper review noted that the play "was received with great applause. The cast includes Edna May, Miss

'Billie' Burke, Pauline Chase . . . Edna May was nervous and out-of-voice . . . Miss Burke made the hit of the evening. . . ." A Harvard man one year ahead of F.D.R. was George Williamson, then about to enter Christ Church college at Oxford. Williamson had close English ties, became a member of a British regiment, and on November 12th, 1914, died in a Belgian clearing hospital—the first Harvard man to lose his life in the war.

∾

"It was a magnificent trip . . ."

[INTERLAKEN]
AUG. 12, 1903,
WEDNESDAY.

[no salutation]

We made the round trip from Interlaken in 1 day—Grindelwald, Wengernalp, Lauterbrunnen. It was a magnificent trip & gave the best possible idea without staying at least a week.

F.D.R.

This was a postal with a Swiss view, and the welcoming legend *Gruss aus Lauterbrunnen.* In his wheeling, one-day sweep around the Alps, he got off two more picture-postcards from Iseltwald and Giessbach; three from Meiringen, showing views of Wengernalp, the Jungfrau, and Grindelwald, all without any message other than his initials; another postal from Meiringen, dated August 13th, saying: "Arrived Thursday 4 p.m."; and a final card from Meiringen, dated August 13th, with a view of Grimsel-Hospiz and the message: "Leave here tomorrow at 6 a.m." Two weeks later, he was home.

∾

"Many hundreds of young men
are today assuming . . ."

(An editorial in the Harvard *Crimson* of Sept. 30, 1903.)

Even as the oldest institution of learning on this continent is growing greater and better every year, so we hope that the

502

class which enters Harvard today will prove the largest and the best which ever came here. Many hundreds of young men are today assuming for the first time much of the responsibility which they will have to face in after life, and it is here that the first, and in many cases the final, judgment will be made of the work of every individual. In the four years of undergraduate life not only can individual careers be made much as they are in the outside world, but the class as a whole will be judged favorably or the reverse, directly according to the success of its separate members.

It is this idea of responsibility which every Freshman should keep constantly before him—responsibility to the University, to his class and to himself; and the only way to fulfill this is to be always active. The opportunities are almost unlimited: There are athletics—a dozen kinds—and athletic managements, literary work on the University publications and the outside press, philanthropic and religious work, and the many other interests that are bound to exist. Surely the average Freshman can choose at least one of these and go into it with all his energy. Every man should have a wholesome horror of that happy go-lucky state of doing nothing but enough classroom work to keep off probation. It is not so much brilliance as effort that is appreciated here—determination to accomplish something.

Thus only can the Class of 1907 come to be known as a "good class." The University is confident that every one of its members will realize his obligations at the outset and that resulting success will attend the class throughout its future.

Thus did the *Crimson,* gravely, admonishingly, voicing a call to the strenuous life, receive the class of 1907, in an editorial written by its new president, Franklin Roosevelt. At this time a *Crimson* president had the responsibility for writing all the editorials; not until 1907 did the system change, and an editorial board begin to emerge. So although F.D.R. must have had occasional assists from his managing editors, most of the editorials through the half-year of his *Crimson* presidency can be with authority attributed to his pen. Selected examples are published here, complementary and relating to the letters.

〜

"I am to make an address to the Freshman class on Friday . . ."

ALPHA DELTA PHI CLUB
OCT. 1, 1903,
THURSDAY.

Dearest Mama—

On Saturday I went to Groton and had a delightful Sunday at the Billy-Wag's—I saw Herman [Rogers] and Hall, who are both getting on finely and are much liked. I saw a lot of Warren and although it poured most of the time we managed to have a walk. All Monday and in fact every spare moment has been taken up with the paper (which by the way I hope you are getting) and I have little time to think about courses. However I have talked it over with a good many Professors who advise Graduate School also with many Law School men who *all* say I would regret it if I went to the L.S. this year. So I am registering today in the Graduate School and will probably take four or five History and Economics courses which really interest me but which are harder than English. I do not in the least expect to get the degree but the training will be excellent.

I am to make an address to the Freshman class on Friday! This is only one of my amusements just now! So glad you enjoy Farmington.

Affec.

F.D.R.

"Hall" was G. Hall Roosevelt, younger brother of his future wife. By registering in the Graduate School, F.D.R. became eligible for a Master of Arts degree—which he did not achieve, his numerous outside activities doubtless standing in the way of the intensive study and high marks required for a four-year M.A. The courses for this last Harvard year were:

(1) *English 11-A.* A half-year course in Bacon, Mondays, Wednesdays, and Fridays at 11, under Assistant Professor Fred Norris Robinson, noted editor of the Cambridge *Chaucer.*

(2) *History 11.* The History of England during the Tudor and Stuart Periods, a full-year course given Mondays, Wednesdays, and Fridays at 12 by Roger Bigelow Merriman, one of Harvard's outstanding historians and later the master of Eliot House.

(3) *History 10-B.* A half-year course in American history: The Development of the West. It was taught by visiting Professor Frederick Jackson Turner of the University of Wisconsin, whose book, *The Frontier in American History* (a collection of historical essays written during this period in his life), had a profound influence upon historians.

(4) *History 16-A.* The History of Continental Europe from the Peace of Utrecht to the Fall of Napoleon I; a half-year course on Mondays, Wednesdays, and Fridays at 9 with myopic Professor MacVane.

(5) *History 16-B.* Second half-year: the History of Continental Europe since the Fall of Napoleon I, same hours, same teachers.

(6) *History 27.* Another course with Dr. Merriman: the History of Germany from the Reformation to the Close of the Thirty Years' War. Held Tuesdays, Thursdays, and Saturdays at 10, second half-year.

(7) *Economics 5.* First half-year: the Economics of Transportation, meeting Tuesdays, Thursdays, and Saturdays at 10 with Professor William Zebina Ripley. The latter was an authority on railroads, served in the Government during and after the First World War, and on the Interstate Commerce Commission from 1920 to 1923. He was the author of a number of influential books on the economic aspects of the railroad industry, and has been described as "a leading advocate of the control of

holding companies for the protection of the small investor."

(8) *Economics 9-B.* The second half-year with Professor Ripley, on the Economics of Corporations.

(9) *Economics 8-B.* A half-year course: Banking and the History of Banking Systems, Mondays, Wednesdays, and Fridays at 10 under the direction of Dr. Oliver M. W. Sprague. Professor Sprague became one of Harvard's leading economists, economic adviser to the Bank of England from 1930 to 1933, and in the latter year joined F.D.R.'s Brain Trust when he became a special assistant to the Secretary of the Treasury. He attended the London Monetary Conference in June of 1933, at which time his name was prominently in the news. The results of the Conference were disappointing to him, and, after expressing strong disagreement with the Government's monetary policy, he resigned and returned to Harvard.

(10) *Economics 8-A.* Second half-year; a general survey course in Currency Legislation, Experience, and Theory in Recent Times, taught by Abram Piatt Andrew.

❧

"Every man at Harvard who takes
any interest in athletics . . ."

(An editorial in the Harvard *Crimson* of Oct. 6, 1903.)

Every man at Harvard who takes any interest in athletics realizes that the football team, in order to be successful, has a peculiarly hard task before it. The lack of heavy men is now even more pronounced than last year: there are indeed scarcely enough playing now to form one team of only average weight and ability. It is certain that many men are in the University who are of sufficient weight to make it an obligation to their fellows to answer the appeal of Captain [Carl B.] Marshall and Coach [J.S.] Cranston. Lack of experience is no excuse for not coming out, and every addition to the squad means improved possibilities for the development of a good eleven.

506

ALPHA DELTA PHI CLUB
OCT. 7, 1903,
WEDNESDAY.

Dearest Mama—

I am now fully in the Graduate School—too deep to get out
or change my mind. I am taking five courses in the Department
of History and Political Economy—which interests me much
more than English but which is also much harder. I have few
hopes of getting an A.M.—indeed I am quite indifferent about
it, but the courses will do me lots of good, whether I get B or D
in them and to do the former would make me work so hard
that I could not do justice to my Senior year.

My courses are History 11, on Middle English History, very
hard but excellent; History 16, the Hist. of Continental Europe from 1715 to today; Economics 8—the history & theory
of banking; Economics 9, the history of Transportation (railroading etc) in the U.S.; and English 11, a course on Bacon
which is good & which I was allowed to take.

After the football game Saturday at which I ushered, I went
to the Beals at Beverly, & attended a small dance at the golf
club. Sunday we spent at the Sohiers camp & had a swim. Alice
Sohier is still on her back after having her appendix removed
last week. I came back after dinner on Sunday & wrote my editorial—What do you think of them so far? The address to the
Freshmen scared me to death but I survived—I drooled on
journalism here & also on strenuousness etc.

Please wire who is coming on the 16th, Friday. Are H.
[Helen] Cutting, Eleanor & Moo all coming to us? I bring
home H. Peabody, Livingstone Davis probably & I may have
one other. Jimmy Jackson can't come. The paper takes every
moment of time.

Ever

F.D.R.

The Freshman Reception was held in Memorial Hall, a large construction completed in 1878 as a Civil War memorial, and consisting of three parts: Memorial Dining Hall (one of the two commons at that time), a transept with commemorative plaques and windows, and an auditorium known as Sanders Theatre. On "Bloody Monday" evening the incoming class gathered in Sanders to hear speeches from members of the faculty and from prominent seniors, on the order described by F.D.R. in this letter. Afterward the Freshmen moved into the Dining Hall for an informal reception. Then the official ceremonies terminated, the official personages looked the other way, and the Freshmen passed out into Harvard Yard, where upperclassmen had arranged a special welcome of their own. The nature of this varied from year to year, and cannot be precisely defined; as good a description as any occurs in Charles Macomb Flandrau's *The Diary of a Freshman,* published in 1901: "A sound of confused cheering reached me the moment I got outside, and when I passed through the gate I could see down the long quadrangle what seemed to be a battle of will-o'-the-wisps—a swaying, shifting, meeting, parting, revolving myriad of flickering lights and lurid faces. I ran until I reached the edge of the crowd, and stood for a minute or two staring and listening. The fellows were surging wildly up and down and across the Yard with torches in their hands, cheering and singing. Whenever enough men got together, they would lower their torches and charge the whole length of the Yard—amid a howl of resentment—like a company of lancers. Then by the time they had turned to plough back again, another group would have formed, which usually met the first one half-way with a terrible roar and a clash of tin torches,—a drench of kerosene and a burst of flame. Two German bands that never stopped playing the 'Blue Danube' and the 'Washington Post' were huddled at either end of the Yard. Now and then a sort of tidal wave of lights and faces and frantic hands would swell rapidly toward them, lap them up, engulf them, and then go swirling back again to the middle. But they never stopped playing,—even when they became hopelessly scattered and horribly reunited."

"... a practical idea of the workings of a political system ..."

(An editorial in the Harvard *Crimson* of Oct. 8, 1903.)

We are reminded by the communication about voting in the New York election that the Political Club here has a field for work which is very large and in which much good might be done. Last year this organization took a good step in arranging a few talks on politics, but these talks would do more good if there were more of them and if they were open to the whole University.

No attempt, however, is made to give a practical idea of the workings of a political system—of the machinery of primary, caucus, convention, election and legislature. With such a large city as Boston close at hand it would be easy to send in parties, under the guidance of some experienced man, which in one day could learn more than through the means of lectures. There must be many among us who, whether or not of a voting age, would be more than glad to gain knowledge by actual experience of the intricacies of Federal, State and Municipal politics.

According to a contemporary *University Register:* "The object of the Harvard Political Club is to educate its members in the subject of politics and to encourage interest in that subject among members of the University at large. ... Several public addresses by prominent men are given each year in order to bring this club and its aim before the members of the University." Membership was open to all, with a small initiation fee. Aside from the public lectures, there were fortnightly meetings for members only. The Political Club was an evanescent organization which appeared and disappeared depending upon how much college interest could be aroused.

". . . waiving my arms & legs before several thousand spectators . . ."

THE HARVARD CRIMSON

F.D.Roosevelt '04, President   P.Dana '04, Business Manager
W.R.Bowie '04, Managing Editor   C.Burlingham '06, Secretary

CAMBRIDGE
OCT. 26, 1903,
MONDAY.

Dearest Mama—

I have been a perfect pig about writing—have been just a goin' to every day, but somehow it never got actually on paper. I wired you yesterday that I still weigh 160 pounds in natal garb—and am otherwise enjoying salubrity. Last week I put in lots of excellent work *outside* of studies. I suddenly became energetic & saw Dr. Morgan twice about my *ocu*lar organs— He says they are really better than they were four years ago. The reason that they have been slightly annoying at times is because my glasses have been too strong—so you see it would have been better if I had not worn them so much lately—! I have ordered new lenses and sh'd get them in a few days. There was a Fly dinner on Saturday, so I spent Sunday in Cambridge. I was one of the three cheer leaders in the Brown game & felt like a D...F... waiving my arms & legs before several thousand amused spectators! It is a dirty job, one gets chiefly ridicule—but some poor devil has to suffer & one can't refuse—

I have looked at one horse—not satisfactory, & am to see another tomorrow. I hope he will do—though I don't know when I'd get time to ride. Next Saturday I go to Cousin Julia's in the evening & return Sunday night. Yours of yesterday has just come. It's too bad Miss C. doesn't improve—What are you going to do? By the way *how* are you going to put *four full grown females* into the apartment tomorrow night? Don't you want me to come & sleep in the bath-tub?! I don't see how

510

I can possibly get off before the midnight train on Monday next—I *have* to be here to see about the paper. Will let you know any way.

Ever

F.D.R.

The fairly prevalent college custom was and still is to choose cheer leaders not for any gymnastic ability, but for class prominence—the idea presumably being that greater recognizability produces a more intense response. The weekend visit mentioned here was to Cousin Julia Delano of New Bedford. There are several evidences that F.D.R. felt strongly about the way Harvard football games were conducted, not only from the aspect of how well the team played but—and the following is excerpted from an editorial in the *Crimson* of Oct. 16, 1903: "[it is proposed that] a separate section be provided where ladies may enter [the stadium] without fear of being asphyxiated. It is undoubtedly disagreeable for ladies to be surrounded with smoke and flying ashes from tobacco which is not always of the best quality."

∽

*"I heard indirectly that two of
Aunt Kassie's men gave out . . ."*

ALPHA DELTA PHI CLUB

OCT. 30, 1903,

FRIDAY.

Dearest Mama—

I can't possibly get off till the night train on Monday as my editorial won't permit me to leave earlier. I will get to Hyde Park at 9-28 on Tuesday and will have to leave again that night.

I don't remember whether I told you my last [letter] that I have accepted the Mortons' invite. Lyman is going also.

Tomorrow I go to Cousin Julias at 5 p.m. after the feetball game at which I again have to lead cheering. I will have to return here Sunday night, as there is so much doing that I have to be on hand constantly.

The weather is nice & warm again and I am wearing summer clothing. By the way I heard indirectly that about 3 weeks ago two of Aunt Kassie's men for this party gave out—but that she had since filled their places!

See you Tuesday—

With loads of love   Ever

F.D.R.

〜〜

"*They are weary of a spirit that will not awake . . .*"

(An editorial in the Harvard *Crimson* of Nov. 2, 1903.)

The Carlisle game was a notable victory for the Harvard eleven. The Indians were actually defeated; they scored only eleven points and the University team scored all of twelve. Of course, the team was satisfied with so excellent a showing. What did it matter that the Indians, some twenty or twenty-five pounds lighter to a man, had literally run over them in the first half? What did it matter that, after Harvard had gained the lead, the Indians were again on the way to Harvard's goal line when time was called? What did it matter that the Indians in speed, quickness and determination conspicuously outplayed a Harvard University eleven? What did it matter? —Harvard won. No wonder the team was satisfied!

But the undergraduates watching the game were not so well satisfied as the eleven. They have grown somewhat weary of the slow, listless play of certain men in the line, who seem to think that their weight is a sufficient certificate of admission to membership on a University team. They are weary of a spirit that will not awake till the team is in a desperate crisis, and goes to sleep again when the crisis is fancied to be past. They are weary and angry—why?—because they know there is no reason why the team should not be powerful, aggressive and, withal, successful if it wills to be. The kind of coaching that will make a victorious eleven is present, the heavy and experienced material that ordinarily would promise a victorious eleven is present; all that is needed is a spirit in the team of aggressive, vigorous determination—a spirit that will begin fighting when the game begins and will not vanish before the game ends. The University believes the team potentially formidable. It is waiting to see the team resolve actually to make itself, by fierce and vigorous playing, as formidable as it ought to be.

How much longer must the University wait?

As a possible goad to this editorial whiplashing, aside from the points noted, one may make mention of an incident of the game. At the opening of the second half, the Warner-coached Indians executed a famous trick. Harvard kicked off, the ball was caught, tucked up under the jersey of a player named Dillon, whereupon the latter proceeded to stroll to a touchdown unnoticed by the Harvard team until too late. The spectators, however, saw the lump on Dillon's back, and began roaring with laughter as the Harvard players raced about bewilderedly. This same trick had been played by the Harvard *Lampoon* on the *Crimson* in their annual football game two years before, and was widely known.

∽

"I wouldn't have missed my first
ballot for anything . . ."

ALPHA DELTA PHI CLUB
NOV. 6, 1903,
FRIDAY.

Dearest Mama—

I had a good trip back and luckily secured a lower berth. I am so glad that I had even those few hours with you, and I wouldn't have missed my first ballot for anything. By the way you say nothing, in the letter I have just received, about the village election. Did Jones get in as road-master—and who is Assembly man, Landon (the crazy man) or Chanler (the lunatic)? On Wednesday I went to Southboro' at 1 and saw the wonderful Groton victory of 35 to 0; Warren was dressed to play but as substitute did not get into the game and so just missed getting his G.S.

The row about Monday's editorial is subsiding—at least half the college think it was quite called for. *Something* of the kind was indeed necessary but *I* shouldn't have made it quite so strong. However I am glad to say the effect has been just what was wanted—it has stirred up the team by making them angry and they are playing all the harder for it. Yesterday I led the cheering in the Square when the team left for Phila. and I am to be head leader on Saturday, so won't sit with the Pattersons—thank the Lord. I will go to the apartment if I have time as you suggest—I have written Mary Morton & probably go up on the 3.30 that day. The enclosed may amuse you—The figure on the forward platform of the car is your son trying to lead cheers

Ever

F.D.R.

This was an off-year state election: in New York City, the Fusionist incumbent, Seth Low, lost the mayoralty race to the Democratic candidate, George B. McClellan, son of the Civil War general; while in the Second District of Dutchess County, where there was an election for state assemblyman, Democrat Robert W. Chanler won an unexpected victory over Republican Francis G. Landon, who had "opposed the giving of passes to legislators." In this election F.D.R. cast his first vote—at the Hyde Park Town Hall, as he was to continue doing for the rest of his life. In his reference to Chanler as "the lunatic," F.D.R. was understandably confusing members of a very confusing family. There were three Chanler brothers, all great-great-grandsons of John Jacob Astor. Lewis Stuyvesant Chanler was elected lieutenant governor of New York in 1906, on the same ticket that saw William Randolph

Hearst (a Democrat) lose the governorship. Robert Winthrop Chanler engaged himself in politics likewise, though attaining less lofty heights. He first ran for sheriff of Dutchess County, reputedly spending $20,000 on his campaign for this reasonably insignificant job, and of course winning the election. He went at his duties with vigor, cleaned out the Poughkeepsie jail to great popular acclaim, and acquired the nickname of "Sheriff Bob." It was the third of the brothers, John Armstrong Chanler, who was the lunatic, and at that he was crazy only in certain parts of the country. He married a very singular Virginian, a lady novelist named Amélie Rives (later the Princess Troubetzkoy), from whom he was divorced, and with surprising dispatch, after this latter event, was committed to the Bloomington insane asylum in New York State. There he acquired the gift of automatic writing while his brothers administered his million-dollar estate, but the exchange he must hardly have felt compensatory, for in 1900, after three years in Bloomingdale, he walked out of the asylum one afternoon and did not reappear. His disappearance was a matter for newspaper headlines during the ensuing period, until he turned up in a Virginia hospital, from which he was released as perfectly sane, and allowed to return to his home near Richmond. He was therefore in the interesting position of being legally insane in New York, and quite otherwise in both Virginia and North Carolina. Chanler proceeded from eccentricity to eccentricity, wrote publishable books and unpublishable verse-dramas, but his immortality derives from a single phrase. His brother, Sheriff Bob, had relinquished politics and gone to Paris, where he had become enmeshed in the toils of the famous soprano, Lina Cavalieri, and signed over his entire fortune in exchange for that lady's artful hand. John Armstrong signalized the event by wiring his brother the deathless question, "Who's loony now?"

∽∽

515

"Hooray for the Dimocrats of
Hoide Park! . . ."

The Harvard Crimson   Payson Dana, '04, Business Manager
The University Daily   W.B.Brigham, '05, Asst. Business Mgr.

CAMBRIDGE
NOV. 10, 1903,
TUESDAY.

Dearest Ma—

It will give me great pleasure to lunch with you on Saturday at 1.30 at Sherry's!

I am too sorry to hear about your cold—you must be careful & get over it entirely and quickly.

Too bad J.R.R. kicks about the wall—but go ahead & have it done. It will be a great improvement & he will appreciate it when it is finished.

Hooray for the Dimocrats of Hoide Park!

I will meet you at 10 West 43rd on Sat. at about 7.30 a.m. Eleanor [Roosevelt] is going to get four seats on the 3.38 up river so don't get any. I will bring Lyman also to wash & dress & have breakfast.

I have been jumping round all day. Tomorrow I try another horse & hope he will suit.

Ever affec
                                                    FDR

How do you like my new writing?

The only date given on this letter is "Tuesday Eve"; its placing in the correspondence is therefore largely conjectural. The wall in point was one which Sara Delano Roosevelt had decided to construct between her estate and that of James Roosevelt Roosevelt which adjoined; a minor squabble—mainly aesthetic—ensued. As for the new handwriting bespoken here, it had a very exaggerated slant, attaining stylish illegibility.

∽

*"I do so want you to learn to
love me a little . . ."*

(A letter from Eleanor Roosevelt to her future mother-in-law.)

8 EAST 76TH STREET [N. Y.]
DEC. 2, 1903,
WEDNESDAY.

Dearest Cousin Sally,

I must write you & thank you for being so good to me yesterday. I know just how you feel & how hard it must be, but I do so want you to learn to love me a little. You must know that I will always try to do what you wish for I have grown to love you very dearly during the past summer.

It is impossible for me to tell you how I feel toward Franklin, I can only say that my one great wish is always to prove worthy of him.

I am counting the days to the 12th when I hope Franklin & you will both be here again & if there is anything which I can do for you you will write me, won't you?

With much love dear Cousin Sally,

Always devotedly

ELEANOR.

Just prior to this letter, F.D.R. had told his mother of his intention to marry Eleanor Roosevelt. It can be assumed that Sara Delano Roosevelt was startled—and, at the prospect of surrendering her twenty-two-year-old son just as he was returning to her after eight years of school, dismayed. At any rate, one result of the announcement was this appealing letter, written from the home of the Henry Parishes, Eleanor Roosevelt's cousins with whom she lived. (The official engagement notice did not appear until one year later.)

〰

"I am the happiest man just now in the world . . ."

DEC. 4, 1903,
FRIDAY.

Dearest Mama—

I have been absolutely rushed to death since I came back, with a thousand things to attend to & meetings of the nomination committee (for Senior Class elections) lasting up to 2 in the morning. I am to be nominated anyway for an office & am naturally delighted— You will be as surprised as I was when you hear *what* office— But I dont stand a ghost of a show of being elected to it—though I am pleased at the honor of nomination.

Dearest Mama—I know what pain I must have caused you and you know I wouldn't do it if I really could have helped it —mais tu sais, me voilà! Thats all that could be said—I know my mind, have known it for a long time, and know that I could never think otherwise: Result: I am the happiest man just now in the world; likewise the luckiest— And for you, dear Mummy, you know that nothing can ever change what we have always been & always will be to each other—only now you have two children to love & to love you—and Eleanor as you know will always be a daughter to you in every true way—

I shall be here over Sunday working all the time but will write you a longer letter then—

Excuse this hurried scrawl, it doesn't express anything but you know what I mean

Your ever loving

F.D.R.

In this letter he refers to his impending nomination for marshal of the class of 1904. There were three marshals chosen, together with a class secretary and a class orator, and to be elected one of these "class officers" was the highest of accolades. Nominations were made by a selected committee, then voted upon by the whole class. The function of the marshals

518

was to lead their fellows in the Class Day parade to Appleton Chapel, then to Sanders Theatre for the award of prizes and diplomas, and later, in the afternoon, through the Yard and out to the Stadium for the Ivy addresses. F.D.R. was not elected a marshal, but shortly afterward was chosen (again by vote of the whole class) chairman of the Class Committee, an important permanent post in the activity of the class as alumni.

〰

"It seems a little hard & unnecessary
on us both . . ."

ALPHA DELTA PHI CLUB
DEC. 6, 1903,
SUNDAY.

Dearest Mama—

Yours of Friday came yesterday & I have been thinking over what you say about next Sunday—I am so glad, dear Mummy, that you are getting over the strangeness of it all—I knew you would and that you couldn't help feeling that not only I but you also are the luckiest & will always be the happiest people in the world in gaining anyone like E. to love & be loved by.

I confess that I think it would be poor policy for me to go to H.P. next Sunday—although, as you know and don't have to be told, I always love & try to be there all I can— I have been home twice already this term & I feel certain that J.R.R. & Helen w'd be sure to smell a rat if I went back for *part of a day* just a week before the holidays, for they would know I had been in N.Y. a whole day. *Also* if I am in N.Y. on Sunday *not a soul* need know I have been there at all as if we go to Church at all we can go to any old one at about 100th St. & the rest of the day w'd be in the house where none c'd see us. Of course I suppose you have told no one you w'd see me Saturday. Now if you really can't see the way clear to my staying in N.Y. of course I will go to H.P. with you—but you know how I feel—and also I think that E. will be terribly disappointed, as I will, if we can't have one of our first Sundays together— It seems a little hard & unnecessary on us both & I shall see you all day Saturday which I shouldn't have done had the great event not "happened".

I have been rushed to death all week & the next will be even more busy—Signet dinner last night—I have managed to get short rides the last four days including today—

I am going to accept all invites for Xmas but don't you think we might have a house party for one or two days— Go ahead & ask whoever you want, we might have two girls & E. & if you name date & telegraph I will try to get two or three fellows— Indeed I don't intend to give up things—it w'd not be right to you or E—& she also will keep on going to things— You can imagine how completely happy I am—it gives a stimulous to everything I do—

I am to be nominated for one of the Marshals of the Class— Don't breathe this to a soul

Ever your loving son

F.D.R.

〜〜

"The election is going on all day . . ."

THE HARVARD CRIMSON

F.D.Roosevelt '04, President   P.Dana '04, Business Manager
W.R.Bowie '04, Managing Editor   C.Burlingham '06, Secretary

CAMBRIDGE
DEC. 16, 1903,
WEDNESDAY.

Dearest Mama—

You will be relieved to hear that there aren't any more diphtheria cases—only 7 or 8 out of 4,000 students isn't bad exactly—I am very well and can't tell you how glad I am that I had Sunday in N.Y. It was rainy in the morning & we didn't see a soul except the Goodwin family in church. Yesterday I bought lots of books for the Club— Dined at the "Fly" with Dr Hale, Prexy Eliot, Dean Hurlbut & A. Lawrence Lowell—

most interesting,—Then had a meeting wrote an editorial &
at 11 appeared at the Bigelow's ball at the Somerset—a huge
affair—I ushered & had great fun. Today I slept till 12.30—
The election is going on all day—I don't stand the least show
—in fact will get less votes than any of the others for marshal—
but I may do better if nominated for a Committee to be voted
on next Friday. The weather has been vile & cold & I haven't
ridden since last week—

I will probably go to N.Y. on Tuesday on the 1 o'clock but
can't tell yet. How about asking E. for the 26th & I will get
L.B. or someone else—. Wire me if Caroline Drayton can
come—if so I will try to get two men——

Ever your affec. son

F.D.R.

Edward Hale was assistant professor of Homiletics at Harvard;
Bryon S. Hurlbut had by now succeeded Le Baron Briggs as
dean of Harvard College. The "huge affair" at the Somerset
was given by the Joseph Bigelows for their daughter Mary.
Caroline Astor Drayton, daughter of J. Coleman Drayton
(at one time United States minister in India), was a first cousin
of Taddy and Helen Roosevelt, and a good friend of Eleanor
Roosevelt. Later she married William Phillips, a career diplo-
mat who was appointed Under-Secretary of State following
F.D.R.'s inauguration in 1933, and served as ambassador to
Italy from 1936 until the declaration of war.

◇◇

*"How is the ice-filling progressing
—also the carload of manure . . ."*

8 EAST 76TH STREET
JAN. 3, 1904,
SUNDAY.

Dearest Ma—

I am alive and kicking—only worrying about your getting
home last night—Uncle W., Jean & Sara went up on the 7
o'clock & got to Barrytown at 2 a.m.!!! Hope you weren't late

521

as the people at the Station said they thought the 3.30 had been
nearly on time.

The theatre-party was great fun & very successful— This
a.m. E. & I went to Church at Calvary & had an uproarious
lunch at the Robinsons & all the relatives came here to afternoon tea—I dined just now at J.R.R's & am off to the midnight. Laura is much better & out today—

How is the ice-filling progressing—also the carload of
manure.

Will write or telegraph within a *month!*—

Ever affec.

F.D.R.

The agricultural inquiries concluding this short note remind
one that Hyde Park was not merely trees and lawn, but a
fairly large and self-sufficient farm, encompassing much land.
A considerable portion of that land was purchased by Eleanor
Roosevelt in 1947 from her husband's estate, and the farm
has begun to operate again—the difference being that it is
now a professional operation and must pay its way or be
given up.

∽

". . . induced to enter New York
politics upon leaving College . . ."

(An editorial from the Harvard *Crimson* of Jan. 9, 1904.)

The series of lectures to be given by the Political Club,
although dealing primarily with New York politics, will be of
value to any one interested in municipal government. The
Committee in New York which has selected the speakers, hopes
that by arousing sufficient interest, men may be induced to
enter New York politics upon leaving College. It promises
that men who so desire, will be given an opportunity to work
for whatever party they wish to join. This is the first time that
so definite an agency for bringing College men into touch with
civic work has been established, and we hope that it will meet
with the success that such a movement deserves.

"Blue-blooded, blue stockinged,
bean eating Boston . . ."

THE HARVARD CRIMSON
JAN. 12, 1904,
TUESDAY.

Dearest Mama—

I wrote you last week and found the scribble in my pocket today— Positively I am the most intelligent man in Harvard without exception! Now I must confess— On Saturday I found I had no engagement & went to N.Y. on the 10 o'clock—E. & I had a quiet evening & went to Church together on Sunday— I lunched at the Parishes' & came on here again on the 3 o'clock getting here at 10, just in time to write my editorial. You know I positively couldn't help it— There was nothing to keep me here and I knew I should be in a much better humor for a short trip to N.Y!

Last week I dined at the Quincy's, the Amory's & the Thayer's, three as high-life places as are to be found in blue-blooded, blue stockinged, bean eating Boston!

Many thanks for the Tuxedo & gloves & smoking apparatus. I have been up every night till all hours, but am doing a little studying, a little riding & a few party calls. It is dreadfully hard to be a student a society whirler a "prominent & democratic fellow" & a fiancé all at the same time—but it [is] worth while, especially the last & next year, tho' hard will be easier— I may go to N.Y. on the 1 o'clock on Friday & hope to find you their on arrival— You will surely stay over Sunday—won't you please—we have so much to talk over about the trip etc.

Your devoted

FDR.

There is reference here to an intended trip. Sara Delano Roosevelt had decided that an alteration of her son's surroundings—from the Cambridge-New York axis to the West Indies—might provide a chance for him to "think the engagement over." She therefore, in February and March of 1904, took him and Lathrop Brown on a Caribbean cruise. Puerto Rico and Cuba were the main ports of call, aboard the same

Hamburg-American Line boat, the *Prinzessin Victoria Luise,* on which F.D.R., his mother, and Teddy Robinson had cruised to the North Cape the summer of 1901. There is no question but what F.D.R. appreciated the tropical seas and scenery to the full; their effect upon his romantic intentions, however, seems to have been nil.

～～

". . . of interest to every man who intends to enter politics . . ."

(An editorial in the Harvard *Crimson* of Jan. 13, 1904.)

President Hadley's address in the Union tonight will appeal to many, not only on account of the personality of the speaker, but also because the subject, "Opportunities for Political Influence," is of interest to every man who intends either directly to enter the field of politics or who hopes to aid in other ways the welfare of the country. Few men are better qualified to speak on such a subject than President Hadley, and he will be received with interest as an acknowledged authority and with exceptional cordiality as the head of the university which has in its history and ideals most in common with Harvard.

Arthur Twining Hadley was president of Yale from 1899 to 1921. An expert economist, particularly in the field of railroads, he served as adviser to a number of Governmental commerce and investigatory committees.

～～

"The man who makes a success of his college career . . ."

(An editorial in the Harvard *Crimson* of Jan. 26, 1904.)

In looking back over the college careers of those who for various reasons have been prominent in undergraduate life in

524

the University, one cannot help noticing that these men have nearly always shown from the start an interest in the lives of their fellow students. A large acquaintance means that many persons are dependent on a man and conversely that he is himself dependent on many. Success necessarily means larger responsibilities, and responsibility means many friends.

But the man who makes a success of his college career like the successful man of business makes his friends not after the hard work is over, but while it is going on, and the time to begin to make friends, is essentially the freshman year, for it is then that friendships are easiest to make. It is then that generally begins the building up of whatever career the future has in store—the time that often decides whether the fates allotted shall be success or failure.

∾

*"I am too sorry I haven't written
for so long . . ."*

ALPHA DELTA PHI CLUB
JAN. 29, 1904,
FRIDAY.

Dearest Mama—

I am rushed to death and will be till the moment I leave. I am *too* sorry I haven't written for so long—I have simply put it off & put it off.

E. & I had a very good time at Groton & the Jones' dance was wonderful—

The Crimson election passed off well but I write eds. till I leave. Don't believe I can get off till Wednesday night & will get to H.P. Thursday a.m. but will let you know definitely later. Will write at more length tomorrow *sure*

Ever yr. affec

F.D.R.

∾

THE HARVARD CRIMSON
JAN. 30, 1904,
SATURDAY.

Dearest Mama—

Last night I dined at the Parkman's, where Alice Parker is staying, and then went on to the Bachelors Ball which was very exclusive, very animated and rather tipsy. I got back at 6 and slept till 11.

Sunday—

I have just heard from E. that Mr. and Mrs. Parish have gone away & I couldn't see her [*i.e.*, no chaperone] if I went to N.Y. on Wednesday. I find I can get off from here Tuesday night and I feel that I must see all I can of E. these last few days—so I am telegraphing you tonight to see if you wont have her up at Hyde Park—coming Wednesday a.m. and staying till Thursday. Nobody need know a thing about it and she wouldn't be any trouble as far as getting off is concerned— for I can pack all my things in half an hour. If you decide not to telegraph her I think I must go down Thursday so as to have all day Friday with her—

The weather is vile and I have been so dreadfully busy that I haven't had much chance to study—a thousand things have to be attended to & all sorts of provisions made about committees, libraries etc.

Today I have been paying calls all afternoon, saying goodbye & I lunched at the Bradley's.

See you Wednesday morning.

Ever yr. devoted

F.D.R.

The "Parkman's" of this letter were the Henry Parkmans, Mr. Parkman being a cousin of the historian. Mrs. Wayne Parker's (*vide supra*) daughter Alice was Mrs. Parkman's niece. Their son, Henry Parkman, Jr., rose to the rank of brigadier general in the Second World War, serving with the Sixth Army Group in Southern France and Germany as assistant chief of staff for military government. The institution of the Bachelors' Ball was roughly contemporary with the Copley-Plaza, where it was held. It was given by about twenty bachelors, no debutantes being invited. The Caribbean cruise followed this letter.

〰️

". . . dropped in to the Automobile
Show for a minute . . ."

ALPHA DELTA PHI CLUB
MARCH 14, 1904,
MONDAY.

Dearest Mama—

Here I am safely after a rather uncomfortable night— The sleeper to Boston now leaves Albany at 11.20 & I didn't get there till 11.30 & so missed it. I was lucky however & got a lower berth on the western train which got in at 12.30 & I got out to Cambridge at eight this morning. The only course I had today was having an hour examination so of course I didn't go, but I have three which I shall attend tomorrow morning.

It is horrid to be back after such a perfect trip—if it only could have lasted longer without being *very* far away from N.Y! But of course today I have been saying "Howdy" to everybody and giving lurid accounts of the West Indies & the entire continent of South America.

I am thinking of you tonight as going to N.Y. but as you didn't mention how long you would stay I shall send this to Hyde Park.

It is a vile sort of day windy & raw. This p.m. I went to town for my trunk & valise & on the way dropped in to the Automobile Show for a minute with Jerry Bradley—

It is 10 now & I am really off to bed

Ever your affec

F.D.R.

〰️

". . . doing some standard reading
for my mind . . ."

ALPHA DELTA PHI CLUB
MARCH 20, 1904,
SUNDAY.

Dearest Mama—

Today it is really warmer though of course everything is knee deep in mud— On Friday I went to the Beals to dinner & to see the "Prince of Pilsen" with Tom afterwards. Yesterday I took a short ride in the afternoon walking in to Boston & out again so got plenty of exercise   In the evening I went to the "Show Girl" with Walter Bradley & supped at the Touraine afterwards—so you see I am trying to make up at the theatres for lost time.

This morning I got rid of some of my correspondence & lunched in town at the Davis' with Livingston, then paid half a dozen calls I owed, including Mrs. Whitman who was not at home. This evening I have been sitting quietly in the Club, doing some standard reading for my mind.

I am so glad Laura is getting on well— If she could only be sent away from her family things might be better all round!

I shall leave Friday by the one o'clock train as there probably won't be any lecture in my Saturday course. Nothing from the office, thank the Lord!

Poor Alice Sohier is laid up again—this time it is her hip— whether rheumatism or something out of joint they don't know. I saw her this afternoon on a sofa & quite unable to walk. So glad you will be in town Friday

Your affec. son

F.D.R.

I may see you this week here & will be ready any day.

Walter Bradley was Harvard '05, and a brother of Leverett. *The Prince of Pilsen,* a musical comedy by Pixley and Luders, had opened on Broadway a year before; it and R. A. Barnet's musical extravaganza, *Show Girl,* were then touring the coun-

528

try with great success. Quite a Boston figure of the period was Sarah Wyman Whitman—patroness of the arts, friend of Isabella Stewart Gardner, and hostess of a notable "salon."

∾∾

"Keep an eye on the silver also
don't let him flirt . . ."

CAMBRIDGE

MARCH 29, 1904,

TUESDAY.

Dearest Marmer

I had a delightful day in N.Y. on the Sabbath—going to Calvary & seeing only the Goodwins, & in the afternoon E. & Hall & I walked in the Park for awhile. I dined at the Harvard Club & had a vile night coming on on the midnight.

Yesterday was simply *wile* here, snow & rain etc & I took only a short walk. Today I spent the morning taking little Charley Brown to see various agents about rooms next year without much success. This p.m. I had a long ride of nearly three hours with Prof. Andrew & C. Bigelow & it was a perfect day for it.

I must get to bed as it is late—will see you in a few days

Lots of love   Ever affec.   F.D.R.

I hope the new serving gent is proving acceptable   I am so anxious to see him in spite of the reputed horrid looks   Keep an eye on the silver also don't let him flirt with that dear Maria

∾∾

"We didn't swim or do much more
than hold a steeplechase . . ."

ALPHA DELTA PHI CLUB

MAY 2, 1904,

MONDAY.

Dearest Mama—

I am sorry not to have written before but Teddy's dinner was rather an interruption but was splendid fun—seventeen of us & we didn't swim or set the house on fire or do much

529

more than hold a steeplechase—some of us at 1 a.m. On Saturday we returned to Boston at noon, lunched at the Touraine, & spent the afternoon at Keith's.

I saw Michelson out here last Monday & talked everything over & all is satisfactory, but he is such a touchy small person that he has to be handled with gloves. He began work Saturday I think & will not have Oscar—I told him not to, but to look up another man he knows of.

I am really very much worried about Eleanor—she has only written two little pencilled notes & we have telephoned several times—but of course from here I cannot tell how bad it really is—I may go to N.Y. on Wednesday by the 1 o'clock & if she is able to go to Tivoli I will go with her—if the doctor is not ready for her to go I will stay in N.Y. till Saturday. At all events if I go I will wire you all about it—

Too bad about Mr. Edgar—I am so glad he will not be permanently injured. I had a nice note from Helen—Must get this into the evening mail

Ever your devoted

F.D.R.

The only dating indication given here was "Monday"; however, since Teddy Robinson's twenty-first-birthday fell on April 29th, a fair guess at the date can be made. "Keith's" was the vaudeville palace. Eleanor Roosevelt had been brought up by her grandmother, Mrs. Valentine G. Hall, who lived at "Oak Terrace," Tivoli-on-the-Hudson, having by now given up her New York house.

〜〜

"I have jumped into a den of
wild animals . . ."

ALPHA DELTA PHI CLUB
MAY 3, 1904,
TUESDAY.

Dearest Mama

I have jumped into a den of wild animals on my return, beginning with a dinner at the Club last Saturday, two private performances of the Pudding show & a crowd of 1903 men here for Herbert Burgess' ushers' dinner & tomorrow we go to his wedding in Brookline.

Yesterday I spent the afternoon judging in the track games on Soldiers' Field & this p.m. I am to drive Toby in the new runabout for the first time & naturally I am much excited. Will you please be sure to bring my spring suits, underclothes & some more shirts, especially all soft ones & one or two white ones—also my white flannel trousers.

I am glad Mrs. Draper has been with you— The weather is perfect today—springlike at last.

I must rush in town to drive—Ever your affec

F.D.R.

Herbert Burgess writes: "I married Jean Kay on May 4th, 1904. The undergraduates, members of our club in Cambridge, came in a body, so to speak, and when they reached the receiving line each one was introduced by Franklin to Mrs. Kay. There was nothing prearranged about this . . . Mrs. Kay was much impressed by his *savoir faire*. His charm and ease of manner were apparent in those early days."

~~~

"I seem to have a good effect on him . . ."

[TIVOLI]
MAY [?], 1904,
FRIDAY.

Dearest Ma,

It has rained almost all the time since I got here, lots of thunder-storms & a steady downpour all day yesterday. On Wednesday E. and I got in a little tennis in the morning but rain stopped our going out again.

Yesterday we went over a lot of books in the library & this morning we walked & are just back now from a drive to Madalin. I saw Mrs. Bob Livingston this morning & she sent you her love. Beyond her we haven't see a soul. Vallie has been exemplary—I seem to have a good effect on him.

Tonight I am off at nine for Albany & the next few days in Cambridge will be very busy.

I am glad you enjoyed the Vassar exercises—many thanks for your note—I don't think Jean or Sara caught on at all!

I will write surely from Cambridge

Ever your loving

FDR

Not far from Tivoli is the town of Madalin. Mrs. Robert E. Livingston lived at "Northwood," nearby. "Vallie" was Valentine G. Hall, Jr., an uncle of Eleanor Roosevelt, of whose attempts to combat an addiction to liquor she wrote in *This Is My Story*.

∽

The correspondence included in *Early Years* ends with this Tivoli letter of undetermined date. In June F.D.R. graduated, with his mother and fiancee attending the Class Day exercises. Also present was his half-niece, Helen Roosevelt—her attention, however, being focused mainly upon Theodore Douglas Robinson, whom she was shortly to marry.

During the summer the unofficially engaged couple exchanged visits at Hyde Park, Tivoli, and Campobello, and Sara Delano Roosevelt became reconciled to their early marriage. On November 29th, F.D.R. wrote the following letter to his old headmaster:

My dear Mr. Peabody,

I think you will be rather surprised when I tell you that my engagement to my distant cousin Eleanor Roosevelt is about to come out. I know you will be glad for my great happiness and consider me a very fortunate man. I had intended going up to School the day after the Harvard-Yale game, but I got jaundice instead and couldn't move from home. I am at the Columbia Law School, trying to understand a little of the work and of course I am going to keep right on. We hope to be married sometime in the late part of the winter and we

both hope that you will be able to help us in the ceremony—
it wouldn't be the same without you.

Always affectionately yours,

FRANKLIN D. ROOSEVELT

Eventually the date fell on St. Patrick's Day, March 17, 1905.
The wedding was to be held at the homes of Mrs. Henry
Parish, Jr., and her mother, Mrs. E. Livingston Ludlow, who
had adjoining houses on East Seventy-sixth Street. Endicott
Peabody came down from Groton; Lathrop Brown, substitut-
ing for James Roosevelt Roosevelt who was away in the South,
stood best man; and, since Eleanor Roosevelt's parents were
both dead, her uncle, Theodore Roosevelt, gave her away.

While the guests in the Ludlow salon were waiting for the
President to put in his appearance (earlier in the afternoon he
reviewed the St. Patrick's Day parade up Fifth Avenue), Peabody, F.D.R., and Lathrop Brown sat in a small anteroom,
bridging over the nervous moments with Groton reminiscence. In fact, so absorbed did they become that someone had
to run in and tell them the President was approaching the altar
with the bride.

First in the procession were Alice Roosevelt and Corinne
Douglas Robinson, followed by Ellen Delano and Muriel
Delano Robbins, lastly by Helen Cutting and Isabella Selmes.
The ushers included Edmund Rogers, Nicholas Biddle,
Charles B. Bradley, Thomas Beal, Lyman Delano, Warren
Delano Robbins, and Owen Winston. The bridal gown, as a
society reporter described it, "was a white satin princess robe,
flounced and draped with old point lace, and with a white satin
court train. The bride's point lace veil was caught with orange
blossoms and a diamond crescent. She wore a pearl collar, the
gift of the bridegroom's mother, and a diamond bowknot, the
gift of Mrs. Warren Delano, Jr. Her bouquet was of lilies of
the valley."

The actual wedding ceremony was restricted to family, but

a large reception followed immediately. The sliding doors between the two houses were thrown open; guests poured in to congratulate the young couple, who stood in front of the mantel in the Ludlow drawing room. Unfortunately, the President of the United States, after briefly remarking to the newly-weds that he was pleased the Roosevelt name was being kept in the family, moved across into the Parish house, whereupon the guests poured right back again after the feature attraction, leaving the bride and groom in more or less exclusive and solitary splendor.

After the reception, F.D.R. and his wife changed into traveling clothes and slipped away for a bedside visit with Robert Munro-Ferguson, the fiance of Isabella Selmes and an old friend of Eleanor Roosevelt. A brief one-week honeymoon was spent at Hyde Park, after which F.D.R. had to return to his studies at Columbia. The couple took an apartment at 40 West 45th Street in New York, and at the end of the spring term sailed for Europe on a real honeymoon trip. At this point the correspondence between Franklin Roosevelt and his mother resumes. In the second volume of these letters, the period 1905-1928—crucial and determining years which culminated with F.D.R.'s election as Governor of New York—will be covered.

INDEX

535

537

Hoover, Herbert, 350n, 362n, 487n
Hope, Anthony, *Phroso*, 88, 89n
Howe, Archibald, 446, 446n
Howe, Julia Ward, 420
Howland, Mary W. *See* Soley, Mr. and Mrs. James Russell
Howland, Rebecca. *See* Roosevelt, Mrs. James (first)
Hoyt, Mr. and Mrs. Gerald L., 270, 270n
Hoyt, Julia, 270n
Hoyt, Lydig, 270n
Hubbard, Miss. *See* Newbold, Mr. and Mrs. Thomas Jefferson
Hubbard, Gorham, 254, 255n, 389, 390, 391, 391n
Huiginn, Reverend Eugene J. V., 268, 268n
Humphreys, Duane, 185
Hurlbut, Byron S., 520, 521n
Huyler's, 278, 279n
Hyde Park, 3, 4, 24n, 67n, 209n, 516
farm, 522n

iceboating, 249, 250, 250n
Illustrated London News, 38, 39n
Indian Mountain School, 488n
infantile paralysis, 100n
Institute of Pacific Relations, 438n
Irving, Sir Henry, 365, 366n

Jackson, Edward, 303, 304n
Jackson, James, Jr., 335
"Jacksons" (examinations), 303, 304n, 305
"Jake." *See* Brown, Lathrop
Jameson raid, 380n
Jefferson, George D., 74, 75n, 279, 280n, 345
"Jennie, Aunt." *See* Delano, Mrs. Warren III
Jernegan, Reverend Prescott F., 218, 219n
John Percyfield, the Anatomy of Cheerfulness, by Charles Hanford Henderson, 493, 493n
Jordan & Marsh, 426n
Joy, Benjamin, 44n
Joy, Mr. and Mrs. Charles, 43, 44n

Kaiser Friedrich, 286, 286n
Kane, Mr. and Mrs. Grenville, 12n
Kane, Marian, 12n
Kane, S. Nicholson, 12n, 24n, 340-41n
Kane, Sybil, 12n
"Kassie, Aunt." *See* Collier, Mr. and Mrs. Price
"Kassie, Little." *See* Saint George, Mrs. George B.
Kay, Jean. *See* Burgess, Mr. and Mrs. Herbert
Kean, Mr. and Mrs. John, 467, 468n
Kean, Lucy, 468n
Keith's, New York, 530, 530n
King, Archibald Gracie, 35, 35n
Kipling, Rudyard, 488n
Kruger, Paul, 380n
"Krum Elbow." *See* Hyde Park
Krumbhaar, Doctor Edward Bell, 55, 56n, 328, 386
Kuhn, Hamilton, 307, 309n
Kuhn, Mrs. Hartman, 307, 309n

Ladd, William F., Jr., 319n
Landon, Francis G., 514, 514n
Lanier, Mrs. Charles, 198, 199n
Lathrop, Lucy, 402
Latin prize, winning of, 413
law, study of, at Columbia, 532
Lawley, George, & Son, 196, 196n, 470
Lawrance, Charles Lanier, 84, 85n

Lawrence, Mr. and Mrs. Amory (Gertrude Rice), 117, 118n, 405, 406, 406n, 407
Lawrence, Amos, 406n, 407
Lawrence, Reverend Arthur, 103
Lawrence, Edith, 406, 407n
Lawrence, Elizabeth Prescott ("Libby"), 302, 304n
Lawrence, Hester, 413, 413n
Lawrence, Mr. and Mrs. James, 30, 33, 39n, 44n, 157, 392n
Lawrence, Mr. and Mrs. John, 413n
Lawrence, Prescott, 30
Lawrence, Richard, 392, 392n
Lawrence, Bishop William, 30, 75, 76, 77n, 118n, 157, 346n, 433
Lawrence, Bishop William Appleton, 76n
Lawrenceville School, 41
"barbarity" at, 364, 364n
Le Bourgeois, Mr., 301, 301n
Lee, Alice Hathaway. *See* Roosevelt, Mrs. Theodore (first)
Lehmann, Lilli, 296, 297n
Lehmann, Rudolph Chambers, 87n, 87-88, 453n
Lemoine, Ashton, 190n
"Libby." *See* Lawrence, Elizabeth Prescott
Life (magazine; old), 369, 369n
Liliuokalani, Queen, 157n
Lindsley, Thayer, 467
Lipton, Sir Thomas J., 339n
"Little White House," 462n
Liverpool, Earl of, 198, 199n, 200
Livingston, Mrs. Robert E., 531, 532
Lodge, Henry Cabot, 164n, 477, 478
London, purchases in (1903), 497
Longworth, Mr. and Mrs. Nicholas (Alice Roosevelt), 128, 128n, 435n, 474n, 533
debut of Alice Roosevelt, 468, 468n
Lord, J. Couper, 242, 243n
Lord, Mr. and Mrs. Sidney Archer (Anne Sturges), 425, 426n
Lorillard, Pierre, and Pierre, Jr., 448, 448n
Low, A. A., & Brother, 137n, 251n
Low, Mr. and Mrs. Abbot A. (Marian Ward), 137n
Low, George Cabot Ward, 120n, 124, 137n
Low, Seth, 137n, 514n
Lowell, Abbott Lawrence, 457n
Lowell, James Russell, 472n
Lowell, Katharine. *See* Roosevelt, Mr. and Mrs. Alfred
Ludlow, Mrs. E. Livingston, 533
Lyman, Catherine, 142, 446n
Lyman, Edward H. R., 250, 251n

MacArthur, Lieutenant General Arthur, 380n
MacArthur, General Douglas, 380n
MacVane, Silas Marcus, 461n, 505n
Magenta, Harvard, 428n
Mahan, Captain Alfred Thayer, 164-65n
"mail niggers" at Groton, 248, 250n, 289
Maine, blowing up, 178, 178n
Making of an American, The, by Jacob A. Riis, 379n
manner, charm of, 531
Marcus Aurelius, *Meditations*, 282
Maria Teresa, 230, 231n
Markoe, Harry, 271n
marks, school, at Groton. *See* Reports, school, at Groton
marks at Harvard. *See* reports at Harvard
marriage, 533-34
marshal of Harvard class of 1904, nomination for, 518, 518n, 520, 521
Martineau, Mrs. Cyril (Muriel Delano Robbins), 20n, 23, 489, 490n, 493, 533

539

Thursby, Emma, 498n
Tilly, Aunt, 66, 67n
"Tip," 423, 425n, 428
Tomkins, Reverend Floyd, 93, 94n
Touraine Hotel, 348-49, 350, 426
"Toutou." *See* Robinson, Mrs. Theodore
   Douglas
Trinity Hall, Harvard, fire, 448
Troubetzkoy, Princess. *See* Chanler, Mr. and
   Mrs. John Armstrong
Truax, Louise, 497, 498n
Tucker, Alanson, 473, 474n
Tuckerman, Mrs. Bayard, 149, 150n, 413n
Tuckerman, Elizabeth, 150n, 412, 413n
"Turned Up," 266, 266n
Turner, Ross, 259, 259n
Turner, Frederick Jackson, 505n
Tuxedo Park, New York, 448n
Twining, Elsie. *See* Abbott, Mr. and Mrs.
   Mather Almon

Union, Harvard. *See* Harvard Union
University Register, Harvard, 509n

Vail Brothers, 298, 299n
"Vallie." *See* Hall, Valentine G., Jr.
Vanderbilt, William H., 154n
Van Wyck, Augustus, 230, 231n
Van Wyck, Robert A., 137n, 230n
Vaughan, Henry, 306n
Vendome Hotel, 280, 280n
Victoria and Albert, 494
vision (eyesight), 393, 394, 510
vote, first, 513

waiting list, Groton, 109n
Walters, Harry, 119n, 261n
Walters, Henry, 118n
Walters, Jennie. *See* Delano, Mr. and Mrs.
   Warren III
war, views on (1914), 251n
Ward, the Honorable John Hubert, and Mrs.
   Ward (Jean Reid), 438n
Ward, Marion. *See* Low, Mr. and Mrs.
   Abbot A.
Warren. *See* Robbins, Warren Delano
Washington, stay in, 38, 39
Washington's Birthday party at Groton, 373,
   374-5, 376, 384, 385
Webb, J. Watson, 153, 154n

Webb, Doctor Leonard, 94n
wedding, 533-34
"Wedding March, The," 375, 375n, 384, 385,
   387
Weekes, Mr. and Mrs. Arthur D., 353, 354n
Weekes, Harold, 353, 354n
Weekes, Mr. and Mrs. John A. (Alice Del-
   ano), 259, 259n, 354n, 464
Weld, George Walter, 453n
West Indies, trip to (1904), 523, 523n
Westmorly Court, Harvard, 389, 418-19, 371,
   372n
Wharton, Edith, 69n
Wharton, William Pickman, Jr., 53n, 68,
   69n, 266n
whistling, Miss Truax, 497, 498n
White House, visit to, 467, 468n
Whitman, Mrs. Sarah Wyman, 420, 528, 529n
Whitney, Mrs., 43, 44n
Whitney, William C., 346n
Widener Library, Harvard, 424n
Wild Animals I Have Known, by Ernest
   Thompson Seton, 373, 374n
Wilhelm II, 473n, 458n
Williamson, George, 500, 501n
Wilson, Woodrow, 480n
window, memorial, for James Roosevelt, 444,
   444n, 447
Windsor, Duke and Duchess of, 24n
Windsor Hotel fire, New York, 283, 283n
Winslow, Mr. and Mrs. Erving (Catherine
   Reignolds), 57-58
Winston, Owen, 484, 484n, 533
Woodford, General Stewart L., 201, 292n
Woods, Arthur, 81, 82n, 490, 491
Woodward, Experience. *See* Pomeroy, Mr.
   and Mrs. Medad
Woolsey, Charles, 127n
Woolsey, Heathcote M., 127n
Woolsey, T. S., 127n
Woolsey, Theodore Dwight, 127n
Wright, Mrs. Isaac, 49n
Wright, William M., 39n, 49n
Wright & Ditson, 349, 350n

yacht captains, 470, 472
yacht races, America's Cup, 339, 339n, 340,
   340n, 342n
Yale University bicentennial, 462n
Year Book, Harvard. *See* Harvard *Year Book*

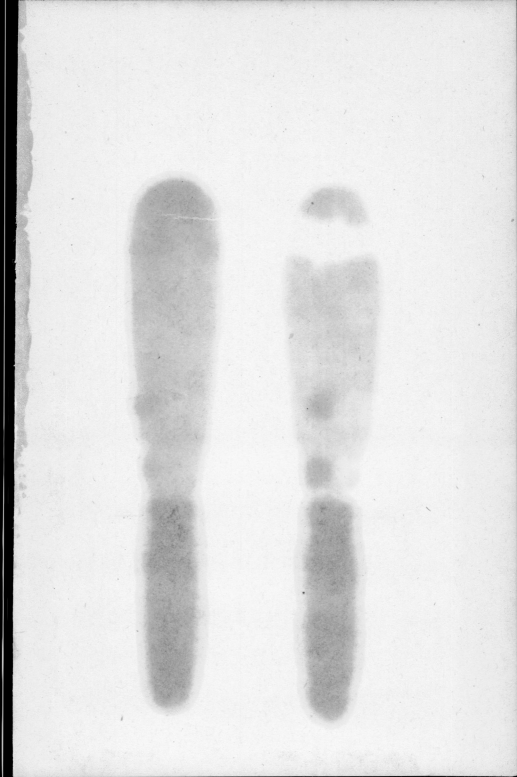